P9-ECI-659

"Peter Popham's vivid new biography, *The Lady and the Peacock*, illuminates the qualities that have made her one of the twenty-first century's great political personalities." —*New York Review of Books*

"[A] rich new biography of Burma's most famous dissident." —*NewYorker.com*

"Peter Popham tells this story superbly in *The Lady and the Peacock: The Life of Aung San Suu Kyi*, by far the best book yet written on this elusive heroine." —*The Wall Street Journal*

"In the latest, and very timely, biography of Aung San Suu Kyi, Peter Popham ably chronicles the incredible story of her life." —*New Republic*

"Peter Popham's life of Aung San Suu Kyi is gripping, partisan and emotional . . . It contains fascinating new material and conveys, better than any other account, the stirring drama of her confrontations with the junta. But perhaps the most interesting thing about it is its timing. . . . *The Lady and the Peacock* is an essential record of the struggle for democracy in Burma before the mysteries and promise of the Thein Sein era: a reminder of the forty-nine long years that preceded eight breathless months of reform." —*London Review of Books*

"Peter Popham's richly detailed biography sheds new light on Burma's heroine and the still-unfolding struggle against military oppression she personifies. An important book." —JOSEPH LELYVELD, author of *Great Soul: Mahatma Gandhi and His Struggle with India*

"A masterly narration of the life of Daw Aung San Suu Kyi . . . She makes one proud to be human in her company. What a gift to our world and what a splendid telling of it in this book. We are deeply indebted to Peter Popham for such a superb account." —ARCHBISHOP DESMOND TUTU

THE EXPERIMENT

BECAUSE EVERY BOOK IS A TEST OF NEW IDEAS

"This is the definitive and superbly written account of one of the most intriguing and admirable political and moral figures of our times."
    —**PANKAJ MISHRA**, author of A*n End to Suffering:*
The Buddha in the World and From the Ruins of Empire:
The Intellectuals Who Remade Asia

"A spellbinding biography of Aung San Suu Kyi . . . provides a complex and nuanced portrait of her on so many levels."   —*Huffington Post*

"Popham paints a sympathetic and well-rounded portrait of Burmese dissident Aung San Suu Kyi in this timely biography. . . . In addition to recounting Suu's remarkable life story, Popham, a foreign correspondent for *The Independent*, deftly outlines the political climate of the troubled nation, and shows how this revolutionary woman became a global symbol of democracy, resolve, and freedom."   —*Publishers Weekly*

"Peter Popham's biography of Aung San Suu Kyi could not be better timed, as the woman who has been the real leader of her country is at last free to participate openly in its politics. This book provides a rich and often surprising portrait of Burma and of Aung San Suu Kyi and her family, which for more than half a century has played a central role in the country's drama. As an age of reform seems in sight for Burma, *The Lady and the Peacock* sheds exceptional light on its prospects and on the experiences that have shaped its coming generation of leaders."
    —**JAMES FALLOWS**, *Atlantic Monthly*, author of *China Airborne*

"We live in a time of political pygmies, but even in an age of giants Aung San Suu Kyi would stand out. Peter Popham's *The Lady and the Peacock* provides a compelling account of her life and career. Her intellectual evolution is deftly sketched, her marriage portrayed without sentimentality and her struggle against authoritarianism carefully outlined. Reading the book, one desperately hopes that by shaking the hand of the 'world' leaders who now line up to meet her, Suu Kyi transfers some of her exceptional courage on to them."—**RAMACHANDRA GUHA**, author of *India after Gandhi: The History of the World's Largest Democracy*

"If the generals think they can control Suu Kyi, they would do well to read . . . Popham's biography."   —*Progressive*

"An inspiring biography and a rare glimpse of what Burma could have been, and could still be . . . In the aftermath of the first, tentative loosening of the military's death grip over the country, Suu Kyi's next chapter remains to be written. For now, enjoy this compassionate biography of an exemplary leader." —*Kirkus*

"Readers interested in modern Asian history and current events will find this book well worth reading." —*Library Journal*

"The most comprehensive, accessible, honest, and fair biography of Aung San Suu Kyi to date, blowing away all previous efforts . . . *The Lady and the Peacock* will leave the reader inspired."—**BENEDICT ROGERS**, author of *Burma: A Nation at the Crossroads*

"A brilliant portrait of the most famous political detainee of our time, Popham's book illuminates not just Aung San Suu Kyi but an entire nation as it makes its twisted, uneasy journey into modernity."
—**SIDDHARTHA DEB**, author of *The Beautiful and the Damned: A Portrait of the New India*

"In this eloquent and evocative biography, Peter Popham supplies fresh insights into the personality of the stoic lady who is the symbol of Burma's democratic aspirations. Aung San Suu Kyi's success or failure is measured in terms of her own ethical yardstick rather than the calculus of state power."
—**SUGATA BOSE**, author of *His Majesty's Opponent: Subhas Chandra Bose and India's Struggle against Empire*

"Suu Kyi emerges as a wonderfully human figure, adding a softer dimension to the remotely beautiful, stubbornly determined, unfailingly polite, and breathtakingly brave woman."—*The Times* (London)

"A portrait both warm and objective . . . it will not be bettered for a long time."
—*Independent on Sunday*

"The first serious biography of Aung San Suu Kyi."
—*Democracy: A Journal of Ideas*

THE LADY
AND THE PEACOCK

Also by Peter Popham

Tokyo: The City at the End of the World

THE LADY
AND THE PEACOCK

The Life of Aung San Suu Kyi

PETER POPHAM

THE EXPERIMENT

NEW YORK

The Experiment, LLC
260 Fifth Avenue
New York, NY 10001–6408
www.theexperimentpublishing.com

Many of the designations used by manufacturers and sellers to distinguish their products are claimed as trademarks. Where those designations appear in this book and The Experiment was aware of a trademark claim, the designations have been capitalized.

The Experiment's books are available at special discounts when purchased in bulk for premiums and sales promotions, as well as for fund-raising or educational use. For details, contact us at info@theexperimentpublishing.com.

The Library of Congress has catalogued the hardcover edition of this book as follows:

Popham, Peter.
The lady and the peacock : the life of Aung San Suu Kyi / Peter Popham.
p. cm.
Originally published: London : Rider, 2011.
Includes bibliographical references and index.
ISBN 978-1-61519-064-5 (cloth)--ISBN 978-1-61519-081-2 (paperback)--ISBN 978-1-61519-162-8 (ebook)
1. Aung San Suu Kyi. 2. Women political activists--Burma--Biography. 3. Political activists--Burma--Biography. 4. Women political prisoners--Burma--Biography. 5. Women politicians--Burma--Biography. 6. Burma--Politics and government--1988- 7. Burma--Politics and government--1948- I. Title.
DS530.53.A85P66 2012
959.105'3092--dc23
[B]
2012004652

ISBN 978-1-61519-081-2
Ebook ISBN 978-1-61519-183-3

Cover design by Susan Mitchell
Cover photograph © Joachim Ladefoged | VII | Corbis
Author photograph © Nick Cornish

Manufactured in the United States of America
Distributed by Workman Publishing Company, Inc.

First US paperback edition published April 2013
10 9 8 7 6 5 4 3 2 1

In memory of Michela Speranza Bezzi

"I have never ceased to be moved by the sense of the world lying quiescent and vulnerable, waiting to be awakened by the light of the new day quivering just beyond the horizon."

—Aung San Suu Kyi, *Letters from Burma*

"If they answer not your call, walk alone. . . .
With the thunder-flame of pain ignite thine own heart,
And let it burn alone."

—Rabindranath Tagore, "Walk Alone"

"Oh this ruler of our kingdom, a pretty thing, a pretty little thing."

—Old lady in Po Chit Kon village, Kachin state,
singing to her grandchild

CONTENTS

ILLUSTRATIONS

36. Monks on the march in Rangoon, September 2007 (*Mizzima News Agency, Delhi*).
37. A monk covers his eyes against smoke during the uprising (*Burma Campaign UK*).
38. Suu with president Thein Sein after their historic meeting on August 19, 2011 (© *REUTERS/Myanmar News Agency/Handout*).
39. Suu welcomes Hillary Clinton to her home on December 2, 2011 (*Khin Maung Win/AP/Corbis*).
40. Suu, addressing Burma's parliament as a newly elected MP on July 25, 2012, demands legal protection for Burma's ethnic minorities (© *2012 AFP/Getty Images*).
41. Suu, pictured in her upstairs office in the NLD's Rangoon headquarters during her meeting with the author in March 2011 (*Mario Popham*).
42. In November 2012, Suu visits monks wounded in a government crackdown on protestors against a copper mine in Monywa, northwest of Mandalay (© *REUTERS*).
43. Houses burned to the ground during ethnic clashes between Buddhists and Muslim Rohingyas in Arakan state, in Burma's far west, are guarded by a soldier in November 2012 (© *AFP/Getty Images*).
44. In the company of former First Lady Laura Bush, House Minority Leader Nancy Pelosi, former Secretary of State Hillary Clinton, and Senate Minority Leader Mitch McConnell, Suu receives the Congressional Gold Medal from House Speaker John Boehner on September 19, 2012, during her first visit to the US in twenty years (© *REUTERS/Jason Reed*).
45. Burma old and new: The reforms have thrown the contrast between the traditional Burmese lifestyle and newly imported trends into high relief (© *2012 Kuni Takahashi/Getty Images*).

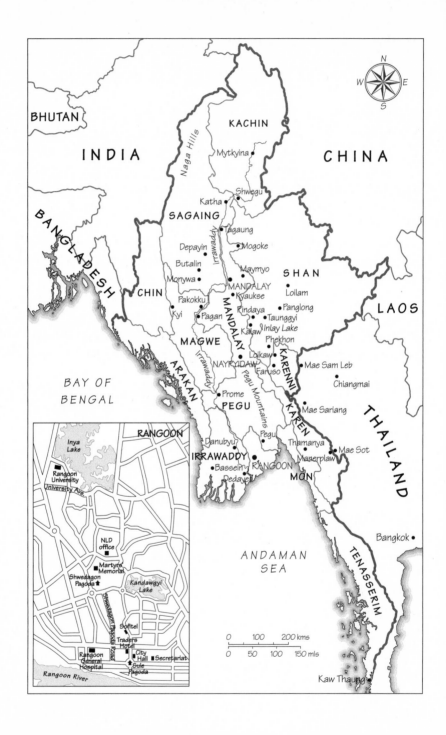

PROLOGUE

IN November 2010, Burma was preparing for its first elections in decades. Aung San Suu Kyi was in detention in her home, as she had been for the previous seven years.

Traveling across Rangoon six days before the poll, I had the luck to hail a taxi driver who spoke some English. I asked him, "Are you going to vote?" "No!" he said, "I don't like it! It is a lie! They are lying to all the people, and all the world. They are very greedy! They don't know what democracy is . . ." Later he said that his wife was going to vote and he was under pressure to do the same: She was afraid that if they didn't they might be killed.

He told me that he had a degree in Engineering from Insein Institute of Technology. So why, I asked him, was he driving a taxi?

"I am driving because I don't want to work for the government, because that means stealing. I want to work for my country and I want to do good. I don't want to steal! Money is not the important thing for our people. The important thing is to get democracy . . ."

It was the strangest election I have ever come across. The party that had won the previous election by a country mile, Aung San Suu Kyi's National League for Democracy (NLD), would have been allowed to participate if it had recognized the new constitution and if it had been prepared to expel Aung San Suu Kyi and all other members in detention or prison. As the party declined to do this, it was de-registered, becoming a non-party. The biggest party, which in the end won handily, had only been in existence for a few months: It was created by the simple trick of turning the Union Solidarity and Development Association (USDA), a regime-sponsored mass organization to which all government employees are compelled to belong, into a party, the USDP. The other parties running included small split-offs from the NLD opposed to that party's decision not to run.

During the weeks of the election campaign, the mood in Rangoon was completely flat. There were no election meetings, no posters stuck up, no loudspeaker vans patrolling the streets blaring their parties' messages. The only indications that something out of the ordinary was under way were a few billboards for the USDP, and daily homilies in the regime's newspaper, the *New Light of Myanmar*, urging people to vote.

"A voter can choose not to vote," one such homily noted, "but a person who is found guilty of inciting the people to boycott the election is liable for not more than one year's prison term or a fine of 100,000 kyats or both."[1]

A cartoon in the paper showed a group of smiling citizens striding towards an arch inscribed "Multiparty democracy general election." Beyond was a modern city of glass and steel skyscrapers, captioned "Peaceful, modern and developed democratic nation." "Join hands," said one of the citizens, "the goal is in sight."

Another article in the same paper recalled that there had been an election twenty years before, whose result had not been honored. "The election was meaningless because it looks like runners starting for the race without having any goal, aim and rule. In other words, it looks like a walk taken by a blind person.[sic]"

Despite the references to the 1990 poll, all mention of Aung San Suu Kyi and her colleagues was rigorously excluded from all printed and broadcast material.

What actually distinguished the 1990 poll was the fact that the polling and the counting of votes were conducted reasonably fairly: That's why the NLD and its ethnic allies won 94 percent of the seats.[2] Subsequently, the regime agonized for nearly twenty years over how to shake off the memory of that humiliation and somehow acquire legitimacy as rulers. This election was the way they finally chose to play it.

It was inconceivable that their proxies would win if the election was free and fair, so they did not want foreigners poking their noses in. Offers from abroad to monitor the polls were firmly rejected, as were visa applications by foreign journalists. I was admitted as a tourist, as on previous occasions.

The most flagrant way the poll was rigged was by regimented voting in advance: State employees and others were dragooned into voting en masse for the regime's proxy party.[3] "We discussed how to take advance votes from members of thirty civil societies in Rangoon," a USDP official told *Irrawaddy*, a news website run by Burmese journalists in exile.[4] Civil servants and members of regime-sponsored organizations including the Red Cross and the fire brigade were among those required to vote in advance. In this way getting out the vote—in many cases days in advance—became a quasi-military operation. In Rangoon constituencies where opposition candidates stood a chance of winning, pre-cooked ballots were poured in to ensure a favorable result. Two days after the poll, without giving any details, a senior USDP official was quoted by Agence France-Presse as saying, "We have won about 80 percent of the seats. We are glad."[5]

By then I and several other undercover reporters had been expelled. I watched the next act of the drama in the office of the NLD-Liberated Areas (NLD-LA) in Mae Sot, on the Thailand–Burma border.[6]

Although Aung San Suu Kyi's eighteen-month detention sentence expired on Saturday, November 13th, it was not clear until the last minute whether she would be released or not. But her party was optimistic: "There is no legal basis for detaining her any longer," said her lawyer.[7] Two days before, women members of the NLD had started cleaning the party's headquarters, which had been closed and shuttered for much of the time she was in detention, and repairing the air conditioners.

Nearly 2,200 political prisoners remained locked up in Burma's jails, but shortly after 5 PM on November 13th, Suu's seven and a half years of detention finally came to an end. At 5:15 PM on that day, the *Los Angeles Times* reported, "Soldiers armed with rifles and tear-gas launchers pushed aside the barbed-wire barriers blocking University Avenue, and a swarm of supporters dashed the final hundred yards to the villa's gate. Twenty minutes later, a slight 65-year-old woman popped her head over her red spiked fence."[8]

The crowd chanted "Long live Aung San Suu Kyi!" "I'm very happy to see you!" she yelled, barely audible over the chanting. "It's been a very long time since I've seen you." Rangoon was a prison camp no more. "Some people sobbed out loud, many shed tears and everybody shouted words of salutation and love," the *Times* of London reported on November 14th. "For ten minutes Aung San Suu Kyi could do nothing but bathe in the acclaim of the crowd."

The previous week an NLD veteran, one of the party's founders, released from prison after nineteen years, had told me, "When I and others were released it was like watering a flower in a pot—the plant is getting fresh, that's all. But when Daw Aung San Suu Kyi is released it will be like the beginning of the monsoon, the whole countryside green and blooming."⁹ And indeed for some days the mood was very much like that.

Burma's military regime had played its best card with great astuteness. In the cacophonous celebrations of the next days, which echoed around the world, the outrageous theft of the election a week before was completely forgotten.

PART ONE
HER FATHER'S CHILD

AUNG SAN SUU KYI emerged from detention in November 2010 as radiant as a lily, as if she had just returned from a holiday. The generals had contrived the election, from which she had been barred, and made sure that their proxy party won. Her marginalization was now official. But none of that made any difference: Her gate was besieged by thousands of supporters, braving the fury of the regime, in the first scenes of mass happiness in Rangoon in more than eight years.

From the earliest days of her political life, Suu has been attacked by the regime as the "poster girl" of the West. If that was a gross exaggeration in 1989, today it would be an understatement: She is by far the most famous woman politician in the world never to have held office, the most famous Burmese person since the late UN Secretary General U Thant and, along with the Dalai Lama, the most feted exponent of nonviolent political resistance since Mahatma Gandhi. She is a familiar figure to millions of people around the world who have no idea how to pronounce her name or where to place Burma on the world map.

But the fact that Aung San Suu Kyi did nothing out of the ordinary before becoming a political star—that she insisted on being described as a housewife—has led many people who should know better to underrate her.[1]

Thant Myint-U, grandson of U Thant, in his book *The River of Lost Footsteps*, casts Suu as little more than a footnote to a narrative dominated down the ages by ruthless military men.[2] Michael W. Charney, in his *History of Modern Burma*, sees her as significant chiefly as the embodiment, for the regime, of the menace from abroad, rather than as a positive force for real change.[3] A previous biographer, Justin Wintle, comes to the eccentric conclusion that she herself is to blame for her fate. "Aung San Suu Kyi has become the perfect hostage," he writes. ". . . Kept in captivity in part brought about by her own intransigence, the songbird's freedom has a price that no one can, or any longer dares, pay. The latest apostle of nonviolence is imprisoned by her creed."[4]

To blame Suu for being locked up for so many years is perverse, like blaming Joan of Arc for being burned at the stake. Yet it is true that her imprisonment has in a sense been voluntary, and this is one of the things that explains her enduring and almost universal popularity with ordinary Burmese people.

Suu's detention was never strictly comparable to Nelson Mandela's twenty-seven years' imprisonment on Robben Island because, unlike Mandela, she was free to leave. At any time in her years of confinement between 1989 and 2009, she could have phoned her contact in the regime, packed a suitcase, said goodbye to her faithful housekeepers and companions, taken a taxi to the airport and flown away; but it would have been with the certainty, if she did, that her passport would have been cancelled and that she would never have been permitted to return. And by flying away to the safe and loving embrace of the outside world, she would have vindicated all the slurs of her enemies, and the worst apprehensions of her supporters.

This choice is something she has rarely discussed, probably because it touches on the most personal and painful aspects of the life she has lived since 1988—on her decision effectively to renounce her role as a wife and mother. But the reality of this choice has also been used by the regime to torture her. This became most brutally true in January 1999, four years after the end of her first spell of detention. The news arrived from Oxford that her husband, Michael, had been diagnosed with prostate cancer and did not have long to live. Despite this, and despite appeals from many well-placed friends including Prince Charles and Countess Mountbatten, the regime refused to grant him a visa to enable him to visit her. The intention was clear: to induce her to follow the dictates of her heart and fly home to his bedside, as nine years before she had flown to Rangoon to the bedside of her mother. Knowing she would never be let back in, she refused to do it. Those in Asia and elsewhere who regarded her as lacking in female warmth felt confirmed in their view. Barely three months later, Michael died.

Justin Wintle is therefore perhaps right to use the word "intransigence" to describe Suu's attitude through her years of confinement. It would have been entirely human, completely understandable, if at some point she had given up and gone home. No one would have blamed her. She would have been hailed and feted everywhere she went. She could have spent precious weeks with her dying husband, and today would no doubt be dashing from conference to conference, banging the drum for Burmese democracy. What difference would it have made if the lights in number 54 University Avenue had gone out for good?

The answer is, a great deal of difference. For Suu's impact has been spiritual and emotional as much as political.

As the letters she wrote to Michael and her essays on Burma both before and after her return make clear, Suu was acutely aware of the suffering of her people long before she returned to live there: of the poverty forced on the inhabitants of this naturally rich land by the idiocy of its rulers, on the stunting of bodies and minds by criminal economic and social policies. When this privileged expatriate flew to Rangoon in 1988 and found herself in the thick of the greatest popular uprising in the nation's history, something clicked. Her people's suffering was no longer something distant and academic: It was a cause she embraced, with the passion to change it. Choosing to form and lead the NLD and fight the election, she made a compact with her country: They were no longer separate, no longer divisible. The harder the regime tried to paint her as a foreign decadent, a puppet of the West, a bird of passage, a poster girl, the more fiercely she insisted that she was one with her countrymen.

It is this decision—a moral much more than a political decision, and one from which she has not deviated in more than twenty years, despite every attempt to blackmail her emotionally—which has earned her an unwavering place in the hearts of tens of millions of Burmese. She could have flown away, and she never did. That has created an unbreakable bond.

But there is far more to Suu's career than simple commitment, however vital that element is. Suu had been thinking hard for many years about what it meant to be the daughter of the man who negotiated Burma's independence. She had a profound desire to be a daughter worthy of him, to do something for her nation of which both she and he could be proud. The tragic first decades of Burma's history as an independent nation, its fragile democracy snuffed out by the army, brought home to her how hard it would be to bring her nation into the modern world without doing violence to its innermost values. In the years before 1988 she had devoted much time and research to that question. Suddenly, against all odds, she had the opportunity, and the duty, to resolve it. She has not yet succeeded. But that is not the same as to say that she has failed.

*

Aung San Suu Kyi was born on June 19, 1945, in the Irrawaddy Delta, the third of three children, during the most tumultuous years in Burma's history. Her father, Aung San, was at the heart of the tumult. Rangoon, the capital, had just fallen to the Allies, and her pregnant mother had sought refuge from the fighting in the countryside.

Aung San was a boy from the provinces, shy, a poor speaker, with abrupt manners, and prone to long unexplained silences.[5] Short and wiry, with the sort of blankness of expression that leads Westerners to describe people from the East as inscrutable, he also had something special about him, a charisma. With a fiery temper and an iron will, he emerged at Rangoon University in the 1930s as one of the most ambitious and determined of the students dedicated to freeing Burma from the British.

Burma was an imperial afterthought for Britain, annexed in three stages during the nineteenth century after one of the last Burmese kings had infuriated them by launching attacks on Bengal, the oldest and at the time the richest and most important part of the Indian empire. Annexing Burma was also an effective way to erect a bulwark against further French expansion in Indochina. But it was never central to British designs in the way that India had become: It was ruled from India as an appendix, and few British administrators took the trouble to try to make sense of Burmese history, philosophy or psychology in the way generations of Bengal-based East India Company officers had done with India. The British simply brought the country to heel, in the most brutally straightforward manner they could, by abolishing the monarchy and sending the last king and his queen into exile. They opened up to foreign enterprises opportunities to extract timber, to mine gems and silver and to drill for oil, and allowed Indian and Chinese businessmen and laborers to flood in.

The process of being annexed and digested by a colonial power was acutely humiliating for every country that experienced it. Nonetheless, in many parts of the British Empire, as the foreigners introduced systems and ideas that improved living standards for many, more and more middle-class and ruling-class subjects would become, to a greater or lesser degree, complicit with the rulers. The pain of subjugation softened with the passing of generations, as the native elite was absorbed into the "steel frame" of the empire, the bureaucratic superstructure that kept the whole enterprise ticking over. That helps to explain why, in some quarters, one can still find nostalgia for the Raj, right across the subcontinent.

But the Burmese experience was very different.[6] It started very late: Lower Burma, centered on Rangoon, was seized during the first Anglo-Burmese War in 1824, and was rapidly denatured as the British threw open the gates. Within a couple of decades Burmese residents found themselves a minority in their own city, bystanders to its transformation. In the north, Burmese kings still ruled: a tradition sanctified, guided and held in check by the *sangha*, the organization of Buddhist monks which had underpinned the nation's spiritual and political life since the eleventh century, retaining that role through innumerable wars and several changes of dynasty.

But in 1885 the British finished the job, storming Mandalay, the last seat of the kings, sacking the palace, burning much of the ancient library and sending King Thibaw and his queen Supayalat into exile in western India. They brought the whole kingdom into the Indian system, governing it from the Viceroy's palace in Calcutta, and supplementing or replacing the local rulers who had been the king's allies with British administrators. They brought in tens of thousands of troops to suppress the rebellions that kept breaking out, until the Pax Britannica prevailed across the country.

But by the time Burma had been subdued, the Indians across the border were themselves becoming restless. The Indian National Congress had been founded in 1885, the year the Burmese monarchy was abolished, and rapidly became the focus for Indian hopes of self-government. The First World War weakened the empire dramatically. The arrival of Mohandas Gandhi from South Africa gave Congress a leader of unique charisma and creativity, and the massacre at Jallianwala Bagh in Amritsar in 1919 brought home the fact that British rule was a confidence trick, with hundreds of millions of Indians kept in check by a threat of force that the few thousand British in residence could never carry out effectively.

Across the Naga Hills, the Burmese drank the fresh ignominy of being colonial subjects to colonial subjects. Peasants tilling the paddy fields were trapped into debt by the Indian moneylenders who fanned out across the country. In Rangoon, foreign shopkeepers and businessmen grew rich exploiting the naïve natives. With the abolition of the monarchy, things fell apart. In lower Burma the British had refused to accept the authority of the *thathanabaing*, the senior monk authorized by the king to maintain the discipline and guide the teachings of the country's hundreds of thousands of monks, and in his absence local Buddhist sanghas lost their direction.[7] Then, sixty years later, King Thibaw was exiled and the monarchy destroyed. It was the coup de grâce.

The first nationalist stirrings in Burma came out of Buddhism and the Buddhist clergy. Traditionally, soon after dawn each morning, in every town and village in the land, monks in their maroon robes would tramp in file through the lanes, their big lacquer bowls extended for alms. They were the potent local symbols of a moral, theological and political system that had governed people's lives throughout Burmese history and which, according to their belief system, gave them their best hope of nirvana. The monks enshrined and sanctified the authority of the Buddhist king, and the people, by giving the monks alms, and by inscribing their own sons in the monastery when they were "big enough to scare away the crows," gained spiritual merit which was obtainable in no other way.[8]

Now all this was smashed and ruined. It was worse than mere humiliation: The nation had lost its compass. In response, the Young Men's Buddhist Association, or YMBA, in imitation of the YMCA, was established. It was a critical first step, less in defying the British than in asserting or reinventing an order that resonated with traditional Burmese beliefs. The most significant figure to emerge from this, in the feverish years after the First World War, was U Ottama: a learned Buddhist monk, who had also traveled around Asia and come back with the news that faraway Japan, another Buddhist country and one that had succeeded in repelling invaders and remaining independent, had actually beaten the Russians, a full-fledged European power, in war.

By the 1920s, under huge pressure from Gandhi and the Congress, Britain had conceded to India important measures of self-government, and the nationalist agitators in Rangoon, advised and cajoled by Indian radicals who had slipped over from Bengal, found that, although their movement was young and raw compared to India's, they had the wind in their sails. By the time Aung San arrived at Rangoon University from his home in the little central Burmese town of Natmauk in 1932, independence no longer seemed an impossible dream. But the more the British conceded, the more impatient the nationalists both of India and Burma became to win full independence.

With his gauche manner, his up-country origins and his clumsy English, Aung San struggled to make an impact among the metropolitan elite of the capital's university. But those who jeered at his contributions to the Students' Union debates and implored him to stop trying to speak English and stick to Burmese, soon learned that this difficult, angular young man had formidable determination. He wouldn't give up a challenge—trying to speak English, for example—until he had actually mastered it. Gradually he emerged as one of the leaders of a group of revolutionary nationalists at the university. Their ideology was hazy, leaning towards socialism and communism but with a deep commitment to Buddhism as well.

They took to calling themselves the "Thakins": The word means lord and master, roughly equivalent to "Sahib" in India. After conquering Burma the arrogant British had appropriated the title. Now these Burmese upstarts were demanding it back. They "proclaimed the birthright of the Burmese to be their own masters," as Suu wrote in a sketch of her father's life; the title "gave their names a touch of pugnacious nationalism."[9]

Aung San and his friends were developing the courage to claw back what the invaders had stolen, beginning with pride and self-respect. He was in Rangoon for the momentous events of 1938 (year 1300 in the Burmese calendar, so known subsequently as the "Revolution of 1300"). Despite the fact that the British had already conceded a great deal, separating Burma from India and allowing the country, like India itself, to be ruled by an elected governing council under the supervision of the British governor, agitation for full independence reached its peak in that year, with peasants and oil industry workers striking and joining the students in demonstrations in Rangoon. During one baton charge to disperse the protesters, a student demonstrator was killed.

Schools across the country struck in protest, communal riots broke out between Burmans and Indian Muslims, seventeen protesters died under police fire during protests in Mandalay and the government of Prime Minister Ba Maw collapsed.[10]

Then the Second World War broke out in Europe, and while Gandhi in India launched his "Quit India Movement," demanding that the British leave at once, and Subhas Chandra Bose in Calcutta began secretly training his Indian National Army, Aung San and the other Thakins decided to look east.

Ever since U Ottama had returned from his wanderings, spreading the word about the achievements of the Japanese against the Russians, the Burmese nationalists had been open to the possibility that liberation might come from that direction. Aung San was no Gandhian: He accepted that Burma would be unlikely to gain its freedom without fighting for it. And in August 1940 he and one other Thakin comrade took the boldest step of their lives when they secretly flew out of the country, to Amoy in China, now Xiamen, in Fujian province.

Their apparent intention was to make contact with Chinese insurgents, either Chiang Kai-shek's Guomindang or Mao Zedong's Communists—anyone with the wherewithal to help them evict the British. But Fujian was already in the hands of the expanding Japanese. And when a Japanese secret agent based in Rangoon, Keiji Suzuki, learned of the two Burmese Thakins roaming the city's streets, he arranged for them to be befriended by his co-nationals. In November 1940 they were flown to Tokyo, where Suzuki himself took them in hand.

It was Aung San's first experience of the world beyond Burma's borders, and he was impressed. Despite misgivings about the authoritarian brutality of Japanese militarism—and his prudish horror when Suzuki offered to provide him with a woman—he was awed by the industrial achievements of his hosts, and pragmatic enough, and politically immature enough, to have no inhibitions about being enlisted by Japanese fascists in their plans for the domination of Asia. After three months in Japan he flew back to Rangoon disguised as a Chinese sailor and set about recruiting the core of what was to become the Burma Independence Army (BIA). Much of 1941 was taken up with the rigorous, secret training of that tiny army, later to be immortalized as the "Thirty Comrades," on the island of Hainan, with Suzuki as commanding officer and general and

Aung San as his chief of staff.

So when Japan launched its air attack on Pearl Harbor in December 1941, and immediately afterwards began its invasion of Southeast Asia, Aung San and his comrades were ready to play their part. Rangoon was shattered by a Japanese bombing raid in the same month, and soon afterwards the Japanese and the BIA entered the country together, streaming up from the "tail of the Burmese kite," the long thin peninsula of Tenasserim that stretches south and east from the Irrawaddy Delta. As they marched, tens of thousands of Burmese joined the new national army until they were 50,000-strong, almost as large a force as the Japanese. The hopelessly unprepared British, routed by the Japanese all over Southeast Asia, fled for the safety of India. Thousands who failed to make it were taken prisoner and forced to build the notorious "death railway" linking Burma and Thailand.

But Burmese misgivings about the Japanese, which had already begun gnawing at Aung San during his first months of exposure to the fascist regime in Tokyo, grew exponentially in 1942, once the Japanese had taken control of the country. They talked a good talk about how the Japanese and Burmese, being brother Asiatics and sharing the same religion, must move together, but the Burmese, Aung San included, were quickly learning that Japanese rhetoric and Japanese intentions were two different things. The Japanese *tatemae*, what appeared on the surface, might speak of Burmese independence, but the *honne*, the unspoken reality, would be that "mighty Nippon" remained firmly in charge behind the scenes.[11] Burma's true destiny, in the Japanese scheme, was to form one of the many obedient and industrious Asian races near the base of the Japanese pyramid, with the Japanese emperor at its apex. Aung San and the other founding members of the Burma Independence Army gradually discovered to their horror that they had swapped one form of enslavement for another. Quietly they began to prepare to fight for their freedom all over again.

It was around this time that malaria and the rigors of building an army and leading the invasion of his own country undermined Chief of Staff Aung San's health, and he was committed to Rangoon General Hospital— an institution that plays a remarkably large part in this story, in one way or another—to recover his strength. The junior nurses were terrorized by his gruff manners and moody silences, so he was looked after by a senior staff nurse called Ma Khin Kyi. He appreciated her expert attentions and feminine graces, and she for her part fell sway to his charisma. A few months later, in September 1942, they married.

In the wedding photograph, Aung San sits like a coiled spring. He and his bride share a large, overstuffed sofa, sitting a good six inches apart. She has jasmine in her hair, a floral garland round her shoulders and a long white robe that sweeps the floor; her black eyebrows offset large, gentle, wide-set eyes. He is shaven-headed and dressed in his army uniform, his knee-length boots brightly polished. He grasps his slouch hat in both hands and leans forward, ready, one feels, to jump up and strike at the first opportunity. It is the portrait of a man who has already achieved a lot, but who knows that he cannot rest, that his work is not even half done.

And so it was to prove. In March 1944 he was flown to Tokyo to be decorated by the emperor and promoted to the rank of major general. In August Burma was declared an independent nation, and the BIA renamed the Burma National Army. But it was all a sham. The Japanese realized that the army they had created under Suzuki was no longer to be trusted and kept moving its units around Burma to make it more difficult for them to organize. Meanwhile Japan was rapidly losing the war, as its lines of supply from Tokyo became impossibly overstretched, and its technological and financial limitations compared with those of the Americans became ever more starkly apparent.

Aung San had now been around the Japanese long enough to know how to play the game by their rules. He accepted their honors with a stiff bow, did as he was told, kept an impassive face—and quietly set about organizing his second war of independence. Soon after his latest trip to Tokyo he made contact with the Allies across the Naga Hills, and began to prepare to open an internal front against the Japanese once the Allies invaded. With their support he secretly set up a resistance movement to work in tandem with his army as a partisan force, the Anti-Fascist People's Freedom League (AFPFL).

But he maintained the pretence of loyalty to his masters. On March 17, 1945, standing alongside senior Japanese officers, he took a pledge at Rangoon's City Hall to launch the Burma National Army's campaign against the Allies, and while a Japanese military band played, his army marched out of Rangoon in the direction of the front. But once outside the city they scattered, following a prearranged plan, to base areas throughout central and lower Burma, and ten days later launched their attack on the Japanese. By August 4th, after tens of thousands of Japanese had been slaughtered by the Allies, now aided by Aung San's "Patriot Burmese Forces" as they were renamed, in increasingly one-sided battles, the war in Burma was over. It was between those two crucial dates that Aung San Suu Kyi entered the world.

Aung San was still only thirty when the Japanese surrendered, but he had matured beyond recognition since his clumsy performances in university debates ten years before. He had shown great courage, determination and cool-headedness as he took the leading role first in forging Burma's first army since the fall of the king in 1885, then turning it, with perfect timing, against the power that had sponsored it. As the war ground on, his popularity among his people grew: To many millions of Burmese he seemed the only young leader with the determination, agility and charismatic appeal to save their country from utter destruction. And when the Allies finally arrived in Rangoon and met him face to face, they took the measure of this man, who had changed sides so nimbly, and decided that he was someone they could work with. Field Marshal William Slim, the British general who captured the Burmese capital on May 3rd at the head of the Fourteenth Army, took the view that he was "a genuine patriot and a well-balanced realist . . . the greatest impression he made on me was one of honesty."[12]

With peace the British returned, reinstalling their former governor, Sir Reginald Dorman-Smith, but they found the situation very different from when they had left in 1941. The country's towns and cities had been devastated by the battles between the Allies and Japanese; in the British parliament, one MP said the degree of destruction in Burma was worse than in any other area in the East. And the Burmese under Aung San and his comrades in the AFPFL, hardened by years of war and hungry for the freedom for which they had been fighting so long, were no longer in a mood to compromise.

Unable to submit to Aung San's demands—which amounted to handing the government of the country over to his League—Dorman-Smith packed the executive council with pro-British Burmese who had no popular following. Aung San responded by calling on the Burmese to launch concerted nonviolent action against the British, refusing to pay rents and taxes or supply them with food. Dorman-Smith was recalled to London, resigning soon afterwards; a Labor government under Attlee replaced the Conservatives, and in early 1947 Aung San and his colleagues were invited to London to negotiate a settlement. During a stopover in Delhi he made no bones about his position. He told journalists that he wanted "complete independence," not dominion status or any other halfway compromise—and that if he was not granted it, he would have "no inhibitions of any kind" about launching a struggle, nonviolent or violent or both, to obtain it.[13]

Once again, his timing was superb: Attlee's government was ideologically committed to freeing as many colonies as it could, and was in any case too strapped for cash to follow any other course. Aung San returned home with a promise of full independence. Burma would be a challenging country to rule: The Burman race to which he belonged was only one of several major ethnic groups within or straddling its borders, and the war had poisoned relations between them. But the following month the Panglong Conference in Shan State, in the northeast, secured the agreement of all of the main ones (except the Karen, who boycotted it, demanding their own state) to the proposed new nation. When elections for the Constituent Assembly were held on April 9, 1947, Aung San's AFPFL won 248 of the 255 seats. Aung San was not only the father of Burma's army and the hero of its freedom struggle but now the preeminent leader of the nation as well.

It would be too brutal to say that he timed his death with equal panache. Little more than three months after his landslide election victory, on July 19, 1947, he was chairing a meeting of the Governor's Executive Council in Rangoon's huge Secretariat Building, the colonial behemoth that still dominates a large part of downtown Rangoon, discussing, ironically enough, the theft of 200 Bren guns from the ordnance depot a week before, when a jeep pulled up outside. Five men in fatigues jumped out, stormed into the building, ran up the stairs, felled the single guard at the door, then burst in and slaughtered most of the council where they sat with automatic gunfire, Aung San included. An embittered political enemy of Aung San's was blamed for the attack, and later hanged. Factionalism and jealousy, "the two scourges of Burmese politics" according to Aung San Suu Kyi, had robbed the country of its most promising leader, less than a year before the independence to which he had dedicated his life was granted.

*

Aung San Suu Kyi was two years old when her father died, "too young," as she put it, "to remember him."[14] In one of the last photographs taken before his death Aung San appears to have mellowed considerably since that nervous, high-intensity wedding picture. He and Ma Khin Kyi smile toothily at each other across the three children, two sons and a daughter, that she has borne him. One of Aung San's hands holds the hand of Aung San Lin, their younger son, his other rests on Suu's shoulder. Suu has protruding ears and looks up at the camera in frank alarm. As in the earlier photograph, Ma Khin Kyi has flowers in her hair, which is coiled in a cylindrical bun, and she looks as calm, radiant and tender as before.

There are numerous strange and ghostly parallels between the life of the heroic father and that of his daughter. It was in 1938 that the so-called "Revolution of 1300" occurred, the nationwide outbreak of strikes and protests that propelled Aung San and his comrades along the road to independence. And it was exactly fifty years later, in 1988, that the greatest uprising in independent Burma's history occurred, propelling Suu to the leadership of the democracy movement.

It was in Rangoon General Hospital in 1941, when he was a patient and she was a nurse, that Aung San met his future wife, Ma Khin Kyi; and it was in the same hospital forty-seven years later, when Ma Khin Kyi was a patient, having suffered a crippling stroke, and Aung San Suu Kyi was nursing her, that she met the students wounded when the army fired on their demonstrations; it was also outside that same hospital, on August 24, 1988, that she spoke to a political meeting for the first time in her life. Two days later she addressed a crowd of hundreds of thousands at the Shwedagon pagoda, the national shrine where Aung San had lambasted British rule before the war.

The vengefulness of Aung San's enemies robbed his family of a husband and father; the vengefulness and fearfulness of the military regime quite as effectively robbed Aung San Suu Kyi's family of a wife and mother.

Aung San won an overwhelming mandate from his people in 1947 but was cut down before he could show what he might have been capable of in government. His daughter won an equally imposing majority but was prevented almost as decisively from doing anything with it.

In these ways Suu's whole life has been haunted by the glory of what her father achieved, by an awareness of how much was left unfinished at the time of his premature death, and by regret for how much was done wrongly or inadequately by those who took his place; for independent Burma, which was to such a great extent Aung San's personal achievement, was launched badly and unhappily, like a wagon with one buckled wheel, after that murderous attack.

When Suu was fifteen the family moved to Delhi, where her mother became the Burmese ambassador. It was an honor, but it was also a way for General Ne Win, the head of the army who would shortly become the nation's dictator, to get a politically inconvenient person out of the way before he seized power.

Intellectually, moving to India proved to be a crucial step for Suu. In the Indian capital she discovered at first hand what a backwater she had been born and raised in, and began to learn how a great civilization, which had been under the thumb of the imperialists for far longer than Burma, had not lost its soul in the process, but rather had discovered new modes of feeling and expression that were a creative blend of Indian tradition and the modernity the British brought with them.[15]

In Burma, colonialism had been experienced as a zero-sum game: The further the foreigners intruded into Burmese life, it was felt, the more the Burmese lost touch with their own traditions, ending up deracinated, demoralized and cynical. But now Suu discovered that just over the Burmese border in Bengal, in the cradle of Britain's Indian empire, a creative renaissance had been set in motion, with the active participation of both Englishmen and Indians, which had resulted in a new synthesis, the forging of new tools to understand and even to mold the developing modern world. In an important essay she wrote many years later, comparing the intellectual life of Burma and India, she sketched what she felt Burma needed, and what it had so far entirely lacked.

"And what should they know of England who only England know?"

Kipling had asked rhetorically, and Aung San Suu Kyi came to feel the same way about her own homeland: Only by leaving it could you really see it, and now she saw its follies and limitations with the clarity of the self-exiled. In an essay written two decades later she quoted the caustic judgment of an early countryman who had traveled abroad, U May Oung, who joined the Young Men's Buddhist Association in 1908 after qualifying as a barrister in London. The modern Burman, May Oung wrote, was "a Burman to all outward appearances, but entirely out of harmony with his surroundings. He laughed at the old school of men . . . he thought there was nothing to be learned from them . . . he had adopted the luxuries but not the steadfastness and high-souled integrity of the European, the lavish display of wealth but not the business instincts of the Indian, the love of sensuous ease but not the frantic perseverance of the Chinaman."[16]

Suu examined her countrymen from her new perspective and saw how right May Oung had been. And she compared the sad figure of the confused and superficial modernized Burmese with the sort of Indians who had emerged from early encounters with the British in Bengal. In particular she describes Rammohun Roy, the eighteenth-century Bengali scholar known as "the father of the Indian Renaissance." She wrote:

> Rammohun Roy set the tone for the Indian Renaissance, which was essentially a search for ways and means of revitalizing the classical heritage of India, so that it could face the onslaught of new and alien forces without losing its individual character or failing to fulfill the demands of a rapidly changing society . . . It was important that social, religious and political aspects of reform should move together . . . But . . . the underlying purpose tended to be the same: to bring India into harmonious step with modern developments without losing her identity.[17]

"To bring Burma into step with modern developments without losing her identity": That could be the challenge of a lifetime. This quotation is taken from a long and subtle essay, first published in 1990, in which Suu compares the intellectual life of India and Burma; but in a sense it was a letter to herself, setting out the sort of mental and emotional, not to mention spiritual and political, development that Burma cried out for, and which, in the first, bruising century of its encounter with modernity, it had almost entirely lacked—and which (the essay implies rather than says it) only someone like Suu herself, a child of Burma who was also steeped in the modern wisdom of India and points west, might be able to provide. These were some of the seminal ideas that an adolescence spent among the brilliant and highly articulate brains of New Delhi had planted and watered.

In New Delhi, and later at St. Hugh's College, Oxford, where she read Politics, Philosophy and Economics (PPE), Suu was developing her ideas of how Burma needed to change so that it could embrace democratic development in the way India had, without losing touch with its identity. But in the real world back home, following his coup d'état, General Ne Win had embarked on a reckless adventure in eccentric, home-grown socialism, nationalizing everything, closing down parliament, terminating the free press and jailing anyone who resisted. Anticipating Afghanistan's Taliban by a couple of decades, he closed down popular entertainments, including horse racing.[18]

Millions of ethnic Indians, many of whom had been in Burma for generations, were forcibly repatriated and Burma's other links with the outside world, such as the Ford Foundation and the British Council, were rapidly eliminated. The sort of ideologically driven economic disaster that overtook much of the socialist world in these years was now enacted in Burma, too, and the "rice bowl of Asia" became a net importer of food. The nation began a long descent through the world's rankings, ending in the ignominious position, twenty-five years after the coup d'état, of having to ask the United Nations to grant it "least-developed nation status," in order to receive the handouts that go with it.

On the other side of the world, Suu graduated from Oxford and worked for three years at the United Nations in New York under the Burmese Secretary General U Thant. Returning to England she married Michael Aris, a Tibet scholar, and they settled down in Oxford with their two small sons. Amid the responsibilities of raising a family on a small academic income, any grand ideas Suu may have entertained about her possible role in Burma shrank in scale.

Yet, as Aris later wrote, Suu had never forgotten who she was and who her father was, had never renounced the idea that sometime, at some unimaginable future date, her country might need her. "From her earliest childhood," he wrote in 1991, "Suu has been deeply preoccupied with the question of what she might do to help her people. She never for a moment forgot that she was the daughter of Burma's national hero . . . She always used to say to me that if her people ever needed her, she would not fail them."[19] In the months before they married, she wrote to him over and over again, and in her loving letters the same anxious theme kept recurring. "Again and again she expressed her worry that her family and people might misinterpret our marriage and see it as a lessening of her devotion to them," he writes. "She constantly reminded me that one day she would have to return to Burma, that she counted on my support at that time, not as her due, but as a favor."[20]

And he quotes from some of these letters—almost unbearably painful to read now, nearly forty years on, more than ten years after Michael's death, and twenty years after she was first confined to her home.

In the end the destiny about which she had such a strong intuition did indeed call. As Michael Aris wrote, there is no indication that she saw it coming. But then suddenly it was there, standing before her, unarguably huge and fearful and compelling. And all she did, all she is still doing, is to answer its call.

PART TWO

THE PEACOCK'S FAN

1
LATE CALL

THEY were practically born on the move, but as the English winter slowly gave way to spring at the end of March 1988, the exotic family that lived at number 15 Park Town, a road of stately Victorian houses in north Oxford, seemed at last to have reached a sort of equilibrium.

After more than twenty years of struggle, Michael Aris was closing in on his ambitions. He had been a lonely pioneer in the madly difficult and obscure subject of Tibetan language and culture; and he had found within that rarified discipline an even more obscure and rarified niche of his own—the history and culture of the kingdom of Bhutan, an offshoot of Tibet high in the Indian Himalayas, the last Tibetan kingdom to open its doors to the modern world. But there is something to be said for obscure niches: For six years, until interrupted by the call of love, he had been able to pursue his studies in the heart of the kingdom itself, as private tutor to the sons of the king.

That night, as their sons Alexander and Kim slept upstairs, Michael was, as usual, deep in a book. If his attention strayed it was perhaps to the comfortable thought that things were looking up. After years of genteel poverty in an increasingly cramped and crowded apartment, they had managed to buy a decent house. His most cherished personal project, a foundation to promote the study of Tibetan, was still no more than a gleam in his eye, but his career was on a firmer footing now: With his doctorate behind him, he had recently obtained tenure at St. Antony's College.

Beside him on the sofa, equally engrossed in a book of her own, was the reason he was no longer in Bhutan, the reason he needed a decent-sized house, the reason a country only very tenuously connected to Tibet called Burma had come to bulk almost as large in his life as Bhutan—the woman he had fallen in love with when he first ran into her in the home of a college friend in Chelsea.

Her name was Suu, pronounced "Sue." One of her best Oxford friends, to distinguish her from other friends with the very common name of

Sue, called her "Suu Burmese." For everyone who encountered her, Suu combined the familiar and the exotic in a way that was uniquely her own. As one who had spent most of her adolescent years in the diplomatic circles of New Delhi, she spoke English like an upper-class Indian—that is to say, with more clarity and precision than most English people have spoken it for about fifty years. And in Delhi she had had the sort of "finishing" normal for privileged young Indian ladies but which, in England, went out with the debutantes: sewing, embroidery, flower-arranging, piano, equitation.[1]

Yet there was nothing Indian about her appearance: Petite, with fine bones, pale skin, almond eyes and pronounced cheekbones, there was no doubting that she came from the other side of the line that divides the subcontinent from Southeast Asia. And despite the graces imparted by an old-fashioned education, she gave off no sense of entitlement, none of the languor common among those with nothing to wait for but a suitable man and a legacy. She was extraordinarily beautiful, and composed, and warm—and funny, too, with a streak of mischief that seemed to go with the unruly fringe that fell across her strong black eyebrows. But there was something else that people noticed when they got to know her a little better: a shadow that fell across her face when she was alone or when the conversation flagged, a grave look that came into her eyes that spoke of sadness and preoccupation beyond her years.

Michael soon learned, as his old-fashioned courtship of Suu proceeded, that she was heir not to an Asian fortune but to a complex and tragic family story. Her father Aung San, brilliant, mercurial and fiercely ambitious, was the father of modern Burma, assassinated with half his cabinet less than a year before he was due to hoist the new nation's flag.

Suu thus bore the most famous name in the country, a name that evoked pride and grief among her countrymen in equal proportions. And as the chaotic teething years of Burmese democracy were swept aside by a military dictatorship, Aung San increasingly became a symbol of Burma's lost opportunities and lost hopes.

Suu was one of three children, but although she was the only girl she was also the only one for whom the family name became an inspiration and a challenge. Her older brother never showed any sustained interest in answering its promptings; the younger one, who was two years older than her and to whom she had been very close, died tragically when he was only five, drowning in a pond in the garden of the family's first house, a death which cast another dark shadow on her young life.

Michael was left in no doubt about how much it meant to Suu that she was her father's daughter, and how much her father's name meant to her countrymen. Their courtship might have been old-fashioned—Suu made no secret of the fact that she believed a woman should never sleep with a man until her wedding night—but it was quintessentially modern in the way that most of it was conducted over thousands of miles of separation. After graduating from St. Hugh's in Oxford, Suu had found work with the UN in New York; Michael, meanwhile, had returned to his job as royal tutor in Thimphu, Bhutan's toy capital. After they became engaged, they exchanged hundreds of letters. Practically all of them remain under lock and key in a private university archive, but telling snippets of some have been made public.

In one of them Suu wrote, "Sometimes I am beset by fears that circumstances might tear us apart just when we are so happy in each other that separation would be a torment . . ."

There was no doubt, although she had not lived in the country since she was fourteen, that Suu felt powerful ties to Burma. But the implication of those ties for her future life remained very hazy. She returned to Rangoon every year, to spend time with her aging mother, to introduce her sons to her homeland, and give them a flavor of its culture and religion. She gave the boys Burmese as well as English names, and on their most recent visit, to cement their second identity, had put them through *shinbyu*, the coming-of-age ceremony which all Burmese Buddhist boys undergo, in which their heads are shaved by a monk and they spend weeks or months in a monastery, learning the rudiments of the religious life.[2]

In these ways she remained in touch with her country—but in the meantime she was a hard-pressed north Oxford housewife. She might continue to wear *aingyi*, the flimsy Burmese cotton blouse with detachable buttons and *htamein*, the ankle-length woman's *longyi*, she might continue to be a vivid, exotic splash among the grey and beige and drizzle of England—but where was she headed, as she wobbled back from the supermarket on her bicycle, laden with shopping?

She was a mother with two school-age sons and a heroically impractical husband, his head high in the Bhutanese clouds, incapable of mending a puncture or changing a fuse—but she was also Aung San Suu Kyi, child of the father of a country under the boot of a military regime whose viciousness was only matched by its stupidity.

One gets a sense, observing the choices Suu made in the late seventies and early eighties, of a woman struggling to understand her destiny, and coming up with a series of unsatisfactory answers. She applied for a second BA degree at Oxford but was rejected. She was commissioned to write slim travel books for children: *Let's Visit Burma*, *Let's Visit Nepal*, *Let's Visit Bhutan*. She wrote an equally slim study of her father, *Aung San*, published by the University of Queensland.

But these must have seemed timid, diffident steps in the direction she wanted to go, because now the restlessness that had taken her to New York after graduating from Oxford attacked her again: In 1985 she won a fellowship in Southeast Asian Studies at Kyoto University, threw herself into studying Japanese, then went with her younger son, Kim, to Japan. She immersed herself in the Burma archives there, to try to understand better the relationship between her father and Japan's militaristic wartime regime, which trained him to be a soldier and took him back to Burma to participate in their eviction of the British.

She then spent several months with the family in Shimla, the north Indian hill station that had been the summer seat of the colonial administration during the British Raj, where she and Michael were Fellows at the Indian Institute of Advanced Study. The result: much the most pregnant and interesting things she had written, two long papers comparing intellectual life in India and in Burma under colonialism, which tried to tease out why India, intellectually speaking at least, had flourished under the foreigner's yoke, while her own country had only languished.

Now, aged forty-two, she had finally begun to find her way home through the medium of scholarship. It was the natural approach for one who had already spent so many years immersed in the academic atmosphere of Oxford, married to a man with a passion for study. Like Michael with Bhutan she would devote herself to making sense of her country: For her own sake, for the outside world, and also for the generations of young Burmese intellectuals puzzled and frustrated by their nation's failure to fulfill its potential. That seemed to be the contribution she could make, while remaining true and useful to her husband and children. As a next step she applied to London University's School of Oriental and African Studies (SOAS) in London to take an MPhil in modern Burmese literature, and was readily accepted.[3] She had already drafted one chapter. Meetings with her supervisor would take her away from home, but not far and not for long: London was little more than an hour away by train.

Meanwhile, like Michael with his center for Tibetan studies, she could dream her dreams. Hers were to launch a chain of public libraries across Burma, that institution taken for granted in England but absent from Burma except in Rangoon and Mandalay, and to set up a scheme to enable bright young Burmese to study abroad. These were the ideas she could brood on while doing the washing-up or sewing name tags on to her sons' school shirts. Even if brought to fruition they would only be a pale shadow of what her father had achieved. But what more could a woman in her situation hope to do?

Michael and Suu were about to turn in for the night—there was school in the morning, they would need to be up early—when the telephone rang.[4] As a consequence of that call, all the plans and expectations of their lives were turned upside down. On the line from Rangoon was an old Anglo-Burmese friend known to everyone in Suu's family as Uncle Leo. He rang with terrible news: Suu's mother had suffered a major stroke and had been taken to Rangoon General Hospital in a critical condition.

Suu went upstairs and packed a suitcase. Years later Michael Aris wrote of that evening, "I had a premonition that our lives would change for ever."

*

The next morning Suu did what she had done so often before, alone or with Michael or the children, in the family's life of frequent, far-flung journeys. She took the bus from north Oxford down to the town center, walked briskly to the station, then took the train down to London and another one on to Heathrow: a journey through the sedate and comfortable scenery of the city that had become her home and the gentle countryside of the Thames Valley, waking now from its winter sleep, with yellow forsythia bursting into life here and there in the gardens. In places like Oxford, England has the gift of appearing immune to change, as if it has always been like this: so quietly sure of its identity and its institutions that it is set for eternity. Of course it's an illusion—nowhere escapes the Buddhist law of impermanence—but it's a persuasive one. The landscape that had been her home for half her life now was not often sunny, not often blazing with joy, but it was solid and safe and decent. And it was the home of humanist values that had affected her profoundly. As she traveled down those familiar railway tracks with her freight of anxiety, there was no way she could know that this was the last sight she would have of semi-detached villas, privet hedges, red pillar boxes, the meandering Thames and the chalk Chiltern Hills for another twenty years and more; that it might be the last time she would ever see such sights in her life.

Back in 1988 there were no direct flights from London to Rangoon; there are still none today. The normal procedure, then as now, is to fly to Bangkok, capital of a nation the Burmans had once, long ago, vanquished in war but whose liberalized, free-market economy now dwarfed its neighbor's, and wait to take another short flight from there.

The country she was going to had become one of the most peculiar in Asia, if not the world: as reclusive and little-known as Albania or North Korea, those hermits of the Cold War. "To the west Burma is still a virtual unknown," *Lonely Planet* wrote in the 1988 edition of their backpackers' guide to the country, "a slightly exotic eastern country that has been on some sort of total seclusion plus mad socialism binge since WWII . . ."

The weirdness, the guide advises, begins at the airport, where an ingenious solution had been devised for the problem of how to equip oneself with the local currency, kyats, pronounced "chats," at the good black market rate (about 35 kyats to the dollar) instead of the terrible official rate (6.6 kyats) without breaking the law. "From Bangkok it goes like this," the book advised. "At the duty-free counter in Bangkok airport buy a carton of 555 cigarettes and a bottle of Johnny Walker Red Label whisky. Total cost $15 . . . the first words you are going to hear from a non-government Burmese are, 'Want to sell your whisky and cigarettes?' You will hear this actually inside the airport terminal . . . You will very soon know what the going price is and will have disposed of both—all seemingly quite legal."

But in one respect the 1988 edition of the guide was already out of date. "In paper currency, K1, K5, K10, K25 and K75 bills are common . . ." the guide advised. But on September 5, 1987, the secretary of Burma's State Council, Sein Lwin, signed an order demonetizing all the higher value notes without warning or compensation. In the first half of the 1980s, Burma's command economy had plunged into a downward spiral, the national debt doubling and the value of exports halving. By abolishing the high value notes, the regime hoped to pull the rug from under the black marketeers whose undercutting of official prices had, they claimed, sabotaged the economy. But like many other measures taken by the incompetents at the state's controls, the effects were quite different from what they had anticipated, and far more devastating. Ordinary Burmese had a deep and well-founded mistrust of banks and preferred to keep their savings under their mattresses, in cash. So the demonetization further pauperized a population that was already one of the poorest in Asia, wiping out 80 percent of the cash in circulation at a stroke, rendering the cash savings of millions worthless overnight.

The demonetization announcement came as Rangoon's students were preparing to pay their annual university fees: Overnight most of their cash became worthless. Their reaction was instantaneous: In a reflex of rage, hundreds of students from the elite Rangoon Institute of Technology poured out of their campus onto the streets, smashing traffic lights and burning government vehicles. Political trouble in Burma always began with the students. The next day, to prevent the unrest spreading, the government ordered schools and colleges all over the country to close, laying on buses to send up-country students back to their homes. The protests died out as rapidly as they had started.

But that was not the end of the trouble. As many other socialist command economies were to learn over the next two years, unrest like that in Rangoon was more than a little local difficulty, to be crushed by a few cans of tear gas and some baton charges. All over the world, centrally planned economies on the Soviet model were suddenly finding it impossible to make ends meet. Within three years of those Rangoon students taking to the streets on September 5, 1987, the political map of the world would be entirely redrawn. And it was with Burma of all places—poor, obscure, out-of-the-way Burma, whose hermit regime had succeeded in insulating their country from the effects of the last geopolitical earthquake to hit the region, the Vietnam War—that it began.

Burma's tragedy is that, although it was the first, it is now the last: While corrupt and tyrannical regimes across the world collapsed, Burma's clung on. It is still clinging on today.

*

After suffering her stroke, Suu's mother, Daw Khin Kyi, had been taken to Rangoon General Hospital, the great red-brick Victorian institution where she had worked during the war as a nurse and where she first met her future husband. Suu found the staff desperately short of everything they needed to do their work. The stroke had left her mother partially paralyzed; her condition was stable but the doctors were discouraging about the possibilities of recovery. Meanwhile Suu and her relatives would be required to provide everything she needed, medicines included. "In Burma health care is ostensibly provided free of charge," she later wrote. "But . . . now [state hospitals] provide merely services while patients have to provide almost everything else: medicines, cotton wool, surgical spirit, bandages and even equipment necessary for surgery."[5] Depleted by decades of economic decline and mismanagement, and systematically starved of funds, the Burmese health system depended on family members to keep their patients alive. Suu prepared for an indefinite period of camping out in her mother's hospital room.

Outside on the city streets, the mood was dark and growing darker.[6] Prices of essentials were soaring, and the anger of ordinary Burmese was rising. The protests in September had been quickly extinguished, but in March a town-versus-gown brawl in a tea shop near Rangoon University had sparked more unrest, which the army stifled by opening fire, killing a twenty-three-year-old Rangoon student called Maung Phone Maw—the first young martyr of 1988.

These were the petty beginnings of the greatest uprising in Burma's modern history, one that still resonates today. Emotions were further inflamed when it emerged in April that the regime had sought and obtained from the UN the humiliating status of "least-developed nation," a fact they had been at pains to keep from the public—because, after all, a mere generation ago independent Burma had been expected to become the richest nation in Southeast Asia.[7] Protests spread rapidly across the city and around the country. The regime replied with extreme violence:

Hundreds of students died, shot dead on the street by troops; dozens were crammed into a van and taken to jail and forty of them suffocated to death on the way. Many of the dead were hauled away and cremated en masse to prevent a clear picture of the fatalities emerging. To stifle the protests the junta again closed the nation's colleges.

By the time Suu arrived in the capital and installed herself in her mother's hospital room, Burma was in a state of suspended animation, quiet on the surface but with bitterness and fury festering underneath. Rumors swirled, as they always swirl there. The summer heated to boiling point, the air was thick with dust, the whole land desperate for rain. In April, New Year was celebrated as usual with the annual bacchanalia of the water festival, called *Thingyan*, when for several days the whole population sheds its inhibitions and arms itself with buckets and hoses to spray and splash everybody else. But when it ended, the hot and exhausting wait for rain—the wait for change—resumed.

If brutality is one of the distinguishing marks of the Burmese regime, the other is complacency: It has long had the bully's serene confidence that fear will triumph. So sure was General Ne Win, known as "the Old Man" or "Number One," that the latest spasm of rebellion had been crushed that on April 11th he slipped out of the country and flew to Europe, to relax in the cool, clean air of his favorite Swiss and West German spas. Meanwhile an Inquiry Commission the regime had appointed to look into the death of the first victim of the violence was going about its work.

The Commission presented its report on May 6th. It admitted that Maung Phone Maw and one other student had been killed by gunfire— but anyone hoping for a clear account of what happened subsequently would have felt badly let down. The report blamed "some students who wanted to create disturbances" for the chaos, gave gross underestimates of the number injured and arrested, and instead invited sympathy for the twenty-eight riot police it said had been wounded by stones. Of the hundreds more students shot dead and the dozens who suffocated in the police van there was not a word. "Rather than soothing the already inflamed tempers," wrote the Swedish journalist Bertil Lintner in his book about the uprising, the report "added insult to injury."[8]

The impudent lies in the report provoked an old critic of the regime, silent for many years, to return to the offensive. U Aung Gyi, aged sixty-seven, a senior brigadier who had been sacked from the army back in the early 1960s for publicly attacking the regime's policies—he had spent two terms in jail, though he still seemed to be on affable terms with Ne Win—suddenly piped up again, sending his old boss a blistering open letter condemning the Inquiry Commission's report and estimating that 282 people had been killed in March. In his conclusion he attempted to draw the sting, exculpating his former boss from direct responsibility— "Sir, may I request you . . . not to get involved or you will regret it," he wrote fawningly.[9] "These violations of human rights will be infamous. You actually were not involved." But even so, his condemnation of the report gave new heart to the growing resistance movement.

At the end of May the silence of the streets persuaded the regime to allow schools and colleges to reopen. This was its final act of folly: Back on their campuses again the students could for the first time see who and how many of them were missing, could hear from the injured the stories of who had died and how, and could once again stoke the fires of anger that had been stifled since the second week of March. Within two weeks the streets again exploded, with demonstrations and running battles which pitched the protesters, who now included textile workers and Buddhist monks as well as students, against the hated riot police.

After almost a week of clashes, the government again slammed down the shutters, ordering classes on all four of Rangoon University's campuses closed—but neglecting to do the same for the two campuses of the Institute of Medicine, one of which was just across the road from the hospital where Suu had for ten weeks been nursing her mother. Without skipping a beat the protests shifted there, taking in also the Institute of Dental Medicine which was next door.

"We held a big meeting on the Prome Road campus [north of the city center] on June 21st," remembered Soe Win, a medical student.[10] "Thousands of people were there and suddenly someone got the idea that we should march down town to the main Institute of Medicine in central Rangoon, where another meeting was being held. We marched off at 1 PM, a solid column of several thousand students. We took our peacock and student union flags and someone went inside the teachers' office [and] brought out Aung San's portrait to be carried in front of the demonstration."

But before the marchers could get close to the city center, they found themselves hemmed in by riot police with rifles and batons and by soldiers with machine guns. Remembering the massacre in March, when the students had been trapped and shot dead by troops, the demonstrators scattered into the lanes and nearby houses before the soldiers could open fire. Most of them survived—but on the same day elsewhere in the city many died.

Word of the new clashes flashed across the city. Down at the Institute of Medicine the student meeting was still in progress, and a witness of the violence further north burst in with the news. Suspected spies inside the hall were pointed out by angry students, and grabbed and hauled to the front of the meeting for summary justice; one of them narrowly escaped being lynched. A hundred or more people died in the clashes that day, according to diplomats' estimates, and many dozens were wounded, and now they streamed into the hospital in ambulances and cars and rickshaws and carried on the shoulders of friends. These were the first protests to erupt since Suu's arrival in the country at the beginning of April, and at the hospital she found herself with a ringside seat. Burma's bloody tragedy was unfolding before her eyes.

The regime acted fast to end the protests, shutting the medical and dental campuses, making hundreds more arrests, and for the first time clamping a dusk-to-dawn curfew on the city. This brought mayhem to markets whose stallholders were accustomed to setting up their stalls and laying out their wares in the early hours of the morning. Forced to start work later, they raised their prices to make up for the loss of trade, adding another new element to the cocktail of misery and fury that was steadily rendering Burma ungovernable.

*

And then the rains came, and Suu and her mother went home.

The month of July has a special meaning in Suu's story, and that of her family: It is the month when her father was killed, the event commemorated every year on Burma's Martyrs' Day. It is when the monsoon, which normally starts in June, increases to its greatest intensity, coinciding with the Burmese lunar months of Wahso and Wagaung. "The word 'monsoon' has always sounded beautiful to me," she wrote eight years later, "possibly because we Burmese, who are rather inclined to indulge in nostalgia, think of the rainy season as most romantic. As a child I would stand on the veranda of the house where I was born and watch the sky darken and listen to the grown-ups wax sentimental over smoky banks of massed rain clouds . . . When bathing in the rain was no longer one of the great pleasures of my existence, I knew I had left my childhood behind me. . . ."[11]

It is the season when Burma is most quintessentially Burmese—hot and sultry and shriekingly green and fertile, when the rain comes down like a waterfall every morning and evening, and sometimes in the middle of the day as well. It is the season in which ecstasy, melancholy and tragedy seem inextricably mixed—for her nation as a whole, and for Suu and her family in particular.

At Rangoon General Hospital, her doctors discharged Daw Khin Kyi: There was nothing more they could do for her. Suu converted one of the large downstairs rooms at 54 University Avenue into a sickbay and on July 8th, she took her home. Mother and daughter were back together in the villa on the shore of Inya Lake, in the north of Rangoon, where they had moved with Suu's brother Aung San Oo when she was eight.

However gloomy the prognosis, it must have been a relief to be back in familiar surroundings. And on July 22nd, to Suu's joy, the family was reunited when Michael, Alexander and Kim flew out to join them. In a letter to her parents-in-law in June, she had revealed how much she missed them.[12] Prior to this, her longest separation from all of them had been a month, and she was looking forward to having them with her again. The house, Michael wrote, was "an island of peace and order under Suu's firm, loving control. The study downstairs had been transformed into a hospital ward and the old lady's spirits rallied when she knew her grandsons had arrived."[13] But the preparations had worn Suu out: "When we first arrived," Michael wrote in a letter to his twin brother Anthony in August, "the boys said that Suu looked as if she had just been released from a concentration camp! She had really exhausted herself trying to renovate the house before her mother's return. She has put on some weight and is looking much better."[14]

The future, though bleak, was now attaining a visible form: Suu would wait out the inevitable, making her mother's last weeks and months as comfortable as possible. Her family would keep her company until the boys had to go back to school. What were their plans once her mother had passed away? Would Suu shut up the house, perhaps sell it, and close that chapter in her life forever, severing her closest ties to her homeland? With the boys still at school in Oxford and both Michael and Suu committed to their academic work in England, that would have been the logical, almost inevitable course.

But then something happened which stunned the nation.

After the last bout of bloodletting, it seems finally to have dawned on General Ne Win that things could not go on as they were. So on July 23rd—one day after the arrival of Michael and the boys—he convened an extraordinary congress of the Burma Socialist Program Party (BSPP), the monopolistic political party he had created and through which he ruled the country. Standing on the podium before the thousand delegates, the blubbery-lipped, muscle-bound, imposing but now fading tyrant made the most remarkable speech of his career, transmitted live on state television.

"Dear delegates," he told the hall, "I believe that the bloody events of March and June show a lack of trust in the government and the party that guides it."[15]

People all over the country watched mesmerized as the man with the power of life and death announced that he was rewriting the rules.

"It is necessary," Ne Win went on, "to find out whether it is the majority or the minority that support the people showing the lack of trust . . . The current congress is requested to approve a national referendum . . . If the choice is for a multiparty system, we must hold elections for a new parliament."

Burma had been awash with rumors about the state of Ne Win's mental health ever since the death of his favorite wife some years before. But now this turkey was apparently voting for Christmas: Had he finally cracked?

The general now handed the microphone to an underling called Htwe Han—who continued to read his boss's speech, still in the first person. And now came the real bombshell. "As I consider that I am not totally free from responsibility, even if indirectly, for the sad events that took place in March and June," Htwe Han read out, "and because I am advancing in age, I would like to request party members to allow me to relinquish the duty of party chairman and party member." As if that was not enough, he added that five other top office-holders, his entire inner circle, the gang who had run Burma for years, would do likewise. "The atmosphere," Michael wrote, "was electric with hope."[16]

Yet anybody who interpreted the speech to mean that the protesters would now have free rein were disabused by his final words—Ne Win had taken the microphone back now—which epitomized the crude menace of his style. "In continuing to maintain control," he said, "I want the entire nation, the people, to know that if in future there are mob disturbances, if the army shoots, it hits—there is no firing in the air to scare."

Nonetheless, the simple message was: All change! "The nation," wrote Bertil Lintner, "and possibly even more so the diplomatic community in Rangoon, was flabbergasted. International wire service reports were euphoric. Public outrage in Burma had forced an end to twenty-six years of one-party rule and one of Asia's most rigid socialist systems . . . Or had it?"[17]

*

As Lintner indicated, things were not as straightforward as they seemed. By the time the congress ended two days later, it had rejected the idea of a referendum on a multiparty system that Ne Win himself had proposed. The Old Man was probably responsible for that, tugging the strings behind the scenes. It had also turned down four of the six resignations he had offered. Ne Win himself was allowed to bow out—but only to be replaced as president and chairman of the party by the most brutal of his underlings, Sein Lwin, the man who had ordered the killings back in March and who had since been known as "the Butcher" to the protesters.

"Sein Lwin's takeover was aimed solely at preventing the loss of [Ne Win's] own power and security," Michael later wrote to his brother.[18] "As Ne Win's hit man and crony he's used to combining the role of court executioner, astrologer, sorcerer and alchemist—literally, not figuratively, in the peculiar mixture of magic and repression that the former regime has depended upon to stay in power, and which will now continue unabated."

It was like offering the demonstrators a carrot—but then cracking them over the head with a stick before they could take a bite of it. It was like opening Pandora's Box but then trying to slam it shut again before anything got out.

For whatever reason, acting on whatever senile, cock-eyed calculation, the Old Man had planted a seed, and nothing would be the
same again. "Up to then," diplomat Martin Morland remembered, "the
student movement . . . was completely unfocused. It was in essence anti-
government: protest against brutality, a frustrated reaction against the
inane policies, the demonetization, the hopelessness of the students, the
lack of any future. There was no focus to it. Ne Win, unwittingly, provides
a focus by calling for a multiparty system, and from there on in, the
student cry is for democracy."

And in that context, substituting the Butcher for the Old Man was like
lighting the short fuse of a big bomb. The curfew, so destructive to the local
economy, had been lifted at the end of June. Colleges remained closed,
but a hard core of protesters had merely moved from their campuses to
pavilions around the Shwedagon pagoda, the nation's most important
Buddhist shrine, where they continued to organize. And when Sein Lwin's
appointment was announced, the protests began almost at once. Martial
law was declared the day after the congress ended, but instead of scaring
people off the streets it simply raised the stakes. "Dissatisfaction among the
public gave way to hatred," wrote Lintner. "'That man is not going to be
the ruler of Burma,' was a common phrase repeated all over the country."[19]
The Old Man himself had acknowledged that his country was ripe for
profound change, and the fact that he had tried to eat those words as soon
as they were out of his mouth could not alter it. He had indicated that the
future did not belong to him and, the Butcher notwithstanding, that it
might not even belong to the army. And quite quickly Aung San Suu Kyi
became a very busy person indeed.

*

How are we to explain the fact that this elegant, scholarly, middle-aged
woman, who had not lived in her country for thirty years and who had
never been involved in politics anywhere, suddenly became the focus of
political speculation and intrigue?

Most countries in Asia that became independent after the Second
World War found themselves, as the first or second wave of independence
leaders died out, confronting the conundrum of legitimacy. When your

country has been arbitrarily ruled by foreigners, backed by the gun, for generations or centuries, how does an indigenous leader convince the people of his rightful claim on power?

In many cases, the solution to which people turned was dynastic. In India, the daughter of the first prime minister had fortuitously married a man called Gandhi; he was no kin of the great Mahatma, but that name plus the Nehru bloodline gave Indira Gandhi a claim to power which none of her rivals could match. Next door in Pakistan, Benazir Bhutto, the daughter of a charismatic prime minister who had been hanged by a usurping general proved to have both the name and the mass clan following to become prime minister twice, even though she lacked the political gifts to become a great leader. And in Bangladesh, Sri Lanka and the Philippines, too, variations on that dynastic theme have had a decisive impact on politics for generations.

In Burma, independent since 1948, Aung San, Suu's father, was venerated in every corner of the land: No town, at least in the areas dominated by Burmans, was without its "Bogyoke [General] Aung San" road or square. No public office was complete without its portrait of the national hero, killed before he could fulfill his destiny and lead the country to freedom, alongside the equally obligatory portrait of Number One. And for months now, in the absence of anyone of flesh and blood to follow, the protests that had thundered up and down the streets of the nation's cities and towns were often spearheaded by a young man or woman holding aloft the portrait of Aung San.

So powerful was the desire for a figure around whom the protesters could unite that in July posters were stuck up all over Rangoon, announcing the imminent return from exile of Aung San Oo, Aung San's oldest child and only surviving son. "He's coming to lead us," went the rumors, "he is the one we are waiting for." But that hope was vain: Many years before Aung San Oo had settled in San Diego with a steady job as an engineer, and had taken American citizenship. During the uprising of 1988 he sent messages of solidarity to Burmese students in Tokyo, where his brother-in-law lived, some of whom cherished the hope that he would galvanize the Burmese diaspora.[20] But the hope came to nothing. He "was not cut out to lead the exiles," says Dr. Maung Zarni, who was a student in Tokyo at the time and read out some of those messages. "Worse still, after his failure to establish himself as the leader of the Burmese exiles he became an annual 'state guest' in Rangoon where he and his wife were wined and dined by the generals."

Maung Zarni, today a sociologist and a prominent activist in the Burmese diaspora, pointed out that the dynastic principle is in fact far weaker in Burma than in many other developing countries, from North Korea to Syria: Neither Ne Win nor his ultimate successor Than Shwe managed to hand over power to their children, despite being the nation's preeminent rulers for a total of more than forty years.

But then in the Burmese context Aung San was unique, as Maung Zarni explained. "According to my great uncle, who was a friend of Aung San and roomed next to him at Rangoon University when they were both undergraduates in the 1930s, Aung San was from his student days consumed by the single-minded pursuit of Burma's liberation by any means necessary," he said. "In place of economic wealth—Aung San left virtually no material possessions to his widow and two surviving children—or a powerful political machine, he left a legacy as unquestionably the most popular and revered nationalist of his time."

And if Aung San was unique, Aung San Suu Kyi was to prove no less so. Though nobody could have guessed it at the time.

Her home on Inya Lake was directly across the water from the huge villa where General Ne Win resided, surrounded by 700 troops, reclusively holding court. And as a new and even more desperate cycle of protest and repression got under way, a host of people with different ideas and agendas began beating a path to her door.

Watching on television that fateful session of the BSPP at which Ne Win resigned, "She, like the whole country, was electrified," Michael Aris later recalled. "I think it was at this moment . . . that Suu made up her mind to step forward. However, the idea had gradually taken shape in her mind during the previous fifteen weeks."[21]

And now it took shape in the minds of many others, too. After Ne Win announced his decision to resign, "Suu's house quickly became the main center of political activity in the country and the scene of such continuous comings and going as the curfew allowed," Aris wrote.[22] "Every conceivable type of activist from all walks of life and all generations poured in . . . She began to take her first steps into the maelstrom beyond her gates . . ."

2
DEBUT

AUNG SAN SUU KYI had not lived in Burma since she was fifteen, nearly thirty years before, but her connections to her homeland were far from tenuous. Her presence was expected on July 19th, when, accompanied by the most senior generals in the Tatmadaw, the Burmese Army, she laid a wreath at the Martyrs' Memorial in central Rangoon, to commemorate her father's death. It was the most resonant day in the young republic's calendar, and Suu was one of the principal actors in it.

There were other reasons, too, for Suu to spend as much time as she could in the city of her birth. Her mother was aging and grateful for regular visits; Suu's surviving brother Aung San Oo came over far less frequently from the United States. On a recent visit she had stayed four months. As a result Suu's Rangoon life was perhaps as rich and full as her life in England. Her Burmese was not merely fluent but up to date and idiomatic. She was in town often enough and long enough to have a social life; she saw the high-ranking people her mother saw. And that gave her access to a very particular set of people.

Daw Khin Kyi's appointment as Burma's first-ever woman ambassador was a signal honor, and one she could hardly have declined. One can understand why General Ne Win wanted her out of the way in the run-up to his coup d'état: Though never a political figure in her own right, she represented a certain vision of her nation, one symbolized by her late husband and by the man who took his place to become independent Burma's first prime minister, U Nu, a vision in stark contrast to Ne Win's. She must also have known the truth behind the rumor that on one occasion her husband, disgusted by Ne Win's compulsive womanizing, had ordered another officer in the Burma Independence Army to kill him.[1] But the officer flunked the task, for which, it was said, Aung San gave him such a ferocious kicking that decades later he still bore the scars.

Despite remaining silent in public, Daw Khin Kyi's disdain for Ne Win and his behavior were well known—which is why it suited Ne Win for her to be packed off to India. Other prominent figures he feared could cause him problems were also given diplomatic appointments far away. Seven years later, as Suu was preparing to sit her Finals in Oxford, Daw Khin Kyi took early retirement and returned to Rangoon.

Back in University Avenue she lived extremely quietly, rarely leaving home except for an annual medical check. As in Delhi, she continued to entertain: Ne Win himself was among the people she invited over for lunch. At least once he and his then wife, Kitty Ba Than, accepted the invitation. Both Suu and her brother were present on that occasion; Suu remembered Kitty Ba Than making light conversation. But Ne Win himself merely ate and said not a word.[2]

Perhaps he had noticed the flag flying at her gate, the original flag of the Union of Burma, with five small stars circling a single large one, which he had abolished and replaced in 1974.[3] It was her discreet symbol of defiance: Over the years, and very unostentatiously, her home on Inya Lake became a point of reference for the growing number of influential people—academics, journalists, senior army officers in disgrace—who had reached the conclusion that Burma was in need of a new direction. And at least a handful of them had encountered Daw Khin Kyi's daughter, listened to her conversation, noted her qualities and drawn certain conclusions.

As early as 1974, when the dishonorable treatment given by the regime to the corpse of its most famous son, the late Secretary General of the UN, U Thant, provoked violent demonstrations, the regime had called Suu in and enquired if she intended to get involved in anti-government activities. "I replied that I would never do anything from abroad, and that if I were to engage in any political movement I would do so from within the country," she wrote later.[4] U Kyi Maung, a colonel in the army who had been imprisoned for years for opposing Ne Win's coup and who later became one of the founders of the NLD, said that he first heard that Suu was thinking of going into politics from a mutual friend in 1987.[5] Twice the friend, U Htwe Myint, mentioned her interest. U Kyi Maung however was unmoved.

The fact is that, until Ne Win's stunning speech of July 23, 1988, there was no way into Burmese politics: With only one party permitted by law, it was the ultimate closed shop. Then suddenly, as the nation's political and economic crisis reached a head, the doors were thrown open. From being a no-man's-land, overnight Burmese politics became a free-for-all. And the elegant and sober lady of 54 University Avenue became the focus of intense speculation.

U Kyi Maung, though he later became one of her closest colleagues, is scathing in his early estimate of her. He met her first, he said, "by chance, at the home of a mutual friend here in Rangoon. It was back in 1986 . . . We spoke for only a few minutes. My most lasting impression was how shy and reticent she was. She seemed like a decent girl who had no interest in frivolous talk or gossip. In fact, I remember thinking how peculiar it was that I never saw her laugh . . . Anyway the point is that she didn't impress me at all. Except by how young she looked. She must have been about forty-two at the time but she could have passed for a girl of seventeen."[6]

But a man known to the Burmese public as Maung Thaw Ka saw far more in her than that. A Burmese Muslim whose tall figure and craggy face betrayed his roots in the subcontinent, he had been a captain in the Burmese Navy;[7] after his vessel was wrecked he survived twelve days at sea without food or water until rescued by a passing Japanese ship. His account of the ordeal became a bestseller. Invalided out of the service, he reinvented himself as a witty and popular journalist and an acclaimed poet. He became head of the Burmese Literary Society, and traveled around the country giving talks about books and writing. He was a known opponent of the regime, and Military Intelligence agents always occupied the first row at his lectures.

It was only natural for the woman now embarked on a postgraduate degree in modern Burmese literature to seek out this substantial literary figure. But whatever information he gave Suu about books and writers, of more immediate value was his detailed knowledge of the first five months of the Burmese insurgency. "He took her around Rangoon," said Bertil Lintner, who subsequently got to know him, "and showed her, 'Look, this is where people were shot.' He took her to the site of the so-called Red Bridge incident, the White Bridge incident, Sule pagoda, everywhere that students were killed."[8] It was a crash course in the political story so far.

*

And there was to be no respite. Within days of "Butcher" Sein Lwin taking over the top job, he made his intentions clear. Aung Gyi, the ex-general who had shattered the taboo against criticizing Ne Win with his hostile open letters, was arrested, as was Sein Win, one of the country's most respected journalists. But the resistance, too, was organizing, its efforts given new focus and urgency by the formerly unimaginable hope of returning to multiparty democracy.

A BBC journalist called Christopher Gunness had flown into Rangoon to cover the ruling party's extraordinary congress in July and stayed on to try to find out what was stirring behind the city's shabby walls—because it was already clear that Ne Win's declaration was not the end of something but only the beginning. "My impression when I arrived was that the situation was extremely tense," he said later. "People were frustrated and angry and there was a feeling of unfinished business; it was easy to sense that something big was about to happen. But there was a feeling of doom as well. I was enormously depressed by what I heard and what I saw."[9]

Gunness became the first foreign correspondent to give the world details of the beatings, tortures and rapes that arrested students had suffered in custody, as well as the medical disasters and the plummeting morale among Burmese troops fighting Karen rebels near the Thai border. But his most vital news was not about the past but the future: The students, he reported, were calling for a nationwide general strike on the auspicious date of August 8, 1988—8/8/88 as the date has been known in Burma ever since: exactly fifty years after a general strike led by militant students, including Aung San, against the British in August 1938. The BBC's Burmese language service had millions of regular listeners in Burma, who depended on it to learn facts the regime preferred to hide. Gunness's report ensured that on 8/8/88 there would be a good turnout.

But the students were not sitting around waiting for the big event: The uprising was already under way. "The first serious demonstration actually occurred on the afternoon of August 3," wrote Dominic Faulder, one of the few undercover foreign journalists to witness it.[10] "It took me completely by surprise as it swept down Shwedagon Pagoda Road towards the city center then turned east going past Sule Pagoda and City Hall, before sweeping round to roar back past the Indian and US Embassies . . . As a display of raw courage it was spine-tingling . . . There were no

security forces in sight and no attempt was made to stop the demonstration, which faded into the wet afternoon with astonishing speed."

That same day, the junta clamped martial law on Rangoon. But the next
day and the day after thousands of demonstrators ignored the restrictions,
marching through downtown, while further north in the capital students
began digging themselves in close to the Shwedagon pagoda, the nation's
Holy of Holies which had been the rallying-point for anti-regime protests
since British days. Demonstrations were now breaking out, not merely
in the capital and Mandalay but across the country. And everywhere
the protesters' indignation and hunger for change were met by casual,
murderous violence.

A fifteen-year-old schoolboy called Ko Ko took to the streets of central
Rangoon on August 6th along with thousands of others. He recalled many
years later:

> Before 1988 I loved the army. My grandfather and grandmother came from
> the same part of the country as Ne Win. So when I saw what they did to us
> protesters I was shocked. At the time we were not demanding democracy.
> We just wanted our friends to be released from prison.
>
> As I joined the demonstration I was afraid, but I thought they could not
> shoot me if I was carrying a picture of General Aung San. So I went into
> a cinema in the city center and asked them to give me the large framed
> photo of Aung San that was hanging on the wall. With thousands of others
> I walked along the road towards Sule Pagoda in the center of Rangoon
> holding the portrait in front of me. We were all shouting slogans, walking
> along in the rain.
>
> We were hoarse from shouting so much and a girl came up offering
> wedges of lemon for our sore throats. I was holding the photograph so she
> put the lemon directly in my mouth. Then I said to her, please hold the
> photograph, I have to re-tie my longyi, so she took the photograph and
> gave me the bag of lemons to hold. And after I had re-tied my longyi she
> kept holding on to the photograph while I held the lemons. Then I heard
> the rat-a-tat-tat of machine gun fire and she was lying on the ground dead
> and the photograph was full of bullet holes.
>
> I was so upset by this event that I ran away from the capital and joined
> the Kachin rebels on the border in the north of the country.[11]

*

The 8/8/88 general strike would have been a big event anyway, given the incendiary state of the nation. But now it had been trailed on the BBC, no one could doubt that it would be the cue for a mass, nationwide uprising.

The protest that day began when dockworkers in Rangoon port marched off the job at precisely eight minutes past eight. The movement that had begun with a student fracas in a tea shop had now spiraled out to include the most vital workers in the economy. Hundreds of thousands marched on City Hall in defiance of martial law.

Throughout the hours of daylight the soldiers and riot police stayed in the background. "Despite its overwhelming superiority of force, the regime is today under siege by its people," Seth Mydans wrote in the *New York Times*, reporting on the cataclysmic day. "The protests . . . have spread to every major city . . . led by students and joined by large numbers of workers and Buddhist monks, as well as by a cross-section of citizens, including government employees."[12]

"No one likes this brutal government," Mydans reported the owner of a curry shop saying. "It has no respect for the people, no respect for human rights. All the people are angry now. All the people support the students."

The huge demonstration, matched by similar shows of popular force all over the country, continued all day in a mood closer to a carnival than a riot. "Happy New Year," Mydans reported one demonstrator shouting to him. "This is our revolution day!" "The euphoric atmosphere prevailed all day," wrote Bertil Lintner. "In the evening, thousands of people moved to the Shwedagon, where a meeting was being held. Meanwhile, Bren carriers and trucks full of armed soldiers were parked in the compound of City Hall . . . But nobody really thought that the troops would be called out."[13]

Then at 11:30, after the last of many "last warnings" issued to the protesters over loudspeakers, the army suddenly went into action. "The tanks roared at top speed past [Sule] pagoda, followed by armored cars and twenty-four truckloads of soldiers," Mydans wrote.[14] "The protesters scattered screaming into alleys and doorways, stumbling over open gutters, crouching by walls and then, in a new wave of panic, running again." The shooting continued until 3 AM. No one knows how many died. The Butcher had lived up to his name.

But if the protesters, who remained as amorphous and apparently leaderless as they had been since the upheaval began, had not achieved the revolution which astrologers had promised and which they had been dreaming of, neither had Sein Lwin succeeded in imposing his will, despite all the bloodshed. The strike continued into the next day. By now the hermit state, till weeks before one of the least-known countries on the planet, was splashed all over the world's news bulletins day after day. While the regime claimed that only a hundred people had been killed in Rangoon, diplomats put the figure ten times higher, while hospital workers in the capital, who were closest to the butchery, said the true figure was more than 3,000.[15] The US Senate, in a shocking blow to Burma's *amour propre*, passed a motion unanimously condemning the regime and the killings for which they were responsible.

Then on August 12th, after less than three weeks in power, the Butcher threw in the towel.

*

Aung San Suu Kyi played no part in the demonstrations.[16] "It's not my sort of thing," she replied with a touch of memsahib haughtiness when asked why not. One might say, given her presence in the country all this time, and the power of her name, that her absence from the protests was conspicuous. As Bo Kyi, one of the leaders of the students, put it, "When we staged demonstrations in 1988, in March, April, May, June, July and August, at that time there was no Daw Aung San Suu Kyi. But all the time that we were holding demonstrations, Daw Aung San Suu Kyi was in Burma . . ."[17]

But she had not closed her eyes to the sufferings of her people. On the contrary, it is clear that she was thinking very hard about what role she could and ought to play.

Sein Lwin's stunning resignation prompted dancing in the street. He was replaced one week later, on August 19th, by Dr. Maung Maung, a London-trained barrister, a former chief justice, an academic who had done research at Yale, one of the very few civilians of stature in Ne Win's circle. But Maung Maung had lost whatever intellectual respectability he might once have claimed when he wrote the official hagiography of Number

One—which included a sly reworking of the life of Aung San, depicting him as a supporter of Japanese-style fascism and an opponent of democracy.[18] If Ne Win and his advisers imagined that the appointment of this ex-military pseudo-moderate would buy off the protesters' anger, they were rudely disappointed. It barely bought them twenty-four hours of calm.

What was now plain was that Burma confronted a gaping power vacuum. And it was during these strange days that a young Rangoon University history teacher met Suu for the first time.

"I was twenty-six," Nyo Ohn Myint remembered.[19] Today, still looking barely out of his twenties, he is head of the NLD-LA's foreign affairs department and lives in exile in Thailand. "I had been a teacher for three years. My colleagues and I were mulling over what part we should play in the uprising. We produced pamphlets and wall posters, stuff like that. Then finally I met her. There were seven of us around the table."

So far the only role Suu had conceived for herself was one behind the scenes. For Nyo Ohn Myint that was not enough. "I raised the fact that our movement really needed a leader," he said. "And she said, no, I have just asked the general secretary of the Burma Socialist Program Party to stop killing the students and other innocent people. That is my role."

Nyo Ohn Myint did not leave it at that. "I appealed to her to meet the student movement. She said no. Then I explained the nature of Burmese political culture to her, which is that you sacrifice a lot. She seemed quite reluctant to do as we asked. Some of us thought that she was an opportunist. She said she just wanted to mediate between the government and the students and the people.[20]

"I said then, 'Okay, so why have we bothered you to come here and talk?' I was quite fed up: I thought, oh my God, I've wasted my time. Because we believed that she was Aung San's daughter, our hero, our mentor, we grew up with stories of Aung San's morality, Aung San's bravery—everything."

Now Suu offered a compromise. "She said to us, 'Why don't you join with me, come and work with me. Come tomorrow, and then every day after that.' She said she would open a small office in her house, in the dining room—the room that became the party's main political office." The others in the discussion group welcomed her proposal eagerly; walking down the road back to the bus stop, they were "very excited that they were going to be working with Daw Aung San Suu Kyi," Nyo Ohn Myint recalled. But he remained unimpressed. "I told my colleagues, 'I'm not coming tomorrow.'" For her to say that she wanted to work with them, he told them, was

> a lie: She's not a leader. She refused to lead. We need a leader. The rest wanted to join with her but I said no, I'm still looking for a leader.
>
> But then two days later a friend of mine who was also a colleague called in on me and said, Daw Suu wants to talk to you. He rang her number and gave me the phone and I said, "How are you, sister?" (because at university it's our custom to call any girl our age or somewhat older Ma Ma, "big sister"). And she said, "Will you come to my home? We need to talk." I said, "No, I already heard you say that you didn't want to lead the movement." She said, "Shall we sit down and talk about it?"
>
> So I went there on August 16th with two others, a high school student called Aung Gyi and a university student, one of the leaders of the student movement, called Koko Gyi, and we sat down with Suu and she explained that she didn't want to be an opportunist, she didn't want to take over a movement that was already going on—but if people really needed Aung San's daughter, she said, "I will do it." But then she said there were so many other considerations, her family life, her two kids, her ailing mother, etcetera. So I said, "The point is, we really need you. We expected your elder brother, Aung San Oo, to be available to help us"—and there were a lot of rumors [about him] in Burma at that point. But he was never interested in Burma or in Burmese political issues or anything. He just happens to be the son of Aung San.
>
> So then she said, "All right, let's start working, because I know something about the Burmese situation through my books and my research, but I have been away from the country so maybe you can fill me in on that part." So we decided to work together as a team. And that's her skill as a leader, as I see it. She never takes the upper hand, she never uses her family background to dominate. She never acts like that.

In fact, in the time it took Suu to persuade this young academic to give her a second chance, she had already made her first political intervention, behind the scenes as she preferred. It was as modest and decorous in form as it was ambitious in content. On August 15th, she and Hwe Myint, one of her earliest political allies, wrote to the Council of State, the circle of elderly generals grouped around Ne Win, to propose that they set up a

"People's Consultative Committee," made up of people outside the BSPP, "to present the aspirations of the people in a peaceful manner within the framework of the law."[21] The letter went on, "In the words of the song which roused the patriotism of our people . . . 'For the good of those to follow/without regard for ourselves,' so is this proposal presented with the good of future generations in mind."

Suu's ad hoc University Avenue think tank was up and running: The proposal carried the endorsement of U Nu, Burma's first prime minister after independence, and other leading politicians from the pre-Ne Win era. But—as so often in years to come when appeals went out to Burma's generals from her address—there was no reply. Clearly, more direct methods would be required.

*

As the democracy movement came into existence around her, Suu was still in the bosom of her family, with all that implied—still nursing her gravely ill mother, keeping her sons up to the mark with their studies, stealing spare moments to resume work on her dissertation.[22] But at the same time she found herself the beating heart of what would soon become the most important political movement her country had seen since independence.

"The boys are in fine form," Michael reported. "Alex is relaxed and happy—trouncing me regularly at squash in the Australian Embassy Club, Kim is swimming, both of them spend time reading to their grandmother . . . There is a constant stream of visitors . . ."

A month later, after the children had flown back home to start the new school term, the life of the house had become even more hectic. "You have no idea how every second of the day is occupied," Michael wrote. "One of my main tasks is to see that Suu gets some sleep."

U Win Tin, a stubbornly contrarian journalist who had been silenced for years by Ne Win and who was at the time vice president of the journalists' union, was one of many drawn to Suu's door.[23]

Three separate groups formed around her, he explained:

In Rangoon everybody knows everybody and all the union strike committees—from the lawyers' union, the doctors' union, the students' union and so on—wanted to make contact with Daw Aung San Suu Kyi. So two or three people from each committee used to come to her house for talks lasting two or three hours, about the political situation outside, the government, the military and so on—that was one group.

After the strike started on August 8th, masses of people started coming into the city from the suburbs of Rangoon, maybe ten miles away, just walking without anything to drink or anything to eat—they did not dare to drink the tap water because there were rumors that it had been poisoned. It was very hard for them because the weather was very hot and humid, but people came down to the middle of town anyway because most of the offices are located in the downtown area. And as they marched and marched they shouted slogans, and anybody passing through from Rangoon's northern suburbs to the center of town has to pass in front of Daw Aung San Suu Kyi's house. So it was very easy for them [to come there] and they shouted slogans and tried to meet Daw Aung San Suu Kyi.

There was a man called Thakin Tin Mya, now he's an old man like me, he's about ninety, he used to be a communist and a leader of the nationalist organization DoBama before the war. He was a very good organizer, he knew almost everybody in Burmese politics, and he formed a group to talk to all these people coming past the house hoping for a meeting: to ask their names and their leader's names and their group's name and whether they are involved in strike action and so on. In the evening he made reports to Daw Aung San Suu Kyi and these reports became a sort of briefing in which he explained the contribution people were making to the strike, not only in Rangoon but also in the small towns and so on. And that was the second group.

And the third group was formed of people like me, senior politicians, journalists, writers and so on: We were her political consultants, thinking what we should do and so on.

The pressure of events—the host of people now clamoring for Suu to take some kind of initiative, and the failure of her proposal for a consultative committee to elicit any official reaction—were steadily pushing her towards the point of no return. Every evening, when all the different advisory groups had gone home, she and Michael sat down to talk over the day's events. Eventually they decided there was no other way out: Suu would have to stand up and be counted. But with troops at every crossroads with orders "to shoot to hit," in Ne Win's words, if the martial law ban on assemblies was broken, the last thing she wanted to do was provoke another bloodbath.

So she took steps to prevent it—and in the process discovered the extent of her influence.

Despite his communist background and the help he was providing to Suu, Thakin Tin Mya, her gatekeeper, was a member of the ruling BSPP and in good standing with the country's political establishment.[24] At Suu's urging he set up a secret meeting for August 23rd between her and U Tin Aung Hein, the Minister of Justice and one of the few people in Ne Win's inner circle not tainted by corruption. Suu confided in the Minister that she intended to make a public speech aimed at bringing an end to the bloodshed in the country—and she wanted him and his boss to know that she had no political aspirations and no hidden agenda.

The Minister replied with a piece of advice: The troops lining the streets regarded Ne Win as the father of the army, he said. "So please don't launch any attacks on him, and don't incite the people to do so, either."[25] Suu readily agreed, but had a specific request to make: To reduce the risk that her first public appearance would precipitate another massacre, she asked the Minister to petition Ne Win to allow the crowd to gather, despite the martial law provisions.

U Tin Aung Hein promised to do what he could. And he was as good as his word. The next day martial law was lifted; Maung Maung, four days into his presidency, announced that, in accordance with Ne Win's proposal in July, a referendum would be held to decide between a one-party and a multiparty system; and Daw Aung San Suu Kyi gave the first public speech of her life.

It was a brief affair, delivered in the grounds of Rangoon General Hospital. Suu stood on a petrol drum to speak, wearing a white Burmese blouse and looking, as U Kyi Maung had observed, about seventeen. At her shoulder stood the shipwreck survivor and poet Maung Thaw Ka, with a quizzical expression on his craggy face. Who can say, he seems to be thinking, what this might lead to?

Grasping the microphone, she expressed her desire to see Burma move swiftly to a political system "in accord with the people's desires." She said she further wished that the people would show discipline and unity and use only the most pacific methods of demonstration. So far, there was nothing to disturb Ne Win's sleep. Then she told them that she would be speaking again at greater length two days' hence—this time at the Shwedagon pagoda.

*

Ralph Fitch, an English merchant who saw the pagoda in 1586, called it "the fairest place, as I suppose, that is in the world."[26] Norman Lewis called it "the heart and soul of Rangoon, the chief place of pilgrimage in the Buddhist world, the Buddhist equivalent of the Kaaba at Mecca, and, in sum, a great and glorious monument." Its special holiness, he explained, "arises from the fact that it is the only pagoda recognized as enshrining relics not only of Gautama, but of the three Buddhas preceding him." The value placed on the huge shrine was made manifest in the treasures lavished on it by successive kings, the guaranteed method—according to the somewhat mechanical dictates of traditional Theravada Buddhism—of speeding one's approach to Nirvana. "It was the habit of the Burmese kings," Lewis goes on, "to make extravagant gifts for the embellishment of the Shwedagon, diamond vanes, jewel-encrusted finial umbrellas, or at least their weight in gold, to be used in re-gilding the spire. The wealth that other Oriental princes kept in vaults and coffers was here spread out under the sun to astound humanity." And its impact on the visitor, Lewis discovered, was quite as powerful as its importance suggested it should be. "I plunged suddenly into the most brilliant spectacle I had ever seen," he reported of his arrival on the pagoda's expansive terrace. "In the immediate background rises a golden escarpment, a featureless cliff of precious metal, spreading a misty dazzlement."[27]

But the Shwedagon is far more than just a brilliant place of pilgrimage. Affirming the centrality of the Buddhist tradition at the heart of the nation's identity, it became the focus during the 1920s and 1930s of the first mass demonstrations against British rule.[28] Aung San delivered some of his most inflammatory speeches here, and is buried nearby. By announcing that she would speak at the Shwedagon, for the first time Suu showed her willingness to throw the charisma of her name behind the uprising. And the regime's response was instantaneous.

Relations between Suu and her mother and the regime had never been less than correct all these years. Suu's frequent appearances at the Martyrs' Day event in July was the extent of their co-involvement, and both sides handled her father's name and fame with great care and respect, exquisitely conscious of how much it meant to all of them. But suddenly, as she stepped into the maelstrom, all that was forgotten. Overnight thousands of leaflets were printed, stigmatizing Suu as the puppet of a foreign power, as a "genocidal prostitute," the whore of a foreign bastard.[29] In grotesque caricatures, the first of many to appear over the years, Suu and Michael were depicted having sex. "Take your bastard of a foreigner," they commanded, "and leave at once!"

Suu and her party left University Avenue at 8:30 AM in a convoy of eleven vehicles. Anonymous bomb scares and assassination threats had heightened the tension of the day. One of her advisers urged her to don a bulletproof vest for protection.[30] "Why?" she retorted. "If I was afraid of being killed, I would never speak out against the government." Already her supporters were getting a glimpse of her mettle. To guard against unpleasant surprises, dozens of the students who had been frequenting her home over the previous weeks, wearing long-sleeved white shirts and dark longyis, formed a large though unarmed bodyguard.

"We didn't go along the main road," Nyo Ohn Myint the lecturer recalled, "because there had been many rumors and we were afraid of being attacked—an army captain was arrested in downtown Rangoon with a lot of machine guns, he had supposedly been assigned to assassinate her. He confessed after he was arrested by members of the public, who then beat him."[31]

Though well into the monsoon season, August 26th dawned sunny and hot. Word of the event had spread across the city, and thousands camped outside the Shwedagon all night to secure a good place. Many tens of thousands more began arriving at dawn. It is a short ride from University Avenue to the shrine—the two addresses are about a mile apart to the north of the city center—and on a normal day it would not take fifteen minutes. But on this day the crowds were so huge that Suu's convoy, with a Jeep in front, herself in a Toyota Saloon and Michael and the boys in another car behind, could not even get close. "We couldn't get through the crowd," said Nyo Ohn Myint. "Michael was in my car and it took something like forty-five minutes because the street was so crowded." They were forced to get down and walk the last few hundred yards, the road ahead of them cleared by students waving flags.

Nobody knows for sure how many people were gathered outside the Shwedagon pagoda that day. It is part of the reporter's informal training to gauge the rough size of a crowd, but massive exaggeration is common in many countries, especially when the meetings are of great political importance; equally massive under-reporting by the authorities is also common, for the same reason. But Win Tin, the veteran journalist and close associate of Suu, insists that his own estimate of the numbers was not distorted by his political views. He said:

> In those days the population of Rangoon was about three million, and about one million attended the meeting on August 26th. The crowd stretched from the pagoda itself all the way to the market, the people were densely packed, so there might have been a million. It was my duty to inform the international press about the event, but when I sent the news to the BBC I said there might be 600,000 people. I didn't want to sound too boastful because when Ne Win held a meeting he only drew 100,000 or 200,000 people. So I didn't want to make too much of the amount.[32]

Faced with such an unprecedented throng, even her closest supporters did not know what to expect from their "big sister," dwarfed on the stage by a stylized portrait of her father. Would she dry up? Would her courage fail this frightening test? Would this long-term expatriate, deeply learned in Burmese literature, be incomprehensible to ordinary people?

"As far as I knew she had never done any public speaking," said Win Tin. "I knew that she could speak Burmese quite well, but we had some misgivings about whether she would be able to speak good Burmese on stage."

The stage was packed with young people, many wearing yellow armbands; a line of young bodyguards wearing headbands sat or crouched watchfully at the edge. A famous film star called Htun Wai, a comfortable-looking figure in a lilac jacket and longyi, stepped to the microphone and introduced her with a vertical flourish of his arm: "Daw Aung San Suu Kyi!" He lowered the microphone six inches and moved to the side. She took his place center stage, her hands clasped over a folder of documents at her waist. And without preliminaries, without hesitation and without even the ghost of a smile she began to speak, in a high, loud voice.

It has been said with some authority that she read her speech from a prepared text.[33] Nothing could be further from the truth. Nor was she reciting parrot-fashion a text she had learned by heart. Instead she spoke spontaneously, without notes, but sticking to a tight and cogent argument; spoke, in other words, on her first real outing, like a seasoned politician.

"She spoke very good Burmese," said Win Tin, "very fluent and very convincingly and very clear. For a normal person it is not so easy to talk to such a huge crowd, a sea of people. She was not reading, and she talked so wittily—something like Obama. We saw at once that she was a born leader: 'a star is born,' something like that."

"It was so direct and down to earth," said Bertil Lintner. "Everyone was absolutely taken aback by that speech. Here was this tiny woman talking and everyone was spellbound. It was amazing. She looked like her father and she sounded like him too."[34]

The crowd stretched away into the monsoon haze, a sea of dark heads. Close to the stage it was slashed by a broad wedge of maroon: hundreds of monks, shielding their shaved pates from the sun with their robes. "The attendance was so big," remembered Win Tin. "Never had so many people come together for a political meeting."

How would this chit of a girl—to judge by her appearance—begin? By regurgitating the consultative committee proposal she had launched ten days before, to no avail? By apologizing for her months of silence and absence? By bemoaning the killings and pleading with the people to return to the path of docility and obedience?

Anyone expecting this sort of thing gravely underestimated the Bogyoke's daughter.

The very first words were like a cannon blast aimed at the regime's monopoly of power.

"Reverend monks and people!" she shouted. "This public rally is aimed at informing the whole world of the will of the people . . . Our purpose is to show that the entire people entertain the keenest desire for a multiparty system of government."[35]

It was a broadside. Here, she declared, were the people—that was incontrovertible—and here and now the people were going to tell, not merely the Burmese authorities but the "whole world"—the world from which she had returned, and which the regime had for a generation done everything in its power to exclude from its calculations—exactly what they wanted. She herself—she had no hesitation in claiming—was the people's mouthpiece. And what they wanted was not the cheese-paring referendum Dr. Maung Maung had announced just two days before, but something very clear. "I believe," she went on, "that all the people who have assembled here have without exception come with the unshakeable desire to strive for and win a multiparty democratic system."

What business did she, thirty years removed from the fray and married to an Englishman, have sticking her oar in Burmese waters? She addressed that issue, the one raised by the obscene posters, head on. "It is true that I have lived abroad," she said. "It is also true that I am married to a foreigner. These facts have never interfered and will never interfere with or lessen my love and devotion for my country." For the first time, two minutes into the speech, applause erupted; the actor Htun Wai at her side beamed and clapped, and Suu paused in her flow.

Love and devotion, however sincere, did not explain her presence on the stage. Unlike the democrats and communists who had spent the decades of one-party rule languishing in jail or fighting Ne Win's troops on the border, Aung San Suu Kyi had been far away from Burma and apparently uninterested in what was happening there. So what had brought her back? "The answer," she said, "is that the present crisis is the concern of the entire nation. I could not as my father's daughter remain indifferent to all that was going on. This national crisis could in fact be called the second struggle for national independence."

This was to step up the attack further. Here was a direct challenge to Ne Win: The standard-bearer of independence, the man who had for so long traded on his closeness to Aung San and who claimed to be his rightful heir, this man—she never named him—was now in her estimation no better than the colonial oppressor, to be resisted and evicted (so it was implied) like the British.

How could she justify such a call to arms? Now she raised the file clasped in her hands and leafed through it to read from a text written by her father. "We must make democracy the popular creed," she read out. Otherwise, "Burma would one day, like Japan and Germany, be despised."

Democracy, Aung San had declared and now her daughter repeated, was "the only ideology which is consistent with freedom . . . an ideology that promotes and strengthens peace."

Deafening applause rolled across the stage. The expression on Htun Wai's face veered between elation and wonderment—with the odd flicker of fright as the speech's incendiary subtext sunk in.

But she had not finished with the army yet. At her secret meeting with the Justice Minister two days before, U Tin Aung Hein had enjoined Suu not to attack Number One, and not to incite the crowd to attack him. She had agreed, and she remained true to her undertaking—though perhaps not so true to the spirit of it.

"I would like to say one thing," she went on, with the first hint of circumspection in her voice. "Some may not like what I am going to say. But I believe that my duty is to tell the people what I believe to be true. Therefore I shall speak my mind . . . At this time there is a certain amount of dissension between the people and the army . . ."

For the first time in the speech, Suu was open to the accusation of understatement: After all, staff at the hospital where her mother had once worked believed the army had killed 3,000 civilians in cold blood—a far greater massacre than any for which the former colonial ruler was blamed.[36] She could not have been unaware that she was now trespassing on the most delicate and at the same time most vital question confronting the people: not what political system the country might adopt, which after all was a question for the coming weeks and months, but the nightmare of murder and mutilation that the country was living through right now, day after day. It could not be ignored.

And again her hands moved to the documents she had brought with her, leafing through to the words she needed. Again the great Aung San, like the ghost of Hamlet's father, pointed his dread finger at his sanguinary successor. "The armed forces are meant for this nation and this people," she read out, "and it should be a force having the honor and respect of the people. If instead the armed forces should come to be hated by the people, then the aims with which this army has been built up would have been in vain."

"My first impression was that she was just another general's daughter," said Nita Yin Yin May, the British Embassy's information officer at the time, "because I'd never met her personally. And then she started talking to the people and I was overwhelmed by her speech. I was shocked: This was the one we were looking for! She was the true leader!"[37] She wiped away tears of emotion at the memory. "I was very much impressed. I thought she was very sincere, very charming, very beautiful, very outspoken. It really hit all of us. It really touched all of us. And then I decided, I'm going to support her no matter what."

There was much more: The crowd listened with keen attention and by the end they were chanting her name. She told them of her "strong attachment" to the army, how soldiers had cared for her as a child. She vowed that she would never be a stalking horse for politicians of the past; echoing her father she exhorted the people over and over again to "unity" and "discipline." She spelled out, naming the hapless Dr. Maung Maung (who was to survive in power for less than a month), her belief that a referendum was not required. "We want to get rid of the one-party system," she said. There is "no desire at all for a referendum . . . free and fair elections [should be] arranged as quickly as possible . . ."

General Ne Win was of course not present at this meeting, and it is not known if he was subsequently given a recording of Aung San Suu Kyi's maiden speech; but if so it is a fair bet that by this point he had switched the machine off, possibly hurling it at the wall. Not only had Bogyoke's daughter come out of nowhere to make a nuisance of herself; not only did she bear a startling resemblance to the man honored as the father of the nation and of the Tatmadaw. But in pronouncing very particular words uttered by the dead man, she had ripped away what shreds of legitimacy Ne Win and his clique could still lay claim to. It was a declaration of war.

3

FREEDOM AND SLAUGHTER

I T is not true that recent Burmese history is an unending catalogue of oppression. Any Burmese over the age of thirty-five can remember a time of perfect liberty, when a free press flourished and trade unions and political parties sprang up like mushrooms after rain.

Unfortunately the Burma Spring lasted less than one month—twenty-six days to be precise. It ended as abruptly as it had begun.

Yet within that brief span in August and September 1988 Aung San Suu Kyi, backed by a shifting and so far nameless coalition of students, intellectuals, old politicians and veteran army officers, succeeded in persuading the regime to push through three reforms which ensured that Burma would never be the same again.

The first was what ushered in the spring, the decision by the Justice Minister to lift martial law—a prelude to and, in Suu's view, a basic precondition, for her public debut at the Shwedagon pagoda: She wanted the regime's assurance that nobody who came to listen to her would risk being shot. On August 24th, the request was granted.

The second reform changed Burma's political matrix forever, even though, more than two decades later, it has yet to produce any of the benefits for which it was promoted: the regime's commitment, not to the referendum advocated by Dr. Maung Maung but to general elections leading to multiparty democracy.

The third was hardly less momentous: the disestablishment of the BSPP, effectively bringing down the curtain on twenty-six years of one-party rule. Burma would never be the same again. And it was Aung San Suu Kyi—the "governess" as she has been labeled, the Burmese "Mary Poppins," the "Oxford housewife," the political ingénue—who brought them about.[1]

*

The effect of the lifting of martial law was immediate. Troops and riot police disappeared from the streets. All over the country people could suddenly do and say exactly what they pleased. Strikers surged through towns and cities throughout the country, no longer defiant, merely euphoric. Twenty-six years before, in the interest of order and discipline, General Ne Win had fastened a straitjacket on the nation. Now it was flung off, and the urges that had been building since March—to laugh, to swear, to scandalize, to join hands, to dream and plan for a future dramatically different from the past—burst forth in all their jubilant diversity.

The regime's indigestible daily rag, the *Working People's Daily*, until the day before full of articles about ambassadors presenting their credentials and generals opening sewage plants, was suddenly publishing daring political comment pieces and pages of photographs of the demonstrations. An unruly crowd of new papers sprang up to offer competition: *Scoop*, *Liberation Daily*, *New Victory*, *Light of Dawn*—their titles alone told of the mood of wild optimism sweeping the country.

Not all the news they published could be relied on: One paper called *Phone Maw Journal*, named after the student whose killing by the army in March had ignited the revolution, informed its readers that a cemetery in a Rangoon suburb where the bodies of many of the victims of army shootings had been unceremoniously buried was now noisily haunted— and that the ghosts were chanting pro-democracy slogans![2] The spirits had also formed a closed shop, barring entry to the mortal remains of members of the ruling party: Anyone brave enough to go close could hear them wailing, "Corpses of BSPP members not to be buried in our cemetery! Stay out! Stay out!"

The movement, which at the start had been the monopoly of students, now drew recruits from every part of society. Martin Morland, British ambassador in Burma at the time, remembered the euphoric mood.

"The Rangoon Bar Association took its courage in both hands and issued a signed protest calling for change," he recalled.[3] "The Medical Association followed suit. The street marches multiplied, with banners identifying the state organization marching. By early September every ministry had joined in. Even the beggars had their march. On the last Sunday before the army struck back even the police band went over to the side of the people and played outside City Hall."

It was the same all over the country. In the little town of Phekhon, in the Shan States in Burma's disputed northeast, a student recently returned from Rangoon called Pascal Khoo Thwe was caught up in the excitement; like many others, it was to determine the course of the rest of his life.[4] He wrote many years later:

> When Aung San Suu Kyi made her great speech . . . on August 26th, she instantly became our leader and inspiration. In the evenings we would listen to the BBC and hope for guidance from our goddess. We formed committees for security, for the food supply, for information, for connecting the different ethnic and religious groups.
>
> Although I busied myself with all this, I knew there was a pompous and officious aspect to it. It also had a dreamlike quality. Only weeks before, to speak in open opposition to the regime would have been unthinkable. Now the whole of Phekhon was talking about the future, about what sort of constitution Burma should have, about the place of the minority peoples. People who had been silent for twenty-six years now wanted to shout, or at least endlessly to debate.

Burma was approaching a state of anarchy, but for a while it worked the way anarchists have always claimed society should naturally work once the state's machinery of repression is sent to the scrapyard, in messy but euphoric harmony. The army had pulled back to barracks and was nowhere to be seen. The feared and hated riot police, the Lon Htein, was likewise invisible. Ministries and government offices had simply closed; the Burmese state had shut down. And the vacuum filled up with people doing their own thing. A young woman called Hmwe Hmwe who had joined the democracy movement in Rangoon traveled to Mandalay to help coordinate strike centers there, traveling by van and pickup truck.[5] "Since everybody was on strike, there was no train service or other regular transport and it was difficult to buy petrol as well," she said. "But spirits were high and we attended meetings all along the way. We slept in the strike centers and there was one in every town we passed through. The people had taken over the local BSPP offices and government premises and managed their own administration . . . There was feverish activity everywhere: people printing leaflets, making posters, publishing their own local newspapers and preparing meetings, rallies and demonstrations."

Older systems of authority re-emerged to fill the place of those that had vanished. Bertil Lintner wrote:

In Mandalay, the young monks' organization . . . had resurfaced.[6] The monks organized day-to-day affairs like rubbish collection, made sure the water supply was working and, according to some reports, even acted as traffic policemen. The maintenance of law and order was also in the hands of the monks—and the criminals who had been caught were often given rather unorthodox sentences. One visitor to Mandalay in August saw a man chained to a lamp post outside the railway station who shouted all day, "I'm a thief! I'm a thief! . . ."

Yet the appearance of a vacuum of power was itself illusory. The military regime was rocking, it is true; its pseudo-civilian governing apparatus was crumbling. But in the months and years to come, proof emerged of a controlling mind behind what was going on during the weeks of freedom—the same cynical and ruthless military mind that had ruled the country for the past generation.

On the same day that Aung San Suu Kyi gave her maiden speech at the Shwedagon, truckloads of troops poured into central Rangoon and removed 600 million kyats from the Myanma Foreign Trade Bank: to pay the army for the coming six months and ensure its continuing loyalty.

The following day, in a cynical coda to the lifting of martial law, Insein Jail, the Victorian panopticon in a leafy Rangoon suburb that is the nation's most infamous prison, evacuated its inmates on what the authorities called "parole," sending them out into the lawless capital with neither money nor food. They were released from the jail after inmates threw in their lot with the strikers outside the walls and attacked the prison guards. The guards replied by shooting the protesters, a fire broke out and it was claimed that 1,000 died and 500 were wounded. Whatever the truth about the riot and its suppression, the mass release of prisoners added a new element of peril and anarchy to the dangerously combustible elements outside. The pattern was repeated around the country, leading to the sudden discharge into the community of more than 10,000 footloose criminals.

The result was predictable—and almost certainly anticipated and indeed plotted by the regime. As Martin Morland put it, "The army evidently hoped that things would get so out of hand that the people would have had enough and beg the old regime to come back."[7] Certainly the sudden appearance en masse of the most desperate people in society added an extra element of terror to the unstable situation, an element to which some of the protesters responded brutally. Lintner wrote:

> On September 5th, four men and one woman were caught outside a children's hospital [in Rangoon].[8] After a rough interrogation, two of them confessed that the gang had tried to poison the water tank outside the hospital, and they were released. But the remaining three refused to say anything and an angry crowd beat them in the street. A man came forward with a sword, decapitated the three and held up their blood-dripping severed heads to the applause of the mob. Public executions—mostly beheadings—of suspected DDSI [i.e. Military Intelligence] agents became an almost daily occurrence in Rangoon. What had started as a carnival-like, Philippine-style "people's power uprising" was . . . coming more and more to resemble the hunt for the *tonton macoutes* in Haiti after the fall of "Baby Doc" Duvalier . . .

But the descent into savagery was strictly localized and, when reported in time, it was strongly opposed. Suu took no immediate steps to capitalize on the success of her performance at the Shwedagon; on the contrary, in her first-ever interviews she expressed reluctance about getting involved in politics. But her home was ever more of a hurly-burly, with throngs of strikers besieging the gates asking to talk to her and think tanks in permanent session in her downstairs dining room-cum-office. Many of the students who had been her escort on August 26th were now camping out in the garden. And when Suu learned of lynch parties at large she repeatedly sent the students to try to restore sanity and calm. Often they succeeded.

The BSPP government was still notionally in power, but the central strike committee in Rangoon called for it to resign and for a neutral interim government to take its place, capable of supervising the free, multiparty democratic elections that were now the goal everyone had in mind. The call was taken up across the country. But President Maung Maung refused to take this step, instead announcing a second emergency conference of the ruling party for September 12th.

The outbreaks of lynching underlined the fact that, if the military had pulled in its claws and the BSPP was on the point of collapse, the democracy movement had yet to take a definite shape or coalesce around particular leaders. The movement's challenge was to prove that the military dictatorship was not merely enfeebled but that it could be superseded. But it was a challenge that it was slow to meet.

The students were the first to make a stab at it. A charismatic biology student called Baw Oo Tun had become their *de facto* leader in many protests, taking the *nom de guerre* of Min Ko Naing—"Conqueror of Kings." In late August they set up the All-Burma Students' Union under his leadership—an initiative weakened by the fact that a quite separate organization with the same name already existed.

Next to throw his hat in the ring was the great veteran of Burmese democratic politics, the first and indeed only prime minister elected under the old multiparty system, eighty-two-year-old U Nu, who had held office until the coup of 1962. At the end of August he defied the constitution by announcing the establishment of Burma's first independent political party in twenty-six years, the League for Democracy and Peace (Provisional). But on September 9th, he critically overplayed his hand, telling the world that he had now formed a parallel government, and calling for general elections. In a press conference to relaunch a career that he had renounced years before in favor of religious devotion, he claimed that Burma's only legal constitution was the one passed in 1947, according to which he was still in charge. "I'm still the legitimate prime minister," he insisted.

If anything was designed to give the democracy movement a bad name, this was it. The announcement stunned U Nu's political friends and enemies alike. "Preposterous" was the verdict of Aung Gyi, the general who had written dissenting letters to Ne Win earlier in the year, while at a press conference in University Road Suu rejected it just as firmly. She was "astonished" by U Nu's claim, she said, adding "the future of the people will be decided by the masses of the people."[9]

This was the theme she had hammered home at the Shwedagon: Burma's future lay in a multiparty democracy; the only way for the country to emerge from the nightmare of military tyranny was for the people to have the opportunity to choose their rulers. And the very next day, in the second important victory she won before even declaring her intention of entering politics, her wish was granted.

The occasion was a second extraordinary congress of the still-just-about ruling BSPP, following the one in July when Ne Win had spoken of his intention to step down. President Maung Maung's offer of a referendum on single- or multiparty systems was still on the table, but as tens of thousands of protesters chanted outside, the congress threw it out, opting instead for "free, fair, multiparty elections." Under Suu's urging and that of millions of other Burmese, the party that had ruled the country very badly for a generation had now written its suicide note.

But it was jam tomorrow, not jam today. The regime, however battered and bruised, clung to what little remained of its authority. There was to be no interim government to see the election process through.

*

The history of Burma is littered with "ifs," and one of the biggest of them looms over the events of the subsequent week.

The democracy movement that had begun obscurely in March—that had been hardened under army fire in which thousands died and that was now groping towards the attainment of some clear political shape—was continuing to grow. With army and police still absent from the streets, the strikers' demonstrations grew larger, more vocal, more militant, more ambitious. So much had already been wrung from the tyrants: One more heave, it seemed, and the rotten superstructure of army rule would come crashing down. What was needed now was for the army itself, or significant portions of it, to switch sides. And with the daughter of the army's founder ever more prominent in the revolt, that was no longer a pipe dream.

Aung San Suu Kyi's emotional appeal for disillusioned members of the armed forces was already apparent. Maung Thaw Ka, the ex-naval officer who had stood alongside her during her speech at Rangoon General Hospital, was one of them. And now other senior figures closely associated with the armed forces were coming over to her side.

U Kyi Maung was to become one of the central figures in Suu's early political life in Burma, the chairman of her party who led it to triumph in the election when Suu and all the other top leaders were in jail or detention. A plump, quizzical figure approaching retirement age with a biting wit and a phlegmatic approach to the terrors visited on him and his colleagues by the regime, he was as devout as he was irreverent: His pithy formulations of how to apply the simple truths of Buddhism to solitary confinement had a powerful influence on Suu herself.[10]

A career soldier, Kyi Maung had reached the rank of colonel before being sacked from the army for opposing Ne Win's coup. He had spent a total of eleven years in jail for his hostility to the dictatorship and had just emerged from a brief third term when he got the message that Suu wanted to see him.

"I thought to myself, let's see what this lady is up to," he said later.[11] "Now is the time, a revolution is stirring . . . I was a veteran jailbird and well over twenty years her senior. Later on I learned that she was watching people, looking in all directions for people who could be trusted—candidates, you know, for the struggle. She was born with revolution in her blood but she needed all the help possible to see it through. So from then on we began to meet frequently." At their first meeting he remembered telling her, "Suu, if you're prepared to enter Burmese politics and to go the distance, you must be tolerant and be prepared for the worst." She listened, he said, "attentively."

Even more ominous to the regime was the arrival at Suu's side of a man who had been one of Burma's most senior and distinguished soldiers before falling out with Ne Win.

Bony and bespectacled, U Tin Oo stood out among the professors and journalists swirling around Suu like a commando at a cocktail party. A decade after being sacked and jailed by Ne Win, there was still a parade-ground gleam in his eye and the abrasiveness of the battle-hardened soldier in his manner.

"From the age of seventeen until nearly fifty, my life was a struggle," he later explained.[12] "I had a very rough life. I had to stay many years in dense jungles during the war. I've been wounded in battle numerous times . . . I lost my father, and my son died at a young age. After being promoted to chief of staff I was betrayed, sacked and imprisoned. I lacked politeness, and felt aggressive."

One of the first recruits to Aung San's Patriot Burmese Forces in 1943 when he was only sixteen, Tin Oo rose rapidly through the ranks. He was twice decorated for valor in battle and was a popular hero of the regime when he was made Minister of Defense in 1974. But during the abortive uprising of that year, his was the name shouted by the crowds calling for Ne Win to step down and be replaced. Two years later, accused of involvement in an abortive coup, he was sacked and jailed.[13]

On coming out of prison, he spent two years as a monk, then took a degree in law. As the democracy revolt erupted around him, he was reluctant to get involved: "My [old army] colleagues urged me to address the public. At first I declined. I wanted to continue living quietly practicing *vipassana* [insight] meditation. I think I was a bit attached to the tranquility and peace of the practice. But my colleagues would not give up, and after many discussions we agreed to form the All-Burma Patriotic Old Comrades' League. Nearly all the retired officers from all over the country came to our headquarters, which was my house, to offer their services."[14]

Tin Oo himself, after much arm-twisting, followed in Suu's footsteps and made a public speech to a "huge, energetic crowd" outside Rangoon General Hospital on August 27th. But although he represented a formidably prestigious sector of this highly militarized society, Tin Oo recognized that the old soldiers could not stand alone. "Although our group was large, consisting of military personnel and some portion of the population, I knew that I could not lead the entire country along with the ethnic races," he said. "We needed a leader, a strong leader, who could lead the whole show . . . We needed somebody who understood democracy, who had really lived it."

A colleague played him a tape of Suu's speech at Shwedagon. "Her words were strong and clear," he recalled, "and there was no hitch at all. Some people who live abroad a long time can hardly speak Burmese when they come back to Burma, but she spoke fluently and with daily Burmese usage. She was clearly a very rare person. I realized that the people were eager for democracy, and that they were thinking that she was the unifying force that could lead the movement. We didn't say 'leader'—she was the lady who could try . . . to guide our people to what they desired so much."

The old soldiers in Tin Oo's League decided that the only hope for the revolution was for the different opposition groups that had sprung up to band together under a single figure. Increasingly Suu was seen as the only plausible candidate. "We agreed that I would meet her," he remembered, "and that I would go alone. . . . When I came to her house she was sitting on the corner of the sofa in the main room. She was alone. I paid my respects . . ."[15]

The old soldier and the daughter of his first commander talked over the desperate straits their country was in. "The way she talked, her complexion, her features and gestures were strikingly similar to those of her father," he said. "She resembled him in almost every way. I thought that she was a female replica . . . I said, 'I listened to your first public speech. We cannot make it alone. We need unity within the struggle for human rights and democracy.' She agreed. 'All right,' she said, 'fine, let's go forward together and work together.' That's all."

It was an encounter of military terseness and efficiency, worthy of Aung San himself, famous for his economy with words. Both were holding in their emotions, but as the general headed for the door, Suu blurted out, "Did you meet my father? Did you know him?"

Tin Oo replied, "Yes of course, I knew him well." Suu asked him how that came about. "I told her that I had known him from my days as a cadet and an officer in his Patriot Force. I said, 'The last time I met your father was at Maymyo, he was the Deputy Chairman of the Governor's Executive Council, and I, a lieutenant. At that time your father was visiting with the Chief of Yawngshwe state . . . And I saw your mother too. That was the last time I saw your father alive.' So she asked, 'Did you notice at that time a small girl being carried by somebody?'" Tin Oo confessed that he had not, but the coincidence further strengthened the bond between them. The general told her how sad it was that Aung San had not lived to bring his work of nation-building to a conclusion. "Now I have to serve and cooperate with you," he told her, "so that you, his only daughter, may enjoy the great fruits of Burma's independence." More than two decades and many years of detention later, Tin Oo remains the most stalwartly loyal of all Suu's colleagues.

The third veteran to stand alongside Suu in the tense days of mid-September 1988 was U Aung Gyi, the gadfly general who, by publishing his anti-regime tirades in the spring, had broken the taboo against open criticism. Aung Gyi himself had spoken at Shwedagon one day before Suu, though his efforts to persuade the crowd to go easy on President Maung Maung were met with stony silence.

Now, for the first time, Aung San Suu Kyi, Aung Gyi and Tin Oo, the emerging leaders of the uprising, banded together. They went to meet the election commission that had been set up following the BSPP's decision to hold multiparty elections, to learn what arrangements were being made to ensure that they were indeed free and fair. But they came away unsatisfied, and in a public letter to President Maung Maung signed by all three they explained why.

They pointed out that new political parties formed to fight the election would find themselves up against the BSPP, which had had a lock on power for twenty-six years and was still in charge. That could never be a fair fight. Furthermore the BSPP had a massive captive vote bank, consisting of the entire armed forces, all of them members of the party by compulsion, as well as millions of civilian employees of the state. Lacking funding and independent supervision, what kind of a chance would the opposition parties have?

The only solution, as the Rangoon strike committee and others had been arguing, was for the replacement of the present administration with an interim government "acceptable to all the people" to be sworn in to see the elections through.

The date was September 13th, a Tuesday.

What is tantalizing, seen from a perspective of more than twenty years on, is to observe how President Maung Maung, in these tumultuous days, seems to be edging towards the same conclusions as his adversaries in the opposition. In a speech after the BSPP's extraordinary congress, the president conceded that his party was not up to the present challenges. "The weakness of the party is that it was born as a ruling party and grew up as one," he told the assembled delegates. "In practice, it lacked the experience of making sacrifices, taking risks and working hard to overcome difficulties." He appeared to be dictating his own party's obituary.

Then, on Friday, September 16th, three days after the publication of the openly hostile letter by Suu and her two colleagues, the regime conceded one of the letter's principal demands. It was the third victory Suu had wrung from them in less than a month. "On September 16th," as Burma historian Michael Charney records, "the State Council announced that since government servants should 'be loyal to the state and only serve the people' and in keeping with the multiparty system that the government now promised to create, all state employees, including the military, could no longer be members of a political party."[16] That meant they could not belong to the BSPP. Another huge clump of the ruined state's masonry came crashing down. Optimists, including Michael Aris, were gladly anticipating the revolution's triumph. "Dear Everyone," he faxed home on September 15th, "an enormous thank you to you all for helping so much with Alexander and Kim . . . We still have high hopes of bringing them here for Christmas . . . Both of us are convinced that by then peace will have firmly arrived. Even now the final cracks in the edifice of this monstrous regime are appearing. Wish us luck!"

Meanwhile the 600 million kyats the regime had forcibly withdrawn from the bank to pay the army's wages appeared to be losing its adhesive power. The regime might discount the arrival at Suu's side of a figure like Tin Oo, long gone from the army and identified with Ne Win's enemies for more than a decade. But what about the sixteen privates from the 16th Light Infantry who marched through Rangoon in their uniforms though without weapons on September 7th, chanting, "Our military skills are not for killing the people"? What of the officers of the immigration and customs police, marching through the capital in their uniforms bearing banners to demand democracy? Or the Railway Police likewise in uniform and marching in formation behind a woman officer carrying the obligatory photo of Aung San?

Small fry, the senior generals might scoff, lower rankers, easily excited but just as easily scared back into line. But what about the air force flyers who started moving in the same direction? On September 9th, 150 airmen of the Mingaladon Maintenance Air Base went on strike followed by airmen from two other units. In the speech in which he pointed out the failings of the BSPP, Dr. Maung Maung had gone on to conjure a hellish image of the barbarous forces of revolt, those determined to "sweep everything aside, bring everything down, rush in on human waves shouting their war cries to the cheers of outsiders, and establish their occupation."[17] But what of these new recruits to the revolt, marching through the capital behind their drummers and buglers in crisp military order, demanding change?

At this point in the story the opposed forces seemed almost perfectly matched: A feather would have been enough to bring the scale down on the side of revolution. "Any high-ranking army officer who had taken an armed infantry unit into the capital and declared his support for the uprising would have become a national hero immediately," argued Bertil

Lintner, "and the tables would have been turned."[18] Rangoon, and Burma, held their breath, waiting.

*

The terrible events of the following few days raise the question: How did General Ne Win and his cronies view the events that had overtaken the country over the preceding months?

In her speech at the Shwedagon, Suu had gone out of her way to honor the army her father had founded. "I feel strong attachment to the armed forces," she had said. ". . . I would therefore not want to see any splits or struggles between the army . . . and the people . . . May I appeal to the armed forces to become a force in which the people place their trust and reliance?" With her long years spent in India and the UK, where the armed forces have an honored place but one that is strictly set apart from the levers of power, Suu was doing what she could to induce the troops to go back to barracks so that a civil and civilized Burma could re-emerge. No threat to the existence or military prerogatives of the army was contained in her message.

But from what took place on the evening of September 18th and the days that followed, it is clear that those in power saw things very differently. Ne Win was the army and the army was Ne Win: An attack on one was an attack on all. The army would not be divided: It had gained too much from a generation in power—too much privilege, too much wealth, a dominant position over the rest of society comparable to the hated British—to risk having it all ripped away. As they saw it, Suu had declared war not on the overweening power of a dictator but on all of them and on everything they had worked so hard to plunder. And now the armed forces responded in kind, with a declaration of war.

*

Sunday, September 18th, was another day of mass demonstrations—the new normality in free Burma. The strike that had begun early in August then spread across the country still held firm. Rangoon's forty-odd daily and weekly newspapers were on sale, brimming with news, rumor and uninhibited polemic. At Rangoon University, students impatient with Dr. Maung Maung's foot-dragging announced that they had formed an interim government—student nonsense intended to prod the president into action. No riots occurred, no beheadings were recorded that day; the capital, its government in limbo, continued to tick over. As Martin Morland recalled, "The city of Rangoon, and indeed the whole country, ran disturbingly smoothly without Big Brother."[19] Over at University Avenue the dozens of students and others who had taken up residence in Suu's house continued to thrash out with "big sister" their vision of the nation's future. It was not all glamorous: Nyo Ohn Myint recalled, "My first job was buying fried rice at the restaurant nearby. And then I was driving. And every day we had so many meetings . . ."[20]

The first sign that today would be any different came at 4 PM when a male voice suddenly broke in to the state radio's afternoon music program. "In order to bring a timely halt to the deteriorating conditions on all sides all over the country," the announcer said, "and in the interests of the people, the defense forces have assumed all power in the state with effect from today."[21]

Martial law was back with a vengeance. With immediate effect, the man said, a curfew was in force between 8 PM and 4 AM. And during the hours of daylight the following activities were now banned: "gathering, walking, marching in procession, chanting slogans, delivering speeches, agitating and creating disturbances in the streets by five or more people, regardless of whether the act is with the intention of creating disturbances or of committing a crime or not."

But over the past month the people had become used to defying the army, and they did so again. "It had started drizzling shortly after the brief radio announcement," Bertil Lintner wrote, "and the late-afternoon sky was now heavy with dark rain clouds. Once again, throughout the city, people began felling trees and overturning street-side wooden stalls to make barricades as they had done in August. Their faces were downcast and the atmosphere electrifyingly tense . . . Electric wires were cut and street lights destroyed to hamper the movements of the troops everyone was expecting to appear at any minute."[22]

Terry McCarthy, a correspondent for the *Independent* who had arrived from Bangkok the previous day on a fake tourist visa, wrote:

Walking through Rangoon was an eerie experience. Most roads were blocked at every intersection with trees, concrete pipes, wooden gates and blocks of concrete. Only a few of the major roads were still passable . . . At every barricade there were young men with an assortment of weapons, including wooden spears, knives, catapults that fire sharpened bicycle spokes, bottles of acid mixed with gravel, billhooks and Molotov cocktails.

The change in atmosphere in the space of a few hours was frightening. Earlier in the day, opposition leaders were talking buoyantly of an interim government being in reach . . . Intermediaries were regularly conveying messages between the opposition and the civilian government of Maung Maung, and students were jubilant as they marched through the streets, calling for democracy.[23]

Now all that was over. Bertil Lintner wrote:

Some people began banging pots and pans inside their houses in a desperate show of defiance. Others took to the streets with their crossbows, swords and jinglees [the sharpened bicycle spokes mentioned by McCarthy, fired from slingshots] ready for a fight with the army . . . Bands of thousands of enraged demonstrators . . . surged down the streets in the eerie evening twilight. Waving banners, flags and crude home-made weapons, they shouted at the tops of their voices "*Sit-khway aso-ya phyok-cha-yay!*" "Down with the dog government!"[24]

The thunderous rumbling, when it finally came, could be heard from afar: Late in the evening hundreds of army lorries, cranes mounted on trucks, armored personnel carriers and Bren carriers left the military cantonment in the north of the city and headed in convoy downtown. And this time there was to be no standoff, no games of chicken, no polite waiting for the crowds to disperse. In July Ne Win had issued his grim warning—"when the army fires, it shoots to hit"—and this time his troops were to obey it to the letter.

"Through loudspeakers mounted on the military vehicles, the people were ordered to remove the barricades," Lintner reports. "If the order was not heeded, a machine gunner sprayed the nearest house with bullets . . . If the protesters themselves had not complied after the first salvo of machine-gun fire, cranes moved in and dismantled the flimsy road blocks."[25]

Anybody out on the streets was in breach of martial law and fair game. "Any crowd of people in sight was mowed down methodically as the army trucks and Bren carriers rumbled down the streets in perfect formation, shooting in all directions," Lintner records. "The dead who were left in the street were trucked away by the army during lulls in the shooting. Sporadic gunfire could be heard here and there in Rangoon throughout that night."

Among the principal targets of the invasion force was Aung San Suu Kyi. For her and her colleagues in the ad hoc opposition movement, the military crackdown had come out of a clear blue sky. A spokesman for Tin Oo commented, "This is a coup d'état by another name. This ruins everything."[26] Suu, Tin Oo and the third member of their triumvirate, Aung Gyi, held an emergency meeting after they had digested the radio announcement, but offered no comment when it broke up. Late the same evening dozens of soldiers and an armored personnel carrier with a .275 machine gun mounted took up position outside Suu's home in University Avenue. No one was allowed to enter or leave, and the phone line was cut.

"All through the night we were kept awake by the noise of machine gun fire," Nyo Ohn Myint, one of the many trapped inside the grounds, remembered.[27]

Suu told the students and others in her compound to offer no violence to the army. "It is better that I should be taken off to prison," she told them. "It is better that we should all be taken off to prison."[28] But Nyo Ohn Myint and the rest quietly ignored her admonitions, and like other activists prepared as best they could for the coming confrontation.

"The machine gun was pointed straight at the front gate," he recalled. "We were very nervous because we only had slingshots to defend ourselves. There were two 14-gallon tanks of paraffin in the cellar, so we made Molotov cocktails with as many bottles as we could find. Our security inside the house depended on self-defense."[29] They made these preparations furtively, without informing Suu, knowing that she would disapprove if she found out. "She didn't know about them," Nyo Ohn Myint remembered. "She was kind of like a mother—when she saw one of the guards with a slingshot she said, don't touch it again . . ."

But Nyo Ohn Myint and his comrades were desperately afraid for Suu. And the young lecturer conceived a cunning plan to save her from arrest or worse—if necessary against her own will.

"The compound next door was the property of Tass, the Soviet news agency," he explained. "And the military was not in that spot. The Russian correspondent for Tass spoke to us over the wall, we conversed in broken English and I told him the regime is very dangerous, they want to kill her. So he offered to give her refuge because his house was the property of the Soviet Union, so it was extra-territorial."

Nyo Ohn Myint raised the idea with Suu. "I requested her to leave if the army started to fire on us. But she said, no. You boys must do nothing to resist, I will talk to the army and I will get arrested. This is the best way to save our lives.

"So I said to my friends—she was very stubborn, we wanted to get her out—I said, let's smack her on the head, knock her unconscious and slip her over the wall to the Tass agency house. Because our focus was on saving her life, and we didn't know if the soldiers would shoot her or not." In the event the siege, which lasted seventy-two hours, ended without violence on either side, and with Suu still conscious, and in her own home.

Despite the blood already shed, the defiant strikers returned to the streets on Monday morning, and the ruthless army response continued. Primed by months of unrest and bloody repression, the outside world was finally paying attention. "At least 100 people—and perhaps four times that number—were shot dead in the streets of Rangoon yesterday," McCarthy reported in a story carried by the *Independent* on its front page, "as the city was plunged into terror a day after the Burmese army seized power . . . As the day wore on, with gunfire echoing all over the city, casualties started to crowd into Rangoon General Hospital. A witness said the scene was unreal. 'There are bodies everywhere. Sometimes it is hard to know who is dead and who is alive.'"[30]

McCarthy went on:

Although most of the confrontations between the students and the military were brief, with the students retreating quickly when the soldiers opened fire, several pitched battles were reported . . . In one incident, reported by several sources, a crowd in the Tanwe district of Rangoon stormed an armed truck and, although suffering heavy casualties, eventually killed the seventeen soldiers and took their weapons. There are also reports, which have been confirmed by official Burmese radio, that two police stations in Rangoon were stormed by demonstrators . . .

As McCarthy's list of crude, homemade weapons underlines, those demonstrators resolved to make a fight of it were pathetically ill-equipped; and most were armed with nothing more menacing than a portrait of Aung San or a peacock flag. But the soldiers behaved as if they were confronting the Vietcong. Bertil Lintner wrote:

> No one in the large column that marched down past the old meeting spot near the City Hall and Maha Bandoola Park saw the machine-gun nests on the surrounding rooftops. As the marchers turned left, [they found themselves] entrapped between three fire points, the troops at the three rooftop positions opened fire simultaneously. No warning was given. Several demonstrators fell bleeding to the street.
>
> Files of soldiers goose-stepped in perfect formation out from different side streets, followed by Bren carriers. At a barked word of command, the troops assumed the prone firing position, as if they were facing a heavily armed enemy . . .[31]

"The Burmese Red Cross was working furiously to gather the wounded and dead from the streets," McCarthy reported. "After one incident in the east of Rangoon, they even asked a Western embassy to send them vehicles to transport the wounded to hospital. 'They have been showing tremendous courage,' a diplomat said."[32]

It is hard to find the correct word to describe what happened on September 18th. It is usually called a coup d'état, but as one disgusted Western diplomat responded, "What coup d'état? The same people are in charge!" Yet it was far more than just another crackdown: There was none of the hesitation displayed by the army in its previous attacks on demonstrators. Nor were there any more indications of wavering loyalties like those that had appeared during the preceding weeks. The troops took up position and fired their guns the way troops are supposed to, without emotion, like well-programmed automatons.

The difference between the army attacks of August 8th and those of September 18th and 19th was like the difference between the first approximate firing of an artillery round and the second, third and fourth firing, when the gunner has recalibrated his sights. In the little town of Phekhon, Pascal Khoo Thwe, practicing his oratorical skills as one of the leaders of the democrats, saw what was happening at the time. During the public meetings, he said, "police mingled with the crowds to observe us, having prudently abandoned their uniforms. We ought to have realized that they were playing their traditional game of letting the leaders surface so that they could be picked off later . . ."[33]

Now the army began putting all the intelligence it had gathered to good use—and thousands of activists, fearing what was to come, fled to the border areas to avoid being picked up or killed. Aung Myint was one who sought refuge in the Karen-held areas on the Thai border. "We fled," he said, "because we realized that this time it was different; not a random massacre as in August. It was meticulously planned and the targets well selected. Because everything had been out in the open during the August–September demonstrations, all the leading activists were known—and the army were looking for us specifically."[34] Now many of those who had stood on improvised stages and urged their fellow students to struggle for democracy turned their backs on all that. Despairing of the nonviolent path, they threw themselves on the mercy of the ethnic armies that had been fighting the Burmese state for years, some of them since before independence. They asked for food, training and guns, and pledged to fight alongside them.

*

By Tuesday night the fight was over; the streets were clear of protesters, the corpses had been carted off, the blood hosed away, might have prevailed again. Ordinary Burmese who wanted to know what had happened were once again thrown back on foreign radio reports: One of the first consequences of the crackdown was the forcible closure of all Burma's newspapers, including the increasingly insubordinate regime mouthpiece the *Working People's Daily*, which only returned to the news-stands, duly castrated, weeks later. But anyone listening to the BBC would have discovered that, since the army takeover, perhaps one thousand people had been killed in Rangoon alone. It was probably an underestimate. Michael Charney wrote, "Suppression associated with the coup led to between 8,000 and 10,000 deaths."[35] It was the worst massacre of civilians in Burma's blood-soaked modern history, and one of the worst anywhere in the world in the postwar era.

This was how the Ne Win regime chose to greet the emergence of Aung San Suu Kyi as a rival for power; it was her baptism of fire. How did the "Oxford housewife" react?

Terry McCarthy spent many hours with Suu in the immediate aftermath of the crackdown and in the days that followed. "I went up there with a couple of other journalists and we had a long chat in her living room looking over the lake," he remembered. "Michael [Aris] was there as well—the two boys had been sent back to school in England some weeks before. I found her so compelling that I went back to her house almost every day after that.

"While we were there the first time the shooting started up—the Burmese army use very large caliber guns, they made a lot of noise and it was clear they weren't shooting at birds. But Suu didn't flinch at all. She was incredibly composed."[36]

At that first meeting she told the Irish journalist that she had been expecting to return to Britain in the autumn, but that the events of the past few months had changed her mind: Now she expected to stay in Burma, "but I would prefer not to remain in politics if I can avoid it."[37] Yet the next moment she acknowledged the impossibility of that. "You can't pick up something and then drop it," she said. "You have to see it through. I realized that after the August shootings.

". . . It's very different from living in academia in Oxford," she conceded, a touch ruefully. "We called someone vicious in a review for the *Times Literary Supplement*. We didn't know what vicious was."

*

The events of September 18th were preceded by the most savage purge of the Burmese government since 1962. On the morning of that day President Maung Maung had been summoned to Ne Win's home and sacked. At the same time, all administrative organs of the state, from the State Council and Council of Ministers at the top down to local authorities throughout the country, were abolished or suspended. They were replaced, not by the neutral, interim administration the people wanted but by the army officers who had been in charge until replaced by a simulacrum of civilian rule in the mid-seventies. The masks of socialism and parliament discarded, the army now confronted the population with its naked power.

Maung Maung's replacement was General Saw Maung, the army's chief of staff, quite as much a creature of Ne Win as the two presidents he had succeeded. When the bodies of the dead had all been burned and the blood hosed from the streets, he took to the airwaves and told the nation that the army had merely been doing its duty—and when that duty was complete, the political evolution of the nation would resume.

The army's immediate job, he said, was to restore law and order and rebuild the state's administrative machinery. Then it would be the responsibility of corporations, cooperatives and "private concerns" to "alleviate the food, clothing and shelter needs of the people." Once these jobs were done, multiparty elections would be held as promised and the Military Council would not interfere with the Election Commission in any way. "We do not wish to cling to state power long," he insisted. On the contrary, he spoke of "handing over power to the government which emerges after the free and fair general elections." "I am laying the path for the next government," he said, and "I will lay flowers in the path of the next government."[38]

But the Burmese were not fooled: Ne Win, they decided, was merely repeating himself through Saw Maung. "It's going back to the 1962 formula," a man near the Sule pagoda in central Rangoon told McCarthy. "Nothing different."[39] After the intense excitement of the past six weeks, a couple of days of hyper-violence had restored the status quo ante. Number One was back on top.

"During the day he carries a revolver," Terry McCarthy wrote of Ne Win, "and sleeps with a submachine gun on the pillow beside him . . . He is moody and erratic, given to fits of anger followed by periods of weeping. He rarely leaves his compound in Rangoon, issuing orders to the military by radio-telephone. His staff are terrified of him. Just as Burma has been cut off from the outside world, so he is cut off from his own people."[40] A former aide told McCarthy: "He thinks killing is routine, in order for reason to prevail—but not our reason, his reason." Another former adviser compared him to a viper. "He is not even like a cobra or a rattlesnake," he said. "They give a warning before they strike."

But despite the similarity of the general repression, several things were starkly different from the Ne Win coup of 1962. For one thing, that first coup was practically bloodless. For another, Ne Win was now seventy-seven, and on record as saying that he wanted to retire. His proxy, General Saw Maung, had endorsed the commitment of the Maung Maung government to multiparty elections, to be held within three months, even while his troops were murdering civilians in the streets.

If paying lip service to that commitment was seen as a way to buy off the outside world, it failed utterly: On September 23rd the United States announced it was cutting off all aid in protest at the massacres. Europe and even Japan, long the junta's most reliable supporter, were soon to follow America's cue. But the commitment to elections was also a perverse way to justify the coup: For elections to be held, first order must be restored, which was why the army was obliged to intervene—as the midwives of democracy! Hence the name that the soldiers gave themselves within less than a week of the massacre: the State Law and Order Restoration Council or SLORC—forever after to be compared to SMERSH, the Soviet counterintelligence agency in the James Bond films.

The regime's pledge to hold elections was bizarre. But amid the terror, the bloodshed, the exodus of students, the general despair, it provided a rare chink of light: There could be a way forward, despite it all. Perhaps that chink could best be appreciated by someone who had spent nearly half her life in England, a country where the words "Glorious Revolution" refer to an event, exactly three hundred years before, in which no lives were lost and which set British democracy on such a big, fat keel that it has been gliding forward ever since.[41]

So it was on Saturday, September 24, 1988, as SLORC was rising from the ashes of the BSPP, and before Ne Win could change his mind, that Aung San Suu Kyi and her allies announced that they were forming a political party.

4

THE FUNERAL

AMONG the hundreds of thousands who witnessed Aung San Suu Kyi's first major speech at the Shwedagon pagoda was a petite forty-one-year-old woman with bright-red lipstick and a piercing gaze called Ma Thanegi. Recalling the day, she wrote:

> August 26, Daw Aung San Suu Kyi makes her first mass public appearance outside the Shwedagon Pagoda, West entrance. Her name is magic: Because she is General Aung San's daughter, there was no one out in the streets who was not curious to see her. The morning was wet and windy, with the field in front of the Western entrance rapidly turning to a mud bath, as I sat with my friends on plastic sheets. The grass had just been cut and we saw small frogs hopping around in panic under our feet. She was three hours late. People who came with her crowded onto the stage behind and around her "to protect her"; but mostly because they wanted to be seen by her side . . .

For Ma Thanegi, who is descended from courtiers in the Mandalay palace and has become one of Burma's best writers in English, it was the start of an intense involvement in the democracy movement.

"Due to a bad sound system we could hear nothing," she wrote of that day. "But even if they could not hear, people instantly took her into their hearts without question, for she was fair-skinned, she was beautiful, she was articulate, and her eyes flashed as she spoke. Above all, she was our General's daughter . . . We were glad to have a symbol, a leading light, a presence bringing hopes and dreams that her father did not have the chance to fulfill . . ."

Before becoming a writer, Ma Thanegi devoted most of her energy to painting. Enthused by Suu's speech, she and her fellow painters began turning out wall posters supporting the democracy movement. When she took samples to show Suu she was quickly recruited to her staff of volunteers.

"About two days after her Shwedagon speech I went to see Daw Suu with my colleagues in the painters' organization, to give her some posters we had produced," she wrote in an unpublished memoir of those days. "She discovered that I could speak English, so soon after this first meeting she asked me to join her personal office staff, as I would be useful in dealing with the foreign media people."

Ma Thanegi began spending long hours at Suu's house, as the new opposition party slowly and chaotically took shape in rooms adjoining the improvised sickbay where Suu's mother, Daw Khin Kyi, still gravely ill, spent her days in bed. She recalled precisely the layout of the house and the people who were then occupying it:

> As one entered there was a staircase going upstairs on the left side of the lobby. A round marble-topped table stood in the middle of this entrance. On the left there was a narrow, closed-in veranda, off which was Suu's office, which had once been the dining room. In fact she used the circular dining table with the Lazy Susan as her desk and as a conference table. Beyond were the bathroom, the kitchen and a store room.
>
> To the right of this office was a small room, and beyond it the larger one where Daw Khin Kyi lay in bed. A back corridor connected this room to the kitchen as well. There was a back door and back stairs, rarely used and fallen into decay.
>
> On the other side of the lobby was the parlor that Daw Khin Kyi kept for her visitors, with sofas, tea tables and a piano. This room, which opened onto the side veranda through French windows and which also opened onto the sick room, was kept locked.
>
> I would arrive at the office around 8 AM and I stayed until 5:30 PM.

But the general strike and the uprising meant that commuting was often a challenge. "By now, some of the roads were blocked with fallen trees so no buses were running and few cars were on the road. Some cars thought to belong to the Military Intelligence had been burned. My house was a few miles away. Sometimes I came on foot.

"At the start two younger women artists in our group helped with the files but both left, one for the US and the other to marry, and I was left very short-handed."

By this time Suu had a small but committed and semipermanent staff. There was an assistant called Ko Myint Swe who paid the bills, ran errands and tracked down books for Suu. Formerly a librarian at Rangoon University, he was "passionate about books," Ma Thanegi recalled.[1] His wife Daw Nwe, a poet, would sometimes stay with him; later the two of them would run the party's public relations section from a shed at the end of the garden. When Suu began making frequent public appearances, her personal assistant Ko Myint Swe would be close at hand with emergency provisions.

The two volunteers with whom Ma Thanegi worked most closely were two brothers, "almost like family to Suu," who had moved into the house and now slept in the main downstairs room. "They were the sons of an ex-army officer called U Min Lwin," she wrote.

> We got along extremely well.
>
> Ko Maw, the elder, was short and wore thick glasses, and talked far too much in a fierce and angry voice. Under his very grouchy exterior he had the kindest of hearts. The younger, Ko Aung, was tall and never spoke unless he was in a good mood. His hooded eyes roved constantly and missed nothing. As time went on, Ko Aung and I learned to work well as a team in any situation—a glance was all we needed to inform each other about something. We relied on each other to get things done—we soon found out that a number of the volunteers preferred the reflected glory of being near Suu to doing any real work. Being extremely bright and street smart, and totally unemotional, Ko Aung was indispensable.

As time went on, more and more shops and offices were shut down by strike action. In the absence of public transport the city became harder to negotiate, with the result that 54 University Avenue at times became a sort of island. "Sometimes tensions would run high in the city and none of us would be able to leave the house for days on end," Ma Thanegi recalled.

> We heard stories about the beheadings, and people brought us newspapers with gory photos of heads displayed on spikes.
>
> One time, when every shop in the city was closed, Suu remarked that she was getting tired of seeing the long hair on everyone. I knew how to cut hair, so I was delegated to be in-house barber. Ko Aung refused to let me touch his shoulder length hair, but the others, including Dr. Aris and Ko Myint Swe, had to suffer the indignity of hair shorn so short that, as Suu remarked afterwards, they looked like convicts.

Ma Thanegi was in the house on the Sunday when military rule announced its return with a bloodbath.

Late in the morning of September 18th, Ko Maw came into the house looking worried. It was a Sunday, so there were no meetings or visitors. "Something's going on," he said. "They are broadcasting military songs nonstop on the radio."

Ko Aung went to fetch a radio which he placed on Ma Suu's round table—the one with the Lazy Susan in the middle—and left it turned on. I made several calls but could not confirm anything, but we all suspected the army was moving in. Sure enough, at 4 PM we heard the announcement that the army was taking over to control the anarchy and that no one was to march in the streets. A curfew was imposed from 8 PM to 4 AM. Government employees were told to report back to work or face dismissal.

Despite the ban on marching, some groups marched out the next day; many were shot and killed. The corpses were quickly taken away and the streets washed of blood.

Ma Thanegi stayed home during the days of shooting and bloodshed when University Avenue was under siege. When calm returned to the streets and she went back to work she found the house in an uproar over how to react to General Saw Maung's promise of multiparty elections.

"There was great excitement in the office over whether we should form a political party. One evening, when there were no other visitors in the house and we were alone, Suu came to me as I was bent over my work to ask if I would want to be involved in party politics. She said she was thinking of getting young people like Ko Myint Swe more involved, by bringing them onto the Central Committee."

Ma Thanegi treated Suu's approach warily: She had played no part in the democracy movement before, and was temperamentally averse to joining organizations. In the end she chose to remain at arm's length from the party, but she was to become intimately involved with Suu as her personal assistant over the coming months as the party came from nowhere to become the most significant political force in the country.

After many meetings and much discussion, the founding triumvirate, Aung Gyi, Aung San Suu Kyi and Tin Oo—Aung-Suu-Tin as they were known for short—announced the creation of the National United Front for Democracy, changed soon afterwards to the National League for Democracy (NLD), the name it retains today. The name change became necessary in late September when the former ruling party, the Burma Socialist Program Party, re-branded itself the National Unity Party—a name too similar for comfort. "All effort is now being put to establish the National League for Democracy, of which Suu is Secretary General," Michael wrote home on September 30th. "There are still troops and check-points in all the streets, but they have stopped indiscriminate shooting it seems. Not a word about negotiations with the opposition . . . After the Malaysian [ambassador] had left, Suu went out to register her party with the Election Commission."[2]

The party's flag was red, with a white star and a stylized golden peacock, head lowered and fan spread—the "fighting peacock." Burmese armies had fought under a flag showing a peacock with a fully opened fan throughout the Konbaung Dynasty, which began in 1700. In the days of the monarchy, "the throne was painted over with representations of the peacock and the hare," according to George Scott, writing under the nom de plume Shway Yoe in his book *The Burman, His Life and Notions*, first published in 1882, "typifying the descent of the king from the solar and lunar races."[3] In the 1930s the peacock also became the emblem of Burma's militant students, who included Suu's father Aung San: He was editor of the student magazine *Oway*, which is the Burmese word for the peacock's harsh cry. Rejecting the bellicose suggestion of the name, Suu preferred the party's emblematic bird to be known as "the dancing peacock."

Suu became general secretary of the new party, Aung Gyi, the retired general, was chairman and Tin Oo vice-chairman. Members of the Central Executive Committee included Win Tin, the turbulent journalist, Kyi Maung, the chubby ex-army officer, and Daw Myint Myint Khin, a woman barrister who was head of the Rangoon Bar Association.

"In addition to Suu, three of them were civilians," Ma Thanegi recalled. "The others were ex-military men, derisively known to the intelligentsia in the party as *baung-bi chut* or 'men-out-of-trousers,' referring to the fact that they had switched back from army uniform trousers to longyis.

"There was mistrust between the two sides from the beginning," she went on. Yet in those grim days of late September there was also great determination and great hope: hope founded on the promise of democratic elections held out by the new generalissimo, and on the "magic name" of Aung San Suu Kyi. Within less than a year almost all those men and women would be silenced, either under house arrest or in jail.

*

What did the very different people now banded together under Suu's name hope to achieve?

Announcing the formation of the party, Aung-Suu-Tin stated that "the basic objective of this organization is to achieve a genuinely democratic government" for which purpose the party was prepared to take part in the elections announced by Saw Maung. A few days earlier, in an article published in the *Independent*, Suu had written, "I am working . . . to achieve the kind of democratic system under which the people of Burma can enjoy human rights to the full. . . . Every country and people must search for a political and economic solution tailored to their unique situation."[4]

So what was Burma's "unique situation," and how might democracy, a concept invented and refined in the West, be tailored to fit it?

The modernization of Burma was a question over which Suu had been wrestling for years, long before she was drawn into the maelstrom in the summer of 1988.

As she told the crowd at the Shwedagon, towards the end of his short life her father made clear that he believed Burma should become a democracy. With the downfall of the Axis powers, fascist dictatorships went out of fashion. The other ideological model, communism, had won a convert in Aung San's uncle Than Tun, who became head of the Burmese Communist Party. But the pitilessly materialistic perspective of Marxism held few charms for the deeply religious Burmese, even after the Chinese over the border turned Maoist. And on attaining independence in 1948, a democracy was what Burma became, and remained until the army takeover.

But what did the word "democracy" mean in the Burmese context?

Inherent in the term as used in the West is the concept of the "loyal opposition." Political parties compete for the votes of the people, which translates into power. The losers in the election remain loyal to the state while putting up steadfast but peaceable opposition to the actions of the elected government in parliament.

Readers will excuse this re-statement of the basic principles of parliamentary democracy because in Burma, as in many other countries outside Western Europe, they originally appeared highly exotic.

Until 1948 Burma had had no experience of democracy or anything like it. The highly autocratic and capricious rule of the Burmese monarchy had been replaced by the diktats of the British in Calcutta, enforced by the gun. The British were eventually supplanted by the Japanese who, despite their sweet words about a "co-prosperity sphere," proved to be every bit as dictatorial as all the others who had ruled the country.

And there was a specific problem with the concept of "opposition." In 1874, King Thibaw's predecessor, King Mindon, on being informed that William Gladstone's Whigs had lost the general election in Britain, remarked, "Then poor Ga-la-sa-tong [Gladstone] is in prison I suppose. I am sorry for him. I don't think he was a bad fellow."[5] "It never occurred to [Mindon]," wrote Burma scholar Gustaaf Houtman, "that, when a political opposition party loses the elections, it might not end up in prison. Indeed, political opposition, unless it is sufficiently strong to extort respect, would appear to necessarily imply exile, imprisonment or death."

As Suu herself observed, the fine social achievements of Burmese Buddhism had tended to close the minds of her co-nationals to the possibility that, in the political sphere, the rest of the world might have anything useful to teach them. "A sound social system," she had written, "can go hand in hand with political immaturity." Burma owes most features of its social system to its experience, stretching back over a millennium, of Theravada Buddhism. There is no room for a caste system in Buddhism: In striking contrast to Hindu practice, the notion that all men are born equal is not only preached but to a large degree practiced. The Burmese had a monarch who ruled over them more or less capriciously, guided and advised by Brahmin astrologers and Buddhist monks, and a chasm of wealth and privilege separated the palace from the people. But the people were not in a state of misery: All Burman children who were Buddhists— which until the British intrusion meant effectively everybody—went to monastery schools where they learned to read and write, and for many centuries Burma had been one of the most literate countries in the world.

It was also infused with religious teaching to an unusual degree: All Burmese boys were inducted into the sangha in early childhood, and for several weeks or months or longer if they chose they lived as monks alongside the adult ones, setting out each morning to collect food donated by local villagers, learning to meditate and read and recite the sutras and perform the many different complicated ceremonies of the temple.

Traditional Burmese society had plenty of faults and problems: People of non-Burman nationality were discriminated against and even enslaved, banditry was common even in the heartland, and it was rigidly hierarchical. But within those parameters there was, for the Burman majority, a broad measure of equality, and the Five Precepts of Buddhism—not to take life of any sort, not to steal, not to commit adultery, not to lie, and not to take intoxicants—were generally observed. And in a country blessed like Burma with fertile soil and plenty of sun and rain, the result for the Burman peasant was simplicity, stability and a general absence of want. George Scott wrote in *The Burman*:

> The Burman is the most calm and contented of mortals. He does not want to grow rich. When he does make a large sum of money, he spends it all on some pious work, and rejoices in the fact that this will meet with its reward in his next existence . . . If any one has escaped the curse of Adam it is the Burman . . . When his patch of paddy land has been reaped, his only concern is how to pass the time, and that is no very difficult matter, where he has plenty of cheroots and betel-nut . . . And so an uneventful life passes away: the greatest ambition to see the village boat successful at the Thadingyut races, and the village champion cock or buffalo triumphant over all others . . .[6]

The downside of the Burman's easygoing contentment, as Suu had pointed out, was a pervasive lack of intellectual ambition. "Traditional Burmese education did not encourage speculation," she wrote, because Burmese were convinced that "Buddhism represents the perfected philosophy. It therefore follows that there was no need either to try to develop it further or to consider other philosophies."[7]

Far away from the peasant in the fields, in the almost unimaginable court, beyond the ken of ordinary mortals, ruled the king, the "Lord of the Celestial Elephant," who if not the son of the previous king—if that king had died without issue—was identified by soothsayers much in the way that child reincarnations of the great lamas of Tibet are identified. "The king," Scott tells us, "emphatically rules by what is called in the Western kingdoms the right divine."[8] But to ensure that right was not infringed upon often required drastic measures: Any potential rivals to power—any latent opposition, to use the language of democracy—had to be got rid of in the most decisive manner.

When Burma's last king, Thibaw, came to the throne, he was persuaded by his mother and consort that "he would never be safe till the princes were put out of the way," Scott writes. "Seventy of the royal blood, men, women, and children, were murdered in the next three days, and buried within the palace, in a long trench dug for the purpose. The eldest prince . . . died shrieking for mercy at the hands of his own slaves, whom he had often tortured . . . The poor old regent of Pegu . . . had his nostrils and gullet crammed with gunpowder, and was thus blown up."

The massacre of Thibaw's rivals was widely reported in foreign newspapers and its bestiality helped the British build the case for ending the Burmese monarchy and imposing their rule on the whole country. But from the Burmese point of view, the clearing away by a new monarch of rivals to the crown was a familiar and prudent custom. "Many Burmans defend it warmly," Scott pointed out, "on the plea that it secured the peace of the country." Otherwise there would always be the risk of those snubbed by the soothsayers staging a rebellion when they felt strong enough to do so.

Burma's royal massacres were startling on account of their scale, but nowhere in the world does a king cut a deal with pretenders to his crown; in traditional monarchical systems, the only place for a royal rival is in exile or under the ground. Burma's tragedy, one which Suu was acutely aware of before she went home, was that history had given the country no opportunity to discover that there were ways in which power could be both asserted and shared.

On the far side of Burma's northwestern border lies the world's largest democracy. India was no less feudal and monarchical than Burma when the British marched in to usurp its history, but it emerged from centuries of colonial subjection with a democratic system that has survived for more than sixty years. Why was India able to sustain such a system while

Burma, despite being encumbered with far fewer social problems than India and with a higher standard of living and rate of literacy, relapsed into tyranny after a mere decade of democratic experiment?

It was a question which Suu had long pondered, and the result was the most mature piece of writing of hers yet to see the light of day: an essay entitled "Intellectual Life in India and Burma under Colonialism," written while she and Michael were in Shimla in 1986.

Democracy was able to sink roots in India, she argued, because the British had deliberately set out to create an intellectual elite educated in English to run their Indian administration. This elite was able to throw off the restrictions of traditional vernacular education and open themselves to international influences, while remaining in touch with their own traditions. The result was people like Gandhi. "Gandhi was of a practical turn of mind that looked for ideas to suit the needs of situations," she wrote. "In spite of his deeply ingrained Hinduism, Gandhi's intellectual flexibility made him accept those elements of western thought which fitted into the ethical and social scheme he considered desirable."[9]

Burma was colonized more than two centuries after Bengal, and when the British cast around for a native elite to help them administer the colony, the Burmans were both outnumbered and outclassed linguistically by the Indians and Chinese to whom the British had opened Burma's door—"peoples," as Suu pointed out, "so much more experienced in dealing with westerners and their institutions."

Then much later, when the British tried to create the University of Rangoon by amalgamating two existing colleges, raising the academic standard and making them residential, they were met by violent protests: "There was . . . in the Burmese mentality," writes Suu, "an ingrained resistance to elitism: . . . education of a national character should be made available to as broad a section of the population as possible." But this salutary motive meant that it was very difficult for Burmese equivalents of the giants of colonial India—people like Rabindranath Tagore, Swami Vivekananda, Gandhi and Nehru, all members of the English-speaking elite—to emerge.

The intense frustration of this failure radiates from an article written by Aung San in the 1930s while still a student. "We are fully prepared to follow men who are able and willing to be leaders like Mahatma Gandhi," he wrote. ". . . Let anybody appear who can be like such a leader, who *dares* to be like such a leader. We are waiting."[10]

It was of course Aung San himself who emerged to lead. But while he was able to lead his country to the threshold of independence, he could not transform its political culture: That was a task beyond the capacity of a single individual, however charismatic, or of a single generation. It was a transformation that, at independence, remained unfulfilled.

The party Aung San headed at his death, and which constituted Burma's first independent government in 1948, the Anti-Fascist People's Freedom League (AFPFL), was not recognizably a party in the Western sense. Rather it was "a loose confederation of political parties and local influential leaders and strong men," according to the American Burma expert David Steinberg. "Its membership ran the gamut of left to left-center positions that were socialist to some degree. More important, the AFPFL included a broad array of individuals reflecting the essential personalization of power; each leader had a power base and his own entourage, and sometimes armed supporters."[11] This "personalization of power," the absence of an ideological coherence that could hold the party together, led to the League eventually splitting into two opposed camps based not on policies but on personalities—which in turn allowed the army to take its first bite of power, four years before the final takeover.

Burma had not digested the concept of a loyal opposition, or of power that could be shared or delegated through society's different strata. As in many other traditional societies, writes Steinberg, "power was conceived as finite." To share power, "from center to periphery, between leaders, etc," was to lose power: It was a zero-sum game. "Loyalty becomes the prime necessity, resulting in entourages and a series of patron–client relationships. Those outside of this core group may therefore be considered potential adversaries—a 'loyal opposition' thus becomes an oxymoron."

Gustaaf Houtman cites three reasons why the concept of "opposition" has failed to gain any traction in Burma. First, "the centralization of power lying with a king or general" means that "the regime views opposition with suspicion and is unwilling, perhaps even unable, to allocate it a place in its political scheme." Secondly, "expressions of opposition are . . . equated with confrontation, and therefore armed force." And thirdly, "opposition is seen as threatening to 'harmony' and 'national unity.' Indeed, the overarching emphasis on national unity means that the idea of opposition is literally equated with the 'destruction of unity.'"[12]

In her speech at the Shwedagon, Suu had repeatedly invoked the need for "unity," as her father had done. Yet from the perspective of Ne Win and his cronies, Suu and her new party embodied a fearful assault on the mystical concept of national unity, and a mortal challenge to their rule—all the more menacing because it was launched in the name of the very man, Aung San, whose achievements were the basis of their own claims to legitimacy.

"In Burma," writes Houtman, "those who declare themselves opponents to the regime are either extremely courageous or extremely foolish—there is little in between."[13] As Aung San Suu Kyi set out to carry word of her new party and its democratic promise to the corners of the country, she would soon discover exactly how courageous she and her colleagues would need to be.

*

If Saw Maung's promise of elections within three months—before the end of 1988—was to be fulfilled, the NLD had no time to waste. Yet almost at once it was embroiled in the factionalism that has been the besetting sin of Burmese politics since the time of Aung San. In this case it was an outbreak of hostilities between the baung-bi chut, the former military men, and the intelligentsia. Almost inevitably it developed into a fight between right and left.

Brigadier General Aung Gyi was the odd man out in the party's leadership. Formerly a close ally of Ne Win and his subordinate in the 4th Burmese Rifles—the regiment that provided all the military elite throughout the Ne Win years—in 1988 he had been the first figure from the military establishment to attack Ne Win's policies openly. He had been purged from the junta twenty-five years before, in 1963—yet he was unblushingly open about his continued affection for the army, and careful to avoid attacking his old boss in person. In the speech he made at the Shwedagon the day before Suu made hers, he urged his audience to heed the words of the new, "moderate" president, Maung Maung. Shortly before the crackdown of September 18th he had "guaranteed" that there would be no army coup, and vowed to commit suicide if he was wrong. It was rumored that he remained on close terms with senior figures in SLORC.

He was in other words a very ambiguous figure to lead the nation's most promising opposition party, and when the rift at the top became open, Suu acknowledged that she had made a mistake in bringing him on board. "I went wrong," she told U Win Khet, one of her close assistants, privately, "but not without a reason. I held a personal grudge against Aung Gyi, but when I started to work for my country I decided to set personal grudges aside."[14]

The general and Suu eventually parted company, but not before Aung Gyi had caused serious trouble to the fledgling party. He had left Rangoon in late September or early October, ostensibly for a "holiday in Maymyo," the British-built hill station northeast of Mandalay. "But on his way there he stopped at every town in between," Ma Thanegi wrote, "held meetings and announced that anyone contributing 30,000 kyats to the National League for Democracy would become a candidate in the election."[15]

This idea, which would have brought in useful funds at the cost of branding the party as an association of the (relatively) rich, would have been anathema to Suu and the rest of the party's leadership. But they only found out about it weeks later, when Suu had to clear up the mess in his wake.

Life in Burma was returning to a sort of blighted normality by the end of October as Suu and her closest colleagues, including Ma Thanegi, set off up-country, defying martial law to hold the first mass political meetings of Suu's career. The general strike which had begun on August 8th collapsed on October 3rd, workers returning to their posts under threat of mass dismissal. Two weeks later Rangoon's banks reopened for the first time since the start of the uprising. SLORC appealed to the 10,000-odd students who had fled to border areas to return, opening reception camps in border areas under government control and promising to treat them not as insurgents but only as "misguided youth"—sending them home to their parents—if they surrendered by November 18th. In an indication of the regime's credibility problem, very few took up the offer, and there were reports that some of those who did were imprisoned, tortured and even executed.

Suu set off from University Avenue with her team on October 30th in a convoy of cars. She traveled in a cream-colored Japanese Saloon owned and driven by Myo Thein, her preferred driver, nicknamed "Tiger." On either side of her in the back were two of the young men with whom Ma Thanegi shared her office duties, Ko Aung and Ko Myint Swe. In the shoulder bag carried by Ko Myint Swe—which to a Burmese identified him as the literary man he was when off duty—were Suu's water bottle, headache pills, smelling salts and tissues, plus a few sweets in case her voice threatened to give out.

It was the first time an opposition political party had set off on the campaign trail in more than a generation, and in this first foray they visited the four states of Magwé, Bago, Sagaing, and Mandalay in the flat and hot Burmese heartland north of Rangoon, meeting the staff of the NLD branch offices which had already begun springing up across the country. But everywhere they went Suu was obliged to correct the picture Aung Gyi had left behind when he had visited a few weeks before.

"At every single rally and meeting Suu had to explain and refute U Aung Gyi's announcement," Ma Thanegi recalled. "By the time we got to the town of Shwebo she was exhausted about it, saying that she had been able to do no campaigning work for the party because her whole time was occupied explaining that Aung Gyi's announcement, inviting contributions in return for becoming the party's candidate, was without foundation. Many people were angry about it."

There were other problems, too. Political campaigning was a phenomenon with which people had no familiarity, but the personality cult of Suu had already spread across the country. "At some places, meetings took too long and we got behind schedule because people at NLD offices insisted on reading out long poems or speeches," she wrote. "This was the same all over the country. Then there were the people who wanted to have their photos taken with Suu, or while they handed bouquets to her, and at the same time not caring if the stalks of the flowers were poking in her face. Others insisted on spraying her with cheap perfume, sometimes spraying it right in her face. Aung Aung"—one of Suu's young student bodyguards—"and I [Ma Thanegi] had to be very rough with these people." Some of the many people who wanted to be seen with Suu would crowd onto the stage with her, alongside her aides and bodyguards.

For a generation the only form of political activity in the country had been that provided by the BSPP; lacking any other role models, the self-appointed leaders of the freshly sprung League branches emulated the former ruling party, Ma Thanegi remembered. "If a township or village had set up a branch of the NLD, its leaders, chairman, secretary and so on, chosen among themselves, welcomed us in expensive style, dressed in silk *gaung baungs* (a sort of turban) and silk longyis, their wives wearing silks and long scarves, all of them looking exactly like apparatchiks of the BSPP, and with the same haughty look on their faces."

But despite all the problems and misunderstandings, it was a brilliant start for the new party. Everywhere they went, Suu and her colleagues drew large, enthusiastic crowds. Party branch offices had sprung up in all the major towns, many of them spontaneously, with no input from Rangoon. There was no doubting the popular desire for change, and Suu had rapidly established herself as the preeminent focus and symbol of it. And although they were trailed everywhere by plainclothes police and agents of Military Intelligence, no one tried to stop their meetings from taking place. On October 26th a small student protest at the Shwedagon was quickly broken up by troops; ten days later an attempted demonstration by monks in the city was also dispersed. But the magic of Suu's name, combined with the fact that she was always careful to emphasize that her opposition to the regime was strictly nonviolent, appeared to have a mesmerizing effect on her adversaries. So far, at least, they let her get on with it.

Perhaps they were banking on her giving up and going home to Oxford and her family before too long; perhaps they were hoping that the growing throng of parties which had signed up for the election, who would eventually number 235, would drown out her voice and stifle her influence. And then there was the Aung Gyi factor apparently working in their favor.

Ever since independence, communism had been the great bogey of Burmese politics. In 1948 the Communist Party of Burma, headed by Suu's uncle Thakin Than Tun, her mother's brother-in-law, had refused to cooperate with prime minister Nu's democratically elected government and had resorted to armed struggle, seizing a large area in the Pegu Mountains northeast of Rangoon and forming an alliance with Chinese communists on the northeast frontier. When Norman Lewis traveled through the country in 1950, large areas were out of bounds because of insurrectionary activity by communists.

Neither in her writings before returning to Burma nor in her political speeches inside the country had Suu given any indication of communist sympathies. But Ne Win loyalists had already condemned the 1988 uprising as a communist plot, and Suu's family connection to the Communist Party, and the presence in the NLD's Central Executive Committee of known left-wing figures such as the lawyer Daw Myint Myint Khin, who had belonged to a Marxist study group in the 1950s, made the insinuation an easy one to make. And the state media, and Khin Nyunt, the bespectacled chief of Military Intelligence, an increasingly influential figure in the junta, made it frequently and boldly. Aung San Suu Kyi was "surrounded by communists" it was claimed; she was "going the same way as her uncle's Burma Communist Party."[16]

Attacks like that could be shrugged off; they were routine, and often laughable—as when Khin Nyunt claimed that the communists had first tried to promote Suu's mother Daw Khin Kyi as the leader of the 1988 uprising, overlooking the fact that the lady in question had been in a hospital bed and close to death since March.

What was far more worrying was when, in early December, Aung Gyi himself started to repeat the allegations: In perfect harmony, both Military Intelligence and the retired, supposedly anti-junta general claimed that eight members of the party's thirty-three-strong Central Committee were communists. Was it possible that Aung Gyi was still in cahoots with Ne Win? Could he be scheming with Number One to weaken or split the new party, or even destroy it?

If he had restricted himself to raising the alarm about reds under the bed, Aung Gyi might have damaged the party severely. But when he began publicly downplaying the importance of Suu in the party, he went too far, fatally underestimating his colleague and the support she enjoyed. At a dramatic meeting of the committee on December 3, 1988, his leadership was put to the vote. He lost, and had no alternative but to step down, taking some of the other baung-bi chut with him out of the party. Fortunately, however, several of the most capable ex-army men on the committee, including Tin Oo and Kyi Maung, stuck with Suu and the civilian intelligentsia, and were to be crucial to the party's later success. Tin Oo, the former Minister of Defense, replaced Aung Gyi as chairman.

*

Her stroke had precipitated her daughter's return home and thereby changed the country's destiny; for months now she had lain semi-paralyzed in her room on the ground floor of 54 University Avenue as a great popular movement came into being around her. Then on December 27th, at the age of seventy-six, Suu's mother, Daw Khin Kyi, finally died, and her strongest remaining link to her father was broken.

If she had died six or seven months earlier, before Suu's Shwedagon speech and all that stemmed from that, her death would have had a very different resonance. It would have been a final, punctuating event in Suu's life: The painful duty that had torn Suu so brusquely away from her family would have been concluded and, however conflicted her feelings about the turmoil in Burma, there would have been no understandable reason for her to prolong her absence from the family home in Oxford.

But now not only Suu but also Michael and the boys understood that the situation had changed definitively. In her final illness, Daw Khin Kyi had been a bridge for Suu: She had passed over that bridge, and on the far shore had found another duty, just as pressing as the need to care for a sick mother, and far more unpredictable in its consequences. Now her fears of separation had been realized, and there was no going back.

For all sides in Burma's churning national crisis, the death of Daw Khin Kyi marked a caesura, a break point, though one with different meanings and possessing the seeds of different hopes.

The regime could yet dream that Suu's entry into politics was a mere fling, a caprice, an aberration, and that now her mother was gone she would pack her bags and depart. They granted Michael, Alexander and Kim, who had returned to England in September, visas to come back, banking perhaps on the emotional tug of home to drag Suu away when they departed.

For the masses of people who had struck for weeks and weeks in the summer and who had been traumatized and silenced by the massacre of thousands of their fellow citizens, the death was by contrast their first opportunity since the events of September 18th to take to the streets en masse and show their solidarity with Suu—and, by implication, their hostility to the regime. Twenty thousand of them flocked to University Avenue after her mother's death to express condolences. Far more were ready to follow the hearse to the mausoleum.

The scene was set, in other words, for another bloody clash. Yet merci-fully, this time around it didn't happen like that. For their part, SLORC made no attempt to relegate the funeral of the widow of the nation's founding father to the capital's shabby margins: In accordance with Suu's request, they sanctioned the lady's burial in a ceremony tantamount to a state funeral, at the mausoleum close to the Shwedagon where the remains of Supayalat, King Thibaw's consort, of U Thant and of Aung San himself were interred. They even paid some money, more than 1,000 dollars, towards the funeral expenses, and approved the building of a new monument to house the remains.

These gracious concessions were further enhanced when the regime's new strong man, General Saw Maung, visited University Avenue the evening before the funeral to sign the condolence book, accompanied by Khin Nyunt, the intelligence chief who was also the Minister of Internal and Religious Affairs. They stayed for tea; referring to the massacres perpe-trated by the army between September 18th and 20th, the president told Suu that he was distressed that his karma had resulted in him presiding over "this blot" on the army's honor, adding that he had no wish to cling to power.[17] What Suu said in reply is not recorded, but it was the closest to a meeting of minds that would ever occur between the two of them.

The public also behaved well. The regime had warned chillingly that the funeral could lead to "another round of disturbances"—words that could have become a self-fulfilling prophecy. But then Suu stepped up to put the matter in more dignified terms. Two days after her mother's death, she issued an appeal for calm, published in the *Working People's Daily* (the regime's English-language newspaper) on December 29, 1988. "As there will be a very large crowd of people at my mother's funeral procession," she wrote, "I humbly request the people to be calm and disciplined in sending my mother on her last journey . . . so that the funeral ceremony may be successful." She added, "I would also like to request the people to abide by the funeral committee's arrangements and security arrangements."

The people, 100,000 of them according to Reuters, did as they were told. The junta helped out by not attending, and by keeping the army in barracks: As so often in the long and strange interaction of the Burmese people and its armed forces, the masses swarmed through the capital in a temporary vacuum of visible force, kept in order by student marshals wearing the same red armbands as during the strikes of August and September. Students sang anti-government songs and waved the NLD's peacock flag. The coffin was carried from Inya Lake in a flower-strewn hearse, led by monks and followed by Suu and the family and a substantial group of foreign diplomats, a walk of two hours under the hot sun. At the end of it the people dispersed peacefully. Suu's relief was immense. "I hope this occasion has been an eye-opener," she told the *Independent* by phone. "If we have cooperation and understanding we can do things peacefully. The people are not out for violence for violence's sake."[18]

Already her thoughts were turning to the future: not Oxford, in the depths of another English winter, but her next campaign tour. Michael, of course, would not be able to accompany her: Even if his visa had permitted such a long stay, his presence was required to look after his sons as they returned to school. So as a second best he suggested to Ma Thanegi, Suu's personal assistant, who spoke such excellent English, that she might like to write a diary of the campaign, to keep him in the picture. Ma Thanegi was happy to agree.

5

OPEN ROAD

THE junta's policies made no sense. General Saw Maung had promised multiparty general elections within three months, had insisted that he would not stay in power long and promised that he would hand over power to the winning party in the election. Dozens of new political parties had registered. Yet it was effectively illegal to conduct an election campaign. Assemblies of more than five people were still banned. Rangoon was still under martial law. All newspapers except the purged and dreary *Working People's Daily* had been closed down. Television, still black and white, stuck just as doggedly to the party line.

How on earth was a political party to get its message out?

Aung San Suu Kyi tackled this challenge in the simplest and most direct manner possible, by merely ignoring the junta's rules and going out on the road to meet the people. She had seen little of her native land other than the major cities, and those she had not visited for many years. And her people, as she was beginning to think of them, had never seen her. With elections due any time—the timetable was in fact very vague—the sooner she got started the better.

It was a form of political action inspired by Gandhi, who like Suu had spent decades in foreign parts but after his return to India devoted years to criss-crossing the subcontinent, to the impotent fury of the British, and these journeys were to become the hallmark of her career. It is tempting to think of them as a series of jaunts, and Ma Thanegi's diary, which is full of humor and acute observation, tends to reinforce that impression. Yet these journeys were always perilous, because every mile of the way Suu and her party were challenging the writ of the regime. On two occasions she came close to being killed. That was a hazard she was keenly aware of from the outset. As Ma Thanegi wrote in her diary about one excursion, "Gandhi is Suu Kyi's role model and hero. Everyone knew it was going to be dangerous: Some of the students had the Tharana Gon sutra chanted over them to prepare themselves for sudden death, a mantra recited in

Buddhist ritual over the body of the deceased. Some became monks or nuns for a few days in preparation."

Suu's attitude was comparable to that of the sannyasin, the Hindu renunciate. Her mother and father had passed away. She had forsworn both the duties and the pleasures of family life for this cause. Burma's democratic future was no longer for her some abstract issue, worthy of her support: It was the cause she was living for and that defined her life, the cause she now identified with totally, whatever might be the consequences.

Everywhere she went, she and her companions were met by huge, ecstatic crowds which had often taken great risks to come out and greet her, defying the orders of the authorities to stay away. And as she moved across the country, to Tenasserim in the south, across the Irrawaddy Delta south and west of Rangoon on repeated trips, to the old capital of Mandalay and points in between, to the Shan States in the northeast, finally right up into the mountains of Kachin far to the north, her party's support ballooned; it was as if she was absorbing the country into her own person, and the country was absorbing her. And every trip she survived, every new crowd that hailed her, the junta's power and prestige shrank proportionately; because, as we have seen, power in Burma is a zero-sum game.

Bertil Lintner captures the mood of those early meetings.

She was coming to open a new NLD office in a suburb on the outskirts of Rangoon. It was scorching hot, April, before the rains. I went out there in a taxi and thousands of people were waiting in this scorching sun for hours—children, old women, people of all ages.

Suddenly you could see a white car somewhere in the distance trailing a cloud of dust behind it, then the car arrived—she had been given the car by the Japanese, a white Toyota, to travel around the country—and the cheers were incredible. And she got out, very relaxed, surrounded by her students, her bodyguards, and smiled at everybody and was garlanded, and she went up on stage and started talking.

And she talked for two or three hours and nobody left. Not even the children left. My Burmese is fairly rudimentary but I could understand what she was talking about, she was using very simple, down-to-earth words. "You've got a head," she said. "And you haven't got a head to nod with, you've been nodding for 26 years, the head is there for you to think." That kind of thing, and people were laughing, it was a family affair. Then she left . . .[1]

The junta felt it bitterly. From the icy courtesy and civilized assurances of January, on the eve of Daw Khin Kyi's funeral, within a few months they were reduced to spreading libels and issuing murderous threats. They made a desperate effort to take the country back—by renaming it; and General Saw Maung was heading for the nervous breakdown which would see him removed from power.

*

On January 20, 1989, Suu and her party set off for the Irrawaddy Delta south and west of the capital, a flat land of endless paddies, dotted with small villages and seamed with wandering rivers, the intensely fertile flat country drained by the British; also the land where tens of thousands were to die in Cyclone Nargis in 2008. It was the first time that Ma Thanegi had kept notes on their progress—and the first time that the right of Suu and her party to move around freely was challenged.

"Great harassment in Bassein," Ma Thanegi wrote of their official reception in one town. "Armed soldiers barred the way out of the house we were staying in, only allowing us out in twos or threes to visit friends etc. . . ." The town, one of the biggest in the delta region, had been flooded with troops by the Divisional Commander, one Brigadier Myint Aung, who seems to have taken the NLD party's arrival as a personal affront. In a letter to her husband, Suu wrote, "Here I am having a battle royal with the notorious Brigadier Myint Aung." The town's harbor was "full of troops, most of the streets blocked, sandbagged and barbedwired . . ." The army had forced markets and offices to close, sent teachers out of the town on so-called "voluntary service" and fired guns in the air to deter local people from greeting them.

The morning after their arrival in the town, they learned that a number of local supporters had been arrested. Suu requested permission to talk to the brigadier: She wanted to register a complaint, she said, and would not leave the town "until I am satisfied there is fair play."

Ma Thanegi wrote in her diary,

Request denied but a lower level meeting permitted, so I said I would go, please put down my name—the army looks down on women and they would think I would be helpless and weak. Ma Suu [throughout the diary Ma Thanegi refers to Suu using the "Ma"—"elder sister"—prefix, either as "Ma Suu" or simply "Ma Ma"] gave permission ("they have no idea I'm firing my first torpedo," she said). Off I went, wearing a demure dress unlike what I usually wore, and slathered in perfume.

Looking all shy and sweet I talked to two midlevel officers and they were hearty with me. Their excuse for not allowing us to go around Bassein was that prisoners had been let out of the jail, two of whom were murderers on death row, and that it was dangerous for us with them out in the town. I'm sure they thought I would be terrified by this explanation—they repeated the word "dangerous for us" three or four times. So far I had been listening demurely but at that point I asked firmly, "If they were convicted of murder and are on death row, why were they let out?" [In Burma's traditional society, women are not expected to ask tough questions of men in authority, army officers in particular.] They gaped at me so I repeated my question. They were furious but could not scream at me as I was talking graciously . . .

When Suu and her party learned that the cars in which they had traveled from Rangoon had been impounded and that they were effectively bottled up in the town, Suu herself broke the deadlock by walking out of the house where they had spent the night and fraternizing genially with the soldiers drawn up on the street. The upshot of Suu's charm offensive, according to Ma Thanegi: "The troops were removed the day before we left and we were allowed to move around freely." It was the first time Suu had come so close to a showdown with the army, but it was not to be the last.

At the next stop, however, their problems melted away. "The minute that we crossed into Bago Division, all harassment stopped," she wrote. "Just over the border, we saw trucks and cars and thought that it was more harassment, but it was crowds welcoming us. Ma Suu gave a speech right there, holding the old type of square microphone that we had seen photos of her father using."

As they were to discover, their official reception varied wildly from place to place, especially in these early months of the campaign, depending on the whim, or perhaps the political inclinations, of the local military authority. Suu and her colleagues adjusted their behavior accordingly. Ma Thanegi reports that in one town they visited they "had some trouble," but in another soon afterwards "the township officer, military, said he was going fishing when he heard we were coming in and did so. So we went in, had lunch, Suu made speeches, and we left: no problem. When there is harassment we try to stay longer or to walk into town singing democracy songs or shouting slogans. If no harassment, just happy to go in quietly in the car and leave quietly."

They returned to Rangoon, but less than a fortnight later they were off again, this time to the Shan States, the rolling hill country which is one of the most idyllic corners of Burma, home to the Shan people, cousins of the Thais.

The Shan States have a special place in the Aung San legend: It was at the town of Panglong, in the far north of the region, in February 1947, that Suu's father signed a historic agreement between the Burmans, the Shans, the Kachin and the Chins—all the most numerous ethnic nationalities in the country with the exception of the Karen—committing them to membership of the new, independent Union of Burma.[2]

The Panglong Agreement was reached immediately after Aung San's successful conclusion of independence negotiations with the government of Clement Attlee in London, and confirmed Attlee and his colleagues in their belief that he was the right man to take charge of independent Burma. So when Suu and her party colleagues set off there exactly forty-two years later, it was a trip of huge symbolic significance.

On February 9th, they were still in Rangoon, making preparations: "An Australian senator came to see Ma Ma at 8 AM," Ma Thanegi recorded. He had also been to see General Saw Maung, "who told him elections would be held soon, after discussions with parties. . . . Spent the night at Ma Ma's place. Ma Ma up and down stairs whole evening, signing letters, seeing to papers, books. Dr. Michael phoned after Ma Ma finished writing a letter to him." Nobody wanted to miss the trip, starting in the morning. "Ko Maw"—Ma Thanegi's small, grouchy, short-sighted colleague— "is ill, but coming along anyway." Others along for the ride included a medical student and democracy activist called Ma Thida. Suu's personal bodyguards on the trip—Ma Thanegi refers to them collectively as "the boys" or "the kids"—were to include Aung Aung, the son of Suu's father's personal bodyguard Bo Min Lwin, and Win Thein, a student who had survived one of the March massacres before deciding to dedicate his life to Suu and the democracy struggle.

*

They set off by car on February 10, 1989, "Tiger" at the wheel as usual, Suu elegant as ever in a mauve longyi and blue jacket, sitting in the back with Ma Thanegi. The journey along Burma's atrocious roads would be long, and the start was brutally early.

> Left Rangoon 4:45 AM, fifteen minutes late. Ma Ma a bit annoyed. She was sleepy in the early part of the morning. I held her down by the shoulders on bumpy roads; fragile and light as a papier-mâché doll. Forced to stop unplanned at Pyawbwe . . . Ma Ma VERY annoyed. Stopped for sugarcane juice at Tat-kone: delicious! Ma Ma loved it. Lunch at Ye Tar Shay. People in the villages amazed and overjoyed to see Ma Ma. Ate lunch, fried rice ordered from Chinese restaurant next door.

Among Ma Thanegi's many duties was ensuring that Suu did not eat anything that might upset her stomach: "Ma Ma looked so wistful when I swiped chili sauce and onions from under her very nose. Later I relented and picked out onions sans sauce for her. Chili sauce v. unhealthy stuff in Burma."

Eleven hours after leaving University Avenue they arrived in the Shan States, high up in the chilly hills, to a reception far grander than Suu was prepared to accept. One is reminded of the ironical remark made about the Mahatma by one of his long-suffering aides: "It costs a lot to keep Gandhi poor . . ."[3]

"Reached Kalaw 5:30 PM and taken to Kalaw Hotel and told about elaborate preparations that have been made for her: New bed, new dressing table. Ma Ma dug in her heels as expected and we all went to stay in a small cottage." The whole party had to sleep in a single, freezing cold room in the cottage. "Darn cold," Ma Thanegi remarked. "Found out later that poor Tiger sat up all night, couldn't sleep. Ma Ma ate no dinner, just some slices of banana and squashed avocado. Very cold, so Ma Ma put on flannel pajamas, long-sleeved thick t-shirt, thick socks; buried under thick quilts. Ma Ma slept badly because the kids [the student bodyguards sharing the room] who couldn't sleep because of the cold kept talking."

"Told me she missed Rangoon. Then she said she missed Oxford: the heating system, and Dr. Michael's (warm) feet."

Despite these privations, the following morning they had another early start.

> February 11: she wore green plaid longyi, white jacket, green cardigan with matching scarf and gloves. Got up (had to) at 4:30. Left for Loilam at 5:30, after I insisted she eat soft-boiled eggs.
>
> At her request I borrowed a tape of Fifties and Sixties songs to listen to on the way, coincidentally the same we were listening to in Rangoon. I remember her singing along loudly "Love you more than I can say" as she scooted upstairs. We sang along with the tape on the way: "Seven lonely days," etcetera.
>
> Ma Ma v. annoyed at easy-going plans. There was supposed to be a convoy on the road "for our protection" but there was no one in sight. We reached Loilam without seeing any. Ma Ma hit the roof.

Later they learned that anti-regime Shan insurgents, a powerful presence in these hills, had chosen a different way to keep them safe. "Found out later that trucks traveling along the road had been forced by insurgents to stay two or three nights at villages. The insurgents were clearing the way for our cars!"

As Tiger negotiated the narrow, winding, potholed road through the hills, Suu reminisced about her family life, about Alex and Kim. "She talked about how [her fifteen-year-old son] Alex had once poured ink all over a carpet, a white one; and how [her eleven-year-old son] Kim, visiting Rangoon with his brother and Michael in January and fed up with all the attention, "said he wanted a notice put in his grandmother's funeral program, 'Do not pet Kim' . . .

"Lunch at Loilam, hurriedly prepared . . . pickled soybeans, we loved them." The work of the tour was getting under way, without impediment from the army—and now they found out why: "Held two or three meetings in Loilam, crowds gathered. One man came up to Aung Aung and said he and his people were taking care of security and not to worry. He was not wearing an NLD badge, so Aung Aung asked who he was . . . reply was 'Shan insurgent' and he left hurriedly. Aung delighted."

By the evening they had arrived in the town of Panglong, where Aung San signed his famous agreement. Suu's preference for spartan accommodation was tempered by an appreciation of modern plumbing which Ma Thanegi shared. "A clean, grand house," Ma Thanegi noted, "with a functioning toilet. 'The flush actually works!' Ma Ma said, very delightedly. 'And there's loo paper, too . . .'

"Discussion with youth etc. after dinner. Preparing for bed she said she'd love to go to Oxford for two weeks, just to recharge her batteries. Seems very homesick because of cold weather. Said she was planning to plead sick and stay in bed for three days after return to Rangoon (she didn't)."

The following day, February 12th, was the anniversary of the Panglong Agreement, to be commemorated with a ceremony, so shrugging off her melancholy Suu "worked late by candlelight preparing her address for the next day" after the electricity failed. After she went to bed the students in the room next door were again talking late, "so I went out to shush them, whereupon they started snoring loudly."

For the ceremony the next day, Ma Thanegi records, Suu wore red. It was held in the morning; NLD central committee member U Aung Lwin, a well-known actor, read out a declaration pledging to strive for democracy, which all repeated. "Young people in the typical costume of various ethnic nationalities clustered behind Ma Ma on the stage. She gave a short speech, then on to a large prayer hall for talks. Gradually audience swelled to about two thousand. I stayed outside the meeting and tended to the toenails of the boys, which needed cutting."

Before lunch they were back on the road. "On to Nan sam, Maipon, Ho-pone. Lunch at Nan Sam. They had prepared Burmese food, pork and chicken curry, soup. We would have preferred Shan food! Most people we met during the tour were very worried about what sort of food we would eat, but in fact we ate anything and everything."

Ma Thanegi seems more interested in recording the practical minutiae of the trip than the political discussions along the way, but she does note down the occasional pregnant exchange: "Someone in the Shan States party said Bogyoke [i.e. Aung San] had forgotten his promise to the Shan States"—his promise to give them wide autonomy within the Union of Burma, with the right to secede from it after ten years. "Ma Ma said no, he didn't forget, he died."

They were driving west now, and arrived in Taunggyi, the capital of the Shan States, in the late afternoon. "Not too cold. Burmese food for dinner AGAIN." They were put up at a monastery: The hospitality and support of the sangha, the community of Buddhist monks, was to become crucial in the history of her party. "At bedtime Ma Ma referred to her pink cotton bed sheet that she had brought from home as her security blanket. 'If it's dirty at least I know it's my own dirt . . .'"

On February 13th Suu wore a grey checked longyi and a "pinni" jacket of the sort that had become part of her party's uniform. "Shan-style breakfast, '*Hin Htoke*,' rice and meat packed in leaves. Ma Ma liked it. I didn't. Nor did the boys: I found them later at a tea-shop, gorging on usual fare of nan bread and cream and tea and buns."

Bad though unsurprising news reached them from Rangoon: a reiteration by the regime of the allegations that the NLD had been penetrated by communists. Ma Thanegi records no particular reaction on the part of Suu to what was becoming the theme song of the junta. "We paid calls on other parties in the town, the local NLD office and the Holy Infant Jesus Convent for Handicapped Children at Payaphyu. Ma Ma v. impressed by it, made a donation of 1050 kyats collected from all of us." Ma Thanegi, who has a very limited tolerance for what she regards as maudlin sentiment, ducked out of the event. "I'm glad I didn't go, couldn't have borne hearing blind boy sing a song he composed about his lost parents. Instead I went to two bazaars and spent time at the house taking up the hems of Ma Ma's longyis."

Like Gandhi, Suu was acquiring corporate sponsors, though on a humbler plane. "Dinner offered by Kyar-Pyan cheroot people," Ma Thanegi records. "Other guests looking dazzling in silk and gold etc, and we trooped in, dusty and rumpled. After our kids [the student bodyguards] were seated, someone said they were not included in invitation, so we (the kids and I, although they implored me to stay) walked out to eat at Chinese restaurant nearby. Pissed off."

Military Intelligence (MI) continued to keep a close eye on Suu, as Ma Thanegi notes, but already she had discovered the knack of how to charm them. "Had fried rice, going Dutch, then went back to the house where Suu was having dinner with the cheroot people, to wait for her. Later, going back all together to the place where we were staying, Tiger lost his way. Our two attendant MI agents were trailing us on a scooter, and Ma Ma told Win Thein to ask them to lead the way back home. They did so willingly and seemed so proud when Ma Ma thanked them sweetly. The two of them huddled together, grinning.

"In bed, lights out, she giggled and said they looked like two crooks from a movie. I said very inferior movie, definitely Grade C."

To try to persuade the Shan that no Burman chauvinist lurked behind her winning smile, Suu wore Shan national costume the next day, though declined the headdress.

> She said she felt funny about wearing fancy dress. Left early for Shwenyaung, then Nyaung Shwe, then Inlay . . . went to Phaung-daw Oo Paya. Then to a monastery: abbot with loud and very dramatically tuneful voice gave blessings and recited prayers, which we had to repeat, during which Ma Ma bravely kept herself solemn, but I couldn't. Disgraced myself with two bouts of giggles, relieved to learn afterwards that most of us nearly in fits.

That night, too, they were guests of a Shan monastery. "Abbot there youngish and so nice and helpful. I don't know if proper to refer to a monk as being 'sweet' but definitely he is." But the monastic prohibition against the close interaction of monks with women caused a small problem. "Men lucky as they could use monks' loo," Ma Thanegi noted, "but Ma Ma and I had to march right outside, to public loo, which consisted of many small rooms high above water, with a very large rectangular hole in the floor of each. Ma Ma terrified, said she was thin enough to slip right through.

"Three of us, Ma Ma, Ma Thida and I, slept on floor on thick mattress in the room of one of the monks, who slept in guest room." Bathing during the trip usually consisted of freezing dips in convenient streams, but the state of the pond here ruled it out. "We couldn't bathe in it. Boys swam in swampy-looking water nearby, and got rashes next day . . ."

They did however enjoy an outing on Inlay Lake, the great tourist draw of the Shan States, famous for floating gardens, fishermen who propel their boats standing up with a single oar, and the Temple of the Jumping Cats. "On boat ride on Lake Inlay, Ma Ma felt the glare of the sun in her eyes and covered her face with white hanky kept in place by hat and hat band. We told her people are going to say Daw Aung San Suu Kyi is VERY fair! Video and cameramen in another boat circled us to get her picture and their jaws dropped when they encountered Ma Ma, face covered!"

Next day they again embarked on the lake.

2/15/1989: sea-green jacket and Arakanese longyi same color. Left Inlay early morning. Just as boat leaving, U Thuriya marched out to supply us with blankets. Ma Ma slept for a while in boat, on and under pile of blankets. Nyaung Shwe NLD people upset because we didn't spend night there. Blamed boys of NLD Inlay for it. Ma Ma explained at length, several times, how it had been fixed in Rangoon by Electoral Commission. This is the sort of thing that annoys her about thick skulls.

After driving for a couple of hours through the gentle, pastoral, almost European countryside, its Asian setting only betrayed by the broad-brimmed hats of the farmers, they arrived at Pindaya, famous for its limestone caves chock-full of Buddha images. "Then to Pindaya cave pagoda . . . stiff climb, all of us except Ma Ma puffing. Cool, beautiful, eerie place. On to Ywet-hla to put up NLD sign. Then to Aungban for overnight stop. Discussions till late. Receive pamphlet denouncing Ma Ma for not being agreeable to armed movement, possibly produced by group in Taunggyi."

That night they stayed in a big wooden house, with what Ma Thanegi describes as "a funny loo—two people can sit facing each other, chatting.

"Bedtime remark: Laughing, Suu said, 'Everyone is attacking me! Whatever possessed me to get involved in all this? When I could have stayed peacefully in Oxford!'"

*

2/16/1989: Red Arakanese longyi; same color jacket. Red flowers in hair. Left Aungban at 7:00 AM. Lunch at Hpe-khon, where we were met by two bands, one of them "western-style" with lovely flutes and drums. Band played "Hail to the Chief" with Ma Ma in step behind them, having to walk slow and looking bashful, hands behind her back, growing red in the face.

Gave us *Kaung-ye* (rice wine) to drink . . . sweet and cool and not strong. In all three villages met by flute and drum bands. One man shouted, "May you become president!" Ma Ma forced to step out of car to walk through crowds which included Padaung women [the so-called "giraffe women" who wear numerous brass rings around their necks]. Two of them, old ladies in traditional dress, separately handed Ma Ma five kyat notes! One of them touched the badge of one of our boys with a picture of Bogyoke on it, and said "This our father." The boy nearly cried he was so touched, said he came out in goose pimples.

Now they were on the homeward stretch, heading south in Kayah state—called Karen state until the regime changed the name—on the road to Rangoon. Ma Thanegi was showing signs of losing patience with the proceedings. "Overnight stop at Loikaw. Got there late afternoon. Meetings held at separate places because two NLD groups in heated rivalry. Meals at separate places; put up at neutral house. A lot of bloody fuss and bloody long-winded meetings."

But there were compensations: "House very nice, clean loo. Ma Ma said I can write loo guide for Burma . . .

"Ma Ma received Kayah style dress, she was feeling silly about all the fancy dress she was expected to wear. I said, since she'd worn Shan national costume it was only fair to wear the others or else they will all be screaming. Told her let's hope she won't receive Naga dress . . ." In a note for Michael Aris, Ma Thanegi wrote, "I hope you know what it's like, Dr. M . . ." Traditionally the women of the Naga tribes on Burma's north-western border went bare-breasted.

Ma Thanegi recorded another of Suu's jocular indications that the controversies into which she was being sucked were getting on her nerves. "Ma Ma said sometimes when everyone is attacking her she would like to have a tantrum like a child and scream 'It's not fair, it's not fair!' . . ."

It was the penultimate day of the journey, and Ma Thanegi allowed herself to kick back a little, to Suu's consternation.

2/17/1989: Dark olive green Arakanese longyi and same color jacket. Left early for Faruso, Dimawso. Talks. Wild greetings at Dimawso in colorful traditional dresses, bands, dances etc. One group of men wearing black shorts with colored woolly pieces and pom-poms and tiny white buttons all over them. I told Ma Ma I am going to get one for Dr. M and she giggled . . . said March 27 his birthday. Lunch at Dimawso, in old chapel. Band played Rudolph the Red-nosed Reindeer while we were having lunch. I had sampled *Kaung-ye* rice wine while she was talking to crowds and was nearly dead drunk only nobody noticed. Thanks to father's training I could handle liquor—father drank like fish.

I warned Ma Ma during lunch not to touch *Kaung Ye* and why.

It was not a warning that Suu was likely to require—she had not touched alcohol since experimentally sampling sherry with Indian friends in the ladies' loo of Oxford's Bodleian Library, more than twenty years before.[4] "She was startled and asked me why I had drunk so much. I said only half a glass. Learnt later it was three-year-old rice wine. If it were any older I'd be under table, father's training or not."

The bodyguards, too, were starting to relax. "Boys very interested in traditional dress, esp. that of the Padaung women, and I'm afraid they asked point-blank how necks were washed.[5] (Strips of straw inserted under brass rings and pulled to and fro.) I dared not ask them what else they asked. . . . Got back to Loikaw . . . huge Chinese dinner. Same dishes for boys, too: I checked. In some places 'top' table dishes better than other tables. Boys ate like horses. Ma Ma ate more than usual and threw up twice during meetings afterwards. She said wryly, 'everything's gone.'" She had caved in to the pleas that she wear tribal dress. "She wore Kayah longyi and big Kayah shawl to dinner."

∗

February 18: Left Loikaw early, 7 AM. Blue checked longyi, blue jacket, red sweater. She had rice gruel for breakfast. Speech at Newma monastery. Said she would love some strawberries but we couldn't get any so we will do so in Rangoon.

Lunch at Kalaw. Trip uneventful to Bawbye. Lovely guavas: Ma Ma said normally she doesn't like guavas but these were huge sweet and crisp. On the way from Bawbye to Kalaw I had eaten a whole guava, a huge one, much to everyone's astonishment, but I think with all the slices Ma Ma ate would be more than one.

The Irrawaddy Delta, which they had already visited, was to be the greatest source of tension during the campaign, and some of the party's members there had already been jailed. But while they were on the road heading home, good news arrived. "We had news that the Irrawaddy Division people have been released. They are out on bail. Much rejoicing."

At Bawbye, the army reacted to their arrival by extending the curfew, so the students in the party felt they had to challenge it, "strolling and talking loudly in front of SLORC's office until 9:55.

"Nice dinner. Ma Ma had double bed to herself with shocking pink lacy mosquito net complete with lacy ribbons." It was the sort of romantic mosquito net targeted at newly married couples. Neither of them took a fancy to it. "I said I would be damned if I would marry any man who supplied me with something like this, I would have to burn it. Ma Ma, lying flat on the bed, said that if she were the bride she would be asking what she had done to deserve it . . .

"February 19: Pale grey outfit demure longyi. At end of long day Ma Ma said it was thoughtless of her to wear such a pale color on a long trip, said she looked dirty, actually she didn't."

At the town of Yaydashe they learned that some members of the former ruling party, now called the National Unity Party, had adopted the dirty tricks first uncovered on the eve of Suu's Shwedagon speech, cranking out semi-pornographic libels against her. "Young NLD people in Yaydashe waylaid us and said they had important matters to discuss. Found out that it concerned dirty anti-Ma Ma propaganda leaflets distributed by the NUP—the people responsible had been caught red-handed and would be prosecuted the next day."

Ma Thanegi recorded, "We all love Yaydashe NLD young people, no fuss no flowers no cameras." She was in such a good mood that she felt moved to help one of Suu's elderly admirers.

> One photographer in his late-70s seemed like a gay old dog, he wanted Ma Ma's photo so I told him to lie in wait and ambush her when she came up. Told me proudly that he had asked her to look this way and she did. He dragged me off to his house opposite NLD office to show me a framed photo of Ma Ma he'd taken during our first trip up country. Caption said, Aung San Suu Kyi, lady builder of democratic nation, daughter of Aung San, architect of Burma. Held my arm in vice-like grip until I had admired the whole effect profusely enough for his satisfaction.

As they neared Rangoon, the pressure of both popular expectation and official hostility began to rise again. The town of Dukgo gave them a reception to remember.

Wonderful sight at Dukgo: As we entered the town the local NLD had issued red NLD caps and we marched in singing a democratic song which was also blared out from one car. We pushed in front of the MI's videos and still cameras. Ma Ma had been saying for days how she was on the brink of losing her voice but it came on full, clear and strong as she started to talk at the NLD office, amplified out into the road, and she sounded darn mad.

While Ma Ma was talking, people crept up to listen at the side of the road. Police and soldiers told them to get back but we told them to come up and listen. Planned for Ma Ma to walk to jail to visit prisoners but when she came out of the NLD office such a large crowd followed her that we were afraid the police—who hurried to the police station and closed the gates—would say we were invading it and shoot us down. So many kids and women in the crowd that we decided just to pass the police station and jail by.

We walked out of town, crowds following, and I was afraid we would be walking all the way home. But at last, with the last goodbye, Ma Ma got into the car.

Had engine trouble all the way: water pipe broke late afternoon. Stopped for a while at Jundasar at a rice mill. Also we had to stop near a stream just before Dai-oo. Large pack of stray of dogs—one of the boys shouted at them about 2/88, SLORC's rule banning groups of more than five gathering together . . .

It was their longest and most draining—yet exhilarating—trip to date, lasting ten days and covering over 1,200 miles, and it was nearly over.

Ma Ma sat in car and asked if I didn't feel a sense of unreality about all we are doing. I said, dealing with stupid people can get us caught up in weeks of stupidity, no wonder it makes us all feel weird . . .

Got home very late about 8:30. Told Ma Ma how I had always hated to travel in crowds and never did so and now I am traveling with a circus, lots of monkeys. Ma Ma said also a few elephants, because some of the boys are really large.

Back in University Avenue at last, Suu "played piano a bit. No bath. Said she must tune piano and play again. Bedtime remark: If my feet are dirty, they're dirty, so what? Said that now she was back in Rangoon she would rest. I very much doubt it, and told her so."

6

HER FATHER'S BLOOD

O N March 23, 1989, Aung San Suu Kyi turned to Ma Thanegi and said with a wan smile, "I must admit, Thanegi, that I am a bit tired." "I said," her friend wrote in her diary, "that must be a gross understatement."

Things were happening so fast: good things, bad things, terrible things. On that very day, for example, Min Ko Naing, the third-year Rangoon University Botany major who had become the charismatic leader of the militant students, was arrested. Five days earlier Aung Gyi, the former general and crony of Ne Win who for a couple of months at the end of 1988 had shared the leadership of the National League for Democracy before being expelled, had renewed his attacks. In a letter released internationally by his lawyers, the regime's former critic repeated his earlier accusation that "eight above-ground communists . . . are dominating in the leading positions of the League," and claimed that Suu and her allies in the party "lied" when they said the ex-general had resigned voluntarily from the party.[1] He maintained that they had expelled him, and had not followed "the provisions of the party constitution" when they did so. The man they now suspected of having cut a deal with SLORC was determined to give the party as much trouble as he could.

It was pressure they really did not need. Thrown together in haste, the NLD had no clear ideology. Some of the founding members had left-wing backgrounds, as Aung Gyi alleged—the intellectuals, people like the veteran opposition journalist Win Tin and his protégé Daw Myint Myint Khin, the leading lawyer—though there has never been any evidence that the party was subjected to "entrist" attack by communists. Then there were the former senior army officers who had long ago fallen out with Ne Win, biding their time for years to take revenge, who were steeped in the conventional, conservative values of the armed forces. In any mature democracy, the intellectuals and the old soldiers would have belonged to different parties. Within the NLD they always made awkward bedfellows.

Then, most disruptingly of all, there was the yeast of the movement, the students who had launched the revolution one year before, who had paid for it by the thousands with their lives in August and September and who now provided the movement with its marshals and bodyguards and poor bloody infantry. Many thousands of them had escaped to border areas after September 18th and were now training in guerrilla warfare with the regime's ethnic enemies. Inevitably, many of those who remained inside the country were full of sympathy for their vanished comrades, and wanted Suu and the NLD to follow the hardest line possible against the regime.

But from the start of her involvement in the revolt, one thing had been very clear to Suu: Nonviolence was a must. She had expressed it on the very day of the crackdown, September 18th, remonstrating with the students in her house not to try to meet the army ranged outside the gate with force. Partly it was Gandhi, partly it was Buddha, but it was also common sense. The military regime had decided to treat the democracy movement as a military threat, the equivalent of the Karen or communist insurgencies on the border: The rebels were to be gunned down, eliminated, exterminated. The moral advantage Suu possessed, like Gandhi and Martin Luther King, Jr., in other times and places, was that she and her followers would never meet violence with violence. This was immensely difficult to sustain in a movement boiling with rage, grief and resentment. Already, in the past months, rebels had resorted to drumhead trials and decapitations. If Suu had given even a hint that she endorsed violent tactics there would have been a surge of righteous delight within the movement—but subsequently SLORC would have found easy justification for any action it chose to take against it; while the party's international prestige, that precious, invisible commodity that perhaps only the well-traveled, cosmopolitan Suu really understood and appreciated, would be forfeit.

Yet at the same time Suu needed to keep the students on board. On February 22nd, Ma Thanegi wrote in her diary, "The NLD youth have been in a ferment for days. They want to form a separate party because they say they need freedom of movement. Ma Ma and the Central Executive Committee promised them more freedom but they want a separate and perhaps in their minds a more powerful status . . ." With fierce arguments—one of the students "burst into protest" after Suu shouted at him—and by adroit use of her own prestige she had succeeded in talking them out of splitting away. But it was hard going. "I don't believe in armed struggle," she told a journalist during these difficult days, "but I sympathize with the students who are engaged in armed struggle."[2] That was the tightrope she had to walk.

But then there was the good news. Despite all the official harassment, Suu and her colleagues were continuing to travel, and everywhere they went tens of thousands of new members flocked to the party: By the spring of 1989, press estimates of membership ran as high as three million, in a total population of around fifty million.[3] The regime was sticking to its promise to hold elections: At the beginning of March it had published the election law, though Colonel Khin Nyunt, the intelligence chief, continued to be evasive about the date, insisting that three conditions would have to be met—the restoration of law and order, regularization of public transport and an improvement in living standards—before they could be scheduled.

And if international opinion was to be a crucial factor in the respective strengths of the two sides—and the army's deliberate shooting of foreign photographers during September's atrocities suggested that the regime was acutely aware of and anxious about its international image—things were looking up. Suu, despite her strange name and the obscurity of her country, was beginning to make her mark.

Terry McCarthy of the *Independent* had got on friendly terms with her back in September, and his paper had scooped the world with an important article she wrote the same month. But the first sign that she was beginning to attract wider attention came in January.

Steven Erlanger of the *New York Times* had first introduced American readers to Suu on January 9, 1989: "the charismatic forty-two-year-old daughter of the country's independence leader," he wrote, "symbolized" the NLD. He reported:

Two weeks ago, after only her second political trip outside Rangoon, to Moulmein in Mon state, thirteen local organizers of her party were arrested. Before the visit, the populace was ordered by loudspeaker not to come into the street to see Ms. Aung San Suu Kyi, not to cheer, give her flowers or shout the traditional Burmese "good health." The warnings proved to be futile, however, as large crowds gathered and inundated her with blossoms.

"The authorities are still trying to deceive themselves," Suu told Erlanger when he visited her at home. "If they're able to face the truth, they must know that this is a great upsurge of popular feeling against an oppressive regime. Yet they keep going on about a communist conspiracy. There is no such thing. The utter lack of confidence in the authorities is very sad. But it is a reflection of how badly people have been treated. Once the waters of a revolution start flowing, you can't push them back for ever . . ."

Two days later Erlanger returned to the subject in the long *New York Times* piece that probably did more than anything else to put her on the world map.[4] "She gave the impression of a sensible politician," he wrote, "articulate and straightforward." If that was a little patronizing, by the end of the piece he was a signed-up fan. She was "charismatic, decisive, altogether admirable," he gushed, "but also very lucky." How so? He quoted an "adviser" to Suu pointing out that "everyone talks about democracy, but this is Asia, and what many people think of her has little to do with democracy. It's like Benazir Bhutto or Corazon Aquino."

Suu laughed at the remark, he said. "I've always accepted that," she replied. "I don't pretend that I don't owe my position in Burmese politics to my father . . . I'm doing this for my father. I'm quite happy that they see me as my father's daughter. My only concern is that I prove worthy of him."

Suu seemed to understand well, Erlanger wrote, that "Burma's military must be preserved as a united institution if the country is to achieve democracy of any sort."

She told him, "I know a split army is against the interests of the nation. In the end we need their cooperation to get where we want, so the people can get what they want with the least amount of suffering. We just want what my father wanted: a professional army that understands that a really honorable army doesn't engage in politics." She was to remind people in many different forums that her father had set his nation a fine example when he resigned his army commission—from the army he himself had founded—to fight independent Burma's first general election, refusing even to take his army pension.

"I have a rapport with the army," she told Erlanger, "I was brought up to regard them as friends. So I can't feel the same sort of hostility to them that the people now feel. And while I understand this anger, I find it very, very sad."

She explained how her involvement in politics had in the end been inescapable. "I obviously had to think about it," she said, "but my instinct was, 'this is not a time when anyone who cares can stay out.' As my father's daughter, I felt I had a duty to get involved." The decision was a long time coming: For the first four months after arriving in the country, she told Erlanger, even after Michael joined her from England, she slept alongside her mother in hospital. But with her growing political commitments, that became impossible—which was "the only thing," she said, that made her wonder if she was making the right choice. "But I'm sure this is what [my mother] would have wanted," she said. She recalled her mother's iron self-discipline after hearing that Suu's younger brother had died in a drowning accident in a pond at the family home. "She stayed and finished her work," she said.

That difficult memory brought her round inevitably to the subject she has veered away from in every interview since, and which has long provided fuel of various sorts to her enemies: her commitment to her own family, in particular to her sons Alex and Kim. "Obviously you have to put the family second," she said. "But the kids are at an important age. Really families need to be together all the time." She paused, then said, ". . . My mother was very ill," and here a tear ran down her cheek, "it was important to be here with her."

It was the conundrum in which she was caught. Her bond to her mother had brought her running across the world to nurse her. But now a family bond which was even more commanding—the care and nurture she owed her sons, both at crucial, tender ages—had been cast off—in favor of what?

As Ma Thanegi's diaries reveal, Suu did harbor doubts in those early days—though if she shared with her friend the agony she felt in being separated from her family, Ma Thanegi, writing the diary for Michael's consumption, was tactful enough to keep it to herself. But the only way to deal with doubt, if you did not intend to surrender to it, was to live your new commitment to the full, holding nothing back at all. The most terrifying test was yet to come.

*

The day after Suu's rare confession that she felt tired they were off again, once more to the Irrawaddy Delta, which drew them as a flame draws a moth throughout the early months of 1989. Here, in the sodden hinterland of the capital, the expectant crowds were huge—but matched by a fierceness of repression seen nowhere else in the country.

Ma Thanegi wrote in her diary,

March 24, left Rangoon 6 AM by boat . . . At Htan Manaing village had to eat lunch in five minutes because someone said he had already told the abbot of the monastery that we were coming and there was no time to waste. Then on to Wa Balauk Thauk village in small boats, along streams winding through swamp-like jungle country, very much like the Vietcong country we have seen in movies. Ma Ma said how Kim would love it.

Reached Kim Yang Gaung in evening but no one came out of their houses. The whole place deserted, people peeping from deep inside darkened huts, only a few dogs going about their business. Learned that a local man who was democratic-minded was shot dead through forehead by army sergeant or corporal one week ago.

From there a long cart ride to Let Khote Kon. Easier to have gone on by boat but one of the NLD organizers felt we should visit that place and he was right. Ma Ma made speech in compound of a dainty little old lady named Ma Yin Nu. A very big crowd. I gave Ma Yin Nu a photo of Ma Ma . . .

Equally long cart ride back to boat, though it felt longer. Soon it became very dark. We never saw such large stars. As usual I pestered Ma Ma, telling her the names of my favorites. Halfway along our cart met a bunch of armed soldiers, five or six, who rudely called out to us, asking who we were, where we were going etc. There were about six carts in our caravan, our boys were traveling behind us but immediately they brought their cart up and parked it between us and the soldiers . . .

Back on boat at 8:30 PM and found out that we couldn't leave because it was overloaded with people—NLD people from the villages we had visited had come along for the ride. Damn. And the tide was going out. Our luggage in Kunchangon where we thought we would stay the night. We slept on moored boat, one corner partitioned off with two mosquito nets where Ma Ma and I curled up unwashed.

March 25: boat left very early with the tide. We arrived in Kunchangon at 4:30, staggered sleepily and dirtily into village, rested a bit then bath and breakfast and on to Ingapu by car.

Back in January when they were in this area the local army commander, Brigadier Myint Aung, had done everything in his power to stop their party from meeting the local people: Suu had told Michael she was having a "battle royal" with him. Now they were on the opposite bank to his headquarters, and none of them had forgotten the feud.

"On the way out to the Irrawaddy river we passed Dedaye on the other side of the bank," Ma Thanegi wrote, "and since it is in Irrawaddy division we talked wistfully about how nice it would be to drop in unexpectedly and annoy Myint Aung, the very tough guy who hates NLD. Toyed with the idea of placing large raft in middle of the river, the boundary line between Rangoon and Irrawaddy divisions, and holding a rally there, people would come in boats and if Myint Aung appeared would slide over to the Rangoon side.

> An hour after passing Dedaye, a boat with two NLD men caught up with us, both hopping mad that we passed close to Dedaye without stopping because they'd been told that we would stop. Utter bewilderment and confusion. Found out they had been assured last night that we would stop and nobody told us anything. They were actually jumping up and down in fury. So back we went to Dedaye where Ma Ma had to go on land to make a speech to hundreds waiting patiently.

They had trespassed on Myint Aung's patch after all, without even planning to. "We were delayed by two hours, but we enjoyed that unexpected fulfillment of our wishes. Back on boat we talked about how mad Myint Aung would be." As they puttered back to Rangoon's Pansodan Jetty and home, they laughed at the brigadier and his rages. Less than a fortnight later the joke would backfire on them, with nearly fatal consequences.

*

The harshest season of the year was upon them: The mildness of Burma's brief winter was only a memory, the relief of the monsoon still a month or more away. The water festival of *Thingyan*, the Burmese New Year, the time when everyone soaks everyone else and all bonds of manners and hierarchy are briefly relaxed, was still weeks ahead; beyond that, a month or more of fierce heat awaited them—and, for Suu and her colleagues, weeks of frantic traveling and organizing.[5]

Back at home, Ma Thanegi squeezed the chores of everyday life into a few quiet hours but Suu hardly stopped to draw breath:

> March 26: I stayed home, did laundry etc, firmly requesting Ma Ma to rest as I left. Not having much faith in her I called in during the afternoon to find out she was holding a press conference which had actually been scheduled for the next day. I rushed over but it was a wonderful show . . .
>
> March 29: Ma Ma upstairs for hours. I thought she was resting but she was cleaning out bedroom and came down at intervals with loads of papers, photos, cards etc and looking apologetic.

More party members were being arrested: The persecution of democratic activists was already growing familiar. And, as Ma Thanegi noted, word of the growing discord between students and their elders inside the party had reached the outside world.

"April 3: In evening met with families of NLD members arrested in Mon state . . . Ma Ma saw *Asiaweek* article about split between students and NLD . . . Someone denied having sent out an open letter about the split . . ."

The next day Suu, Ma Thanegi and their convoy were on the road again, back to the Irrawaddy Delta for the fourth time since January—heading for the encounter which would imprint forever an image of almost unbelievable courage on Suu's name.

"April 4: left home at 5:30 and had to wait for an hour at Insein jetty. We took two cars, Tiger's car and a green pickup. Arrived at Meizali village, army said we could not stay there." They set off again, stopping by the roadside to drink sugar-cane juice while they waited for the green pickup, which had fallen behind, to catch up.

Leaving Rangoon they had driven almost due west; at Meizali they joined a river which they now followed as far as the next village, Hsar Malauk: "A long village," Ma Thanegi recalled, her descriptive powers failing her for once, with "a nice loo." "Ma Ma stood on a table at the front door of the NLD office," she added, "to address public."

But trouble was brewing again.

Near end of her speech two cars arrived and parked on either side of the crowd, and started blaring on about decree law 2/88 etcetera [the martial law provision banning public assemblies, of which Suu and her party were flagrantly in breach everywhere they went] and making such a racket. Ma Ma talked through this and the crowd which had until that point listened in silence started clapping and cheering and whistling. Then one car after another in turn repeated the announcements. We all made a show of listening carefully, Ma Ma included, turning our heads to each car in turn, then when one of them was a bit delayed Ma Ma called out "Aren't you going to start?"—at which they gave up and went away.

Ma Ma said goodbye to crowd and we went home to lunch. A lot of reserve firefighters and people's voluntary forces standing around but looking sympathetic. Lovely lunch of nice seafood—sellers in market had cut prices to get rid of their wares faster so they could listen to the speech. Ma Ma able to rest in the afternoon, boys had football match on the beach in evening. Lovely dinner also, fish, fish.

Next day they left Hsar Malauk and drove north alongside a waterway so broad you could barely see the far side, to the township of Danubyu, where in 1824, during the First Burma War, the Burmese Army had lost a critical battle to the British. The authorities here, under Suu's old enemy Brigadier Myint Aung, had decided to make things difficult for them. As at the village of Kim Yang Gaung, which they had visited on March 24th, the army had ordered the population at gunpoint to stay indoors— though not all obeyed. And at the entrance to the town Suu's convoy was stopped and told they could not drive through the town's main street but must take a different, circuitous route to reach the party's office.

"April 5," Ma Thanegi wrote, "arrived in Danubyu and found there were certain roads which we were not allowed to pass through. They had given us a longer alternative route." The two sides parlayed tensely over the arbitrary restriction, until Suu discovered the perfect loophole, an excellent legalistic reason why they could not obey: The new route "unfortunately meant we had to go the wrong way down a one-way street. Ma Ma firmly said we must not break traffic rules, so joyfully Tiger turned into the forbidden road leading to the market past cheering crowds and then to NLD office. Local SLORC secretary followed and parked a little way off, looking furious." Win Thein, one of the student bodyguards, remembered seeing scores of soldiers lined up in front of the party office, guns at the ready.

The officer in charge of the troops, Captain Myint U, acting under the orders of Myint Aung, told Suu that Danubyu was under martial law and that she was therefore forbidden to address the public. Suu was obliged to compromise. "Ma Ma made a speech inside NLD office, then we all left the office to walk to a jetty nearby, intending to take a boat to some of the outlying villages." With the local supporters who had joined them, Win Thein remembers there being some eighty people in the group—but under the dire regime of Brigadier Myint Aung, even walking in a group was a violation of martial law. "As we walked along, SLORC followed in a car warning us not to walk in a procession," Ma Thanegi wrote in her diary. "Three warnings were given to the effect that if we did not break up they would shoot to kill."

It was the first time they had been subject to such a direct threat to their lives.

"Order was given to load and aim. Arms loudly loaded by soldiers standing near officers as we passed and we looked calmly at them and walked on. Ma Ma told one soldier, 'Hey, they are telling you to load, aren't you going to, soldier?' They raised their rifles on first warning but after that we were at jetty and already on boats."

They were on the water, and safe. "Stopped at villages, glorious lunch which I sat through with gritted teeth while party supporters recited two poems. With the exception of very few I would like to hit poets who are writing poetry, usually very bad, about doing this and doing that in the movement and reading them aloud . . ."

The military presence did not stop at the town limit. "Armed soldiers all along the way," Ma Thanegi wrote. "Two majors followed in their own boat and one soldier on it grinned and nodded several times when we waved at him."

Despite all the intimidation they had experienced in Danubyu, they planned to return to the town in the evening and spend the night. Not everyone in the party thought this was a good idea: Win Thein says that he was among the voices urging Suu to pass the town by and land further downriver; their cars could drive down from Danubyu and pick them up there. But Suu insisted on sticking to the original program.

Sure enough, the army was there on their return to the town, in the form of a single guard, forbidding them to disembark. "Came back to Danubyu at 6 PM," Ma Thanegi wrote, "when armed and lone soldier tried to stop us from landing. But we said no we are landing. You mustn't come on land, he said, yes we will we said. And we did."

They set off through the almost deserted streets to walk back to the NLD office for dinner. But even though the market was long closed and the townspeople were indoors, the army was still determined to impede their progress. "On the way we were told by one military policeman that the road in front of market was not allowed to us." The order seemed ridiculous to Suu—just another attempt to bully and humiliate them. "Market closed by that time and streets almost deserted. Route given quite a bit longer . . ." Again Suu flatly ignored the army's command. "Ma Ma said 'We'll take shorter one.' MP shouting angrily after us as we passed him."

By now the sense of danger was acute. "I quickened pace to get ahead of Ma Ma and boys . . . I managed to get right out in front beside Bo Lwin, our very tall, very dark and very nice cameraman and Win Thein, our hot-tempered bodyguard who was carrying the flag." Meanwhile an army jeep roared up and screeched to a halt at the end of the road down which they were walking.

I kept one eye on Win Thein and one on Captain Myint U, who had halted his jeep at the top of the road. Six or seven soldiers jumped down from the jeep and took positions, three or four kneeling, three standing. The kneeling chaps pointing guns somewhat low, at our midriffs, standing ones guns pointed upwards. Someone on jeep turned on a song about army not breaking up etcetera—we had heard the same song played from afar this morning as Ma Ma spoke at Danubyu's NLD office.

A furious captain swung around to shout and the music stopped in one bar. I felt a bit giggly at this but only for a moment. Captain Myint U came towards us, one arm outstretched and finger wagging, shouting at us to stop walking in procession.

People react to terrifying situations in unpredictable ways. Ma Thanegi's reaction was to get angry herself. "How the hell did this fool expect our group of forty to walk?" she wrote. "Indian file and ten paces apart? We were just hungry, hot and longing to rest. I thought I had better tell this fool the true meaning of 2/88, and called out to him that I would like to talk with him. I shouted this several times but he didn't hear, he was too intent on shouting to Ma Suu that he would shoot if people blocked road."

Suu now offered a compromise. "Ma Ma called out to us to walk at the sides of the road—I didn't hear because I myself was still shouting at the captain. But somebody came up beside me and pushed me towards the side of the road."

Suu herself recalled,

In front of me was a young man holding our NLD flag. We were walking behind him in the middle of the street heading home for the night, that's all. Then we saw the soldiers across the road, kneeling with their guns trained on us. The captain was shouting to us to get off the road. I told the young man with the flag to get away from the front, because I didn't want him to be the obvious target. So he stepped to the side. They said . . . they were going to fire if we kept on walking in the middle of the road. So I said, "Fine, all right, we'll walk on the side of the road . . ." And they all moved to the sides.[6]

But for the irate young captain, the gesture was too little, too late. "Captain Myint U said he would still shoot if we were walking at the sides of the road," Ma Thanegi wrote.

At this point Ma Ma walked out into the middle of the road, the boys after her, and by that time she was so close to the soldiers that she brushed past them. They stood petrified, clutching their arms to their chests and looking pale.

I had such a stab of sick fear when I saw her pass through but within seconds she was safe.

Just before this I vaguely heard someone shouting, "Don't do it Myint U, don't do it Myint U!" and I thought it was one of our NLD people, not knowing it was one of the majors who had been ambling behind after us." She learned later that his name was Major Maung Tun of 1-08 battalion. "He came up running and ordered Myint U not to fire—the captain tore off his epaulettes, hopping around in the dust raised by our group and his own feet and shouting, "What are these for, what are these for?"

I listened for a few minutes thinking he was speaking to us but then realized it was not so. Then I followed Ma Ma and others home to the NLD office . . .

Why did Suu walk back into the middle of the road, risking death? She explained that the captain's rejection of her proposal to walk at the side of the road struck her as "highly unreasonable." "I thought, if he's going to shoot us even if we walk at the side of the road, well, perhaps it is me they want to shoot. I thought, I might as well walk in the middle of the road . . . . I was quite cool-headed. I thought, what does one do? Does one turn back or keep going? My thought was, one doesn't turn back in a situation like that."[7] In a later interview she said of that split-second decision, "It seemed so much simpler to provide them with a single target . . ."[8]

She added, "I don't think I'm unique in that." In situations of sudden danger, "you can't make up your mind in advance what you'll do; it's a decision you have to make there and then. Do I stand or run? Whatever you may have thought before, when it comes to the crunch, when you're actually faced with that kind of danger, you have to make up your mind on the spot . . . and you never know what decision you will take."

She remembered noticing the reaction of the soldiers who had been aiming at her. "We just walked through the soldiers who were kneeling there. And I noticed that some of them, one or two, were actually shaking and muttering to themselves, but I don't know whether it was out of hatred or nervousness."

It was this incident which, more than any other, created the mystique of Aung San Suu Kyi, while at the same time—in this land of the zero-sum game—effectively dismantling that of the army. If anyone still doubted that she was her father's daughter, true-born child of the man who had defied both the British and the Japanese and come out on top, they could doubt it no more. When, on July 19, 1947, assassins burst into the conference chamber where he was holding a cabinet meeting, Aung San's response—as instinctive as Suu's in Danubyu—was to stand up and face them: Their bullets tore apart his chest. That was heroism, and returning to the middle of the road in Danubyu and keeping on walking was heroism, too. Suu may be right in saying that she is not "unique" in the way she reacted to a moment of grave peril, but her whole prior life had been a preparation for that moment.

"Ma Suu and I were once tidying the glass-fronted cabinets where [her mother] Daw Khin Kyi's clothes were kept," Ma Thanegi later recalled. "She took out a white scarf with a large patch of dried blood on it, and said that when her father died all her mother could say was, 'There was so much blood! There was so much blood!'

"It was her father's blood. I broke out in goose pimples; I was trembling, with tears in my eyes, to be touching the blood of our martyr, our hero, our god. That must be the most memorable moment of my life."

Word of what had happened and what had so nearly happened helped to consolidate Suu's reputation among the deeply superstitious Burmese public, many of whom now began to consider her a female bodhisattva, an angel, a divine being. The fact that she had survived the army's attempt to kill her was proof positive of her high spiritual attainment: only someone "invulnerable to attack," "guarded by deities" and "subject to adoration" could have come through alive.[9] She was "a heroine like the mythical mother goddess of the earth," one admirer wrote three years later, "who can free [us] from the enslavement of the evil military captors."[10]

In January Suu had told the *New York Times* reporter, "I don't want a personality cult; we've had enough dictators already." But it didn't really matter whether she wanted it or not. Now she would be stuck with it, forever.

7

DEFIANCE

In a letter to her husband written soon after the near-death incident at Danubyu, Suu tried to make light of the risks she was now running, making her High Noon encounters with the army sound more like a rather mucky Girl Guide camp. "Alas, your poor Suu is getting weather-beaten," she wrote, "none of that pampered elegance left as she tramps the countryside spattered with mud, straggly-haired, breathing in dust and pouring with sweat."[1]

The self-portrait does not convince: It is very hard to imagine the sylph-like Suu, the very embodiment of Kipling's "neater, sweeter maiden in a cleaner, greener land," running with sweat; Ma Thanegi, herself a very ladylike Burmese, was awed by the way Suu sailed through these journeys. "Hours and hours of travel, with stops for her speeches, meetings with supporters etc., and she could do that for days on end, still looking fresh and peaceful," she noted in her diary.

But even less persuasive is the jolly, carefree mood Suu evokes in the letter. Brigadier Myint Aung's intemperate captain may have been particularly melodramatic in the way he tried to enforce the regime's martial law provisions, but he was not out of step with SLORC—a point borne out by the honors he was later to receive from the regime. The truce between the two sides after the death of Suu's mother in December was no more than a memory now; both were bitterly aware that they were heading for a showdown in which only one would remain standing. A joke current in Rangoon in those days went that Ne Win's favorite daughter Sanda had challenged Suu to a duel. Suu declined, saying "Let's just walk down the street together unarmed and see which of us gets to the other end alive."[2]

Of course the contest was absurdly unequal. The army had already shown itself capable of terminating the democracy protests by the simple stratagem of slaughtering a few thousand demonstrators. Since those bloody days in September, very few people had ventured out into the

streets to protest. Yet this impertinent woman held public meetings day
after day, in flagrant breach of martial law, and her presence provided the
pretext for thousands to come out and greet her. Why not do what Captain
Myint U had so nearly done in Danubyu and simply eliminate her?

Two factors stayed the regime's hand. One was who she was. Because
of her father and his unique and central place in independent Burma's
founding myth, she was the closest thing the nation possessed to royalty.
The generals felt the tug of that themselves—hence the presence of
General Saw Maung and Lieutenant General Khin Nyunt on her doorstep
in December, offering condolences on her mother's death. For forty years
the Burmese state had elaborated and glorified the cult of Aung San; Ne
Win's chief claim to legitimacy was that he had been that fiery young
general's comrade in arms. It was what ensured the loyalty and unity of
the armed forces, however crassly the Old Man and his underlings might
govern. Pull down that column and the whole house could come crashing
down.

The second factor was that, as young American protesters had chanted
at the National Guard on the streets of Chicago in 1968, the whole world
was watching. Despite coming to politics so late, Suu was quick to realize
that her familiarity with the outside world, her fluent English and her ease
at communicating with foreigners gave her a huge advantage over her
insular, monolingual and deeply paranoid antagonists.

Burma's encounters with the outside world had for a century and a half
been unremittingly bruising, from their serial humiliations by the British
to the catastrophe of the Second World War, which saw the country
devastated twice over. By bottling the country up, Ne Win had insulated
it from most of the turbulence which shook Southeast Asia during the
postwar years: He had saved it from being sucked into the Chinese civil
war and the Vietnam War. But in Suu the army had an enemy who had
spent half her life abroad and for whom foreign parts held no terrors.
This advantage of hers was constantly to throw the regime off balance:
They could never be sure what their treatment of her might provoke the
foreigners to do. Fear that the United States could attack them was one of
the motives for moving the capital from Rangoon to an up-country site
well inland in 2006. As recently as 2008 they seem to have been genuinely
afraid that the Americans could use Cyclone Nargis as a pretext to invade.

So while keen to reassure Michael that the worst that menaced her was mud and sweat, on her return to Rangoon Suu was also quick to make sure her diplomat friends knew all about what had happened. She paid an urgent visit to Martin Morland, the British ambassador, at his residence, to brief him, while Ma Thanegi also got busy. Nita Yin Yin May, the embassy's information officer and a friend of Ma Thanegi's, immediately sent news of what had happened to the BBC. Within a few days, Danubyu was fast becoming a legend both at home and abroad.

"April 7th," Ma Thanegi wrote on her first day back in the office, "early to work and managed to send word of Danubyu incident to Bangkok through a family friend of Ma Suu . . . She typed the weekly news release herself and also sent letter to *Asiaweek* which she had translated herself . . . . Central Executive Committee meeting, very long one. Wrote out draft of very gentlemanly and furious letter to SLORC about Danubyu incident. All very worried at close shave."

*

Meanwhile the show had to go on, the schedule was set. The very next day they went back once more to the Irrawaddy Delta—this time bound for the village where Suu was born. Though her parents' home was in Rangoon, her mother had taken refuge here with her two young sons in the last weeks of her pregnancy after Aung San had defected to the Allied side in the war. And now the people of the village were eager to welcome their most famous daughter.

"April 8: left Rangoon 6 AM from Nan Thida Jetty," Ma Thanegi wrote. The last and longest stretch of the journey was "by cart, a very long way under blazing sun . . . Lovely lunch at monastery. The village donated 20 bags of rice to NLD. Ma Ma was feeling guilty about taking them until they assured her they have enough food for themselves.

"April 9: got up at 4:30 to leave Dedaye by 5:30. Ma Suu said, 'What a scandal if I said '*Matabu, matabu,* I'm not getting up, I'm not getting up and went back to sleep . . . ' I said no scandal, everyone else would cheer and go straight back to sleep."

After passing through many small delta villages they arrived at last at the tiny spot where Suu was born.

Arrived at Hmway Saung Village where Daw Khin Kyi gave birth to Suu while hiding from the Japanese. That village so proud of it.

First we went to monastery then to large stage built in the fields. No shade for the audience yet they had waited in that summer sun for hours. Whenever Suu apologizes and tries to cut short her speeches because of hot sun and people sitting in their full rays they call back no, no, it's not hot, denying the very existence of that fiery ball.

Since we came by car we couldn't see the place where Daw Khin Kyi landed over forty years ago. So three of our boys including Win Thein, the hothead who had carried the party flag at Danubyu, went to investigate in the name of historical research.

But the Burmese capacity for taking it easy got the better of them. "They saw some boats moored and decided to snooze in them a while. They can nap anywhere and under whatever conditions. They were still sleeping when we unknowingly left after about one and a half hours. There were so many cars and so many NLD supporters hanging on to the cars welcoming us or seeing us off from place to place, sometimes we feel like a circus traveling with its audience.

On to Hmone Gyi village and a speech there . . . Discovered three boys missing and Ma Ma worried sick. I wasn't so worried. They eventually caught us up by boat, arriving a little after 10 PM.

April 10: Ma Ma wore a yellow jacket, brown longyi. Left Pyapon village 5 AM by boat. Kyontar village and Kyowar Kyauk village welcomed us with music from the full traditional orchestra. Long boat ride, nearly seven hours, changing boats twice, small fast ones.

As the NLD party puttered on through the muddy waters of the delta, Burma's biggest annual holiday was stealing up on them: *Thingyan*, the annual water festival, ushering in the new year, when problems large and small are forgotten and for a few wild days everyone says exactly what is on their mind, however unthinkable that may be the rest of the year.

But a full year of revolt had put the festival in a new and menacing light. The temptation for the students to let rip with their true feelings about the regime would be hard to resist—and in fact to channel and encourage those emotions the NLD had organized a competition for the most humorous and hurtful anti-regime slogans, to be bawled out by contestants outside the party's head office during the festival days. But could the army be relied on to take the abuse lying down, as those in power had laughed off such acts of *lèse-majesté* in years past? Ma Thanegi was not at all sure they would. "I felt apprehensive about this Thingyan thing," she confided to her diary, "as it is a good excuse for SLORC to start gathering up our NLD people."

"April 11," she wrote, "Ma Ma wore pink jacket, red Shan longyi, left Kadon Kani at 5:30 by boat arrived at a village where people very scared . . . Arrived in Bogalay 1 PM, big crowd, flowers, arrived Maung Kyaw town at 6 PM for overnight stay." The students in the party were already getting in training for the festival. "Our boys shouting anti-regime Thingyan slogans at tops of lungs, practicing for slogan competition to be held in Rangoon.

"April 12, first day of Thingyan. Left Mawkyun at 6 AM when we were supposed to leave at 5. Boat trip the whole day . . . Passed by Bon Lon Kyaung village, Thingyan songs played from loudspeakers and two very rough-looking types danced in welcome. All through day water splashed on our boat."

Now they were heading back to Rangoon for the culminating days of the festival. But the city, normally a scene of wild celebrations at this time, was sullenly silent, closely guarded by the army.

Spent night on boat, traveling all night when we were supposed to be back in Rangoon that night.

April 13: Arrived 6 AM at Nandigar jetty in Rangoon. Driving through city, saw the streets were deserted, no water festival pandals of any kind—there were only about three in town.[3] As we came home in the back of the pick-up truck, a couple of the kids with us waved the big NLD flag.

We all went first to Ma Ma's house where we got down. We noticed a large stage at gate of 54 and enormous loudspeaker system. I don't think Ma Ma realized to what an extent this slogan competition had grown.

We chatted a bit at the house, then went with seven boys in car to go home. As we got near to a restaurant almost opposite the NLD office a MP [military policeman] stopped us and we saw an army truck parked nearby. One army captain strode towards the car and told us angrily to get down. We got down. The captain kept asking who had been waving the flag from our car. One of our boys had run towards the house as soon as we were

stopped so Ma Ma received the news that we had been stopped. By that
time a crowd had gathered across the street. We were searched then told
to get in the army truck and taken to Tatmadaw park, to the Army outpost
there.

Though now under army arrest, they affected the relaxed, light-hearted
manner that had become Suu's trademark. Ma Thanegi noted:

> Very pleasant place, hollyhocks, some white geese, green grass. We were
> asked the usual and none too intelligent questions, name age etcetera . . . we
> answered the questions very casually and not at all worried, we said what
> lovely geese and so on, made the young thin MI guy furious.
>
> We heard later that first Ma Ma and then [party chairman] U Tin Oo
> had arrived at the scene of our departure and were sitting down by the side
> of the road refusing to move until we were released . . . A lot of wireless
> calls, rushing to and fro of army etcetera, and a chastened captain took us
> back to NLD, we were stunned to see the crowds there, Ma Ma sitting on
> a kerb stone. Ma Ma thanked the captain and we marched home, Ma Ma
> making sure we walked ahead . . .

The stress was beginning to tell. Suu gave an impromptu press
conference at the house to protest at the detention of her colleagues, then
Ma Thanegi went straight home and stayed there. She wrote:

> Worried about the Thingyan pandal and slogan competition. I kept
> phoning to see if everything all right, everything okay.
>
> April 14: Stayed home to paint. Very hot and constantly worried. Ma Ma
> ill, stayed in bed till evening when she went to see the slogan competition.
>
> April 15: Apparently all okay at NLD . . . Ma Ma better, stayed in bed a bit.
>
> April 16: Competition still on . . .

Though Ma Thanegi was not there to see it, the competition had
become yet another stand-off between the party and the army, with the
NLD office ringed by rifle-toting soldiers, who were obliged to listen as
one student after another, drunk with the reckless festival spirit, bawled
out poison and defamation about them and their masters. The regime
took the opportunity to arrest several of them, but the blitz Ma Thanegi
had been dreading failed to materialize.

That afternoon, Suu fought off her illness to attend the finale.

"Ma Ma made closing speech at competition, saying it was a tradition of Burmese to let off steam every year by shouting political slogans during water festival, government should have sense of humor and grace about it or words to that effect, SLORC probably foaming at mouth and shrieking."

Probably—but they were also taking emergency measures to ensure that the spectacle was never repeated, and that those responsible paid the price. On April 16th, as Suu was making her plea for tolerance, they set up what they called the Committee for Writing Slogans for Nationals, whose goal was to make sure that any and all slogans bellowed during Thingyan "aimed for national unity." Within a week, NLD members accused of dreaming up the offending slogans were being hauled in.

There were still moments, however, for taking consolation in the simple, elegant customs of Burmese tradition.

"April 17: New Year's Day, to office, cleaning up reports and letters and stuff. To NLD hq in afternoon for Buddhist ceremony." Burmese Buddhists believe they gain merit—take steps along the road to Nirvana—by releasing fish and birds from captivity, and New Year's Day is an auspicious time to do it. "Our boys and girls released fish and birds," Ma Thanegi wrote. "Two brown doves either would not or could not fly, and we brought them back to house. Ma Ma was holding one cuddled against her and they sat and preened and ate rice at the marble-topped round table where she has her meetings. I was visualizing them sitting on CEC heads during meetings and happily dropping liquid bombs." But she was duly punished for her malicious thoughts. "As I went home on bus I was soaked with water thrown by somebody—it never happened on New Year's Day before."

*

Within days Suu, Ma Thanegi and their colleagues were packing for yet another trip: the last leg of a nationwide journey that had more in common with a triumphal circuit than a campaigning exercise.

In her diary a few days earlier Ma Thanegi had recorded the return of an NLD party from Kachin state in the far north of the country, "looking dirty, bedraggled and exhausted." They had been arranging Suu's most ambitious tour yet, this time to the Kachin region in the far north, whose ethnic army, fighting for the autonomy of this overwhelmingly Christian corner of the country, had for years been one of the best-trained and most formidable of the regime's ethnic enemies. It was another pilgrimage in Suu's father's footsteps—he had visited the regional capital, Myitkyina, in December 1946.

The first leg of the journey, to Mandalay, took thirteen hours. Now the punishing schedule of the past months was telling on practically everyone.

> April 24: Ma Ma wore pale blue plain longyi, blue lavender print jacket, looked very lovely. Left Rangoon at 4:30 AM in two cars. Arrived in Mandalay at 5:45 PM and shocked at heat of everything, air, dust, furniture, water, even reed mats which are supposed to be cool.
>
> On the way Tiger had been very sleepy twice so U Win Htein took over the wheel . . . I have been so busy these days that I felt sleepy as never before on a trip. Ma Ma insisted I lay my head on her shoulder while she held me. Preparing for bed, I told Ma Ma that when we are over 80 we will be laughing over all this craziness. Ma Ma said that if anything goes wrong we won't be able to laugh.
>
> April 25: Ma Ma wore mauve longyi and darker jacket. Spoke at two monasteries . . . Back to house, lunch, long baths and to the station at 3 PM.

Low-intensity official humiliation, sometimes apparently decreed directly by Ne Win himself, was becoming an everyday experience, though sometimes it backfired.

"SLORC or, as we were actually told, 'orders from above,' state that Aung San Suu Kyi must queue up at the station and buy her own ticket. They thought it was an insult but we know it to be good publicity. Crowd stood around to watch, offered sweets, drink, food, sandwiches . . ."

It was the first time they had traveled in Burma's notoriously slow and cranky trains. They managed to obtain two sleeper berths between the whole party, which they used in shifts "We all took turns sleeping, Ma Ma and I slept from 12 midnight to 6 AM next day."

But if the regime was determined to make them suffer as they moved around, their ever-swelling body of supporters made them feel like kings and queens.

> At every stop NLD and public were there to give flowers, food and expensive dishes, Seven-ups, Cokes etc., each can cost 30 kyats, we've never

had so much Coke in our lives. Icy cold too. Even in the dead of night local NLD members turned up smartly dressed, I remember elderly men in perky gaung baungs and large matrons dressed to kill in silk and nets, and there we were as usual a bedraggled, dusty, dirty, sweating, untidy bunch of wild-looking people.

Once our train stopped alongside an army train and troops craned their necks to see Ma Ma, most of them smiling. . . . Ma Ma was in upper bunk where at first she didn't want to sleep; we insisted as window too close to lower bunk.

The precaution was justified. "After midnight as we settled down in our bunks with lights out we heard men at the next stop shouting 'Where is she, can't see her!' and shining torches all over the place. They were just friends, Ma Ma and I giggled and kept very still.

April 26: spent more than half the day on the train. We had heard horror stories about people climbing in through the windows and squatting everywhere with their black market goods and chickens but our trip went smoothly: No crowds, no long halts, but whistle stops at unscheduled halts so crowds could welcome Ma Ma with huge smiles and sky-raising shouts, "Long live Aung San Suu Kyi," "Good health," "God help Daw Aung San Suu Kyi," "May her wishes come true," they would chorus. Or where there is forced labor working as porters for the army, they chorused, "May she be free from the Six Evils."

A traditional Burmese salutation is to wish one's friends free of the "five evils": government—Burma's problem with oppressive rulers is nothing new—fire, thieves, water and enemies. "Number six, the latest addition," Ma Thanegi explains, "means the Army."

Several of the most senior NLD people maintained a daily routine of vipassana meditation—but it was hard to keep it up on a journey like this.

"Uncle U Hla Pe tried his best to meditate but I wonder how far he got with our monkeys around. We heard small beeps coming from somewhere among our luggage up in the racks, Aung Aung finally located it as coming from a brown holdall, we asked who owned it and no one owned up . . ."

In the carriage the reaction to its discovery was hysterical.

Local people are so used to KIA [Kachin Independence Army] blowing up trains etcetera that they panic at the slightest beep. I was getting worried, people in some compartments so alarmed they shrieked and ran out near to the loo, we thought it was a time bomb.

Aung Aung was just about to throw [the holdall] from the window when Uncle Hla Pe came out of his meditative trance and yelled that it was his. Close shave, he nearly had to travel a month with just the clothes on his back. It was his alarm clock, he couldn't shut it off and it gave us trouble all the way, it would beep on and on at every dawn driving Ma Ma wild. I and others just snored on.

Late that afternoon they arrived in the Kachin capital, Myitkyina, and the usual round of large public meetings got under way, some of which required a change of costume.

April 27: In the afternoon Ma Suu changed into Lisu costume: very wide skirt, jacket and lots of beads and a cute beaded head dress, all this to visit Lisu party office. I was away at the market when she was changing, I came back to find her sitting among our kids, blushing furiously. It suits her very well, she always says she hates to look a fool in fancy dress, but she never looks foolish.

April 28: At one Kachin house Ma Ma was given a gift of a basket of food to symbolize blood relationship, just as one was given to Bogyoke [Aung San] over 40 years ago. It is a large basket to be slung on the back in which were food including rice, salt, meat, vegetables, bread.

April 30: Po Chit Kon village: one old lady after seeing Ma Ma half sang to her grandchild, "Oh this ruler of our kingdom, a pretty thing, a pretty little thing . . ."

Hopin, Nan Cho, Ywa Thit Gyi, Lwin U, Nant Mon, Maing Naung, Ma Mon Kaing, Yan Ton, Nant Pade, Takwin, Myo Thar, Leimee, Kyunpin Thar, Alei Taw . . . Village after village after village, interspersed by monasteries and pagodas, and at each stop an ecstatic crowd, a presentation of gifts, a speech—yet another speech, of the 1,000-plus Suu was to deliver during this six-month epic of traveling. It was becoming less a journey, more an extended hallucination. This was what happened to national heroes returning from conquest—not to "a pretty little thing" steadily and vengefully pursued by the nation's rulers.

May 1: Someone presented Ma Ma with whole peacock tail cut from killed bird, such a pity, that large unwieldy thing traveled with us getting frayed and dirty.

. . . Nearly trampled to death by about 30,000 shouting welcome . . . Ma Ma went all the way on the bonnet of the jeep, half leaning half sitting.

Next place stayed in large house—just before bedtime Ma Ma found out owner was a Scrabble freak and said she wanted a game. I said no Scrabble it's bedtime. She half sang out "Okay Ma Thanegi!" and jumped into bed.

May 2: Old lady Buddhist yogis danced slowly in a circle. While Ma Ma was speaking SLORC tried to lure people away with free video show. Apparently nobody went along.

Ma Ma shampooed hair at 10:45 PM, only place to plug in hair dryer was shrine room so dried it there.

May 3: One old lady waved us on and stood there crying . . . Through dust got a glimpse of one old lady sat on side of the road, making bowing obeisance to our car as if to a monk . . .

During long discussion speech I and a few boys went upstairs and had nap, boys on large mat, me on my wrinkled wrap in the corner. We have been going on rough roads in heat and dust and not getting enough sleep, we tend to curl up like kittens and catnap when we get the chance, of course Ma Ma can't do this.

They descended from the Kachin hills to the fiery heat of the Burma heartland.

Into Sagaing division and immediately it became very hot . . . Winding rough tracks of journey through semi-jungle . . . As always meetings until bedtime for Ma Ma, everyone exhausted. Some of the boys are ill.

May 4: dark blue longyi and dark blue jacket, got up at 5:30, thankful for small blessings as not 3:30 or 4, had to travel in high lorry as road too rough for jeep. Stopped at villages along way where they asked Ma Ma to speak, served tepid sticky cold drinks which we didn't have the heart to refuse.

A lot of us coughing . . .

May 5: beige longyi, beige jacket. Left Inndaw at 5:30, huge cheering crowds everywhere with flowers and banners and music.

Tagaung was like a kiln. A shop nearby selling tamarind juice and we bought it by the potfull. So many people lining the road it took two hours to drive from outskirts to NLD office.

Very hard to get any kind of privacy, people will peer and peep in everywhere, once even when Ma Ma was on the loo unless boys and I can scout and stand guard . . .

*

For the next leg of the journey they went by boat, and Ma Thanegi's longer, more meditative entries reflect the different pace of traveling by water. All of them got their breath back.

May 6: Blue jacket, dark blue Kachin longyi. As I said to Ma Ma, It's horrible to get up at 3, she said you're telling me. We walked to jetty at 4 AM, not many NLDs up as they didn't believe we would get up at 3 even though we said we would. On boat Ma Ma sometimes sewed names on boys' longyis as we sat in small cabin . . .

At Shwegu, NLDs there unable to handle crowd, I was nearly trampled on as I tried to make my way to the car, then I wasn't able to climb on board until Tiger took me by the waist and threw me in head first, this my usual entry into cars or boats when public too enthusiastic.

Ma Ma stood up in front, I just behind ready to punch anyone too vigorous about greeting her. You wouldn't believe how people grab her hands and once one stupid girl pulled her head down to kiss her so hard Ma Ma nearly hit her head on the jeep frame. We were furious. Aung Aung and I would punch them in the chest just to get these girls off Ma Ma.

May 7: Orange jacket, dark blue longyi. We heard early call to prayer from mosque. Talking lightly about "God," Ma Ma suddenly remembered how Kim said "bless me" whenever he sneezed. Her face really lights up and she loses her tired look whenever Alexander or Kim are mentioned. When she is tired but unable to rest I try to turn the conversation to the boys . . .

The thousands of miles spent crammed together in transport of every kind were bringing the women very close together. Ma Thanegi confided:

I love Ma Ma, but it's not a personality cult, not because she is Daw Aung San Suu Kyi but because she is herself. I've always been a loner without much attachment to family and I never thought I would think of anyone as a true sister as I do her.

Aung San, his wife Ma Khin Kyi and their first baby, Aung San Oo (Oo means simply "first").

Aung San, his wife Ma Khin Kyi and their three children, Aung San Oo, Aung San Lin and Aung San Suu Kyi (left).

A silkscreen depicting Aung San, Aung San Suu Kyi's father. It decorated the stage during her debut speech at the Shwedagon Pagoda and is now on a wall in her house.

Above: Aung San Suu Kyi with friends in the cast of *Anthony and Cleopatra.* Suu, whose early ambition was to write, made a precocious start at Delhi's Lady Sri Ram College, writing and acting in a spoof of Shakespeare's play.

Left: Tin Tin and Khin Myint, sisters who went to the same elite school in Rangoon as Suu and Ma Thanegi.

Below: St. Hugh's College, Oxford, where Suu was a student.

Right: Suu and Michael on their wedding day in London, January 1, 1972.

Below left: Michael Aris (left) with his identical twin brother, Anthony.

Below right: Suu and baby Alexander.

Suu with Michael's siblings and brother-in-law, plus dog. They all struck up a warm relationship with the family's new member.

Suu and Michael in Bhutan with their new puppy, forever to be known as Puppy, to which Suu became very attached.

Suu, Michael and Alexander with Daw Khin Kyi, during their first visit to Burma after the wedding. Despite her initial doubts about Suu marrying an Englishman, Daw Khin Kyi got on well with Michael.

Suu with Hugh Richardson, Michael Aris's mentor in Tibetan studies and the last British resident in Lhasa before the Chinese invasion. In 1981, after his death, Suu and Michael co-edited a volume of essays in his memory.

Above: The Shwedagon Pagoda, Rangoon, outside which Suu gave her crucial debut speech.

Left: A statue draped in gold inside the Shwedagon shrine.

Below: Pagan, the medieval city which is Burma's most famous historical site.

A page from the campaign diary kept by Ma Thanegi, Suu's friend and companion. On the campaign trail Suu's fans developed a penchant for spraying her with cheap perfume. Here, Ma Thanegi quotes Suu telling her, "You know, Ma Thanegi, I've gone up in the world—they sprayed me with Charlie instead of Concord!"

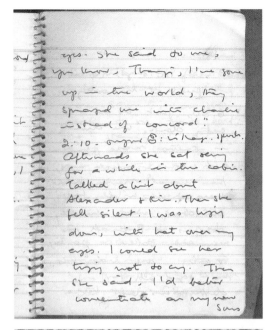

Suu on August 17, 1995, with her friend and assistant, Ma Thanegi. Despite the broad smiles, the friendship would soon end in bitterness.

Suu, U Tin Oo (third right) and other members of the NLD's Central Executive Committee outside Suu's house in early 1989.

Bertil Lintner, the veteran Swedish Burma-watcher based in Thailand, photographed in November 2010 in Chiangmai. Lintner's book *Outrage* documented the uprising of 1988 and its bloody repression in great detail.

Nita Yin Yin May, OBE, courageous information officer at the British Embassy and NLD activist imprisoned in 1989 when she was already pregnant. She gave birth in prison. She now lives in London and works as a producer for the BBC.

Suu's estranged elder brother Aung San Oo at the Martyrs' Memorial, Rangoon, with his wife Lei Lei Nwe Thein in July 2007.

At Bamaung we learned that during the night the army cars had thrown anti ASSK leaflets all over town. Speech at Bamaung NLD then to house where we will stay, very hot . . .

For past few days boys have been bragging about swimming in cool cool rivers, Ma Ma and I green with envy, that night we decided to evade nanny, which is Aung Aung, and sneaked off for a dip with only two or three boys in the know.

We somehow managed to evade forever-gaping friends of Ma Ma because she was wearing a cap and thanks to lack of electricity in Burmese towns it was quite dark, also first day of new moon.

The water was lovely, almost ice cold, and we would discover warm and cold currents and tell each other exactly where with great excitement. Never enjoyed a bath so much before, so different, Ma Ma, said from pouring water over yourself.

Suu had now been back in her homeland for more than thirteen months, much the longest period since her childhood, and whatever illusions she may have held about her people were falling away.

Ma Ma getting to know well the Burmese character, the bad side. Said she is fed up to the teeth with pushy egoistic stupid people. She is getting to know the true Burmese character and is getting depressed by it. I have a feeling she is too idealistic and emotionally vulnerable. Easy-going as we Burmese are, we are totally selfish, ostrich-like in dealing with unpleasantness and very short-sighted.

When she is in a pensive mood I would search her face and feel a deep sorrow that so many burdens are on this frail-looking and gentle person. I think she needs to be more cynical to deal with the Burmese and of course hard-hearted to some extent. She feels hurt when people complain about the rudeness of our boys, I tell her politeness would not penetrate the thick skulls and dim minds of these people.

She came back after a hot trek in the sun to some village or other smelling strongly of cheap scent. It's usual for enthusiastic ladies to spray Ma Ma with perfume that they all think great, and the perfumes are either something called Concord or Charlie, Charlie is slightly more expensive, or Tea Rose, the scent of rose, and we are beginning to recognize these three. Ma Ma is more often sprayed with Concord and we hate this spray business. These ladies are not too careful where they aim the nozzle. Sometimes it gets into her face or her mouth, she has to be careful about moving her face or it would go into her eyes. She said you know Ma Thanegi I've gone up in the world, they sprayed me with Charlie instead of Concord.

May 9: Couldn't stop so Ma Ma made speech from boat without going ashore. They gave us packets of fried noodles.

Onboard boat cabin very hot so Ma Ma sits on deck and chats to boys or reads travel book by Patrick Leigh Fermor, saying she likes to remind herself that there are other lives than the crazy one she's leading.

But then there was the risk of plummeting into memories of the life she had lost.

"After giving a speech from the boat she sat sewing for a while in the cabin, mending some of the boys' shirts." The mundane domestic task whisked her back to Oxford, and the home she couldn't go back to; "the happy highways where I went/ And cannot come again."[4]

"In the small, grimy cabin we shared, she talked for a while about Alexander and Kim. She said that she used to sew name tags onto her sons' shirts for school, then she fell silent. As she sewed she had tears in her eyes, she said nothing more. I was lying down with my hat over my eyes, I could see her trying not to cry. Then she said, I had better concentrate on my new sons.

"She never let on, except as jokes, how much she missed her family."

*

Min Kyaung Kon village: speech at monastery. At 6:30, just as it was getting dark, we arrived in Katha, lots of women and children, much more than before, never before seen such wildly happy children. They told us happily that all the men have been taken as porters so only we kids left. Ma Ma said all her depression left her when she saw them. Loud cheers. Three or four kids squatting on sloping bank to see into the boat stood up in turn, Ma Ma at the railing, they told Ma Ma that they would carry on and were not afraid, Ma Ma said in that case she would come to Katha to be protected by these kids if she runs into trouble in Rangoon. Loud cries of we'll protect you, we'll look after you.

Archway of red flame-of-the-forest flowers, lovely. Ma Ma and I and others slipped away to ancient pagoda to pray. It was the birthday of her brother Aung San Lin, the one who died so young. She would say to me, "what we could have done together . . ."

May 11: Left Tagaung at 5 AM, hot even at dawn. Ma Ma could not find her lipstick and kept saying, where are you you damn thing. She remarked to me, I know I'm tired when I get to the point of talking to my lipstick. Boys talked and yelled in their sleep last night, she said they have no lipstick to talk to.

That town had been razed by fire a few weeks ago. Met some old ladies who escaped with just the clothes on their backs. Cheerfully told us they have nothing now as they sat puffing on big cheroots with fragrant *nakao* on their cheeks.[5]

May 12: Left 5:30 by our own cars. When we saw our cars yesterday evening we were so glad, I kissed our car and said I love you car. Tiger, the owner/driver of that car said it was like meeting his girlfriend.

On our way to Mogoke . . . 6:40 AM arrived at Hsar Hpyu Taung village . . . Ma Ma had taken a sleeping tablet and was nearly out, she felt so sleepy, I held her as she napped in the car. At villages where we had to stop she would collect her wits, think rapidly and make speeches, no mistakes, no blurred words, she just looked a bit bewildered.

We put up at large old house at Mogoke. Old as it was the house had bath and loo attached, to Ma Ma's joy, she would jump up and down and clap her hands at news of such luxury. A double bed for her, with as usual a lacy net, white this time. She lay back on the bed and said, just my luck, my bed always festooned with bridal lace and here I am all alone!

Wherever they went the masses of supporters and the wild acclaim were the same.

May 13: She was wearing a sequined jacket and sequined Arakan longyi. Left Kyut Pyin at 7 AM for Mogoke. Cloudy and cool. People from Mogoke met us on the way in cars then followed us, about 50 cars in all. Near Mogoke we met about 40 kids on BMX bicycles and also dozens of motorbikes. One fat lady waiting by the side of the road thrust 3,000 kyats in cash into Ma Ma's hands.

Ma Ma stood up in green pickup sheltered by umbrella against drizzle. It took over two hours to get to the football field, people screaming greetings all the way. At the football field near lake and pagoda there were so many people who sat in the rain, keeping their umbrellas closed so that people behind might see Ma Ma. She stood on table under large colorful beach umbrella. It reminded me of the first time I saw her at the Shwedagon assembly last August: mud, rain and a packed field.

Such a crowd came out to hear Ma Ma that all the stores closed, including the ruby exchange, which never closed for any reason. Local people spoke with awe of the ruby exchange closing for Ma Suu.

At entrance to town army made an appearance, stopping motorbikes, taking down names of those without helmets, etc. Well, they had to do something. Never saw such crowds in my life . . .

*

Wherever she went, north, south, east or west, Suu was met by vast crowds who hailed her as their ruler, their savior, their redeemer; "This ruler of our kingdom," as the Kachin grandmother chanted, "a pretty thing, a pretty little thing . . ."

Did it go to her head? In some respects, clearly not. She remained touchingly, enchantingly human, as Ma Thanegi's diary brings out so well. She would get down from the stage after another triumph—and go into the kitchen of the place where they were staying and slice mangoes for the bodyguards. With the applause for her latest speech ringing in her ears, she would duck into the squalid little cabin of the boat in which they were traveling and sew patches on "the boys'" shirts.

But where was it all heading? How well did she read her adversaries?

Ma Thanegi, who was later to fall out with her bitterly, had a better opportunity than anybody to observe her at close quarters, warts and all. "With her idealism and high standards of honesty," she wrote long after the rift, "she sometimes seemed to me so much like a small child, with that deliberately composed dignity you see in young children when they are not sure of things and sensing (but at the same time not really aware of or understanding) the manipulations or shrewd dealings or lies of adults . . . In spite of her strength of character I see her as vulnerable, an innocent cast to the wolves."

Two things were happening at once. On the one hand the National League for Democracy, the officially registered political party of which she was secretary general, was touring the country, meeting the people, preparing as best it could for multiparty elections to be held under the auspices of the ruling military junta, when they would be ranged against the former ruling party and a host of others. So far so legitimate, so almost normal.

But at another level there was a war going on—a war for the future and for the identity of Burma. Her country, Suu said, had gone dramatically off the rails, and now it was her duty, as her father's daughter, to put it back on the right track.

This pitted her not against the other political parties but against the army itself—and against the Burmese state that the generals had fashioned. It was all wrong, she said, they would have to start again from scratch.

Overwhelmingly, the people were on her side. No one could doubt it. But how did you get there from here? What process did she envisage?

By casting Ne Win and his circle as the ones responsible for leading the country to perdition, she cut away the ground from under them. The deal offered by General Saw Maung was multiparty elections leading to democratic rule, a process to be supervised by SLORC. But by heaping doubt on the legitimacy of the army's rule, she undermined their role in the process.

She had every reason for doing so, given the many thousands of unarmed protesters the army had massacred to stay in power. It was a revolutionary posture: It echoed the calls for the overthrow of army rule emanating from the ethnic armies on the border, and the thousands of students who had joined them there. Yet the difference was that she was in the heart of the country, with the army watching her every move, and she had committed her party to nonviolence.

So what did she foresee? A march on Rangoon by millions of her supporters, herself like the French Revolution's Marianne, brandishing the party flag? Ne Win and Saw Maung and the rest clambering on board the last helicopter and flying away, like the Americans leaving Saigon, like Ferdinand and Imelda Marcos fleeing Manila? Khin Nyunt tamely surrendering the keys to the kingdom like Poland's General Jaruzelski?

Looking back on those hectic months from more than twenty years later, knowing, contrary to the excited claims at the time, that history did not in fact end after all, it is easy to underestimate the intoxication in the air.[6] It is with the wisdom of hindsight that we see her and her party's errors. But one wonders if wiser counsel might not have seen that they were headed, quite fast, into a cul-de-sac.

According to Ma Thanegi, there were some in the party's Central Executive Committee who argued the case for cutting a deal with the army, for the sake of effecting a democratic transfer of power. She singles out Kyi Maung, the former army officer who had been with Suu from the outset and who was to lead the party to its election victory after Suu and the other top leaders were detained. "Around that time, I was talking to U Kyi Maung and U Win Tin," she wrote in her diary, "and U Kyi Maung said to us that what we must have is a democratically elected government. If in exchange we have to guarantee the generals' security or their wealth, never mind: We must give them anything they want."

But harsher voices insisted on ratcheting up the pressure, and they were to prevail.

*

The party set about undermining the regime at the most fundamental level: by hijacking the calendar. March 27th was Armed Forces Day, the annual occasion for a Kremlin-style parade of military hardware through the center of Rangoon. This year it also marked General Ne Win's return to the spotlight, his first public appearance since his explosive speech to the party the preceding July. But the NLD succeeded in stealing the show, despite Number One's cameo: They told the world they were renaming the event Fascist Resistance Day—the name given it by Suu's father—and making it the occasion for popular demonstrations *against* the "fascist" army. In the first major demonstrations since the September bloodbath, thousands of students took to the streets of Rangoon and Mandalay.

Two weeks earlier the NLD had sprung another constitutional ambush on the regime by declaring March 13th Burma Human Rights Day—the first anniversary of the killing of student protester Maung Phone Maw, the outrage that precipitated the uprising. More new holidays were to be declared as the year wore on. Every nation is defined by the holidays it marks; it is the way the story of the nation punctuates the passage of time. By proclaiming these new or revived national holidays, the NLD tried to wrest that function away from the regime, further weakening its legitimacy.

Then there was the question of religion. As her threat to the regime increased, Suu's enemies continued to claim that she was surrounded by communists. In Burma's simplified political landscape, the opposite of a communist was a Buddhist, and the best way to prove that your enemies lied was to play up your piety. In fact this came easily to the NLD. Everywhere they went the monks provided hospitality. They also accepted Suu's alms and turned out in sizeable numbers to listen to her speeches, steadily building a spirit of fraternity and complicity between the party and the sangha.

The monks had been central to the legitimacy of the Burmese kings: The palace sustained the sangha in material ways, paying for the building and maintenance of their pagodas and monasteries; conversely the sangha, by receiving alms from the court and performing ceremonies and rites at the king's behest, endorsed his right to rule. That was the rock on which the pre-modern Burmese state rested.

The destruction of the monarchy by the British smashed that symbiotic, sanctified model of governance—which is the main reason the monks were in the vanguard of protest throughout the colonial period. Burma's first prime minister, the pious U Nu, had strongly revived the bond with the monks—but the self-consciously "modernizing" Ne Win had spurned it as an anachronism, leaving a fine vacuum for the NLD to occupy.

Then there was the whole question of what democracy might involve. When SLORC had announced multiparty elections in September 1988, it seems to have been acting on two assumptions: One, that the mass of people would vote for the only party they had ever heard of, the BSPP, rebranded the National Unity Party (NUP); and two, that the votes of those that didn't vote NUP would be so divided that they would have no weight. General Saw Maung, the regime's new figurehead, promised that after the elections the army would return to barracks and have no further political role; and when he saw that 235 political parties had registered for the election, he must have congratulated himself on the success of his plan. Burma could emerge from this democracy charade with international esteem—and with the army still in charge behind the scenes, as before.

But during Suu's epic journeys in April and May 1989, that prospect began to change. The NLD began to consolidate its position, building bridges with other parties and ethnic groups that threatened this comfortable scenario. Aung San Suu Kyi, wrote Gustaaf Houtman, "had such success making alliances between many political and ethnic groups, much like her father . . . that it looked as if she had the ability to unify the opposition in a manner that would leave no political role" for the army.[7]

On every front the army was getting squeezed. It was time for it to fight back.

*

For the regime, Aung San was now the problem. Fundamental to the creation of a modern Burmese identity in the preceding half century, he had now been hijacked by his daughter and her followers. Far from being a benign symbol of military rule, he was becoming the rallying cry of the revolution. It was time to unhitch Burma from Aung San. That this was an urgent necessity became clear from the One Kyat Note fiasco.

Practically all currency notes in Burma since independence bore Aung San's image—just as every town had its street and square named after him, every public office had its framed portrait of him, every schoolchild had his or her head full of his courage and wisdom. But when the regime introduced a newly designed one kyat note in 1989, the designer showed his anti-regime feelings in a very delicate manner.[8]

The note was to bear a watermark with Aung San's image—the usual high cheekbones, pursed lips and chilseled jaw of the national hero. But by subtly softening the lines of the jaw and making slight modifications to the nose, mouth and cheeks, the father's image morphed into the likeness of his daughter.

The note was printed and in circulation before this elegant act of subversion came to the regime's notice: All around the country people hoarded the notes, whispered about them, and pointed out how the designer had also incorporated the figures 8/8/88, the date of the general strike, into his design of concentric petals on the watermark. As soon as the scandal was discovered the note was withdrawn from circulation— and from then on no Burmese banknotes ever bore Aung San's image again.

Nothing was said about it, there was no Moscow-style airbrushing of the past, but Aung San's legacy began to fall into disrepair like an abandoned pagoda. The museums dedicated to the hero were no longer kept up. While Aung San Suu Kyi was attacked as a vassal of the colonialists and a sexual libertine whom her father would have disowned or killed, the museums in the village of Natmauk, in the restored house where he was born, and in the grand house at 25 Tower Lane, the family's Rangoon home at the time of his death, were allowed to run down. Every year in the run-up to July 19th, Martyrs' Day, the date of his assassination and the biggest national holiday of the Burmese year, Rangoon University professors used to fan out into the city's schools to give lectures on the meaning and achievement of the hero's life. But not this year, and not ever again.[9]

So in the absence of the founding father, what did SLORC have to offer? It was a subject that was clearly preying on the generals' minds—and on May 30th, less than a week after Suu's return from the far north, they hit on something original.

On that date they set up a twenty-one-member "Commission of Enquiry into the True Naming of Myanmar Names."[10] Though notionally a scholarly body, all but four of its members were from the military. If Aung San had forged an identity for the nation in the chaos of the Second World War, the challenge for the generals was to go much further back—by building a bridge to the line of kings that the British had deposed.

All over South Asia the postcolonial era has seen the rejection of names associated with the imperialists: Ceylon became Sri Lanka, "Holy Lanka," Bombay became Mumbai, Madras became Chennai, Calcutta Kolkata and so on. Often these changes were promoted by populist tub-thumpers, but the governments that enacted them were democratic ones, and the decision followed a period of study and debate.

Not so in Burma: There was no consultation, no attempt to test the people's mood on the subject—and precious little time for the commission to do its work. Less than three weeks after it was set up, the "Adaption of Expressions Law" came into force, changing Burma to Myanmar, Rangoon to Yangon and so on for every town and village in the country.

The change made very little difference to Burmese people themselves: The words "Bama" and "Myanma" have both been used by Burmans for their country for centuries. The change was intended for international consumption: It was a way of saying that, far from being a transitional set-up as originally conceived, SLORC planned to stay in power and had every right to do so because it was rooted in the ancient past, in the proud era of kings, long before the land was contaminated by the colonialists. It was a way to insist on international respect and recognition—and five days later, despite the rushed process, the UN (and the *New York Times*) duly recognized it.

*

All the while the repression of the democracy movement continued as hundreds more activists and protesters were locked away. By the end of June the number was said to be 2,000—by the end of July it had escalated to 6,000. The mood of confrontation was building rapidly.

The question for Suu was, how to combat it? How to oblige the regime to stick to its promise of elections, ensure that they were free and fair, and then guarantee a handover of power?

Yet in the increasingly frenzied atmosphere, that goal—which would have required the regime and the party to be on speaking terms—was lost sight of. Perhaps it was taken for granted that the elections would be a farce. Perhaps it was merely that the rapidly increasing rate of arrests, and the growing mood of mutual recrimination, made talks of any sort between the two sides out of the question.

And so rather than moderating her side's expectations, Suu chose this moment to up the ante further.

As dialogue was impossible, this was a war in which slogans had become the ammunition. All over the country SLORC began erecting huge signs with Orwellian calls to discipline and patriotism; they dot Burma's towns and cities to this day. The NLD retaliated during the water festival with their competition to produce the most pungent anti-regime slogans anyone could think up. Now, Suu announced, her party's defiance of the regime would be enshrined in all its literature, in a permanent call to nonviolent resistance.[11] Speaking on June 5th, she inaugurated what she called her party's campaign of civil disobedience. The campaign's slogan, exhorting the Burmese public to "defy as of duty every order and authority not agreed by the majority" would be printed in all the party's literature starting the next day, June 6th. The right of the regime to command obedience would be denied at every turn.

It was a move that some of her colleagues had resisted. The campaign, originally suggested by U Win Tin, the veteran anti-regime journalist on the party's Central Executive Committee, was under discussion, Ma Thanegi remembers, but notes in her diary that "before it was decided on another CEC member called U Chan Aye presented a paper saying the NLD should instead try to work with SLORC. I heard that Daw Aung San Suu Kyi was thinking about it. But then some of the students in the party asked her if she was afraid—and she discarded the idea of dialogue at once. It is very easy to push her buttons."

The civil disobedience campaign was a watershed for the party. After that, said Ma Thanegi, "Everyone knew it was going to be dangerous. Some students living in Ma Suu's compound had monks chant a special mantra for the deceased over them, in preparation for sudden death. Some of them became monks or nuns for a few days."

Some people in the party's office who did not want to face the consequences melted away, and quietly severed their ties with the party. "But," said Ma Thanegi, "almost all of us around Daw Aung San Suu Kyi felt it would not be loyal to abandon her in the face of danger."

The regime's reaction was furious and instantaneous: On June 6th they threatened action against any printers who followed the NLD's instructions, and soon afterwards launched a countrywide blitz on NLD publications. A week later 800 printers and publishers were summoned to a compulsory meeting and warned unequivocally to toe the SLORC line. "Decisive action" would be taken, they were told, against any of them who "slandered" the junta or the army.

Both sides were painting themselves into their respective corners. A military spokesman said martial law would remain in place even after elections had been held, and that it would not surrender power until a new constitution had been agreed by parliament. Suu countered by saying that the NLD could not participate in elections "until the question of the transfer of power is resolved."

Then, in a speech delivered on June 26th, Suu broke the taboo that had retained its force throughout this year of tumult: She attacked Number

One by name, spelling out the charges which could be read between the lines of her address at Shwedagon.

"General Ne Win," she declared, "[who is] still widely believed to control Burma behind the scenes, was responsible . . . fashioning the military into a body answerable only to him . . . The opinion of all our people is that U Ne Win is still creating all the problems in this country." He "caused this nation to suffer for twenty-six years," she pursued, "and lowered the prestige of the armed forces."[12]

It was a breathtaking assault: the distillation of a lifetime of antipathy, dating back to the effective exiling of her mother when she was sent to be ambassador to India in 1960. Suu could not guess the consequences of these words, but she knew enough about their target to guess that they could be severe. This was the all-powerful dictator who had not hesitated to have civilian protesters murdered in their hundreds and thousands. And even trivial annoyances provoked him to wild, disproportionate violence. One of his several wives had deserted him for good after he hurled a heavy glass ashtray at her in a rage, injuring her. When the peace of his lakeside villa was disturbed by a Christmas party at a nearby hotel in 1975, he had personally stormed round with a platoon of soldiers and taken part in beating up and humiliating the guests and destroying the band's instruments. When a European woman stood up to complain, he grabbed her party dress, ripped it down the front, and threw her back into her chair.[13] And this was the man whom Suu now chose to seize by the horns.

*

In the same speech, Suu rolled her party's siege engine up to the junta's walls. She introduced Burma's new calendar of martyrdom. The generals might demand that their country be called by a different name now, but if the NLD had its way they would have to swallow a raft of holidays to commemorate atrocities for which they were responsible: The people's uprising of 8/8/88, the Saw Maung crackdown of September 18th; Martyrs' Day, July 29th, with the list of martyrs brought up to date; and the most immediate, and the one aimed most precisely at Ne Win, the twenty-sixth anniversary, on July 7th, of the demolition by high explosives in 1962 of Rangoon University's Student Union building with an unknown number of students inside, the event which had ushered in Burma's authoritarian era. Each of these dates, Suu told the press conference, would be marked by mass demonstrations.

What, besides reminding the world of how the army had treated its own citizens, would be the point of these demonstrations? For SLORC, which continued to believe, or claim to believe, that Aung San Suu Kyi was a puppet of the communists, it was as clear as day: This was the planned revolution. "They [the NLD] planned to start a mass uprising," General Khin Nyunt, number two in SLORC, told a press conference in early August, "by inciting the people at Shwedagon pagoda as part of the confrontation campaign of Daw Aung San Suu Kyi on July 19th, Martyrs' Day. Should that instigation have failed, they planned to try again on the anniversary of the 'Four-Eights' [8/8/88]. Had the mass uprising taken place, they planned to garner more forces from within [the country] to oppose the government while from the outside the members of the Democratic Patriotic Army trained by the Communist Party of Burma would move in. They planned to move politically as well as militarily until an interim government was established."

There is no indication that the NLD had prepared such a plan; Suu's commitment to nonviolence had been so consistent and was by now so well-known—and endorsed by the pacific and disciplined behavior of NLD rallies, even the huge ones—that a violent takeover with Suu at the head was literally unthinkable. "We don't have any intention to seek a confrontation," Suu insisted to the *New York Times'* Steven Erlanger in a telephone interview. "We intend to carry on peacefully with our rallies. We do not want any trouble."[14] At a rally outside the Sule pagoda in downtown Rangoon on July 3rd, attended by more than 10,000 people, she urged SLORC to agree to hold talks with opposition parties in order to "thrash out existing misunderstandings."

But there had never been much talking between the two sides. And this time the regime's answer came not in words but deeds: the arrest the following day of Win Tin, the journalist who had been there at the creation and who was one of the most combative and articulate figures in the party. It was a blow that stunned his colleagues, Suu included, and from which the party struggled to recover. He was to remain in prison for nineteen years.

More answers came within days. The army rolled back into town, sealing the university completely to prevent the gathering for the planned commemoration of the destruction of the Student Union building. And lest anyone question the need for that many troops to control a nonviolent movement, bombs started going off, one that same day at an oil refinery in Syriam, killing two refinery workers and badly injuring a third, a second on July 10th at Rangoon's City Hall, killing three and injuring four. Three young NLD members were picked up and accused of the refinery bombing. "Now it is obvious who is behind the recent bombing," said Khin Nyunt, "and plans to disrupt law and order."[15] The allegation, given the NLD's nonviolent track record, was laughable— but menacing. As a foreign diplomat remarked, the bombings could be terrorism—or the work of agents provocateurs, providing the excuse for another crackdown.

A bare week remained to Martyrs' Day: The Burmese state's founding rite was now embroiled in bitter recrimination. The aim of the ceremony was to recall those who had died for Burma's independence and inspire the country with gratitude and patriotic pride; instead it now threatened to add yet more pages to the martyrs' roll, and further stain the nation with blood and hatred.

SLORC decided to pretend that nothing had happened in the intervening year. On July 16th, reverting to the mode of icy protocol last glimpsed on the eve of Daw Khin Kyi's funeral, they sent round an invitation to University Avenue, politely requesting Aung San Suu Kyi's presence at the Martyrs' Mausoleum, near the Shwedagon, for the usual annual event. Also included in the invitation was U Soe Tint, an old friend of Suu's family, the principal of Rangoon's State School of Fine Arts and Daw Khin Kyi's regular escort at the event in years past.

The leaders of Suu's party convened to consider the invitation. "After CEC meeting," wrote Ma Thanegi, "Ma Suu decides she will not attend. She will march with her followers later, after the official ceremony, when the mausoleum is opened to the public." She was sticking to the party's plan, come what may. "NLD was quite sure it could control the masses— but SLORC almost accused NLD of planning a mass revolt," Ma Thanegi wrote. One Burmese journalist, a veteran stringer for Agence France-Presse called U Eddie Thwin, desperately tried to obtain the regime's assurances that it would not slaughter the marchers as long as they remained peaceful. "He was at the daily press conferences of SLORC and kept asking questions to find out if we would be safe if we simply marched and did nothing else." After great persistence he was rewarded with a reply in the affirmative. "Finally he got the reassurance, I think on the evening of 18th," she wrote. "He called me and I told Ma Suu about it."

But at almost the same moment SLORC sent army trucks with loudspeakers round the city to send out a very different message. There was to be no marching: People were free to pay their respects to the nation's martyrs on July 19th as usual, but only in ones and twos. A new martial law decree, number 2/89, laid down that any groups approaching the mausoleum consisting of more than five persons would be subject to three years' imprisonment, life imprisonment, or death, sentences that could be imposed by army officers on the spot, with no need for a court hearing.

That evening, too, Burma's brief experiment with *glasnost* came to an abrupt end. The last accredited foreign correspondent to leave Rangoon was Reuters reporter David Storey—perhaps the first and last correspondent to be deported from the country despite having his visa in order. "I was picked up at my hotel at night on the 18th, after curfew, although I had a valid journalist visa," he recalled. "I was treated firmly but politely and it was clear that they did not want any journalist to cover the events that followed. I was taken to the airport in a jeep, guarded by a section of the troops, and had to spend the night on a cot on the floor in the departure lounge. The following morning I was put on the first flight to Bangkok."[16]

So subscribers to the Reuters wire service were not to learn what happened late on the evening of July 18th: The thousands of fresh troops rumbling into the city, including battalions that had been used to crush the protests the previous August; the road blocks set up on main roads and the barbed wire stretched across them; the hundreds of what Military Intelligence deemed to be troublemakers picked up; the particularly ugly detail of the city's hospitals being told to prepare for an influx of casualties. Telephone and telex lines to the outside world were cut, and Burma went back into its shell.

*

It was at dawn on Wednesday, July 19th, Martyrs' Day, that Suu and her colleagues learned of the army's preparations.

"I arrived at Ma Suu's home around 7:30 AM," Ma Thanegi wrote in her diary. "By tradition a food offering for monks took place at the party's headquarters at dawn on the 19th of every month. Present at the offering was a party member called Soon Kyway who had arrived on foot from Tharkayta, a satellite town. She told Daw Aung San Suu Kyi that she saw many checkpoints on the streets and feared for Ma Suu's safety. Others, too, urged Suu to reconsider her plans."

The dreadful massacres of September 18th and 19th, 1988, which had also been preceded by army warnings, were still a garish memory. There was no reason to suppose the army would behave any differently this time.

"Daw Aung San Suu Kyi then decided she would not march out," Ma Thanegi went on. "She wrote out a message, which she had someone type up on wax duplicating paper, saying that in order to protest people must stay home and boycott the ceremony. She signed it, then hundreds of copies were printed and people sent off immediately to distribute them all over town." Explaining the decision, Suu told her party colleagues, "We do not want to lead our people straight into a killing field."

Before the age of Facebook it was not simple to call off a major rally at the last moment. And, anyway, after days of feverish preparation, many students were unwilling to fall into line.

"Thousands of students disregarded Suu's message," Ma Thanegi wrote. "For days now they had been hyped up over the march. They did not meet at the football field as planned but marched out from their own meeting places."

The army stopped them from approaching the mausoleum. "Many beaten up with batons and many thrown in jail," she wrote. "All through the morning we got news of students being chased and beaten up on their way to the mausoleum."

A surprising number succeeded in evading arrest. "About 10:30 AM Moe Hein came running to Ma Suu's house to tell her about how many had managed to escape from the army by running away. Her only comment was, 'Why did they run? Why didn't they sit and take it?' before stalking off into her office. I thought, she's thinking about Gandhi and the salt march."

No deaths were reported on July 19, 1989—in contrast to the thousands massacred exactly ten months earlier. Suu's hastily duplicated flyer had helped to avert a bloodbath. But the real confrontation still lay ahead.

*

Nobody could be sure what was going to happen next, but it was clear that it would be nothing good: The rift between the two sides had gone too far to be mended. Many people in the movement were already in prison. The rest would not have long to wait.

"The next day Aung Aung [Suu's head of security] called me very early," wrote Ma Thanegi, "saying it was not wise to come, things looked bad. I said in that case I should be there.

"When I got to the house, Ma Suu told me that the previous night she could not sleep until she had decided that she should be arrested." If that was to be the fate of her colleagues, Suu was determined that she would share it. "Then, she had a good sleep and she had just told Aung Aung to call the local authorities to tell them to come and arrest her [. . .] The party's Central Executive Committee arrived for a meeting around 9 AM and by 9:30 the compound was surrounded by troops and no one was allowed in or out. I heard that U Nu, Burma's first democratic prime minister, came to the gate in his car but was turned away by the soldiers." An inveterate opportunist, the man who a year before had insisted that he was still the legitimate prime minister had turned up wearing a rice farmer's bamboo hat, the NLD's electoral symbol.

Into this moment of high drama stumbled Suu's two sons, visiting their mother for the first time since Christmas—without their father, who had had to stay behind in Scotland where his own father had just died. They brought a surreal air of boyish normality with them. "Ma Suu had a lunch meeting with the CEC," wrote Ma Thanegi, "while I ate with Kim and Alexander. I kept Kim company, playing Monopoly with him." It was the family's favorite game, and had been the occasion for Suu and Michael's rare clashes of temper (for which reason they had given up playing).

"The army allowed the CEC to leave around 2 PM," she went on, "and after that we sat around chatting while some of the boys [the student bodyguards] took naps." The surreal mood persisted; a perverse, infectious mood of gaiety stole up on them. "We all agreed that Suu would not be put under house arrest," Ma Thanegi recalled, "as people might march up and rescue her." Nonetheless, that Suu would be arrested was now taken for granted.

> We wondered where she would be taken to. No one seemed at all worried; we chatted amiably and cheerfully, cracking jokes. Suu asked us who would stay with her and everyone said they would. I said I would, I only needed to have my art materials brought in for me.
>
> Around 4 PM an army officer came to the gate and asked permission to see her. We all walked out to the gate, Ma Suu and I first dabbing on some perfume which I had with me in my holdall. We said to each other that we refused to be arrested without French perfume.
>
> She and her sons were escorted into the house and the rest of us into the large bamboo shed at the end of the garden used for classes and meetings. We sat around, and one MI asked Ko Myint Swe to make a list of who would like to stay in the house. He did so, but we knew that was not going to happen. It grew dark; we could see moving bright lights in the house and knew they were taking videos.
>
> We were then herded out onto two large trucks parked near the front of the house. I went inside to take my bag of clothes that I keep under my desk, and my holdall. Ma Suu ran to fetch lavender soap and a large tube of toothpaste for me plus her expensive leather sandals which she said were very good for trekking. I told her I doubted if I would be walking anywhere but she insisted. We hugged and told each other to take care. Neither of us had a look of sadness, despair, or fear on our faces.

Ma Thanegi and her colleagues were taken to prison. Aung San Suu Kyi was put under house arrest for "endangering the state," Section 10(b) of the penal code.

Nine months later, despite the fact that all its senior leaders were under lock and key, the NLD won the general election by a crushing majority, gaining 392 of parliament's 485 seats. Overall, parties opposed to SLORC and army rule won more than 94 percent of the seats.

But Suu remained in detention, and the army remained in power.

She was not to emerge for nearly six years.

PART THREE
THE WIDE WORLD

1
GRIEF OF A CHILD

BUDDHISM teaches that nothing is permanent, nothing is fixed, all is in flux. If Aung San Suu Kyi had metamorphosed within a year from an Oxford housewife into her nation's longed-for leader but was now a prisoner in her family home, her earliest days were no less mercurial. Raised the child of the most honored family in the country, she had been born a fugitive.

A photograph in Suu's short biography of Aung San shows her father as Minister for War in Japan's puppet Burma government in 1943. Shaven bullet head, tunic tight on the Adam's apple, lower lip thrust out, what one would have to call a fanatical gleam in his eye: a model servant of the God-Emperor.

Yet the picture is misleading: Like his colleagues in the Burma National Army, which he had founded, Aung San was already discovering that, as one of his followers put it, "If the British sucked our blood, the Japanese ground our bones."[1] "He became more and more disillusioned with the Japanese," wrote William Slim, commander of the Allied Fourteenth Army. "Early in 1943 we got news . . . that Aung San's feelings were changing. On August 1, 1944, [as the Japanese and the British were still fighting it out for control of central Burma] he was bold enough to speak publicly with contempt of the Japanese brand of independence, and it was clear that, if they did not soon liquidate him, he might prove useful to us."[2]

"Liquidation" was a lively danger, even though Japanese resistance to the Allied counterattack was rapidly disintegrating. Then in March 1945 Aung San's Burma National Army (BNA) defected to the Allied side, surprising and killing some Japanese officers, and Slim responded by providing Aung San with arms and supplies and bringing his small but useful force into the Allied scheme.

The collaboration seemed to be working when, on May 16, 1945, with the aplomb he showed all his life, Aung San presented himself to Slim in person. There followed an interview so extraordinary that Slim felt it worth recording verbatim in his memoirs. He wrote:

> The arrival of Aung San, dressed in the near-Japanese uniform of a Major General, complete with sword, startled one or two of my staff. However, he behaved with the utmost courtesy, and so, I hope, did we. He was a short, well-built, active man in early middle age, neat and soldierly in appearance, with regular Burmese features in a face that could be an impassive mask or light up with intelligence and humor. I found he spoke good English . . .
>
> At our first interview, Aung San began to take rather a high hand. He was, he said, the representative of the Provisional Government of Burma, which had been set up by the people of Burma through the Anti-Fascist People's Freedom League . . . He was an Allied commander, who was prepared to cooperate with me, and demanded the status of an Allied and not subordinate commander.[3]

Slim's eyes were surely widening in amazement. "I told him that I had no idea what the Anti-Fascist People's Freedom League was or represented . . . I pointed out that he was in no position to take the line he had. I did not need his forces; I was destroying the Japanese quite nicely without their help, and could continue to do so . . ." He went on to remind Aung San that he was wanted on a civil murder charge, for which there were witnesses, and that Slim was being urged to put him on trial: During Aung San's progress through southern Burma with the Japanese in 1942, it was alleged that he had personally executed a village headman he accused of betrayal. "Don't you think you are taking considerable risks in coming here and taking this attitude?" he demanded with some heat.

"No," Aung San replied.

*

While Aung San in newly liberated Rangoon was giving a textbook demonstration of chutzpah, dozens of miles to the west, taking refuge in the simple, huddled villages of the Irrawaddy Delta, his wife Ma Khin Kyi was heavily pregnant. Protected by five soldiers in Aung San's Burma National Army, she, her sister and her two toddlers had fled Rangoon in March, all disguised as poor civilians, as her husband prepared to defect to the Allies: If any Japanese forces remaining in the city had identified her and her children, their revenge could have been terrible. There, on June 19, 1945, in the tiny village of Hmway Saung, Aung San Suu Kyi— her name, she explains, means "strange collection of bright victories"— was born.

Aung San's improbable gambit with Slim succeeded: He won his trust, and even his affection. He had had the temerity to claim equality with the Allied army commander despite being a Japanese collaborator who was wanted for murder "because you are a *British* officer" as he put it, a reply that made Slim laugh. Aung San had a shrewd idea that the Allies would want to make use of his force; he also showed remarkable insight into British psychology. Slim wrote:

> He went on to say that, at first, he had hoped the Japanese would give real independence to Burma. When he found they would not, but were tightening the bonds on his people, he had, relying on our promises, turned to us as a better hope. "Go on, Aung San," I said. "You only come to us because you see we are winning!'
>
> "It wouldn't be much good coming to you if you weren't, would it?" he replied, simply.
>
> . . . I felt he had scored again, and I liked his honesty. In fact I was beginning to like Aung San.[4]

With the shattered and scattered remnant of the Japanese Army trying to flee east into Thailand, the Allied forces aided by the BIA had retaken Rangoon without a fight, entering the city in the first days of May. And now with charm, daring and exquisite timing, Aung San had established himself in the good books of Burma's newly returned masters—after nearly four years fighting for the other side. Soon after Suu's birth he had a note hand-delivered to his wife: All the Japanese were gone and the city was again at peace. The family was reunited in Rangoon.

The home in which Aung San Suu Kyi started life was 25 Tower Lane, a large but plainly decorated villa in its own grounds, built some fifteen or twenty years before for a Chinese or Indian merchant, located in the salubrious suburbs of the capital north of the commercial center and a mile from the Shwedagon pagoda. Here Suu learned to crawl, then to walk, then to read; she discovered the meaning of friendship and of physical courage and also—twice before the age of nine—the meaning of grief.

For many years it was possible to explore Suu's first home, because after the family moved out, in 1953, it became the Bogyoke Aung San Museum. But the slow and surreptitious unhitching of the regime from the person of Aung San, described in the previous chapter and which began with the scandal of the "Aung San Suu Kyi" One Kyat Note, has now reached its apogee: The house is still standing, just, but when I visited in 2010 I was waved away by a man in the grounds; the family in residence took shelter indoors to avoid being filmed. The garden is overgrown and the house is in the last stages of disrepair. A man in the tea shop nearby told me it opens only once a year, on July 19th, Martyrs' Day—the last remaining vestige of the national cult.

Suu came to consciousness in what must have been a warm, bustling, loving, stimulating home. Her brothers Aung San Oo, the eldest, and Aung San Lin, were aged two and one respectively when she was born. A second daughter, Aung San Chit, was born subsequently but died after only a few days.

Tower Lane was the first, proper, permanent home the family had enjoyed, following a series of temporary lodgings. Peace had come; independence was surely on the way, and Aung San, the undisputed leader of the nation, who soon resigned his commission in the army to concentrate on politics, would be a shoo-in for prime minister. Important visitors thronged in and out, debating the issues of the moment with Aung San in the big reception room downstairs. But Suu's mother was no purdah wife, lurking deep indoors polishing the silver: Ma Khin Kyi was articulate, well-educated and strong-willed, heir to the Burmese tradition of robust, emancipated women. The domestic tasks were taken care of by Indian Christians, who continued to work for the family for decades.

Aung San must have been a fleeting presence in the family during these feverish days, the broadly smiling but distracted man who flew out to his chauffeured car in the mornings, laden with files and burst back into the house in the middle of the day for a high-speed family lunch; till late at night the children in their beds upstairs—the eldest, Aung San Oo, was only four when Aung San died—would have sniffed the cheroot smoke of his important guests and heard the urgent, impassioned murmuring of adult voices as the nation's future was discussed and dissected downstairs by the Burmese men in whose hands it would shortly repose.

But none of that lodged in the memory of the small girl with the protruding ears and staring eyes, the baby of the family, who was just two years and one month old when her father went away one hot morning in the wet season and never came home again.

"My father died when I was too young to remember him," she wrote in the Preface to her book on his life.[5] That was honest of her, and honesty was the principle most fiercely inculcated by Ma Khin Kyi. Because the memories she did retain she no longer trusted. "I have a memory of him picking me up every time he came home from work," she told Alan Clements. "I do seem to remember that whenever he would come back from work, my two brothers and I would come running down the stairs to meet him and he would pick me up."[6] But that memory, she decided, was unreliable. "I think this may be a memory that was reinforced by people repeating it to me all the time. In other words, I was not allowed to forget. So it may be a genuine memory or it may be something I imagined from what people kept telling me."

Yet flashes of true memory emerged from time to time, perhaps at moments of exhaustion or great stress. In her diary of their journeys, Ma Thanegi records Suu telling her that one time she had refused to kiss her father, "because she had a cold," she said—which was a fib. And once when he failed in his daily attentions, she remembered ordering him, "Please pick up the child!" and when he said, "Which child?" replying petulantly, "*This* child, *this* child!"

Not recalling him with any vividness, how badly did she miss him? Not at all, if her own account is to be believed. "I don't remember my father's death as such," she told Clements. "I don't think I was aware that he died."[7] But once again Suu's tough and unsentimental honesty masks a more complex psychological reality.

On the one hand, his death was hardly a surprise: Ma Khin Kyi knew she had married a destiny as much as a man of flesh and blood. In February 1946, when Suu was eight months old, Aung San said to Britain's Governor in Rangoon, Sir Reginald Dorman-Smith, "How long do national heroes last? Not long in this country; they have too many enemies. Three years is the most they can hope to survive. I do not give myself more than another eighteen months of life."[8] In his disarming and rather brutal way, with a shouted laugh, he must have said something very similar to his wife—and after her flight to the delta and the crazy vicissitudes of the war, she would have believed it.

On the other hand—what a loss for a family to sustain! This vividly physical, scintillating presence, bold enough to conceive and then strenuously set about building a future, not merely for himself and his loved ones but for his entire nation. It was a loss you would never get over. It is arguable that Suu never did.

*

Life went on, and in many ways it went on unchanged. Visitors continued to stream through the house, though they no longer stayed till late in the night, trying unsuccessfully to argue Aung San into the ground. Now they came with sorrowful looks and pitying glances for the tiny orphans: Aung San's surviving political colleagues, including Nu, the first prime minister after independence, and the survivors among the Thirty Comrades, the first recruits to the independence army who had accompanied Aung San for training under the Japanese, and many others whose lives he had touched.

Despite the loss of paterfamilias and breadwinner, this was no sad nucleus of a family: Ma Khin Kyi's father, a Christian convert, lived with them for the rest of his life, and Suu cites him as a tower of strength in her childhood. "I never felt the need for a dominant male figure," she told Clements, "because my mother's father, who lived with us, was the ideal grandfather. He was very indulgent and loving. During my childhood he was the most important male figure in my life."[9] There were also aunts and great-aunts and nieces and nephews and cousins—the large and shifting cast of characters of the typical extended Asian family.

At the heart of it were the three small children. As the eldest—the "Oo" part of his name means simply "first"—Aung San Oo was rather apart from the other two; he slept in a room of his own, and he is strangely absent from Suu's story, except in recent years when he cast a malevolent shadow on her, suing her, allegedly at the behest of the regime, to try to stop her repairing the family home, which they own jointly. Aung San

Lin—Ko Ko Lin, "big brother Lin" to Suu—shared a room with his baby sister, and they grew very close.

With her father gone, Ma Khin Kyi became the most important figure in Suu's young life. She was well suited to the role. "She was such a dignified woman with a very distinctive voice," remembered Patricia Herbert, one of the very few Westerners, besides the diplomats, who lived in Rangoon during the Ne Win years, and who became her close friend.

> It was a very clear voice, very authoritative without being domineering: You paid attention to what she said, and I think in that sense she must have had a huge influence on her daughter.
>
> Her face was a perfect oval, and her hair was always beautifully done, she often wound it around a gold comb. She wore very traditional aingyi, the Burmese cotton woman's blouse, with detachable buttons which might have gold or diamonds in them, which picked up the color of the htamein, the woman's longyi.
>
> She was a wonderful hostess, the meals were always beautifully prepared by her cook, but above all I remember her as being motherly. Of course she wasn't my mother, but in my memory that's what it felt like. She had that ability to make everybody feel special.[10]

Suu credits the woman she became on the consistently high standards her mother set. "My mother was a very strong person," she told Clements. "My mother's relationship with me was quite formal. She never ran around and played with me when I was young . . . She tried very hard to give us the best education and the best life she could . . . She was very strict at times. When I was younger I felt that was a disadvantage, but now I think it was a good thing because it set me up well in life."

"How was she strict?" Clements asked her.

"Highly disciplined, everything at the right time, in the right way," she replied. "She was a perfectionist."[11]

Any middle-class child of the 1950s remembers being told to sit up straight at meal times. Ma Khin Kyi took it that little bit further: Suu told Ma Thanegi that her mother would not allow the children's backs to touch the back of the dining chairs. The medicine worked: Her perfectly erect carriage was a source of wonder at Oxford, that asylum of slovenliness. And she did her best to pass it on. Ma Thanegi wrote in her diary: "I used to slouch a lot when we were traveling together, and Ma Suu often said to me, 'Don't slouch, Ma Thanegi, how many times must I tell you?'" At home the children were required to walk round and round the garden lawn, to practice walking with straight backs.

Ma Khin Kyi had been brought up under the influence of both Christianity and Buddhism, but Aung San was a traditional Burmese Buddhist and Ma Khin Kyi made sure that the children were exposed to the rites and doctrines of the religion of the overwhelming majority of Burmese from early on. "There was a Buddhist shrine room at the top of the house," said Tin Tin, one of Suu's friends at her first school in Rangoon, "and she told me that her mother made them go up to that room and pray every night—she was laughing when she told me about it, but later on she became a very devout Buddhist."[12]

There were other rules, too, designed to impress on the Bogyoke's children the need to behave just so. "She told me that when she was young, her mother would not allow her to lick stamps," Ma Thanegi recalled. "Instead they had to be moistened with a sponge." Nor could they indulge in the custom (popular all over the Indian empire) of pouring hot tea into the saucer to cool it, or dunking biscuits in the tea. "Whenever she did any of those things," said Ma Thanegi, "she would giggle and say 'I can do it now, I'm grown up!'"

Suu suspected her mother of favoring her elder brother, a suspicion confirmed for her when Ma Khin Kyi gave Aung San Oo a ruby ring that Suu had coveted. But despite her severity as a parent, Suu claims she never resented her mother. "I asked her once if as a teenager she had problems or arguments in her relationship with her mother," says Ma Thanegi, "because I did: I also have an elder brother, who was mother's pet, so I sympathized. But she said, no, she never had any such problems."

On the contrary, she remembered her mother being always available.

My mother was very good [at answering questions]. She never once told me not to ask questions. Every evening when she returned from work, she used to lie down on the bed because she was rather tired. And then I would walk round and round her bed, and every time I got to the foot of her bed, I would ask one question. You can imagine, it doesn't take long to walk round a bed. And never once did she say, "I'm too tired, don't go on asking me these questions." Mind you, she couldn't answer a lot of my questions.

I remember asking her, "Why is water called water?" Now it's very difficult to find an answer. But she would never say, "Don't ask me such nonsensical questions." She would try to answer or she would simply say, "I don't know." I respected her for that.[13]

She was not available when she was out at work, however. And if she had not been out at work, perhaps the second tragedy in Suu's young life might have been avoided.

It has always been Suu's proud boast—casting a baleful eye at the grossly corrupt generals who lord it over Burma today—that when Aung San resigned from the army to go into politics he did not claim an army pension, setting what he intended to be a good example to those who trod in his footsteps. When he died, however, that demonstration of rectitude posed a problem for his widow, who had no independent means of her own. The surviving kin of those wiped out in the July 19th massacre were all given a one-off condolence payment of 100,000 kyats, but that was no substitute for an income. To keep the family above the breadline Ma Khin Kyi made inquiries at her old employer, Rangoon General Hospital. But she was saved from a return to the bedpans by the personal intervention of U Nu, the prime minister. Better, more important work must be found for the widow of the Bogyoke, he decided. Ma Khin Kyi was therefore brought into the civil service, taking the role of director of the National Women and Children's Welfare Board.

The small children were therefore left more and more to their own devices, supervised rather distantly by the domestics. Number 25 Tower Lane was a wonderful home for a small boy or girl. The small shrine room at the top of the house, which looked over to the Shwedagon, had a glass roof. Suu never forgot the day she summoned the courage to climb up to the roof.

It was Ko Ko Lin who led the way. Ma Thanegi wrote in her diary, "She told me how when they were children her brother would climb up to the ceiling and into the circular roofed pavilion with glass around its walls, built right in the center of the roof for natural light to enter. Aung San Oo did nothing of the kind, but Aung San Lin did. Once, he urged and helped her to do the same. She said she was terrified but she trusted him, and he told her what to do every step of the way, so she actually made it."

Heights were not the only thing she was scared of, this child who was to grow up to become the Lioness of Danubyu. "When I was a child I was afraid of the dark," she said, "whereas my brothers were not. I was really the cowardly one in the family. This is probably why I find it very strange when people think I am so brave . . ."

Brother and sister grew very close. "Ma Suu's and Ko Ko Lin's beds were next to each other and they would whisper to each other in the night," Ma Thanegi said. "Aung San Oo had a separate bedroom. Ma Suu said Ko Ko Lin made her feel safe.

But when Lin was nine and Suu was eight, they were separated for ever. On January 16, 1953, in the middle of Burma's best season, the two were playing in the garden of their home. Suu had gone inside for a while; Lin dropped his toy gun at the edge of the pond near the drive that led to the front door. He retrieved it but in the process got his sandal stuck in the mud at the pond's edge. He ran to find his sister and tell her what had happened and give her the gun while he went back to fetch the sandal. Suu told Ma Thanegi that she remembered nothing at all after that. The next thing anyone knew he was discovered dead, floating face down in the pond.

Suu was too young to fully comprehend what had happened or to grieve like an adult, but Ko Ko Lin's death was a source of profound sorrow which returned to her frequently in later years. "I was very close to him," she said, "closer than anybody else. We shared the same room and played together all the time. His death was a tremendous loss to me . . . I felt enormous grief." What upset her, she said, was "the fact that I would never see him again. That, I think, is how a child sees death: I won't play with him again, I'll never be able to be with him again."[14]

The sense of loss was to remain with her, as if her own choices in life might have been less cruel, less weighty, with him at her side. She felt he had qualities that could have made him an exceptional man. "During campaign trips or when we were having problems with the military or with disagreements between NLD members," Ma Thanegi recalled, "she often said, 'Oh, how I wish Ko Ko Lin were here! He was so brave and clever, he would have made a great leader.'"

Two deaths within six years; two of the family's five members taken—three if you include Suu's little sister, dead within days of her birth. Yet

Ma Khin Kyi and her remaining children found the strength to move forward. "It was not something that I couldn't cope with," Suu said of Lin's death. "There must have been a tremendous sense of security surrounding me. I was able to cope—I didn't suffer from depression or great emotional upheaval. I was not utterly devastated by it. I did not go to pieces."[15] And she could not understand why her mother now insisted that the family move house. But you did not have to be a very superstitious person to see Ma Khin Kyi's point: Three deaths in the family at Tower Lane was three too many. Soon after Ko Ko Lin was cremated the family moved to the home with which both mother and daughter were to become intimately familiar: 54 University Avenue, overlooking Inya Lake, another gracious merchant's villa, a gift of the government of Burma and one of the best addresses in Rangoon. For the Bogyoke's family, only the best would do.

*

By now Suu was at school. First she went to a private Catholic girls' primary school and then to the English Methodist High School opposite the British residency: the school of choice for Rangoon's westernized intellectual and social elite.

As a growing child she was not, she insists, such a special person, and the recollections of her school friends confirm that impression. She kicked against the severity of her mother. "When I was young," she said, "I was a normal, naughty child, doing things that I was told not to do, or not doing things that I was supposed to do. Like running away and hiding instead of doing my lessons. I didn't like to work or study. I preferred to play all the time."[16] She contrasts her "normal" attitude to the extraordinary application of her father. "My father was one of those people who are born with a sense of responsibility, far greater and more developed than mine. From the very moment he started going to school he was a hard worker, very conscientious. I wasn't like that."

Ma Khin Kyi persisted in her efforts to turn Suu into a refined young lady. "My hands were never allowed to be idle," she told Ma Thanegi. "I had to be doing something all the time, whether sewing or embroidery or practicing the piano." But the impression she made on her first friends at the English Methodist High School was far from ladylike. With the two most important males plucked from her life, it seems that the growing girl sought unconsciously to compensate by turning into a boy.

"Ours was a mixed school," her friend Tin Tin remembered, "but Suu was not interested in boys. In fact she looked very much like a boy herself. Our uniform was a maroon skirt with a white top, but under them she wore a boy's shirt and vest instead of girl's ones."[17] She had her hair in plaits and wore black lace-up shoes like a boy, her legs were stout and boyish and, according to Tin Tin, she even walked like a man.

She was also very tanned, Ma Thanegi (who was two years her junior at the Methodist High School) remembered, which was not the mark of an aspiring lady. "She told me it was because she was always playing in the sun." But all these tomboy tendencies might be explained by the fact that she was a keen Girl Guide—her mother being the founder of the Burmese Guides. She has made little of this biographical fact, but her cheerful survival of thousands of miles of campaigning in conditions that would be an insult to the average pariah dog suggest close familiarity with the two-finger salute and the tireless quest for badges.

Her dead father already weighed heavily on her mind. According to Tin Tin, "Suu was always speaking about her father and always saying how she respected her father, and saying she has to follow her father's line." And in fact her first ambition was to follow in his footsteps quite literally. "When I was ten or eleven I wanted to enter the army," she said. "Everyone referred to my father as Bogyoke, which means general, so I wanted to be a general, too, because I thought this was the best way to serve one's country, just like my father had done." At some point someone must have gently pointed out to her that the Burmese Army did not recruit girl soldiers.

Suu's fame as the daughter of the Bogyoke brought her no special status or privileges at the Methodist school, where practically all her peers had something to boast about. "The children of three out of four of our presidents, of Prime Minister U Nu, of many branches of the royal family, of most politicians, of diplomats before there was an international school, and of old money Rangoon aristocracy—they all went to our school," said Ma Thanegi. "Our school was the only co-ed mission school, and the best school in the country. Most conservative people did not want to send their children to co-ed schools so our parents were the most progressive, liberal-minded and westernized in Rangoon."

The English Methodist High School was, in other words, living on borrowed time. Though founded only after the return of the British at the end of the war, it was a throwback to the days of Empire—days that were to last only until 1948. And when the English travel writer Norman Lewis visited Rangoon in 1950, when Suu was five, the signs of decline and fall were already hard to miss.

*

Like most cities of the Indian empire on which the Raj left a strong mark, Rangoon is divided into three distinct parts. Out of sight to the north, behind well-guarded walls and fences, is the Cantonment, the army base. Spreading across the hills further south, intersected by winding lanes and boulevards and luxuriantly planted with parks and gardens, are the leafy residential areas reserved for the administrators and the native middle class and their servants. It is these areas, damaged but by no means destroyed during the decades since independence, and with the Shwedagon's dazzling stupa visible from all directions, that give modern Rangoon its delightfully tropical character, making it for Western visitors one of the most charming cities of modern Asia.

But it was the commercial heart of the city down by the river that monopolized Norman Lewis's attention, both because its character was so strikingly at odds with the civilization in which it was set, and because it had so patently seen better days.

This tightly planned section of the city was "imperial and rectilinear," he wrote in his vivid account of his journey through Burma, *Golden Earth*, "built by a people who refused to compromise with the East." It "has wide, straight, shadeless streets, with much solid bank-architecture of vaguely Grecian inspiration . . . There is much façade and presence, little pretence at comfort, and no surrender to climate. This was the Victorian colonizer's response to the unsubstantial glories of Mandalay."[18]

But the Victorian glory days were also gone, Lewis found. "These massive columns now rise with shabby dignity from the tangle of scavenging dogs and sprawling, ragged bodies at their base." The main streets have acquired a squalid incrustation of stalls and barracks, and through these European arteries now courses pure oriental blood. Down by the port it is an Indian settlement. Over to the west the Chinese have moved in with their outdoor theatres and joss houses . . . Little has been done by the new authority to check the encroaching squalor. Side lanes are piled with stinking refuse which mounts up quicker than the dogs and crows can dispose of it . . . Half-starved Indians lie dying in the sunshine. Occasionally insurgents cut off the town's water supply . . . Wherever there is a vacant space the authorities have allowed refugees to put up pestiferous shacks . . .

Amidst this fetor the Burmese masses live their festal and contemplative existences . . . They emerge into the sunshine immaculate and serene . . .[19]

For the privileged Burmese students of the Methodist High School, life did not however conform to the "festal and contemplative" cliché of folklore; their school was disciplined yet privileged and comfortable in a way that would have been perfectly recognizable in Putney or Georgetown. "The school was on Signal Pagoda Road in the middle of town, north of the pagoda," said Tin Tin.[20]

Ordinary people in Rangoon went around by bicycle rickshaw, but we were taken to school by private car—ours was a Morris Oxford. People had all sorts of imported cars.

It was a very expensive private school with a tennis court and all the best modern amenities, run by American Methodist missionaries. At that time most of the elite could speak English: Our parents' generation had grown up under British rule so their English was very good, and because we went to this private English school our English was much better than the students elsewhere. At school there was a rule that except in Burmese class we had to speak in English. Even in the playground and the canteen, the prefects would be monitoring us and they would pull us up if they caught us speaking Burmese.

On Wednesday we had to go to the church which was in the school grounds. But there were a lot of Muslims [Tin Tin's family is Muslim] and Hindus in the school, and although we had to attend the church, nobody tried to convert us.

And because in those days Rangoon possessed no international school, pupils grew up with an easy familiarity with other races and tongues:

Hindi, French and German were among the languages spoken by the pupils, as well as Burmese and English.

Having shed her ambition to be a general, Suu next decided she wanted to be a writer. This was again following in her father's (intended) footsteps: He dreamed aloud, towards the end of his short, frenetic life, of getting out of politics and taking up writing full time. That was not as escapist an urge as it may sound: ". . . in Burma," Suu pointed out, "politics has always been linked to literature and literary men have often been involved with politics, especially the politics of independence."[21]

The urge to write was "the first serious ambition I had," she said, and it went in tandem with a growing passion for literature. She graduated rapidly from Bugs Bunny to Sherlock Holmes, and from Holmes to Maigret and George Smiley. She remains a devotee of crime fiction, including P.D. James and Ruth Rendell, but by her early teens she was also gorging on the English classics: Jane Austen and George Eliot and Kipling, whose *Kim* provided her second son's name and whose great poem of moral exhortation "If" was a source of strength in her first years of detention. "When I was about twelve or thirteen I started reading the classics," she said. "By the time I was fourteen I was a real bookworm. For example, if I went shopping with my mother I would bring a book along . . . The moment the car stopped anywhere I would open my book and start reading, even if it was at a traffic light. Then I would have to shut it, and I couldn't wait for the next stop."[22]

She was open to whatever the world had to offer that might touch her mind or move her heart—but for her generation in Burma that was the natural state of affairs. Only now, looking back after a half century of isolation, the deliberate rejection by the Burmese regime of the rest of the world and all its works, its determination to keep its people as ignorant as possible, does it seem an aberration or a miracle.

"Before the coup Burma was the one country in Southeast Asia with a really good economy," said Tin Tin's sister Khin Myint. "People came to Burma from all over Southeast Asia to do shopping. Rangoon was the jewel of Southeast Asia: You could buy anything there."[23] And the culture of the West flowed in without impediment: From the English classics, which had for generations been the foundation of an upper-class Indian education, to the raucous new music born in the USA. "At the weekend we had jam sessions," remembered Tin Tin, "with dancing, very modern, rock 'n' roll, sometimes played live."[24]

Did Suu dance too? There seems little doubt that she did. As Ma Thanegi recorded in her diary, Suu asked her to find music cassettes to while away the hours in the car, and sang along loudly to hits of the late-fifties and very early sixties which she remembered from her early teens.

When she suddenly emerged into Burma's public life in 1988, Suu spoke Burmese as her co-nationals did, but she was *not* Burmese as they were. That was because, while the defining experience of Burma for the past fifty years has been political and cultural isolation, the defining fact of Suu's life has been the opposite: continuous exposure to the world outside Burma in all its variety. Her father had learned to speak English fluently, had traveled to China and Japan, trained as a soldier in Japan, learned Japanese, then later traveled to London via India to parlay with the colonial oppressor-turned-liberator. His daughter had had the good fortune to grow up in Rangoon during the only years of its postwar history when it was an international town. Then she went abroad, and the exposure continued, and never stopped.

*

Burma, however, was about to turn in the opposite direction: inwards. The diversity and openness of Rangoon as they knew it would prove to be very fragile commodities.

Their country had suffered more in the Second World War than anywhere else in Asia. It had been deliberately smashed to pieces twice over, first by the British, fleeing from the Japanese, then by the Japanese, as they died in huge numbers opposing the British return. While the Burmese huddled in the ruins of their towns and villages and looked on in shock, the two warring empires blasted the country's ports, bridges, power stations, factories, mines, oil wells and government offices, and its cities, towns and villages to pieces. When it was all over there was little left of the calm, self-sufficient, increasingly prosperous colony of the prewar years. Then Aung San, the only man who might have succeeded in pulling it all together, was murdered; and then the end for which he had worked so strenuously, independence, was handed to his successor, U Nu, on a plate by the bankrupt Attlee government, divesting itself of its costly foreign commitments—or "scuttling" as the Tory opposition preferred to put it—as fast as they could manage.

Rarely has there been a truer case of being cursed by what you wish for. "The Burmese," writes Michael Charney, "had achieved independence without a revolution, which prevented the emergence of internal solidarity or the squeezing out of rival groups and ideologies."[25] Burma was not merely prostrate economically and industrially, it was also bitterly divided. While he lived, Aung San had failed to win over the Karen, the large ethnic group concentrated around the Thai border and in the Irrawaddy Delta, to the cause of national unification: His Burman-dominated BIA, while still allied with the Japanese, had been accused of numerous anti-Karen atrocities, and the Karen held out for their own homeland, "Kawthoolei," which literally means "Land Without Evil."

Aung San's Panglong Agreement of 1946 had won round other important "races" of Burma, including the Shan, the Chin and the Kachin to the national project. But after the war a more formidable enemy to national unity presented itself in the form of the Burmese communists. They split into two factions, the "White Flag" faction, the BCP, led by Aung San's brother-in-law Than Tun, and the "Red Flag"—but both committed to overthrowing the democratic government in Rangoon. And where communist insurgency was not a problem, *dacoits* (bandits) and other armed and disaffected groups tore at the country's integrity.

Norman Lewis experienced all this at first hand. "The last occasion when Burmese affairs had been strongly featured in the British press," he wrote, "had been in 1948, when the Karen insurgents had taken Mandalay and seemed to be about to overthrow the Burmese government. Since then, interest had died down . . . In July 1949, the Prime Minister had announced that peace was attainable within one year. Having heard no more I assumed that it had been attained."[26]

Lewis envisaged a leisurely tour of the whole country, preferably arriving in the northwest from Manipur in India and working his way down. His delusions did not last long. They "were stripped away . . . within thirty-six hours of my arrival. On the first morning I bought a newspaper and noted with slight surprise that a ferryboat crossing the river to a suburb of Rangoon had been held up by pirates and three members of the crew killed."[27] In a village twenty miles away, "the whole population had been carried off by insurgents. Serious fighting seemed to be going on, too, in various parts of the country . . . there were a few extremely vague reports about the government troops capturing towns . . ." The most perilous part of his severely foreshortened journey was when he insisted, against all advice, on traveling from Mandalay to Rangoon, Burma's two principal cities, by train.

The Burmese government's problems in combating communists and other insurgents were aggravated by the absence of Aung San. His successor, U Nu, was enormously popular with ordinary Burmese on account of his sweet face, his charming temperament and his Buddhist piety. But he had none of Aung San's steel, and only a fraction of his political savvy. The party he had inherited from Aung San, the AFPFL, was less a coherent party, more a ragbag of rivals from different parts of the political spectrum, each with his entourage. And as the communist and ethnic insurgencies continued to rage and the country struggled to recoup the prosperity it had enjoyed before the war, the AFPFL began to come apart.

Confronted by a bitterly divided party after the general election of 1958, U Nu found himself obliged to invite the army to take over temporarily to restore order in the country. General Ne Win duly became temporary prime minister and the army went to work cleaning up the squalor Lewis had observed in the streets of Rangoon, which had got much worse over the years, and enforcing a degree of tranquility in the rest of the country. In 1960, true to his remit, Ne Win politely handed power back to U Nu, who, popular as ever despite his failings, won another large mandate in that year's election.

But U Nu's new government was never to complete its term. Ne Win had enjoyed his taste of power, and now he wanted some more. Heavily influenced by the chauvinistic, anti-Western Japanese during his years of training there with Aung San, bitterly prejudiced against Burma's prosperous Indian community after an early business failure, and with a strong puritanical streak which sat oddly with his taste for the pleasures of the flesh, he saw much that he wanted to do with his country. And after returning to his barracks in 1960, he began plotting to take power, not at U Nu's invitation but on his own initiative, and permanently.

It was a move that required careful preparation: He wanted the takeover to be peaceful, so potential rivals and enemies of army rule needed to be dealt with well in advance. One of these was Aung San's widow. Aung San had always opposed the idea of army rule, which is why he resigned his commission before entering politics. His widow was close to the prime minister, who had not only found her a new home and turned the previous one into a museum but had also set her on a high-profile career in public service.

The appointment of Daw Khin Kyi as ambassador to Delhi in 1960, the first time a woman had been made a Burmese ambassador, would normally have been described as a great honor for the woman who was now chairman of the Social Planning Commission. So it was—but it was also an excellent way of removing a person of enormous symbolic importance from the scene; a figure who, even if she remained politically taciturn, could easily become a focus for enemies of army rule. In the old days, the first and crucial step for a newly crowned Burmese king was to dispose of potential pretenders. These days they did not roll them up in scarlet carpets and have them trampled by elephants; instead they sent them far away, on honorable state business.

Thus, in 1960 Aung San Suu Kyi and her mother boarded a plane for Delhi. Suu's years of exile were about to begin.

2
THE GANG OF FIVE

THERE is a certain irony in the fact that the house where Daw Khin Kyi and her daughter set up home in Delhi is today the headquarters of the Indian National Congress party—and as such is plastered with smiling images of the woman who, thanks to her close family connection to the man who negotiated the nation's independence, has for years been the most powerful person in India: Sonia Gandhi.

Even in 1960 that elegant bungalow at 24 Akbar Road, in the gracious, leafy heart of Lutyens's Delhi, was in the Nehru family's gift. Jawaharlal Nehru had seen in Suu's father Aung San a comrade and a fellow spirit; when they met in Delhi as Aung San was on his way for crucial negotiations on independence in London, he gave him sound advice and a new set of clothes. When his widow arrived nearly fifteen years later with her daughter to take up her appointment as Burma's ambassador—her son, Suu's surviving brother, Aung San Oo, was by now at boarding school in England and only visited in the holidays—he made sure she was set up in style. The bungalow was temporarily renamed Burma House.

India and Burma were about to move in different directions, the army taking Burma down its lonely path to a peculiar form of single-party socialism while India remained committed to multiparty democracy and was still firmly in the grip of the party that had struggled for and won independence. But in 1960 the similarities between Rangoon and Delhi would have been far more noticeable than the differences.

Flying in from Rangoon, Suu would have noted the same fiery weather, and similar brilliant flowering trees lining the streets; the same broad boulevards, built by the former colonial power and ideal for military maneuvers if required, and a huge military cantonment within easy reach of the city center, just like Rangoon's.

Even the ethnic composition of the capital would not have been unfamiliar, for a majority of Rangoon's population was of Indian descent until Ne Win began compulsory repatriation. A dozen years after both countries had gained independence, traveling from Rangoon to Delhi was like moving from the provinces to the center. English was the lingua franca of the elite, a language Suu was already quite at home with, thanks to the English Methodist High School; the privileges of the political and diplomatic caste she belonged to were quite as much taken for granted as the poverty of the masses; and in both cities modern Western culture seeped in, filtered but not entirely blocked by distance and Asian morality.

Yet Delhi was a center as emphatically as Rangoon was a province, and Suu's four years in the city gave her a perspective on the land of her birth; her discovery of Gandhi, Rabindranath Tagore and the other giants of India's struggle for political and cultural emancipation were to prove a vital stage in her intellectual development, one which bore fruit twenty years after she left India for England.

India and Burma both shook off British rule in the late-1940s, within five months of each other; but India had borne the colonial yoke for the best part of three centuries—with consequences for the nation's development that Suu slowly came to appreciate as Burma grew steadily more oppressive and claustrophobic under army rule.

But for the time being what mattered was that she was abroad, but without the disorientating sense of being an alien. She was fifteen and a half on arrival, and her mother enrolled her in the closest Delhi equivalent to the school she had just left, run not by American Methodists but Irish Catholic nuns: the Convent of Jesus and Mary, with sections for boys and girls, "separated appropriately by the cathedral," as one of her best friends put it.

That friend was Malavika Karlekar. The daughter of a senior Delhi civil servant, she was to remain close to her for the next seven years, and is still a friend today. She and Suu formed two-fifths of what Malavika called "a gang of five," their friendship forged in the rigors of "a dreadful school." "I don't think Suu liked it either," she added.

"I soon hated my new school and till well into adulthood would avoid going anywhere near it," Malavika wrote in a memoir of her childhood. "I hated the teachers . . . and though I made friendships that have lasted through the years, felt constantly inadequate."[1]

Although the school was packed with students from different religious backgrounds, many of them Hindus, the Irish Jesuits tirelessly thrust

Roman Catholic Christianity down their charges' throats. "There was no proselytization but when the gong rang at midday we were all made to kneel and say the Angelus, we had to say the Lord's Prayer in the morning, and Hail Mary," Malavika remembered. "Scripture was a compulsory subject for the Senior Cambridge exam, and we studied the Gospel according to St. Mark. Though not an official subject for the final examination, there was also Moral Science, a hodgepodge of dos and don'ts, all with a strong Christian undertone."

Some teachers were also racially condescending, a reminder that the entrenched racism of colonialism was only a few years in the past. Their English teacher was called Mrs. Ince: "a good teacher," Malavika concedes, but a racial snob. "One day, Mrs. Ince had the arrogance to punish the entire class for something or other and shout, 'What kind of families do you girls come from?' at a class of forty-plus girls standing with their heads down. She was greeted by silence from the daughters of senior armed forces personnel, bureaucrats, diplomats and businessmen. Clearly we were not taught to question or answer back—either at home or in school."

Malavika continued, "The best thing about school was the new set of friends I made": three Indians and Suu. Previous friendships were thrust into the margins: "Life with my school friends took over."

Despite having flown in from the other end of the ex-empire, Suu was embraced without any strain. "She was not at all exotic," Malavika recalled in an interview at Delhi's Habitat Center, "and she was extremely plain! You wouldn't ever think so, but she was extremely plain. She would come to school in the ambassadorial Mercedes driven by Wilson, their driver, her hair in two neat plaits and just a trace of arrowroot on her face." What looked like arrowroot was actually *thanaka*, a paste produced by grinding a type of tree bark, which has been used by Burmese women for centuries as a face cream.

Soon the five of them—Malavika, Suu, Anjali, Kamala and Ambika—were spending much of their free time together, outside school as well as in. Malavika said:

> There was a lot of coming and going between people's homes. We were very close, as kids are. Her mother was a friend of my parents: It was a very small society. The five of us would spend lazy Sunday afternoons gorging

on delicious khao suey, rice with prawns, at Suu's house. Daw Khin Kyi would get this great big meal organized, she'd be there and she'd come and say hello to us. We were scared of her: Suu was under her strict supervision.

We never felt Suu was any different from us [. . .] We didn't talk about Burma or the fascination of her father, but her mother would say to her, you must remember who you are. Of course we knew who her father was, my parents all knew about Aung San, it was part of the postcolonial discourse in South Asia. There's no question about that. But to us she was no different from any of the rest of us. It wasn't, "Oh, she's the daughter of an assassinated leader"; rather, "She's the daughter of an ambassador."

While we were always aware that she was the daughter of the maker of modern Burma, she never spoke of a life in politics. In fact, if I remember right, her interests were highly literary. But what I do remember is her upright posture, never an adolescent slouch, and great pride in lineage. "I will never be allowed to forget whose daughter I am," she would often say. History proved her right.

Harriet O'Brien, the daughter of a British diplomat then based in Delhi, visited 24 Akbar Road around this time and was powerfully struck by the refined atmosphere.

"Delhi, characterized by much heat and disorder, seemed to evaporate as we walked into the Burmese Residence," she wrote years later.[2]

The living room was divided by elegant lacquer screens and was cool and very exotic with finely worked silverware on coffee tables. India outside was dirty and earthy in comparison to the neat and delicate sophistication of Daw Khin Kyi and her house. She wore longyi and aingyi and her hair was pulled back into a tight bun on the top of her head where it was ornamented with an ivory comb, a gold pin and a single flower.

In a later interview, O'Brien recalled the same occasion: "Her daughter appeared and was introduced simply as Suu. I remember being struck by how she plunged into the conversation about politics. She was seventeen or eighteen and was already a commanding person . . . Her mother was shrewd, funny and generous; she said she felt that Suu was surrounded by people who deified her father, which she didn't think was a good thing. Her mother was a bit more relaxed than Suu. You could have a good chuckle with her. Suu was more correct."[3] Erect, correct, obedient, "under her mother's strict supervision," "extremely plain" . . . so far in her story there are few glimpses of the woman who would one day galvanize her nation. Perhaps the docile, slightly hangdog impression that emerges from these years was the fault of those nuns. But soon all that was to change.

After two tough years under the thumb of the Jesuits, high school was over and all five friends went on to Lady Sri Ram College, Delhi's first degree college for girls. For Malavika it was a great improvement.

"The Convent of Jesus and Mary was horrible in the sense that I felt I was in a straitjacket," she said. "So when we went to Lady Sri Ram, which again was like a nunnery, we thought we'd come to heaven. All our respective interests and talents flowered, Suu writing plays, all of us acting . . ."

In Delhi's rather buttoned-up, old-fashioned society—"we had post-colonial Victorian upbringings," Malavika said, "more than half a century after the great lady passed on"—Lady Sri Ram was a breath of fresh, relatively modern air. Founded only six years earlier, and with three hundred students, it offered Delhi's brightest young upper-class ladies proper first degree courses in serious subjects, in surroundings that allowed them considerable freedom.

"Lady Sri Ram was different in that you didn't have to wear uniform," Malavika went on. "There were horrible gates that were locked and you weren't allowed out of them, but there was no uniform, we wore saris and we could do what we liked; for example there was a canteen where we could go and sit. It was just so different."

Although Malavika echoes Suu's own assessment of herself as a girl with the literary bug, Suu took political science at the college—but then so did her friends. "All five of us studied Political Science," said Malavika. "I wanted to do Chemistry honors because that's what my father had done and I had got a distinction in that at the Convent, but my father said, 'Chemistry . . .?' Remember, this was in the early Sixties. You don't do science, you don't go all the way to the dirty great university and hang around with boys, you go to a nice girls' college and do Political Science."

There was a similar prejudice, Malavika remembers, against studying English. "Suu was a reader, and I think that English Literature was more of an interest for her than Political Science. She had a literary bent and a literary mind—why she went into Political Science I don't know—but for some reason reading English Literature in those days was regarded as something we shouldn't be doing. I don't know why."

But although the girls' parents had strong opinions about what their daughters should and should not study, there is no sense that they wanted to circumscribe their ambitions. Like the parents of Suu's friends in Rangoon, these were the most progressive and Westernized people in the city, and hoped and intended that their daughters, while remaining genteel and cultured, would go on to further study and then into significant careers.

Meanwhile Lady Sri Ram allowed them, in the most genteel way, to let their hair down. "We were all the teachers' pets," admitted Malavika. "We were good students, nice obedient girls from appropriate homes. We didn't cut classes. We were not rebellious against our teachers—there was no arguing about Plato's *Republic*, or why did Rousseau say this rather than that—none of that . . ."

But there was clowning—and Malavika gives a tantalizing glimpse of the funny, irreverent Suu who was later to tease both her tormentors and her supporters in Burma—the self-aware, self-mocking Suu who was to share so many jokes with Ma Thanegi as they traveled around the country.

"She wrote this spoof on *Antony and Cleopatra*," she recalled. "It was very cleverly done. She had an extremely intelligent turn of phrase. And she certainly acted, in the usual ham-handed manner we all did . . ." A couple of photos of the production survive, with Suu erect and very elegant in a waisted satin robe and sandals, and with a haughty look on her face. Malavika firmly denied that Suu played Cleopatra, but to judge by the appearance of the girls in the cast photograph, she seems the most plausible candidate for the part.

"In a sense Lady Sri Ram was a finishing school," said Malavika. "But that's not entirely true: My family had a long tradition of Oxbridge and that's what my father wanted me to do. It wasn't as if he was going to shove me off into an arranged marriage or anything. No way." Instead Malavika, like Suu, was to take a degree in Politics, Philosophy and Economics at St. Hugh's College, Oxford.

While the rest of the gang remained at Lady Sri Ram for two years and emerged with degrees, Suu stayed only one year, and much of it she spent applying for and then preparing for her move to England. The British High Commissioner in Delhi at the time was Sir Paul Gore-Booth; he and his wife Lady Pat Gore-Booth had been friends of Daw Khin Kyi when Sir Paul was posted at the embassy in Rangoon. Now they very gladly acceded to Daw Khin Kyi's request to act as her daughter's guardians while she was in England.

Although Suu was so warmly accepted by her Indian friends, this girl from the edge of the empire had a lot to learn—and India had a lot to teach her. She and her mother were on friendly terms with Prime Minister Jawaharlal Nehru, though he was aging now and preoccupied with the problems that were shortly to flare up into war, first with China and then (after his death) again with Pakistan. She also met his daughter Indira, soon to become prime minister herself, and her sons Sanjay and Rajiv.[4]

Suu and her mother of course had Burmese friends, too, including a monk called U Rewata Dhamma who had come to India to study in Varanasi, and who many years later was to play a significant role during Suu's detention. But their social set stretched far wider than that, encompassing the whole diplomatic strata of the city. Given the fame of Daw Khin Kyi's table, the generosity of her hospitality and her qualities as a hostess—"always full of good gossip about the latest political intrigues which she dispatched with much wit and humor," as Harriet O'Brien recalled of her a few years later in Rangoon—24 Akbar Road must have been as lively a political salon in those years as 25 Tower Lane in Rangoon had been while Aung San was alive.[5]

It is a little-known fact—little known except to those who have lived there—that Delhi is a very intellectual town. The conversation at dinner parties in the smart districts of London is never far from degenerating into chatter about property prices and celebrities, no matter how brainy the guests. Delhi, by contrast, where the intellectual elite has a sort of copper-bottomed stability guaranteed by the caste system, is much readier to plunge into the sort of political, philosophical or religious questions that are taboo on the other side of the world. And Suu, straight-backed, wide-eyed, and with an increasingly well-stocked mind, was paying attention.

And she was learning to hold her own, as Harriet O'Brien noticed. In Rangoon, although the sexes were in many ways relatively equal, youth deferred to age, women did not contradict men, and harmony was valued over the contentious pursuit of truth. In Delhi Suu learned, at an impressionable age, the ways of "the argumentative Indian": the Indian delight in passionate, long-winded and often ferocious discussion, with no concern for the tender feelings of those on the other side of the table.[6] It became a part of her character—one that was to cause her endless trouble twenty years later, back in the far more protocol-heavy atmosphere of Burma.

In 1962 the trajectories of India and Burma split apart permanently: In India the Congress under Nehru won another general election, though with a reduced majority, while in Burma General Ne Win launched a carefully planned and all-but bloodless coup d'état and propelled the nation down the Burmese path to socialism. Suu must have asked herself why the two countries—both steeped in Asian philosophy and wisdom, both recently freed from the colonial yoke —should have such contrasting modern destinies. Studying the lives of Gandhi, Nehru himself, Nirad C. Chaudhuri and particularly Tagore, she was already noting the differences and ruminating on the different results they produced.

There was the English language—regarded as a colonial imposition in Burma, and one that was only grudgingly accepted, while for educated Indians it was a vital and ready tool, to be appropriated and used. There was the willingness in India to accept Western ideas without surrendering your own, and the self-confidence and creativity to make from the two a new synthesis. Tagore and Gandhi had had a serious falling out, but Nehru, the family friend of Suu and her mother, succinctly expressed what the two great men shared in common, in words written during his imprisonment in the Second World War.

"Both in their different ways had a world outlook," Nehru wrote in his book *The Discovery of India*, "and both were at the same time wholly Indian. They seemed to represent different but harmonious aspects of India and to complement one with the other."[7]

They were also giants of their age—and Suu cast her eyes homeward in vain to find any contemporary Burman of comparable stature. Back home General Ne Win was rapidly closing the nation's doors and windows, expelling the Indian population, closing down the newspapers and the opposition political parties and imprisoning those who spoke out against him. Meanwhile in Delhi Suu was discovering the great cry of freedom, written in English, of Rabindranath Tagore:

> Where the mind is without fear and the head is held high;
> Where knowledge is free;
> Where the world has not been broken up into fragments by narrow domestic walls;
> Where words come out from the depth of truth;
> Where tireless striving stretches its arms towards perfection;
> Where the clear stream of reason has not lost its way into the dreary desert sand of dead habit;
> Where the mind is led forward by Thee into ever-widening thought and action—
>
> Into that heaven of freedom, my Father, let my country awake.[8]

3

AN EXOTIC AT
ST. HUGH'S

A UNG SAN SUU KYI's timing, like her father's, has always been
good. She left her homeland just in time to be spared the slow death
of her country by military rule. She arrived in Delhi in time to experience
the last years of Nehru and India's transition from dynastic politics. And
she arrived in England in the middle of the biggest explosion of popular
culture the country had ever seen.

It was 1964, the year the Beatles had number 1 hits with "Can't Buy Me
Love," "A Hard Day's Night" and "I Feel Fine." Harold Wilson became
Labor prime minister one month after her arrival, ending "thirteen wasted
years of Tory rule." Men's hair was creeping down to their shoulders, their
trousers were acquiring bell-bottoms and their shirt collars expanding to
the point of absurdity. Skirts were racing up girls' thighs, and erotic boots
were closing the gap. Dingy, foggy, smoky London, gloomy and sarcastic,
woke up to find it was suddenly trendy. A man called Moulton invented
a bicycle with tiny wheels.

And Suu blossomed like a lotus flower.

She had left Lady Sri Ram College after only one year, while the rest of
the Gang of Five stayed a further year to complete their first degrees there.
And when Malavika saw Suu again—they were to take the same course at
St. Hugh's, Oxford, but one year apart—her friend's transformation was
remarkable.

"This sophisticated Suu emerged," she remembered. "Before she had
worn her hair in a ponytail, but now she cut it in a fringe, she wore these
tight white trousers and had a Moulton bike . . ."

Back in Rangoon, Suu's old classmate Tin Tin helped out a painter
friend who was looking for a model: He wanted a pair of hands to paint.
But when the smart new Suu returned for a visit, the friend took one look
at her and pleaded with her to sit for a portrait. "I was really annoyed!"
said Tin Tin. "Suu looked so beautiful with jasmine in her hair and the

fringe—she painted Suu's portrait and it was very, very nice . . . The ugly duckling had turned into a swan."[1]

On her arrival in London, Suu stayed for a few weeks at the Chelsea home of her guardians, the Gore-Booths, then went up to Oxford as a fresher at St. Hugh's to start her course in Politics, Philosophy and Economics.

She made an immediate splash. Large-scale immigration from the Indian subcontinent had yet to get under way: England was still predominantly a white, Anglo-Saxon country, and Suu, who may have been the first student in the history of the college to turn up for classes in longyi and aingyi, was petite, beautiful and exotic.

She had changed from a stiff, over-protected adolescent into an elegant and fashionable young woman. Shankar Acharya, an Indian student who was also studying PPE, a friend of Malavika and her gang, got to know Suu well during her first year, though they were never more than friends. But he conceded, "Every male who met Suu had a little bit of a crush on her. So let's not pretend that that dimension was totally absent."[2]

Yet although something in the Sixties' air had brought on Suu's transformation—her release from Daw Khin Kyi's strict supervision was doubtless another factor—she found herself strongly out of sympathy with the moral relativism growing rampant all around her, of which Swinging London was the most famous manifestation. Malavika described the mores in which she and her friends in Delhi's elite were raised as "post-colonial Victorian" and there is something of the prim and puritanical Victorian about the way Suu reacted to her new environment. But if it had only been that, if she had just been a provincial person with a lot of catching up to do, she might have shed those attitudes after a while, as others did. Instead, as her new English friends were to discover, her moral certainties were firmly rooted.

"She had strong views about her country, and about right and wrong," said Robin Christopher, another Oxford contemporary and friend. "She had a high sense of moral rigor, an almost visible sense of moral purpose. She would not do anything that she considered was wrong: She just wouldn't! That shone through in an almost naïve way, but always touched with humor." But where did her certainties come from? "She was very widely read in literature—it was she who introduced me to Jane

Austen, and me an Englishman," he said. And as Christopher saw it, Suu's morality was "a mixture of her own traditional Burmese background and identification with bits of English literature. It was very curious . . ."[3]

Over the years, a handful of Suu's women friends have been strongly enough affected by Suu to record their memories of the friendship with a special eloquence and affection. Ma Thanegi in Rangoon many years later was one; and at St. Hugh's she encountered another. She was Suu's close contemporary, a few months older but starting the same course in the same term. Her name was Ann Pasternak Slater, the niece of the great Russian novelist.

"We got to know each other in Oxford, as freshwomen at St. Hugh's College, in 1964," Ann wrote in a memoir of the friendship.

> I have to admit that I first approached her simply because she was so beautiful and exotic. She was everything I was not. I came from an Oxford home and Oxford schooling . . . I had spent the long summer between school and university in statutory fashion—hitching round Greece, picking grapes and maize in Israel, traveling deck-class across the Mediterranean with *Anna Karenina* for a pillow. Suu's tight, trim, longyi and upright carriage, her firm moral convictions and inherited social grace contrasted sharply with the tatty dress and careless manners, vague liberalism and uncertain sexual morality of my English contemporaries.[4]

How did Suu herself regard Oxford, and herself in it? For most British students, to gain a place at Oxford or Cambridge was and remains the great prize, the foundation of a good career, a priceless opportunity to build a network of useful contacts; it is an achievement in its own right, cause for jubilation. Yet there is nothing in the record to suggest that Suu saw it this way.

She did not appear to be in awe either of Oxford or of England: She was doing what her mother wanted her to do, and what a girl of her age and class and intellect was capable of. And far from being a social climber, she seemed to pick her friends merely on the basis of liking them.

"When I first got to know her as a student I can remember her talking very proudly about her father, and teaching me how to pronounce her name," Pasternak Slater said in an interview at her home in Park Town, opposite Suu and Michael's last family home in Oxford.[5] She continued:

All of that was a very important part of her total personality. But she was not a social climber in the least. She was extremely sort of democratic in her friendships. They were multiracial and included a Ghanaian girl who I didn't find very interesting, outside the Indian social and intellectual elite who were the other people she knew.

Then there was the matron of St. Hugh's who she was very kind to and who was very kind to her, and an elderly lady, a friend of our family, who was a terrible bore, a single Jewish spinster artist who Suu was extremely kind to, always hospitable and always polite—just as she was, with less effort I hope, to my mother, who was another foreign oddity.[6] In this way she made friends with people who were of no possible use to her, and she was not looking over their shoulders at a party or something, on the contrary.

Suu was an anomaly from the outset: an exotic belle who showed no interest in testing the value of her looks and breeding—who on the contrary was fiercely hostile to the prevailing morality of the university.

Suu had arrived at the most sheltered and peripheral of Oxford's five single-sex women colleges, founded by Elizabeth Wordsworth, great-niece of the poet, in 1886. It lacked the classic medieval cloisters of the city's more venerable colleges, and its buildings were unremarkable and generally undistinguished. In compensation it was endowed with spacious grounds and plenty of trees and greenery.

Its north Oxford location "was popularly dismissed as 'too far out,'" wrote Pasternak Slater in her memoir of Suu, "a full three minutes" bike ride from Balliol or St. John's," and the college had "a demeaningly high reputation for hockey. As freshers we were housed in the heavy main building. Dark brown doors; long, dim corridors; bleak sculleries where the homelier students simmered hankies and bedtime cocoa."

Talk of sexual liberation was all around—this was, after all, four years after the Lady Chatterley trial and two years after the Beatles' first LP— but at St. Hugh's at any rate it was rarely more than talk: For most of the freshers it was more a torment than a promise.[7] "When we first arrived," Pasternak Slater's memoir continued,

> there was an active myth that news of the rare male visitor used to be tapped out on the central heating pipes running from room to room. Only a decade or two previously, another rumor ran, when men came visiting, the women's beds had to be moved out into the corridor until their guests

had left. We certainly had to be in by 10 PM, or sign a late pass releasing us until midnight at the latest. A warren of nervous adolescent virgins and a few sexually liberated sophisticates made for an atmosphere airless and prickly as a hot railway compartment.

In this setting Suu was delightfully antithetical, an original who was at once laughably naïve, and genuinely innocent. All my memories of her at that time have certain recurring elements: cleanliness, determination, curiosity, a fierce purity. How do I see her? Eyebrows furrowed under a heavy fringe, shocked incredulity and disapproval: "But *Ann! . . .*" We are in the basement laundry room, starching piles of longyis and little sleeveless blouses. She is teaching me to iron. She is teaching me to eat rice neatly by hand . . . She is showing me how to carry off long dresses plausibly . . . She taught me to twist and tie a longyi round my inappropriately broad, unoriental waist; to sit on the floor, legs tucked away so that not even an ankle showed; to walk upstairs with only a slight furl of skirt twitched aside, not a great heaved armful in the English manner. Even with familiarity, much remained exotic—her proud parentage, above all. But no less evocative now is the tiny tuft of silky hair under her chin, the block of sandalwood she ground for face powder, the abundant scraps of sample silk she collected for dress trimmings, the fresh flower worn daily in her high pony-tail . . .

There were tea parties of interminable oriental decorum, whose wit and finesse were imperceptible to my coarse western ear. And then the long night gossip in other students' rooms, where Suu's assumptions seemed merely absurd.

Everyone was on the hunt for boyfriends, many wanted affairs, sex being still a half-forbidden, half-won desideratum. Being laid-back about being laid was de rigueur—except that most of us were neither laid back nor laid. There was excitement and anxiety about the unknown, an atmosphere of tense inexperience dominated and dragooned by the few vocal and confident sexual sophisticates. It was extremely difficult to preserve any kind of innocence in such a setting. To most of our English contemporaries, Suu's startled disapproval seemed a comic aberration. One bold girl asked her, "But don't you want to sleep with someone?" Back came the indignant reply—"No! I'll never go to bed with anyone except my husband. Now? I just go to bed hugging my pillow." It raised a storm of mostly derisive laughter.[8]

If Suu's reaction to the new moral consensus ushered in by the pill struck her Oxford contemporaries as hilariously anachronistic, her shock at the ethical quagmire in which she had landed was unfeigned.

England might have been the colonial oppressor, but both in Rangoon and Delhi she had learned that it was also the fount of learning and wisdom, the land of Jane Austen and George Eliot, of John Locke and Wordsworth and John Stuart Mill. Gandhi, asked for his opinion about Western civilization, said he thought it would be a good idea, but that was just a quip: He carried around one of the works of John Ruskin, and his social philosophy was based as much on primitive English socialism as on anything suggested by the Vedas.[9] But on her first direct encounter with England, not in some benighted slum but at the high altar of scholarship, Suu learned that the moral values with which she identified England were crumbling.

For the first time she found herself in a country where Aung San and the Burmese independence struggle meant very little; and where Buddhism meant less than nothing to the vast majority, while those few who thought they understood it were mostly quite wrong. It was a moment of lonely self-definition. If we can locate the moment when Suu discovered the need to dig in her heels and declare her own moral convictions, however mocking or baffled the reaction, this was it.

At least one of her teachers found her unforgettable for that reason. Yet even Mary Warnock, the distinguished philosopher, could only make a failed, groping attempt to work out what she was all about.

Reviewing a book about Suu many years later, she wrote:

Aung San Suu Kyi was, briefly, a pupil of mine when she was reading for the honors school of PPE.

She was unlike any undergraduate I had taught before or have taught since. She was highly intelligent and articulate, though quiet and enormously polite . . . She was totally untouched by the sexual aspirations of her friends, naive in a way, but sure-footed and direct in all her dealings. She was also extraordinarily easily amused, and found many things hilarious, not least her philosophy tutorials.

She had been brought up severely by her mother in a Buddhist tradition. I never knew how religious, in the ordinary sense, she was. Once in the course of a very standard tutorial on personal identity, starting from the text of John Locke, we . . . were considering the proposition, put forward by Locke, that one is the same person only as that person whose past acts one can remember. Suu said, "But I am my grandmother." Her [tutorial] partner and I fell upon her with questions about how she knew this. She smiled, with a look of incredible mischief, and refused to be drawn.[10]

Suu was discovering that, despite close encounters with Asia going back some three hundred years, Britain, as represented by the brains she found around her at St. Hugh's, had largely failed to get to grips with Asian religious and philosophical ideas. If a philosopher as distinguished as Warnock could write hazily about "a Buddhist tradition" yet be amazed that a practicing Buddhist should subscribe to a belief in reincarnation, what could she hope for from her peers?

"Morality," ventured Warnock, seeking to put Suu's beliefs in a nutshell, "consists in aspiring to the traditional Buddhist virtues, especially loving-kindness and honesty. She is a living illustration of the truth that to be moral entails essentially wanting to be good, rather than bad." It would be hard to imagine a lamer attempt to sum up the truths of Buddhism. Listening to such stuff, the "enormously polite" Suu must have heaved a quiet sigh and bitten her lip. What would be the point, with this Oxford philosopher, of, say, proposing a discussion of the basic principles of Theravada Buddhism—of the three characteristics of conditioned beings, for example, namely suffering, impermanence and non-self? Better to save your breath.

*

Yet if Suu found Oxford intellectually frustrating and in steep moral decline, she did not react by retreating into her Burmese shell. On the contrary, she was quite as determined to master the exotic customs of the country as she had been to climb up to the glass roof of 25 Tower Lane with her brother fifteen years before. Ann Pasternak Slater wrote:

> She was curious to experience the European and the alien, pursuing knowledge with endearing, single-minded practicality. Climbing in, for instance. Social kudos came with climbing into college after a late date. One actress friend was a precociously blasé habitué of late-night scramblings: By her second year she spent full nights and days away from college; by the third she was breaking college rules by renting a pad shared by a variety of boyfriends. After two demure years in Oxford, Suu wanted to climb in too, and requested a respectable friend to take her out to dinner, and then—as any gentleman should—hand her over the crumbling college garden wall. No infringement of university regulations could have been perpetrated with greater propriety.[11]

Pasternak Slater also identified the precise moment of Suu's white jeans metamorphosis—and the very practical reason for it. It was the summer of 1965: Suu had just emerged from her first northern winter, which must have struck her South Asian soul as unspeakably long and dark; the country was pulsating to the beat of "(I Can't Get No) Satisfaction" by the Rolling Stones, "Mr. Tambourine Man" by the Byrds, "California Girls" by the Beach Boys and the new Beatles album, *Help!* And a cool new Suu emerged. "Most students have bikes," Pasternak Slater wrote, "it is a practical way of getting about, but tricky in a longyi. In the first summer term Suu bought a pair of white jeans and the latest smart white Moulton bike with minute wheels. One sunny evening spent on the sandy cycle-track running alongside the University Parks and that was mastered."

Rather more challenging was the art of punting, in which her Indian friend Shankar Acharya instructed her, and took an embarrassing photograph of her trying to do it.

Like cycling, Pasternak Slater pointed out, punting was "another essential qualification for an Oxford summer," and Suu would not be found wanting. But she quickly discovered that it is more difficult than it looks. "A punt is a flat-bottomed, low-sided tray of a boat," wrote Pasternak Slater. "Its weight, inertia and ungainliness defy description. It is like sailing a sideboard. It really is difficult learning to punt, especially on your own. The boat swings in dull circles that modulate to a maddening headstrong zigzag from bank to bank, until you learn to steer, like a gondolier, by hugging the pole tight against the punt as you push, and letting it swing like a rudder.

"Suu set out, a determined solitary figure in the early morning haze, to return at dusk, dripping and triumphant."[12] But Acharya's snap of Suu afloat seems to have been taken before her mastery was complete. It may be the most unflattering photo of her ever published. The ugly duckling plaits have made a comeback, crowned by a white cap. Her dark jeans are wrinkled, and the profile they give her bears out Pasternak Slater's remark to me that "she was not completely blemishless—she had quite fat thighs and was still quite chubby when I knew her." Rather than the grave, poised, vertical posture recommended by the experts, with the pole held as close to the breast as a walking staff, Suu is bent at the knees and holds the pole in her outstretched hand and looks as if she is planning to vault out of the boat and onto the bank.

Then there was alcohol. Buddhism's Fifth Precept requires the Buddhist to abstain from alcohol. Although it is not exactly a commandment as it is for most Muslims, and plenty of Buddhist laypeople drink in moderation, for Suu it has always been non-negotiable. But at Oxford everyone did it, often to excess, and Suu decided she must try it once. "She was curious to know what it was like," wrote Pasternak Slater.

> At the very end of her final year, in great secrecy, she bought a miniature bottle—of what? Sherry? Wine?—and, with two rather more worldly Indians as *accoucheuses* and handmaids at this rite of passage, retired to the ladies' lavatory in the Bodleian Library. There, among the sinks and the cubicles, in a setting deliberately chosen to mirror the distastefulness of the experience, she tried and rejected alcohol for ever.[13]

Despite her shyness and her strict rules, Suu's circle of friends gradually expanded. Her punting teacher, Shankar Acharya, offered the comfort of familiarity: He was from the same top civil service drawer as her Indian friends in Delhi, but as he had spent the previous four years at school in London, where his father was a diplomat, he was more familiar with British ways.

"She was more comfortable with Indians than with Brits to begin with," he remembered, "because they were similar to her own cultural background, vaguely Victorian."[14] Both he and Suu were studying PPE, and soon after Suu arrived at Oxford they became friends. "Our backgrounds were quite similar and we hit if off easily and well," he said. "These things happen. Basically she had led a sheltered life in terms of dealing with the opposite sex: She had been to an all-girls' college in India, and presumably her life at Oxford was fairly cloistered, too, in terms of going around with boys. I think she was quite a shy person. I was less shy as I had already been in England."

Although Acharya did not deny having "a little bit of a crush" on Suu, "like every male she met," their friendship remained on the calm, platonic plane; soon he was courting the Indian student who later became his wife. When Suu had overcome any awkwardness she experienced in dealing with English people, that sort of relationship, founded on common interests but going no further than simple affection, proved to be one she had a gift for.

Robin Christopher, who later became a diplomat, said of his relationship with Suu, "It wasn't a romance. It was an utterly genuine friendship. But we were very close as friends—she came and spent Christmas with my family, down in Sussex. It was a lovely friendship. We worked together mornings and afternoons and very often had lunch together. I'd see her virtually every day."[15] Suu was close enough to have, Christopher said, "no inhibition about criticizing my choice of girlfriends." But that did not, it appears, mask an ambition to displace them.

In the same summer that she discovered the joy of cycling, Suu had a very different experience which, in the longer perspective of her life, was to be much more significant.

A vitally important figure in Suu's life, almost a guardian angel and certainly a role model, was a middle-aged Burmese woman called Dora Than É. A striking beauty in her youth, and an acclaimed singer, she became nationally famous in the 1930s as one of Burma's first recording stars. When Aung San came to London to negotiate independence, Ma Than É had become friendly with him, and at his request sang at the farewell reception thrown by the Burmese party in England. Also at his request she selected and purchased on his behalf souvenirs for him to take home to Rangoon. When she met Suu many years later she was pleased to learn that the large doll she had chosen for her was still in good shape.

After marrying an Austrian documentary film-maker, Ma Than É moved to Europe, and in the second half of her career had a succession of jobs with the United Nations. The first was in Delhi, where she managed the UN Information Center and became close to Daw Khin Kyi and her family. Then she was transferred to newly independent Algeria, where she set up a similar center in the capital.

She was living in Algiers while Suu was at Oxford, and Suu flew out to meet her there in the summer of 1965, arriving a few days after President Ahmed Ben Bella had been ousted from power in a bloodless coup. The authoritarian backlash to colonial rule that had occurred in Burma after Suu and her mother moved to India was now unfolding before her eyes among the date palms and sand dunes of the Mahgreb. Suu had just turned twenty, and if the dusty texts on politics which she was required to read at Oxford did not inspire her, the striving and suffering she saw all around her in Algiers were a different matter. Here was the politics

of liberation, being enacted before her eyes in all its passion and difficulty. For the first time in her life her sympathies and energies were fully
engaged, however briefly, as a participant in the sort of struggle that she
was to find waiting for her in Burma twenty-three years later.

Suu "was much more interested in getting to meet Algerians and in
what was happening in the country than in the many parties to which she
was invited," Ma Than É wrote later. "We got in touch with an Algerian
organization which ran several projects to help those affected by their
long struggle."[16] Volunteers were needed to help build houses for the
widows of freedom fighters, she learned. Suu joined other volunteers
from around Europe and North Africa laboring on the project at a large
camp and stuck with it for several weeks.

Back at Oxford, her student life resumed. But it was not working out
well. She was committed to a course of study that did not really interest
her, imposed by her mother. "She didn't want to be doing PPE," said Ann
Pasternak Slater, "she tried to change, she wanted to do Forestry, which
would have been useful for Burma, and the stupid Oxford authorities
wouldn't allow her."[17] Then she wanted to do English, which she would have
loved and which (Pasternak Slater is sure) she would have got "a perfectly
good Second for," but they wouldn't allow that, either. In the end she
obtained a third-class degree, which is perhaps an indication of the extent to
which she had lost interest in the subject: Her friends are in no doubt that
she could have done much better. (As she told Alan Clements many years
later, "I would study hard only when I liked the teacher or the subject.")

But she was also living and making new friends, and towards the end
of her second year she fell in love. "She got to know a young Pakistani
student by the name of Tariq Hyder, who went on to join the Pakistani
Foreign Service," Shankar Acharya remembered. "He was in Queen's
College. We knew each other but were not chums."[18] Mr. Hyder, who
recently retired after a distinguished ambassadorial career, and now
writes on foreign affairs in the Pakistani press, declined to be interviewed
for this book. As Suu has never spoken publicly about the affair, it is hard
to know how much it meant to her; but it is clear that her affection for him
lasted a considerable time, and that, at least in the end, he did not requite
it. One university friend mentioned that she was still talking about him
"at least a year after she left Oxford."[19]

Some of her Indian friends did not approve of Hyder.[20] "He was a bit of a sleazeball," said one. "Not a terribly nice guy. Let's put it this way, we weren't terribly happy that Suu was going around with him. He just didn't come across as someone you'd want to be very friendly with." Whether the antipathy was partly a reflection of the ongoing tensions between India and Pakistan, who had fought their second war since independence in 1965, is not clear.

A problem was slowly crystallising for Suu, and her lingering and unhappy love affair with Hyder points it up: Her path ahead was by no means clear. For her friends from the civil service elite of the subcontinent, by contrast, it was plain sailing. The careers of two of them are exemplary.

After obtaining a good degree at Oxford, Shankar Acharya went on to do a PhD at Harvard, which led to an important post at the World Bank. Eleven years later he returned to Delhi, where at the climax of his career he was appointed chief economic adviser to the government—one of the most important civil service jobs in the country. Malavika Karlekar returned to India after graduating from St. Hugh's, where she took up important university positions and edited the *Indian Journal of Gender Studies*. Both of them married Indians who had shared their experience of study in Britain. Back home they slotted neatly into the stimulating and comfortable life of the Indian ruling class.

For other friends like Ann Pasternak Slater the future was even easier to map out. Born and raised in Oxford, she married a fellow student, Craig Raine, who went on to become one of Britain's best-known contemporary poets. Both she and Raine became dons at the university, and today they still live in the house where Ann grew up, five minutes' walk from St. Hugh's.

But no such straightforward course presented itself to Suu. She went back to Rangoon more than once during her undergraduate years, and given her age and beauty and bloodline there was great excitement about finding her a suitable mate. But whether because of Mr. Hyder or for other reasons, the chemistry was not there.

Her school friend Tin Tin was tangentially involved in one attempt. "She would discuss these things with me when she came to Burma," she said.

They were trying to make a match for her with someone from the university, I'm not going to mention names. Unfortunately he was a bad one, and I said, "Oh no, don't think of marrying him, he's an idiot!" His brother was in our class and he was quite intelligent, but a girl is supposed to marry someone older than herself and his elder brother was not so intelligent. I said, "You will be bored, you know," and she said "Okay, okay," because she wasn't in love or anything. I said, "That's my honest opinion but it's entirely up to you . . ."[21]

Suu was in full agreement.

Compared to her friends at Oxford, the choices for Suu were both stark and unappetizing. Soon after coming to power Ne Win had begun closing down Burma's links to the West, banishing the Ford Foundation and the British Council and other similar organizations, banning the teaching of English in schools, making it more and more difficult for Burmese to travel abroad and for foreigners to visit Burma—in every possible way turning the clock back a hundred years to what some sentimental nationalists conceived as the Golden Age of Burmese isolation, before the British turned up and blew the doors off. These policies led slowly and inexorably to the tensions that resulted in the uprising of 1988. But in the meantime they had a more immediate impact for the likes of Suu: They made a return home, after the richness of her experiences in India and England, deeply unappealing.

Yet Burma was once again where the home was, if not the heart: In 1967, the year Suu graduated, Daw Khin Kyi decided to retire as ambassador to Delhi. She was not recalled to Rangoon, but the lack of sympathy between her and the regime made it more and more difficult for her to represent her country. On her return she was served with a tax bill for 40,000 kyats, even though serving diplomats, who were paid risibly small salaries, were exempt from tax. It was a typically petty act of vengeance by the dictator she had spurned.

A diplomat to her fingertips, Daw Khin Kyi never spelled out the true reasons for her decision to retire, but it is likely that, in the developing policies of Ne Win, she saw the steady erosion and betrayal of her husband's legacy. At the same time the ever more extreme political positions taken by her fugitive and estranged brother Than Tun, leader of the outlawed Burma Communist Party, under the influence of Beijing's Cultural Revolution, may well have increased tensions further.

The man who had made an economic success of the army's first bite at power, from 1958 to 1960, was General Aung Gyi—the same Aung Gyi who was to become the first to go public with biting criticism of the regime in 1988, later briefly becoming Suu's colleague at the head of her new party.

Aung Gyi had been a subordinate of Ne Win's in the 4th Burma Rifles during the war, and when the army seized power permanently in the coup of 1962 he was given the job of Minister of Industries, overseeing what was intended to be Burma's rapid industrialization.[22] A moderate socialist, he was in favor of keeping a private industrial and trade sector going in tandem with the nationalized industries.

But Ne Win came increasingly under the influence of another of his former junior officers, Tin Pe, the so-called "Red Brigadier," who favored a far more radical, communist-inspired approach to the economy. In 1963 the Revolutionary Council, which now ran the country, issued its answer to Mao Zedong's *Little Red Book*, entitled *The System of Correlation of Man and his Environment*, "a mixture of Marxism, historical dialecticism and Buddhism" according to the historian Michael Charney, which spelled out the conditions for creating a socialist Buddhist paradise in the country—though, in deference to the Buddhist doctrine of *anicca*, impermanence, it was conceded that this would not be a final but only a provisional paradise.

This document has baffled generations of Burma scholars and is usually described as an indigestible hodgepodge. But its principle message could not be plainer: It parrots the far-left truisms of the People's Republic of China next door—for, as a famous Burmese maxim has it, "When China spits, Burma swims."

Charney summarizes the document's thesis:

> The only reliable classes were those who contributed to the material needs of society, such as the peasants and the industrial workers . . . As these productive forces attempted to change the economic and social system, those whose greed was satisfied by the existing system oppressed the material and spiritual producers. This oppression was responsible for

class antagonisms. To abolish these class antagonisms, the conditions that created them must first be abolished. Only then could a socialist society without exploitation be established . . .[23]

With the publication of *The System* . . . the writing was on the wall for "capitalist road-ers" like Aung Gyi: Tin Pe's economic notions gained more and more prestige, Aung Gyi's various posts were stripped from him, and in June 1965, while Suu was laboring under the Algerian sun as a volunteer, he was arrested.

The way was clear for Tin Pe to enact the sort of root-and-branch communist reforms that had already taken place in China, nationalizing the domestic rice market, the import and export trade and all private companies, from large to tiny: The bitter joke in Rangoon was that even the little noodle carts on the street were ripe for being taken over by the state. Burma's course was set for economic disaster—though of course it did not look like that at the time. Two years later, thoroughly fed up, Daw Khin Kyi headed home from Delhi.

On graduating, Suu could have rejoined her there. But given the way Burma's academic world had been eviscerated, she would have had no prospect of capping her university studies with an appropriate academic career. Or she could have taken the even less attractive course of allowing a matchmaker to find her a suitable boy and buckling down to life as an Asian wife, in what was becoming an increasingly stagnant Asian backwater.

Probably her mother hoped that she would follow one of these two courses. Instead she decided to do something completely different. She may well have encountered opposition: In a letter written years later, she indicates that her mother and brother considered her to be often "wayward" in her choices.[24] But if that was the case now, Suu was grown-up enough to have few qualms about defying the formidable Daw Khin Kyi. And instead of going home she decided to follow the example of her beautiful and charismatic friend Ma Than É, the woman she came to describe as her "emergency aunt," who despite her fame in Burma had left home and made a life abroad, and see what happened.

4
CHOICES

SOME people know exactly where they are going in life, and go there; for others, life is more of a puzzle. Suu's elder brother, Aung San Oo, who was studying electrical engineering at Imperial College in London while Suu was at Oxford—"he has all the angles of his father and none of the charm of his sister" was the tough verdict of a London acquaintance—was one of the former: He proceeded to a career and marriage (to a Burmese woman) in the United States with speed and dispatch, renouncing his Burmese citizenship in favor of American along the way.

Aung San Suu Kyi however was one of the latter. Her puzzlement and difficulty can be sensed in photographs taken of her in those years. In one taken in her Delhi home in 1965 she stands beneath a photograph of her father in uniform. She is elegant in longyi and aingyi and already wears a flower in her hair, but her expression is quite blank; she is merely standing there, as requested. Five years later she attends a party at the home of the daughter of UN Secretary General U Thant in New York. It is quite a grand affair and Suu looks spectacular in a starched white aingyi with baggy sleeves; but while her hostess, Aye Aye Thant, beams at the camera with an animated expression, Suu's gaze, pensive under powerful eyebrows and the famous fringe, is elsewhere, the expression on her full lips almost sulky. She was raised in privileged circumstances, at home in diplomatic enclaves and grand apartments, and she had spent three years in one of the world's great universities. But this world, her blank expression seems to convey, is not my destiny. She was passing through, picking up clues as she went, but well aware that she was miles from her destination.

Her Oxford friend Ann Pasternak Slater worried for her. "Fragmentary memories of that period lie like fanned-out photographs—some of them, indeed, real snaps from her letters," she wrote. "Suu in London, head high in a green armchair, serious, sad, uncertain where to go, all determination and an unknown void to cross . . ."[1]

She left Oxford and took her disappointing degree down to her guardians' place in London, which had been her surrogate home since arriving in England. Lord and Lady Gore-Booth, as they now were, lived in a handsome Georgian house, 29 The Vale, off the King's Road in Chelsea, in one of the most elegant and fashionable corners of London. Suu had a cozy self-contained flat there under the rafters, and was treated like one of the family.

She found part-time work as a tutor, and for a spell also worked as an assistant to Hugh Tinker, a Burma scholar who happened to be a friend of the Gore-Booths. It was a useful connection and one that kept her in touch with events at home. But from the perspective of a career it was a way of treading water, no more.

Pat Gore-Booth, now an elderly lady but still, at the time this book was being researched, deeply engaged in Burmese affairs, regards Suu almost as a daughter. "She called me Di Di," she remembered in an interview with me at her home in London—the affectionate Indian term for "aunty." "She was a great adapter, and became a full member of the family. She was always the first to offer to wash up, she was very interested in cooking . . . She was a very dutiful honorary daughter, she respected Paul very much for his supposed wisdom, his mixture of Irish whimsy and Yorkshire grit. She bore her third-class degree very well—at home she supervised the kids' homework, did the crossword . . . She still retained all the traditional graces of her race and yet she was full of charm and fun and very intelligent."[2]

The traditional good manners so essential in Burma can sometimes convey an impression of servility when translated to the West, and the way some of her English acquaintances describe her, Suu runs the risk of coming across as too good to be true. Yet as Ann Pasternak Slater and her other Oxford friends found out, she had a tongue in her head when required, and no inhibitions about using it. When Suu's brother visited her at her guardians' home, the froideur between the siblings was palpable. "Why were her relations with her brother so bad?" Pat Gore-Booth mused. "Perhaps he was envious of her charm. His English was not nearly as good as hers. They were polite with each other but no more than that."

It was in this period that Suu quietly burned whatever bridges may have remained between her and Burma's military regime. In addition to being a murderous tyrant, Ne Win was also a hypocrite. He imposed a joyless regime on his people yet at the same time he continued to indulge in the pleasures he had forbidden at home on his frequent trips abroad. He married three times, salted away a considerable fortune in Swiss banks, relaxed in Austrian and German spas, went to the races at Ascot and owned several fine homes abroad, including one in Wimbledon.

Yet for all his wealth and power, he would not be able to count the daughter of Aung San among his flatterers: When he summoned both the hero's children to an audience at his Wimbledon home in the spring of 1967, Suu declined the invitation, on the grounds that she was busy preparing for her finals. Pat Gore-Booth, with a lifetime as a diplomatic wife and mother behind her, is in no doubt that this was a faux pas, and that she should have pointed out the fact to Suu at the time. "From a diplomatic point of view, we should have said 'Go,'" she said. "But at the same time we were proud of her independence."[3]

*

Lord and Lady Gore-Booth had twins two years older than Suu called David and Christopher. David Gore-Booth studied at Oxford, then, after graduating, followed his father Paul into the Foreign Office, and crowned his diplomatic career with the post of High Commissioner to Delhi— where in 1997, during the Queen's visit to the subcontinent, he collided spectacularly with Labor Foreign Secretary Robin Cook. Christopher by contrast, who went on to become a croupier, was studying at Durham University, where he became friendly with one of another pair of twins. And on one occasion when Christopher brought this friend down to his parents' home in Chelsea, Suu happened to be present as well, and Christopher introduced them.

A tall, rumpled, gentle, amiable man, Michael Aris was one year younger than Suu though he looked considerably older, and concealed a vast and unusual ambition beneath his air of easy-going geniality. He and his identical twin brother, Anthony, were born in Havana, the sons of an English father, John Aris, and a French-Canadian beauty, Josette Vaillancourt, whom he fell in love with and married while working as ADC to the Governor General of Canada, Lord Tweedsmuir (better known as the thriller writer John Buchan).[4] The twins and their older sister, Lucinda, had a peripatetic childhood between the Italian Alps, Geneva and Peru before settling in London. The twins were sent to a Catholic boarding school, Worth School, where they were taught by Benedictine monks.

After leaving school, Michael went to Durham University to study Modern History. His choice of subject is puzzling because by this time he had become intrigued by a subject well off the track of the curriculum: the culture, language, religion and history of Tibet.

This arcane interest had been accidentally implanted by his father when he brought a Tibetan prayer-wheel back from a trip to India. Michael became fascinated, less by the function of the device—one of the many ways invented by Tibetans to express their devotions—than by the mysterious letters inscribed on a piece of paper he found inside it. As it happened, one of their teachers at Worth School, Andrew Bertie, knew some Tibetan, and helped Michael to decipher it. A lifelong fascination was born.

When Suu came down from Oxford, we know that her unhappy love affair with her fellow student Tariq Hyder was still on her mind, and continued to weigh on it for another year. There was to be at least one other candidate for her love, and Pat Gore-Booth recalled how she got to learn of it. "Paul and I were on a tour of South America," she said, "when we got a message from Suu saying I would like to marry so-and-so, a Burmese man. As a very dutiful honorary daughter, she was not asking permission, just running it past us." But like the Hyder affair this one, too, came to nothing—and just as well, it would seem: Though notionally, like Suu, from the faction opposed to Ne Win, "he proved to be a turncoat," Pat Gore-Booth remembered, "and later became a minister in the regime."

Yet somewhere between these failed liaisons, an interest in the lanky, tousle-haired Aris boy took root and began to grow. And for Michael, it seems, there was never any doubt: This delicate young Burmese lady with an Oxford degree and a flower in her hair was the most enchanting thing he had ever seen. "He was smitten from the word go," said his brother Anthony.[5]

Like many East and Southeast Asians, the Burmese are hostile to foreign liaisons, particularly if they involve the recently departed imperial oppressor. Suu's mother Daw Khin Kyi, however sophisticated and experienced in the ways of the world, was no different from the rest of her race in feeling this way. But for Suu it was all rather different. She had come of age in the sixties, where in the West prejudices of every sort were being discarded. For years she had been moving in cosmopolitan circles, where interracial relationships were common. Her Indian friends were in this respect more hidebound: The pressures and expectations of caste still tended very largely to dictate their choice of partner. In Burma, where caste in the Indian sense does not exist, the chief obstacle to overcome was xenophobia pure and simple—plus the view that, as Norman Lewis put it, "through failure to spend a token period as a novice in a Buddhist monastery, the foreigner has never quite qualified as a human being."[6]

By falling in love with Tariq Hyder, she had already shown her willingness to consider a mate who would have caused all sorts of difficulties back home in Rangoon. There is, after all, no arguing with the human heart. The candidates who were on the face of it more promising had problems of their own: The Burmese youth, dismissed by Suu's friend Tin Tin as an "idiot"; the other Burmese fellow who became a turncoat.

And then there was this Aris boy she was getting to know, and who was already in love with her. The qualities he was to bring to their marriage must have been already apparent: He was considerate, thoughtful, patient. If he was not an alpha male like Tariq Hyder or David Gore-Booth, not exactly ambassadorial material, if he was a touch on the dreamy side, then perhaps that was no bad thing: When she herself was so uncertain about the way ahead, another seeker was perhaps what she needed for her partner, rather than someone like her brother who knew exactly what he wanted and how to get it. With someone like Michael, a woman would stand a chance of building a life on equal terms, rather than merely tagging along.

There was her mother to be brought round: She was firm in her view that Suu should marry someone Burmese. But Suu had lived apart from her mother for three years now, and had learned to stand on her own feet. She had discovered the strength of mind to turn down flat the invitation of the most powerful man in Burma; she would find a way to win her mother over. And in this respect Michael Aris's fascination with Tibet, which would have seemed eccentric to many, was an important asset.

Most people Suu knew at Oxford had only the vaguest notion about the religion in which she had been raised. Michael Aris already knew more about it than any Englishman she had ever met.

*

They began their romance, in fine modern style, by flying off in opposite directions. They were to be united only very briefly over the next three years. The Internet did not exist, international phone calls were prohibitively expensive and reserved for emergencies, so Suu and Michael Aris carried on their love affair by airmail. That they were still together at the end of this period testifies to the strength of their feelings for one another.

It is sometimes an advantage to be fascinated by something that fascinates only a very few other people. Though his degree was in Modern History, Michael employed his spare time at Durham learning as much as he could about Tibet's history, culture, religion and language. "While he was still at Durham he formed a friendship with Hugh Richardson, a great authority on Tibet who had been the last British Resident"—or official representative—"in Lhasa before the Second World War," recalled Michael's brother Anthony, and Hugh "became his mentor."[7] He also came in contact with another outstanding figure in Tibetan studies, Marco Pallis. Now that he had graduated, Michael wanted more than anything to get to the country he knew so much about and become a real expert. But Tibet, never easy to enter, had been totally barred to foreigners since the Chinese communist takeover in 1951.

There were however several "little Tibets" on the fringes of the Tibetan plateau, high in the Himalayas, which preserved the ancient culture and language of the country and which were more readily accessible: Ladakh, for example, now a part of the Indian state of Jammu and Kashmir; Sikkim, at the time a protectorate of India; and Bhutan, an independent Buddhist monarchy, closed to tourists and very little known to the outside world.

With one of those strokes of luck by which careers are made, Marco Pallis learned that the royal house of Thimphu, the Bhutanese capital, was looking for a tutor for the royal children. In Michael Aris he had a young man he regarded as the ideal candidate: already with a considerable knowledge of Tibetan, but with a high level of general education as well. Aris seized his opportunity and set off. He was to remain in Bhutan for six years.

Suu meanwhile flew off the other way, to New York. There was never a more exciting time to be in the Big Apple than the late 1960s, with Andy Warhol and the Velvet Underground, Robert Rauschenberg and the Abstract Expressionists, the Buddhist Beats and the Last Poets and the Black Panthers all competing for attention. But none of this held any appeal for Suu: What induced her to cross the Atlantic was her dear Burmese friend Ma Than É, the famous former singer, who had returned from Algiers and was now working at the headquarters of the United Nations. She invited Suu to share her tiny flat in midtown Manhattan.

There was good reason for the move from the point of view of Suu's career: Despite her poor degree, Ma Than É had persuaded Frank Trager, professor of International Affairs at New York University and an expert on Southeast Asia, to take on Suu as a postgraduate student. She could live down that third, get a postgraduate degree, enjoy a taste of the New World, prove beyond doubt her independence and self-sufficiency—and at the same time relax in the company of her cosmopolitan, worldly wise Burmese friend.

Yet there was a flaw in the strategy, and it is the same flaw that dogged Suu throughout her on-again, off-again academic career. What did she want to study and why? What was the end in view? Her mother had browbeaten her into taking a degree in Politics, Philosophy and Economics, which failed to engage her fully. The university had prevented her from changing to a more congenial subject. And now she had found what appeared to be the perfect way to recoup; but instead she hit the buffers.

Suu began commuting from Ma Than É's apartment uptown in Beckman Place, round the corner from the UN at First Avenue and East 49th Street, to NYU, which was centered around Washington Square in Greenwich Village. But after a few weeks it seemed that it was not working out.

"Getting to and from New York University meant a long bus ride," Ma Than É wrote in an essay about her friend, ". . . and it was a trial for Suu, who was given to giddiness on bus rides. There were also the hazards from toughs who frequented her route from the bus stop across the park to Washington Square and the classes she had to attend."[8] So she simply gave up.

But knowing what we do of Suu's story since 1988, the explanation fails to convince. "I see myself as a trier," Suu told Alan Clements.[9] "I don't give up." And for a trier there would have been ways of sticking to that commitment. Never mind the giddiness-inducing bus: From Ma Than É's flat on Beckman Place it was a five-minute walk to the Lexington and 53rd Street subway stop, then eight stops downtown on the E train to West 4th Street, and a couple of minutes' walk to class from there. New York was rougher in 1968 than it is now, to be sure, and there were many parts where it was unwise for a young female to go alone—but Beckman Place and the NYU campus were not among them. Professor Trager's offer of a postgraduate place would have been like gold dust for an ambitious student. If the commute (it takes less than twenty-five minutes each way) was such a problem, a really motivated student would have found a room of her own close to the campus, and paid the rent by waiting on tables. Ma Than É's account is a kind attempt to save her friend's face, but the true explanation must be that, once again, Suu's heart was not in it.

A more compelling explanation is that, within those few weeks, Suu discovered that Professor Trager was on friendly terms with high officials in the Ne Win regime.[10] She was learning that attentions from the other side of the political fence, such as apparently innocuous invitations to Wimbledon, were to be handled with great care.

But meanwhile the man who was without doubt the greatest Burmese statesman on the international stage since the death of her father was at large and in control just a couple of blocks from her New York home: U Thant, who had been Secretary General of the United Nations since 1961. If the university didn't work out, for reasons of giddiness or something else, perhaps there was a far more promising prospect on the doorstep. "The UN was about six minutes' walk from where we lived," Ma Than É recalled. "Why shouldn't she try for a job there and do her studies later? After applications, recommendations, interviews and the usual delays and difficulties, Suu was in."

*

U Thant is little remembered today, but for anyone growing up in the 1960s he was a figure of enormous fame and stature, his curious name and smooth, sensitive, rather worried-looking features as familiar as those of any national statesman. These were the days, with the cataclysm of world war less than two decades away and the Cold War raging, when earnest intellectuals still dreamed that the United Nations could usher in a new era of World Government, when all conflicts would be resolved without resort to arms. U Thant, who held the closest job ever invented to President of the World, seemed the ideal person to bring it about.

He held the post from 1961 to 1971, thrown in at the deep end when the first holder of the office, Dag Hammerskjöld of Sweden, died in an air crash in the middle of the Cuban nuclear missile crisis—the closest the world has ever come to all-out nuclear war. U Thant's sharp wits and cool, low-profile negotiating skills helped pull Kennedy and Khrushchev back from the brink. He went on to play a key role in ending the war in the Congo, and had a crucial part in resolving many other international conflicts. U Thant was also centrally involved in launching the UN's humanitarian, environmental and development missions. In 1965 he was awarded the Jawaharlal Nehru Award for international understanding. While in office he successfully spiked the Soviet Union's proposal that there should be three Secretary Generals, one representing each of the major power blocs, a recipe for permanent impasse. Perhaps the greatest testimony to his charm and suppleness is the fact that at the end of his term, already gravely ill, he was still on speaking terms with the leaders of both Russia and the United States.

The UN's gain was Burma's loss: If democracy had survived in Burma it is hard to imagine that U Thant would not have been at the center of it. Norman Lewis, who met him in Rangoon a decade before his dramatic elevation, was impressed: As Permanent Secretary at the Ministry of Information in 1949, he advised the English writer on his prospective journey around the country. U Thant "saw no reason why I should not go wherever I wished," Lewis wrote. "Later I found that . . . this was his first experience of a request to travel about the country . . . any doubts were veiled beneath more than even the normal measure of Burmese charm."[11]

Even at this early stage of his career, U Thant had mastered the art of spinning awkward news: "U Thant said that the railway service from

Rangoon to Mandalay was working. It was perhaps a little inconvenient because of a break in the line. Proper arrangements were made to carry passengers across the gap . . . either in lorries or bullock carts, and if they were sometimes held up it was only to extract a kind of toll. That was to say, no violence was ever done . . ."[12]

As his record at the UN—and his rapidly deteriorating relations with the United States, as the Vietnam War span out of control—proved, U Thant was profoundly hostile to colonialism and neo-colonialism, and as Secretary General he did everything he could to make the newly independent ex-colonies feel at home in the UN. But he was not an embittered nationalist fanatic like Ne Win, not bent on tearing down the good that the colonialists had done along with the bad, and Ne Win's hostility to him is further proof of his small-mindedness. U Thant represented that cadre of civil servants, so important in the creation of independent India and so badly missed, because so few in number, in Burma, who were able to carry on, administratively speaking, where the British left off. "Thant's dream," wrote his grandson, Thant Myint-U, "had been to become a civil servant in the British Burma administration."[13] Instead he became right hand man to prime minister U Nu, his friend since university, secretary of the Asian-African Conference at Bandung, Indonesia, in 1955, and a founding father of the Non-Aligned Movement which the conference inspired.

For most of the 1950s he was U Nu's secretary, his closest confidant and adviser, keeping his often wayward and capricious friend to the diplomatic script. Then in 1957, in the waning days of U Nu's last government, U Nu asked him to go to New York to be Burma's permanent representative. Whether or not Ne Win—who the following year took over control of the country, in his dry run for military rule—was behind the proposal, its effect was to remove the prime minister's most capable adviser from national politics for good. Four years later U Thant was catapulted into what was then regarded as the most powerful job in the world.

*

This was the man whom Suu now found herself working for, in a humble and very junior capacity, as part of the staff supporting something called the Advisory Committee on Administrative and Budgetary Questions—"in real life no less dreadful than it sounds," according to Thant Myint-U, who himself later became a UN diplomat.[14] She also got a taste of the real New York by volunteering, many hours every week, at Belleview Hospital, a short bus ride from home, where she read or chatted to or otherwise helped out some of the many prostitutes, derelicts and incurable patients that the enormous hospital housed.

If she ever got seriously homesick, she was now within easy traveling distance of the most influential and civilized colony of Burmese anywhere in the world outside Rangoon—U Thant's gracious home overlooking the Hudson river, which was also home to his children and grandchildren and where Suu and Ma Than É were sometimes invited for Sunday lunch or family birthdays. The Secretary General's official residence was "a rambling seven-bedroom red-brick house, partly covered in ivy and set on a grassy six-acre hillside along the Hudson River," wrote Thant Myint-U, who grew up there.[15]

> On the map it was part of Riverdale, but in most other ways it was a small slice of Burma . . . There was always an assortment of Burmese houseguests, who stayed anywhere from an evening to many months, and a domestic staff (all Burmese as well) of nannies and maids, cooks and gardeners, as one might expect in any Rangoon pukka home. Burmese dancers and musicians sometimes performed at parties on the lawn. A Buddhist shrine with fresh-cut flowers graced a special area on the first floor, and a constant smell of curries drifted out of the always-busy black-and-white tiled kitchen.

"U Thant and his family would be warmly welcoming," Ma Than É remembered—but even when the parties to which they were invited were intimate, the Secretary General declined to be drawn on the political issues of the day.[16] Not for nothing had he succeeded in climbing to the top of diplomacy's greasy pole.

As the most powerful Burmese diplomat in the world, though with no official ties to Rangoon, U Thant was duty bound to keep in the good books of all the different Burmese factions on his doorstep, including the Ne Win appointees at the embassy. Doubtless they and the fiercely anti-regime émigrés among his guests—people such as Ma Than É and Aung San

Suu Kyi—eyed each other venomously over the fish curry: Factionalism, as Aung San had noted many years before, was the besetting vice of the Burmese, and the polarizing policies of Ne Win made it very much worse.

The permanent Burmese representative at the UN in those days, U Soe Tin, was in this respect unusual in that, although umbilically tied to the regime, he maintained friendly relations with those on the other side, and Suu and Ma Than É were often invited to his own, less imposing home in Riverdale for Burmese functions. "We liked him and his wife and children," wrote Ma Than É. "He was a liberal type who did not divide us into sheep and goats . . . At his house it was possible to discuss, debate and argue, sometimes heatedly but in the main with much good nature."[17] But Soe Tin was on Ne Win's payroll and orders were orders—hence one particular, very uncomfortable lunch party the pair of them had to sit through. It was Suu's introduction to the ugly menaces which were the general's political stock-in-trade.

It seemed to Ma Than É like just another run-of-the-mill lunch invitation to Riverdale, arriving during a session of the UN General Assembly. "Some members of the [Burmese] delegation had said they would like to meet us," she wrote.[18] They arrived at Soe Tin's home to find "a whole battery of Burmese ambassadors attending the current General Assembly," all of them seated on chairs and sofas which had been ranged against the walls. Suu was put at one end of the room, seated between two of these worthies, her friend far away. "We made some slight inconsequential remarks," she wrote. "U Soe Tin was smiling politely but looked uneasy. It became clear to me that the company was preparing to sit in judgment on Suu. But for what?"

The chief of the Burmese delegation to the General Assembly took the floor.

How was it that Suu was working for the UN? What passport was she using? Since her mother was no longer ambassador, Suu should have given up her diplomatic passport. Was it true that she had not done so? She must be aware that she was holding her diplomatic passport unlawfully. It was most irregular and should be put right as soon as possible. The whole company listened to this tirade with a sort of sycophantic deference, turning their eyes on Suu and murmuring agreement.

Ma Than É recorded Suu's reply—a very modest dry run, though no one could have guessed it at the time, for her speech before a million people at the Shwedagon more than fifteen years later. She wrote:

> Suu's calm and composure were for me very reassuring. She replied with great dignity and in very quiet tones. She had long ago applied for a new passport to the embassy in London but had not received a reply up to now. She could not say what could be the reason for this extraordinary delay. She had come to New York to study and therefore had used her old passport . . .
>
> The ambassador from London then stood up to confirm that Suu had indeed applied months ago for a new passport . . . All of us in that room knew, of course, of the bureaucratic confusion and incompetence in Burma which had created similar delays . . .[19]

The genteel court-martial ended with the chief delegate, comprehensively humiliated, promising to sort out the confusion when he returned to Rangoon. Suu had learned a useful lesson: Despite her youth and her sex, she was not obliged to kowtow to fools in office.

It is debatable, however, whether she fully appreciated that this was a special dispensation that applied to her and her alone, because of who she was, and not to any disaffected Burmese with the nerve to rock the boat. Ma Than É remembers a friend in the permanent delegation at the UN, one with whom they were in the custom of having knockabout political debates, saying to Suu teasingly one time when he felt she had gone over the top in her critical remarks, "You not only have the courage of your convictions—you have the courage of your connections!" It was the courage that was to carry her all the way from the Shwedagon to house arrest.

*

Buddhism is a curious religion. All the different schools acknowledge the same founding teacher, Gautama, the Seer of the Shakyas, the Enlightened One, and the same teaching, the same Fourfold Noble Truths, the same moral precepts. Most of them have sitting meditation as a central component of the religious practice. But they have been separated from each other for many centuries, since the destruction of the great monasteries and universities of Buddhism in northern India and the disappearance of Buddhism from the Indian mainland. And despite all they hold in common they have had very little to do with each other since. As is the way with all creeds, there is a tendency for adherents of each particular school to believe that they are the ones on the right track, but mutual indifference is the best way to characterise these non-relationships. There is no persecution, as Islam's Sunnis persecute the Shiites and vice versa, no accusations of heresy or efforts to convert—but neither are there ecumenical efforts to build bridges or make compromises.

The most celebrated of those few efforts that there have been is the exception that proves the rule: When the American Buddhist convert Colonel Henry Olcott, who was also the cofounder with Madame Blavatsky of the Theosophical Society, tried to make all the Buddhist branches into one church. He succeeded, in Sri Lanka, in writing a Buddhist Liturgy, accepted by the Buddhist authorities on the island, and he designed the beautiful Buddhist flag, composed of oblong strips, red, pink, white, indigo, saffron, comprising the colors of the Buddhist robes of the different Asian countries, which is vastly popular in Burma even today. But of his efforts to bring all these groups together, little remains. What, they would probably have asked him, is the need?

So although Michael Aris, in faraway Bhutan, was becoming more and more familiar with the Bhutanese variant of Tibetan Buddhism, that didn't in itself bring him materially closer to a young woman steeped in the related but distinct and very different traditions of Theravada Buddhism. Yet something convinced her—perhaps we can just say "love" and leave it at that—that Michael was the man for her.

The two of them had kept in touch by letter since their early meetings in London. What those letters say remains a closely guarded secret. What we do know is that in the summer of 1970, when Aris came home to Britain from Bhutan on holiday, he also visited New York, where he and Suu became formally engaged. The following spring Suu kept a promise she had made and visited him in Thimphu, the Bhutanese capital, where he had now been working for three years and where they planned to live once they were married. The trip went well: Soon afterwards she was writing to thank her brother-in-law-to-be, Anthony Aris, for giving his formal approval to their union—a requirement in the Burmese tradition—while lamenting, though without too much apparent anxiety, the fact that her mother and brother had yet to give theirs.[20] She also expressed her happiness and pride at the prospect of becoming part of a family she was already fond of. "At the end of her third year of service in the UN Secretariat," wrote Ma Than É, "Suu made a choice. She decided that a husband and children would be greatly preferable to a career in the UN, however brilliant it was promising to be."[21]

With six months' more hard slog in a city she had learned to dislike thoroughly before she could start her new life, Suu began writing to Michael with remarkable intensity.[22] During the eight months between her visit to Thimphu and the wedding, she wrote to him more than once every two days: a total of 187 letters.

Some of them were tough letters to write, and tough to receive. If Michael had any doubt that he was marrying a person with very particular baggage, these letters would have removed it.

Given the indifference of one brother and the death of the other in childhood, Suu was the only one of her generation left to carry the family flame. What did that mean? She had no idea. She was not a soothsayer. But she felt the weight of her father's legacy on her shoulders; and she had already discovered what sort of weight it carried in Burmese affairs, even today, more than twenty years after his death. Ne Win would ask her to tea, and whether she accepted or refused, her response mattered. She obtained a humble job in the United Nations, and the passport she carried became a diplomatic incident. This was a weight you could shrug off only by deciding that it didn't matter what your father had said or done or believed: by doing like her brother, becoming a foreign citizen, settling elsewhere and turning your back on the whole thing. But even in the midst of her early adult doldrums, that was not a position Suu showed any sign of adopting.

Marrying an Englishman was not the obvious way to stay true to the legacy, it would not make it any easier to stay true to it—but she was in love and that was that. So the only thing to do was, by the force of her will, to ensure that she did stay true, regardless, and that her fiancé was well aware of that and fully accepted what it might mean, well in advance. Because otherwise this marriage was not going to happen. It was the mother of all pre-nups.

"Recently I read again the 187 letters she sent to me in Bhutan from New York," Aris wrote twenty years later.[23] Then he quoted from the letters: lines that, among Suu's worldwide supporters and admirers, have become famous:

> I only ask one thing, that should my people need me, you would help me to do my duty by them.

> Would you mind very much should such a situation ever arise? How probable it is I do not know, but the possibility is there.

Michael Aris accepted these terms without demur. There could be no finer proof of his love. They married in London on January 1, 1972.

SUPERWOMAN

T HEY were married in a Buddhist ceremony in the Gore-Booths' home in Chelsea, guests wrapping sacred thread around the couple as they sat cross-legged on the floor while a Tibetan lama, Chime Youngdroung Rimpoche, blew on a conch shell. "It was a lovely ceremony," recalled Sir Robin Christopher, one of Suu's closest friends from Oxford. "I was one of those who walked around them with the holy thread. What a wonderful bond that was to prove to be!"[1] It was charmingly romantic: two anglophone Buddhists, conjoined a few hundred yards from the World's End and Gandalf's Garden—before flying off together to make their home in Shangri-La.[2]

But few romantic stories are quite as enchanted as they appear, and there is none without its shadow. The ceremony was a gracious nod to Suu's roots and Michael's fascination with Buddhism, but there were absences that were ominous given Suu's stature as the Bogyoke's only daughter. The Burmese ambassador did not show up: The froideur between Suu and the Ne Win regime was now official. More upsettingly, nor did Suu's brother or mother. Despite the evocative ceremony and the reception at the Hyde Park Hotel afterwards laid on by her generous guardians, it was more like the wedding of an orphan than Burma's most honored child.

There is no doubting the strength of the love that Suu and Michael Aris felt for each other: There is a gleam in Suu's eyes in the photographs taken in the early years of their marriage that we have not seen before. Gone is the blank correctness of her expression when she was an Oxford student visiting her mother in Delhi, the air of gloomy abstraction she wore in New York, "serious, sad, uncertain" in the words of Ann Pasternak Slater.[3] In a photograph taken in 1973 during their first visit to Burma together, Suu glows in a way that is quite new. She and Michael are pressed together on the floor in a room washed with sunshine, both dressed in white, gazing at the camera. Michael appears dazed with happiness, Suu looks practically beatific. In a photograph taken the same year in Nepal, she cradles her baby boy Alexander and beams open-mouthed at the camera from under her fringe, showing her sparkling teeth, and looking more like a Burmese Audrey Hepburn than one would think possible.

They look like the perfect modern couple: Buddhist to a degree—both steeped in its ideas and ceremonies and art works—but never in thrall to superstition, unmistakably secular, late-twentieth century young people, their differences of race and upbringing dissolved in the hot sun of their love for one another; the conventional expectations of an older generation— settling down, finding a career—rendered irrelevant by the wonderful prospect of setting off together on a great adventure. And the adventures really happened: A year in Thimphu, where hardly any foreigners had spent even a fortnight; the best part of another year in Nepal, tiny baby in tow, with side-trips to Burma; later long trips to Japan, to the Indian Himalayas.

That's the bright side of the picture. What of the shady side?

It is the story of many a modern woman who finds herself in what turns out to be, almost by default, a rather traditional marriage—often despite the best and most enlightened intentions of both partners.

Since they had first met in Chelsea, Michael had got his lucky break and run with it: He had spent nearly five years immersed in the language, culture and history of Bhutan and Tibet. Those years were to be as funda- mental to his future career as the voyage on the *Beagle* was for Charles Darwin. From now on, no one in Tibet studies would get away with calling him a dabbler.

And Suu? She had taken a mediocre degree, done a little part-time tutoring and a little temporary research work, obtained a postgraduate position in New York which she abandoned weeks later; and then had used her name and connections to get a semi-menial job in the United Nations, from which she resigned after three years to get married. She was the proud daughter of a great man but had achieved next to nothing on her own account—and, more disturbingly, did not seem to have a compass of her own. Unable to forget who she was, she had attached ferocious condi- tions to her marriage ". . . should my people need me . . ."—but in the meantime she was that unfortunate creature: a trailing spouse.

*

They flew off to Bhutan, where Michael, now thoroughly at home, continued as tutor to the royal family while deepening his knowledge of all things Bhutanese. During his free time they trekked through the kingdom's vertiginous valleys, sometimes on foot, sometimes on ponyback; at least once they were obliged to ride on the roof of a lorry, and snacked on the fruit of the Asian gooseberry trees they passed under.

For Michael it was the coda to his years of primary research: By the end of it he had enough material, he believed, to write the doctoral thesis that would be the next vital step in his career. For Suu, by contrast, it was an exotic interlude but not much more. The scenery was magnificent, though repetitive; the local cuisine, in which pork fat and chilies played a dominant role, was largely inedible, she confided to a friend in Rangoon—"we were hungry all the time," she said.[4] In response to her appeals, her mother sent that eye-watering staple of Burmese cuisine, fried *balachaung*—pounded dried shrimp and fish paste deep-fried with sugar, chili and tamarind paste—packed in empty Horlicks bottles. On one occasion the package arrived but the bottle was cracked at the bottom; they debated whether they should throw it out because of glass shards but ended up eating it at a single sitting.

Keeping Suu company during Michael's frequent absences was a Himalayan terrier puppy called Puppy, a gift of the king's chief minister. Suu became extremely attached to her new pet. It accompanied them back to England, and was with them throughout the family's years together— a talisman of their togetherness, as cherished pets often are. When she learned that Puppy had finally died at an advanced age in her absence— word arrived while she was traveling around Burma in 1989, campaigning for her party—the news broke her heart.

Bhutan joined the United Nations while Suu and Michael were in residence, and Suu advised the kingdom's minuscule Ministry of Foreign Affairs on the mysterious ways of that body. She also taught English to a class of royal bodyguards, but her fierce efforts to keep order reduced them, by her own admission, to cowering shadows of their normal hulking selves. Michael learned to drive on Thimphu's almost empty roads, but his attempts to pass on his new skills to Suu were not a success. Then in August, eight months after their arrival, Suu discovered she was pregnant, and they decided to go home.

By Christmas they were back in London. Michael wanted to write a doctoral thesis at SOAS on the early history of Bhutan, based on what he had learned during his years of residence there; his supervisor was to be the man who was already his mentor in Tibetan studies, Hugh Richardson. With Michael's family's help they bought a tiny flat in Brompton, not far from the Gore-Booths, and on April 12, 1973, Suu's first son Alexander was born.

As any parent knows, the first year of a child's life is a unique time when many things are possible that become unthinkable afterwards, and within a few weeks of Alexander's birth Michael and Suu were heading back to Asia with their baby. Word of Michael's special expertise was getting around the world of Tibetologists, and he had been asked to lead an expedition to Kutang and Nubri, two remote areas in northern Nepal having much in common culturally with Bhutan. They were away from Europe for nearly a year.

Probably more significant for Suu were the two visits they paid to Rangoon during that period, the first one to introduce Alexander to his grandmother. If the couple were anxious about what sort of reception to expect from Daw Khin Kyi, they were to be relieved: Despite her earlier misgivings, she decided that she was well satisfied with this genial and learned young man. "She was very pleased with him," wrote Suu's former personal assistant Ma Thanegi in her diary. One thing she appreciated were his old-fashioned English manners. "When Suu was out somewhere, Michael would not touch his food until she returned," she went on. "Once when Michael was out, Suu was so hungry she wanted to sit down to eat right away. Her mother reminded her gently that *he* always waited for *her*. So she felt she had to wait, too."

*

Daw Khin Kyi must have been glad of their company, because her life since her retirement from Delhi in 1967 had become one of almost total seclusion: She left 54 University Avenue once a year, for an annual medical check-up, but otherwise remained there all the time.[5]

She did not live like a hermit: She had always been a generous and amusing host, and intellectuals, former politicians, disgraced army officers and foreign diplomats streamed through her living room, avid for the latest gossip about who was in and who was out, who up and who down. But she gave no ground in the silent war she waged with the tyrant across the lake.

Both Daw Khin Kyi's resistance and her reticence—her refusal to give an inch to the regime, while at the same time declining, hedgehog-like, to expose herself to any sort of attack—indicate a deep understanding of the pitiless nature of the political game as played in her country, and as mastered by Ne Win. In this game, the illustriousness of an opponent was not a reason for holding back, but on the contrary a reason to attack with every weapon that came to hand until victory was total. The most flagrant example of this was the way Ne Win humiliated the corpse of U Thant, a few months after Michael and Suu's second visit.

*

Suu's old boss at the UN had retired as Secretary General in 1971, not long before she herself left the organization. Already unwell, he told the General Assembly that he felt "a great sense of relief, bordering on liberation" at relinquishing "the burdens of office": His last years in the job had been particularly testing. He died of lung cancer less than three years later, in November 1974. His daughter and son-in-law and their young son accompanied his coffin on the then long and tedious air journey back to Rangoon for burial.

It is not clear what sort of reception the family expected to receive in Burma, or if they were fully aware of the depth of the rift that had opened up between U Thant and Ne Win. But when their charter plane taxied to a halt at Mingaladon Airport, no government officials were on hand to welcome them, nor was there a government hearse or limousine to collect the coffin and the mourners.

The deputy education secretary, U Aung Tin, turned up—but only because he had been a pupil of U Thant's when the great man was a provincial headmaster and he could not bear to be part of the systematic snubbing that was under way. When, at a cabinet meeting, he proposed that the day of the funeral be declared a national holiday in the dead man's honor, he was sacked on the spot.

The coffin was eventually collected from the airport by a beaten-up Red Cross ambulance and taken to an ad hoc wake to the former racetrack, so the ordinary people of the city could pay their respects. A floral wreath placed nearby was signed, eloquently enough, "seventeen necessarily anonymous public servants."

Enmity between the two most powerful Burmese of their generation had been festering for years, but according to U Thant's grandson Thant Myint-U, who as an eight-year-old boy accompanied U Thant on his last journey home together with his parents, what had tipped Ne Win over the edge was the behavior not of U Thant himself but of the man to whom he had for years been secretary and close adviser, U Nu.

U Thant was exquisitely diplomatic, long before becoming the highest-ranking diplomat in the world; back in the 1950s he had single-handedly rescued a prime ministerial visit by U Nu to Russia from disaster after the Burmese prime minister had unilaterally, and for no reason that had anything to do with Soviet–Burmese relations, taken it into his head to attack Khrushchev for his government's repressive policies towards Soviet Jews. After several outbursts on this theme by U Nu, followed by private Soviet complaints, U Thant had managed to make his boss see sense, rewriting all his pending speeches to save Burma's relations with the second superpower from hitting the rocks.

Given the loose-cannon propensities of the former Burmese prime minister, it was unfortunate that U Thant should have been away in Africa in early 1969 when both U Nu and Ne Win, already settled enemies, visited New York at the same time. U Nu was in the early stages of trying to rebuild his political career, and he took advantage of his old friend's absence from town to call a press conference inside UN headquarters at which he fiercely denounced the Ne Win regime and all its works, and called for a revolution.

"Never before," wrote Thant Myint-U, "had a call for the overthrow of a UN member state government been made from inside the UN."[6] U Thant called U Nu, rebuked him, and extracted an apology, but it was too late to salvage the *amour propre* of the paranoid and irascible dictator. "General Ne Win was upset," Thant Myint-U wrote, "and became sure that U Thant was now conniving with U Nu. He told his men to consider Thant an enemy of the state." When the Secretary General went home on a private visit the following year, Ne Win refused to see him; when he needed to renew his passport, the regime made it insultingly difficult. But Ne Win's best opportunity for revenge came when U Thant was dead.

The coffin lay where it had been placed on the uncut grass in the middle of the disused racetrack. More and more people thronged to the site to say goodbye to the dead man, but the next day the state media claimed that the family had broken Burmese law by bringing the body home without permission and could face legal action. Eventually—U Thant had been dead a full week by now—permission came for a funeral, but the burial ground for Burma's greatest statesman was to be a small private cemetery.

The family, their grief now exacerbated by fear, anger and stress, would have swallowed this final humiliation for the sake of getting the great man into the ground and the whole miserable business concluded. But it was not to be.

It so happened that 1974 was a watershed year for the Ne Win regime. Tin Pe, the so-called "Red Brigadier," had for years been the most powerful figure in the Revolutionary Council (which was replaced in 1972 by a pseudo-civilian government with the same cast of characters). Advocating a rapid conversion of the economy to Marxist orthodoxy, he oversaw the nationalization of practically everything, including, crucially, the purchase and distribution of rice. The destruction of the market and its replacement by a command system had the same effect in Burma as everywhere else: Productivity plummeted, and the black market boomed. In British days Burma had been known as Asia's rice basket, but now productivity was falling year by year. As early as 1965 Ne Win, in one of his moments of startling frankness, admitted that Burma's economy was "a mess" and that everyone would be starving if the country were not so naturally fertile.

By 1970 the Red Brigadier's luck had run out and he was forced to retire, but the evil effects of his reforms continued to be felt. The price the state paid for rice was so low that farmers either hoarded it or sold it on the flourishing black market. This forced the government to reduce the ration of low-priced rice, forcing consumers to supplement it by buying more on the black market—for twice the price. It was a vicious circle.

The result was unprecedented social unrest, which began with strikes in the state railway corporation in May and spread rapidly to other industries. Massive demonstrations were brutally suppressed by the army. In August the whole situation became very much worse when widespread monsoon flooding led to an outbreak of cholera.

And then the corpse of U Thant came home—and its treatment by Ne Win gave the students, who were as usual at the sharp end of the protests, the symbol they sought. Here was a man regarded by millions of Burmese as a national hero being dealt with like a pariah by the man who was dragging the whole nation into poverty and enslavement. It was intolerable.

On the day of the funeral, Thant Myint-U was left behind at the home of his great uncle: His parents feared that the funeral procession might encounter trouble, and they did not want their son to be exposed to it. So Thant Myint-U was not on hand to witness the extraordinary—and, for the family, deeply upsetting and traumatic—events of that day. He wrote:

> The Buddhist funeral service went as planned, but then, as the motorcade began driving towards the cemetery, a big throng of students stopped the hearse carrying the coffin. They had been arriving all day long in the thousands, with thousands more onlookers cheering them on. Through loudspeakers mounted on jeeps they declared, "We are on our way to pay our tribute and accompany our beloved U Thant, architect of peace, on his last journey." One of my grandfather's younger brothers pleaded with them to let the family bury him quietly and to take up other issues later, but to no avail. The coffin was seized and sped away on a truck to Rangoon University.[7]

One of the students involved, now a senior editor in Rangoon, said, "We put the coffin on a truck and thousands and thousands of us marched towards Rangoon University campus. First we put it in the Convention Hall—we had no plan—and then we started asking for a burial ground in an honorable place and we said we will bury him, and people started giving us money to make a huge tomb for him . . ."[8]

So began a stand-off that lasted for days. The coffin was "placed on a dais in the middle of the dilapidated Convention Hall, ceiling fans whirring overhead in the stifling heat," Thant Myint-U wrote.[9] Tens of thousands of people poured into the campus, and the mood of hostility took on a political complexion as students stood up to condemn not merely the regime's treatment of U Thant but their repression of dissent and their disastrous economic policies as well.

Eventually the regime offered a compromise: There would be a public but not a state funeral, and U Thant would be buried at the foot of the Shwedagon pagoda. But as the coffin was about to be transported for the second attempt at burial, the students hijacked it again. The former activist recalled:

> We took it to the site of the Students' Union building, near the gate of the campus, which Ne Win had blown up in 1962 with students inside, a few months after his coup d'état, and we buried it there. We called it the Peace Mausoleum. That infuriated Ne Win, and the thing escalated.
>
> Finally after five days the troops stormed onto the campus in the middle of the night and started shelling us with tear gas. We picked up the shells and threw them back but we were outnumbered, and then they started using guns, shooting live ammunition. So we went deeper into the campus where there were some hostels for students, and we tried to defend ourselves with Molotov cocktails, but they were much cleverer than us. They surrounded the buildings, and when we started throwing stones and Molotov cocktails at them they took the students who had already been arrested and used them as human shields, so we couldn't attack. And then they started shooting at us with real bullets and everything so we surrendered and got arrested.[10]

At least nine students were killed that night, and the true figure may be much higher; hundreds more were arrested, and many ended up serving long terms in jail. As the coffin was taken under an escort of troops and armored personnel vehicles for its second interment, more riots broke out in various parts of the city, destroying a police station and wrecking a government ministry and several cinemas. Troops again opened fire to quell the protests, and the city's hospitals were inundated with the wounded.

U Thant was finally laid to rest at the Cantonment Garden near the Shwedagon pagoda as the riots and the fiery military backlash continued. "At about six that morning we were woken up at our hotel by a phone call," Thant Myint-U wrote. "The caller, who identified himself as a government

agent, said that U Thant's body had been retrieved from the university . . .
They said there had been no violence and only tear gas had been used. My
family was allowed to pay their last respects. We were asked to leave the
country and about a week later headed back to New York. Only much later
did we realize the full magnitude of what had happened that day."[11]

The aftermath of this explosion of student fury was a crackdown
by the regime on the entire student and youth population, militant
and otherwise. Martial law was declared and Mandalay and Rangoon
Universities were shut down and did not reopen for five months. And
there was cultural repression, too—Ne Win's Taliban streak coming out
again. Trousers of all sorts but particularly jeans were outlawed, along
with all other imported western fashions, and all male students with long
hair were forced to have it cut short. And this did not mean a trip to
the beauty salon. "The abiding image I have of the U Thant riots," wrote
Harriet O'Brien, who was then living in Rangoon with her diplomat
parents, "[is] of a student friend with his hair cut off in tufts . . . He had
been dragged from the street by soldiers who had forcibly hacked off his
hair with their bayonets."[12]

*

Suu and Michael learned to their horror how the last rites for Suu's
old boss had given rise to the bloodiest political confrontation since
independence. But there was never any question that this scholar's wife
with her new baby would make some kind of public declaration about
the affair. Indeed she had explicitly promised that she would do nothing
of the sort. A few months earlier—after the rice protests but before the
floods and U Thant's death—Suu and Michael were visiting Daw Khin
Kyi for the second time together, Alexander being at the time a little over
one, when officials of the government called Suu in and asked her whether
she planned to get involved in "anti-government activities."[13] She told
them that she would never get involved in Burmese affairs as long as she
continued to live outside the country. She was as good as her word.

But already it seems she was brooding on her duty. On a visit to
Rangoon the following year she met retired Brigadier Kyaw Zaw, one of
Aung San's Thirty Comrades. "Uncle, I've heard that these days you are

mostly looking after your grandchildren," she told him chidingly. "Do you think you have completed your responsibilities to your country?" Kyaw Zaw, who recorded the exchange in his memoirs, replied, "Rest assured I will continue to meet my obligations to the nation—but you also need to do your part."[14]

*

As Rangoon was getting its first taste of People Power, Suu, Michael and Alexander were back in England, and in some uncertainty about what to do next. The Brompton flat that had been just adequate for two was impossible when there was a third who was already toddling. Michael was in discussions with the staff at SOAS about his PhD but so far they were inconclusive. So to find the peace and quiet he needed to organize the results of his six-year stay in Bhutan, the family moved in with Michael's father and stepmother, John and Evelyn Aris, in the large home in Grantown-on-Spey, in the Highlands of Scotland, where they had retired. They remained there for several months, and when they went south again it was to settle not in London but Oxford. SOAS had accepted Michael's proposal for a PhD on the historical foundations of Bhutan, and St. John's College Oxford had awarded him a Junior Research Fellowship which would give him a modicum of financial backing.

The family moved first to a cottage in the village of Sunninghall outside Oxford—"a pretty but impractical house" Ann Pasternak Slater called it—but then in 1977 St. John's gave them a college flat around the corner from Suu's old college.[15] That same year their second son was born and named Kim, in honor of Suu's favorite Kipling character. Ten years after graduating, she was back in her old neighborhood, with a husband and a family. And because many people who study at Oxford contrive to stay on indefinitely afterwards, there were friendships to be dusted off.

"Memories of that time are still sunlit but with a sense of strain," wrote Ann Pasternak Slater, whose home in Park Town was less than half a mile from the Arises' flat in Crick Road. "The flat was on the ground floor of a pleasant North Oxford house. But its apparent spaciousness was deceptive. Apart from the large, south-facing living room, where all the family life took place, on the gloomier northern side was a tiny kitchen, one bedroom and a box-room doubling as a nursery and frequently occupied spare room."[16]

Suu believed in the open-armed tradition of Burmese hospitality that she had grown up with: Visitors to the flat included Ma Than É from New York, who spent long periods with them every year, and numerous visitors from Burma and Bhutan. But Suu was welcoming them all—without the help of the servants who had been a fixture of her childhood homes—in the harsher climate of England, with two small children to look after and a husband who was otherwise engaged. She became fantastically busy.

"On my way to the library I often saw Suu laboriously pedaling back from town, laden with sagging plastic bags and panniers heavy with cheap fruit and vegetables," Pasternak Slater wrote.

When I called in the afternoons with my own baby daughter, I would find her busy in the kitchen preparing economical Japanese fish dishes, or at her sewing machine, in an undulating savanna of yellow cotton, making curtains for the big bay windows, or quickly running up elegant, cut-price clothes for herself. Michael was working hard at his doctorate. Alexander had to be cared for without disturbing him. There were endless guests to be housed and fed. Still Suu maintained a house that was elegant and calm, the living room warm with sunny hangings of rich, dark Bhutanese rugs and Tibetan scroll paintings. But battened down at the back, hidden away among the kitchen's stacked pots and pans, was anxiety, cramp and strain.[17]

"Michael and Suu complemented each other, it was a marriage made in heaven," said Peter Carey, an Oxford don and a close friend. "Not because it was all roses, because it wasn't, it was a very rocky road."[18] Robin Christopher has a memory of Suu ironing everything in sight, including Michael's socks: "It was a role she performed with pride," he said, "and with a certain defiance of her more feminist friends."

Suu became close friends with another academic wife, a Japanese woman called Noriko Ohtsu whose husband was also on a research fellowship at the university.

"It was actually her husband Michael who I got to know first," Noriko said. "I met him in 1974 when we were both students of Tibetan at the School of Oriental and African Studies [SOAS] in London. I liked him from the word go: No one could call him exactly handsome but there was a big-hearted gentleness about him that made people feel comfortable."[19] He told her about his years in Bhutan, and she found something comically appropriate about it: He reminded her of the Abominable Snowman. "With his unkempt hair and his great height he looked like a giant who had just emerged from the Himalayas. The first thing he said to me, with evident pride, was 'My wife is Burmese.'"

As chance would have it, we all moved from London to Oxford in 1975: I and my Japanese husband Sadayoshi, an expert on the economy of the Soviet Union, and Suu and Michael and their toddler Alexander. As a result we all got to know each other much better. It helped that both Suu and I were from Asia, in a city where people from our part of the world were few and far between. There was an intimacy to our friendship that I found with none of my other Oxford friends.

My first sight of Suu when I met her in London was of this beautiful young girl pushing a pram, wearing Burmese dress, her hair in a pony tail with a fringe hanging down over her forehead. She looked like a teenager: I couldn't believe she was twenty-nine, one year older than Michael, who looked old enough to be her father.

Suu was already interested in Japan because of her father's deep involvement with the country before and during the war. And despite the many differences between their two nations, there was also much in common: instinctive courtesy and self-effacement, for example, and a habit of diligence and graceful attention to everyday tasks.

"We exchanged recipes and went shopping together in Oxford's covered market," Noriko remembered.

We went window-shopping for Liberty prints then snapped them up when the price came down in the sales and Suu would run the fabric up into longyi.

Michael was trying to make ends meet with his research about Tibet but their income was very small, and Suu would say to me, "Noriko, we're down to our last £10! What on earth can I do?" But she was brilliant at making delicious meals out of cheap ingredients, and I helped out whenever I could by inviting the family round for a Japanese dinner.

The multiple challenges of running the family single-handedly—
"Michael couldn't cook properly," Noriko recalled, "it was always Suu
that cooked"—brought out a trait of puritanical perfectionism in Suu,
Pasternak Slater recalled. "She could be very critical and very disapproving—to me and certainly to Michael," she said.

> I remember me driving her down to some rather tatty budget furniture
> shop and me saying, "Why on earth do you want to buy this sort of crap?
> Why don't you buy an antique?" And she would say, "This is perfectly
> good, there's no need to be spending money on antiques." I was spending
> money on pine blanket boxes and the like while she was getting stuff
> from this cheap place and she probably thought I was a kind of cultural
> snob, I suppose. It was part of her practicality: There was no need to have
> something grandiose, it's just children's furniture, what the hell.[20]

On cut-price food, by contrast, she was unbending. "Her pride did
not permit any compromise with fish and chips, burgers or other such
fast-food solutions," said Noriko. "She always tried to feed her family with
freshly cooked home-made food."

She was also becoming a stickler for traditions, including those not her
own. She didn't like Christmas pudding, and never ate it, but nonetheless
she ritually made one six months in advance. When she visited Noriko in
Japan, years later, she even took one with her as a present—even though
neither of them liked the stuff. She showed no signs of converting to
Christianity, but she is remembered by another Oxford friend as the first
person to get her Christmas cards out every year. And she visited the
Victorian severity of her mother on her own children and their friends.
As her babies grew, Ann Pasternak Slater, who now had four children
of her own, remembered, "It was Suu who gave the copy-book parties
with all the traditional party games—except that the rules were enforced
with unyielding exactitude, and my astonished children, bending them
ever so slightly, once found themselves forbidden the prize. To them Suu
was kindly but grave, an uncomfortably absolute figure of justice in their
malleable world."[21]

She was equally unbending about telling the truth, even at the risk of
offending people, and was appalled and uncomprehending when Michael

did otherwise. Noriko remembered one conversation in which the subject of British social hypocrisy came up.

She and Suu were in agreement about the abysmal quality of much British food. Suu said to her in Michael's presence,

> Noriko, as you well know, some British food is really awful. When we get invited out to eat and the food is bad, I don't say it's delicious: I'm a person who does not tell lies. But if they ask Michael, he always says, "Thanks for the delicious meal!" Staring at Michael she added, "Why does he always do that?"
>
> Michael replied, "It's a matter of courtesy, it's a way of expressing my gratitude." "There's no need for it," Suu retorted, "I wouldn't do it." She turned to me. "Michael was brought up eating bad British food in boarding school," she said, "so he's become insensitive to it." Michael just rounded his eyes, looked up at the ceiling and shrugged.
>
> That was Suu and Michael's life encapsulated in one scene. Whatever you said to Michael he would just smile. Because he knew that as long as he and Suu were together he would get home-cooked food to eat.

He was a lucky man and he knew it. "For the first fifteen years of the marriage it was all Michael," said Peter Carey, "the fellow of St. Antony's, the fellow of St. John's, the great scholar of Bhutan and Himalayan Buddhism. He was the breadwinner, the core of the marriage, and she was the helpmate, the north Oxford housewife. She was her father's daughter, but she had transmogrified into this north Oxford inheritance."[22]

With her closest friends, Suu expressed some of her frustration. In 1978 Michael completed his dissertation and obtained his doctorate, but Suu felt that subsequently he did not try hard enough to capitalize on that hard-won achievement.

"I think Suu thought that he could actually have pushed his way a bit more," said Ann Pasternak Slater. "She felt that he was not proactive enough. She said I was very lucky to have a husband who was a bit more of a wheeler-dealer. It was partly him not being as go-getting and achieving as my husband was—I didn't need to tell Craig what to do but she felt she had to be pushing Michael and she said she envied me a husband who didn't need that."[23]

Suu's was the common lot of the modern mother who, despite her qualifications and professional experience, finds herself laboring away at menial tasks while her husband is absorbed in the—painfully slow—construction of his glorious career. But in Suu's case there was an extra twist: With both her sons she was unable to be as complete a mother as she felt was both her duty and her right. As Michael struggled with his Tibetan texts in their cramped flat, Suu struggled and failed to breastfeed her second child.

Pasternak Slater recalled:

> She had been unable to breastfeed Alexander, too, and Kim was very, very difficult. Michael was understandably desperate to finish his thesis and this created a lot of friction because there was this baby who wouldn't sleep and Suu trying to feed him and so it was very hard. She wasn't able to in the end, she had to give up. I doubt whether the anguish she felt can be understood by anyone who has not had the same experience. Especially because at that time everyone was saying breast is best, it was very much the thing. So in the end Kim had to be taken into a pediatric unit to try and spend nights away from Suu so he didn't scream all night long.

Both boys ended up being bottle-fed. It was a telling demonstration of how Suu's indomitable willpower could sometimes backfire on the whole family. Her pain, said Pasternak Slater, was "the inevitable result of her rooted reluctance to accept defeat, or to allow herself the indulgence of a second-best way."

*

By 1980, the family's situation was beginning to improve. Michael's doctorate had been rewarded with a full research fellowship provided by Wolfson College, which also came with a bit more money. They had moved from the tightness of the college flat to their first—and, as it turned out, only—proper family home, across the gated gardens from Ann Pasternak Slater and her family in Park Town. Alexander had started going to the Dragon School, a posh preparatory school in north Oxford; Kim would follow him there soon. And Suu was at last able to raise her eyes from the sink and the sewing machine and consider her options.

"She was very much casting around for a role for herself," remembered Carey. "She said, is this my destiny to be a housewife, the partner of an Oxford don?"[24] Ann Pasternak Slater said, "She was becoming more serious, more focused, more determined, more ambitious."[25]

She started helping Michael in his work, and in a volume of essays dedicated to Hugh Richardson, who had died in 1979, she was named as co-editor.[26] She found a part-time job in the Bodleian, Oxford's famous library, working on its Burmese collection. She made another effort to go back to college, applying to take a BA in English, but her third-class first degree was held against her and she was turned down. "All those years spent as a full-time mother were most enjoyable," Suu said in an interview many years later, "but the gap in professional and academic activity—although I did manage to study Tibetan and Japanese during that time—made me feel somewhat at a disadvantage compared to those who were never out of the field."[27]

So instead she set about realizing one of her earliest childhood ambitions and turned herself, in a modest way, into a writer.

She wrote three short books for schoolchildren about the countries she knew best, Burma, Bhutan and Nepal, books she rightly dismissed later as potboilers. More significantly, she also wrote a slim biography of her father, Aung San of Burma, published by Australia's University of Queensland Press in 1984. In his biography of Suu, Justin Wintle described it as "idealized." It is certainly not iconoclastic, and it is too brief to stand as a major work of scholarship, but it is written in a clear, limpid style and is shot through with insight and affection.

Aung San, she wrote, "has left an unflattering description of himself as a sickly, unwashed, gluttonous, thoroughly unprepossessing child who was so late beginning to speak that his family feared he might be dumb ... While his three brothers started their education early, he refused to go to school 'unless mother went too' ..."[28]

In the last paragraph of the book's concluding chapter, she described what it was about Aung San that had made him such a popular and successful leader. The words were an implicit denunciation of what, under Ne Win, leadership in Burma had come to mean; they would also become a sort of manifesto for herself. She wrote:

Aung San's appeal was not so much to extremists as to the great majority of ordinary citizens who wished to pursue their own lives in peace and prosperity under a leader they could trust and respect. In him they saw that leader, a man who put the interests of the country before his own needs, who remained poor and unassuming at the height of his power, who accepted the responsibilities of leadership without hankering after the privileges, and who, for all his political acumen and powers of statecraft, retained at the core of his being a deep simplicity. For the people of Burma, Aung San was the man who had come in their hour of need to restore their national pride and honor. As his life is a source of inspiration for them, his memory remains the guardian of their political conscience.[29]

As her children grew, her thoughts were turning again restlessly to Burma. She had been going back most summers, alone or with the family, to keep her mother company and pay homage to her father on Martyrs' Day. Later—one year before her mother's devastating stroke—she took the boys back for shinbyu, the ceremony all Burmese Buddhist boys undergo between the ages of five and about twelve, when they re-enact the Buddha's renunciation of his royal heritage and his decision to embrace the life of the spirit. Suu had not taught Alexander and Kim to speak Burmese but they both had Burmese as well as English names and passports. And now they also had the most important Burmese rite of passage behind them.

It was on one of these visits that she struck up a friendship that was to prove important to her later on. She visited Rangoon University to seek out copies of Burmese classics on behalf of the Bodleian and got talking to one of the senior librarians, whose name was Ko Myint Swe, a friend of her mother's. "You must help our country," he told her. "But how, uncle?" she replied.[30] Myint Swe was not sure: But he was one of several voices in Rangoon reminding her who she was, and that she might yet have a role. When she took the plunge and entered politics in 1988, Myint Swe became one of her closest aides.

Both her boys were now at school, and Suu decided that the best way to re-engage with her country was as a scholar. Following in Michael's footsteps, she applied to SOAS in London to do a PhD on Burmese political history, which would give her the opportunity to expand the slim biography of her father into a full-blown scholarly work. But again her cursed third in PPE came back to haunt her and she was rejected: Her assessors felt that her grasp of political theory would be insufficient to see her through.

Suu was livid at this new rejection, but then it was suggested that she might write a thesis on modern Burmese literature instead. She took a one-year course at SOAS in preparation, reading numerous works in Burmese, working one-on-one with her tutor Anna Allott, and finally sitting an exam.

"We read several novels together," said Allott, "and I asked her to write essays about them and what she wrote was very illuminating because she wrote from a Burmese point of view."[31] The exam tested her command of the language and her knowledge of modern Burmese literature and she passed easily.

At SOAS she also learned about a research fellowship offered by the Center for Southeast Asian Studies at Kyoto University in Japan. Suu applied and was awarded a research scholarship for the academic year 1985–86, to study Burma's independence movement. This would be her opportunity to delve into the Japanese archives and learn firsthand what experiences her father had undergone in Japan. Her plan to write the big biography of her father may have been shunted aside but it had not been derailed. With her customary determination she plastered the bathroom at Park Town with blown-up *kanji*, Japanese characters, and set about learning to read Japanese in world-record time.

The family was on the go again: Suu was to move temporarily to Japan, taking eight-year-old Kim with her—he would undergo a very challenging year in a Japanese primary school—and at the same time Michael went with Alexander to Shimla, high in the Indian Himalayas, where he had won a two-year fellowship at the Indian Institute of Advanced Studies. The four of them would get together for the holidays.

*

She was back in Asia: She had not spent so long in an Asian country since leaving Delhi for Oxford eighteen years before. Japan was in the middle of the biggest economic boom in its history—a phenomenon that interested her as little as the hippies of London or the Velvet Underground in New

York. But to be in the country which had offered so much to Burma, and delivered so little, and so ambiguously—that was interesting, and difficult. It was a brother nation to Burma, it had offered liberation from the white man and fellowship in the Greater East Asian Co-Prosperity Sphere, but on closer acquaintance that had proved to be an even more onerous form of colonialism under a fancy name.

Suu loved Japanese food and appreciated Japanese diligence and culture, but she was critical, too. She found the people arrogant and obsessed with making money, and she couldn't understand why, despite their great aesthetic sense, they built such hideous modern cities. Her father had been shocked to be offered a prostitute during his stay in Tokyo—and she was appalled at the way Japanese men bossed and bullied women, in a way that would not be tolerated in Burma.

She shuttled between Kyoto and Tokyo to interview war veterans who had known her father, and dug for raw material on Aung San in the libraries of the Self-Defense Forces, the National Library and elsewhere, plundering them for anything she could find on him.

Yet in the opinion of Noriko Ohtsu, her Japanese friend from Oxford who had returned to live in Kyoto, her hometown, the academic slog was in the long run less important than her own transformation. In an interview years later, Suu said, "When I was young I could never separate my country from my father, because I was very small when he died and I'd always thought of him in connection with the country. So even now it is difficult for me to separate the idea of my father from the concept of my country."[32] And those months of immersion in her father's life and work were, in her friend's opinion, crucial for Suu: a first *kikkake*, as she puts it, a turning-point, in the fitful, unplanned process of realigning her destiny with Burma's.[33]

At the weekends, Suu and Kim sometimes visited Noriko and Sadayoshi at their place in the countryside overlooking Lake Biwa, and during the months in Japan Noriko witnessed a transformation come over her friend. At the university she encountered Burmese exchange students who treated her with a mixture of deference and vague yet intense expectation that was quite novel to her.

"She and Kim were staying in International House, Kyoto University's residence for scholars," Noriko said, "and there were young Burmese scholars staying there, too, nice, clever boys. Their attitude towards Suu was totally different from other people, because of the respect in which they held her father."

Yoshikazu Mikami, Suu's first biographer, noted a similar effect. "In Japan she had her first encounter with Burmese students," she wrote, "and they were all talking about the country in the same way—nostalgia, nationalism, respect for her father . . . She came to Japan to follow her father's shadow—but then the image became clearer and became imbued with reality. And her sense of mission began to grow."[34]

Noriko remembered one student in particular: In Japan he was nicknamed Koe-chan. "Koe-chan was one of the boys who respected her. Then he went home to Rangoon and at the airport he was surrounded by soldiers and they took a pistol out of his bag and he was sentenced to seven years in Insein Jail.

"He had a weapon illegally: That was the reason they gave." But for Noriko and Suu it was ridiculous, unbelievable, scary. "Koe-chan was a serious student, he was studying classical Japanese literature. Firearms are totally banned in Japan—even we Japanese cannot obtain a pistol or any such thing in Japan, it's totally illegal. So maybe a soldier put a pistol in his bag, to incriminate him." The dark suspicion she and Suu shared was that the students at International House were being spied on by one of their number, and Koe-chan was punished for being friendly with Suu.

In Britain, Burma would always feel like a faraway, exotic country, its problems and realities having little bearing on everyday British life. But in Japan, the country which had maintained the closest diplomatic and commercial ties with Burma since independence, and which had been Ne Win's most consistent sponsor, she was back in the same parish. There were Burmese spies here; more to the point, there were Burmese students who knew exactly who she was and why it mattered.

Noriko said,

> She became aware of the mixture of respect and expectation with which they regarded her. Koe-chan was one of them. He was such a clever, promising boy. It's quite difficult to get a PhD at Kyoto University. I think she felt some responsibility or guilt when she heard what happened to him. And her thinking about her life and her potential role began to change.

That is one of the reasons why she went into politics. It's a very interesting coincidence: Aung San stayed in Japan, and Suu stayed in Japan, and both father and daughter went on to have the same experience, both had a revolution to fight. It's a coincidence, isn't it. But I really felt that that is what Suu was feeling.

At Christmas Michael and Alexander flew out to join Suu and Kim in Kyoto. Christmas is a non-event in Japan, but New Year is the biggest festival in the calendar, and on New Year's Eve the whole family went out into the country to see their friends from Oxford.

"We took them to a nearby Buddhist temple where they all rang the big temple bell in the Japanese tradition called *joya no kane*," Noriko remembered. "The next day I had a vivid insight into how much Suu missed Burma. I had heard of a temple not far away with a Burmese Buddha on the altar; I mentioned it to Suu and she asked if we could visit it. The gate was locked because of the holiday so I went round the back and asked for advice."

A caretaker opened up the temple for them.

There on the altar was the Burmese Buddha with a gentle and delightful smile. Suu said "Ooooh!" then fell silent. Although she had always been very careful with money, she offered the priest 5,000 yen to say a prayer service, then prostrated herself on the earthen floor in front of the Buddha and went up and down any number of times, her hands together, chanting in Burmese.

It dawned on me that Suu and I had only known each other in England and Japan, never in Burma: I had only known her as a foreigner, with all that involves. Now, in a rustic village in Japan, coming face to face with a Burmese Buddha, suddenly she revealed her Burmese heart.

I had an intuitive feeling that she could only really fulfill herself in Burma. Would it be better for Suu to spend her whole life in comfortable Britain? Whatever the dangers and difficulties, would she not be happier immersing herself in her own country again?

Michael and Alex flew off, Kim went back to school and Suu resumed her research, but a seed had been planted. "One day towards the end of her stay in Japan she came to see me again, bringing some of our favorite *manju* cakes to eat with green tea," Noriko recalled. Noriko was in the habit of speaking bluntly with her friend:

> Over the tea I said to her, "Suu, if I were you, I would go back to Burma. Your country needs you. There are lots of things you could do there—your English ability alone would be very valuable. Michael could get a research job at some Indian university so you would not be far apart, you could put the children into boarding school . . . don't you agree?"
>
> Normally Suu was lightning quick with her replies, but now she merely stared down and said nothing. But I knew the answer.
>
> Eventually Suu looked up. "Noriko, you're right," she said.

Two years later, for reasons that had nothing to do with politics, she found herself back there. And the rest of her life began to unfold.

PART FOUR
HEIRS TO THE KINGDOM

1

ALONE

O N the day they placed me under arrest," Suu told an American journalist who visited her at home in 1995, "this garden was still quite beautiful. There were lots of Madonna lilies, fields and fields of them, and frangipani, and fragrant yellow jasmines, and gardenias, and a flower from South America that changes its color as it matures and is called 'yesterday, today and tomorrow.'"[1]

But after she was detained Suu did not want to look out on flowers any more, and she did not want their scent in her nostrils.

On July 21, 1989, a SLORC spokesman announced that Aung San Suu Kyi and U Tin Oo, the NLD chairman, were to be confined to their homes for a minimum of one year "because they have violated the law by committing acts designed to put the country in a perilous state." They had been detained under the new rules enacted earlier in the year permitting summary justice by the military without recourse to the courts.

That was bad enough. But all Suu's closest comrades, the forty-odd men and women, including her friend and companion Ma Thanegi, who had spent Martyrs' Day at her home together as the army once again clamped the capital in an iron grip, had been taken off to Insein Jail. Only she and Tin Oo had been left on the outside.

Suu demanded to be taken to join them in prison. When the regime refused, she went on hunger strike. She would eat nothing, she said, unless they agreed to her demand and put her in jail with the rest. In the meantime she would take only water and fruit juice.

Alex, now sixteen, and Kim, eleven, were with her at home—Michael had sent them on ahead while he attended to essential business following his father's death—but now they found themselves spectators to a battle of wills that had nothing to do with them, and that they must have struggled to comprehend.

When news reached Michael of his wife's detention, he set out to join his family as quickly as he could. Fortunately he already had a valid

Burmese visa in his passport, so he was able to leave almost at once, informing the authorities that he was on his way. But when he landed at Rangoon's Mingaladon Airport on July 24th, he discovered that he had arrived in the thick of a major crisis.

"As the plane taxied to a halt," he wrote, "I could see a lot of military activity on the tarmac. The plane was surrounded by troops . . ."[2] Aris would not have been human if he had not been a little apprehensive: The assassination of Filipino opposition leader Benigno Aquino, Jr., shot dead on the tarmac of Manila's airport as he returned from exile, was only six years in the past. But no violence was offered him. Aris was escorted away by an army officer, forbidden to make contact with the British Embassy, and told that he could join Suu and the boys if he agreed to abide by the same terms of detention as Suu. He consented promptly and was driven from the airport to University Avenue, where he found the house surrounded by troops. He wrote later:

> The gates were opened and we drove in. I had no idea what to expect.
>
> I arrived to find Suu in the third day of a hunger strike. Her single demand was that she should be allowed to go to prison with all her young supporters who had been taken away from her compound when the authorities arrested her. She believed her presence with them in prison would afford them some protection from maltreatment. She took her last meal on the evening of July 20th, the day of her arrest, and for the following twelve days until almost noon on August 1st, she accepted only water.[3]

It was another Danubyu, another stand-off, in the series of confrontations that have punctuated Suu's political career, but for the first and only time her husband found himself thrust into the role of go-between. It was clear that the authorities had no intention of agreeing to her demand. So either the family could sit there and watch their wife and mother waste away and die, or they would have to find a compromise.

Dying, he insisted to her, would do no good to the imprisoned students or anybody else. So under her husband's persuasion, Suu agreed to moderate her conditions: She would agree to stay where she was and break her fast on condition that she was given the regime's solemn word that the NLD members who had been locked up would not be maltreated in prison.

The house no longer had a working telephone—to Suu's and the boys' amusement, some soldiers had turned up with a large pair of scissors and snipped the cord after her detention began—so Michael passed on his wife's terms to the officers who came to the compound regularly to look in on Suu. They listened to what he had to say, then went away: Clearly the matter was beyond their competence.

Meanwhile Suu was dwindling away. Already back in February she had been "fragile and light as a papier-mâché doll," according to Ma Thanegi's diary. Throughout the self-imposed ordeal Suu was "very calm," Aris wrote, "and the boys too. She had spent the days of her fast resting quietly, reading and talking to us." But Aris himself was at his wits' end. "I was less calm," he confessed, "though I tried to pretend to be." Finally the agony of waiting was broken and he was summoned to a full-dress meeting of senior army officers at Rangoon City Hall to present Suu's demands, recorded by the military's video cameras for posterity. And on August 1st, a week after his arrival and twelve days after the start of her fast, the tension was broken.

"A military officer came to give her his personal assurance, on behalf of the authorities, that her young people would not be tortured and that the cases against them would be heard by due process of law," he wrote. "She accepted this compromise, and the doctors who had been deputed to attend her, whose treatment she had hitherto refused, put her on an intravenous drip with her consent. She had lost twelve pounds in weight. I still do not know if the authorities kept their promise."[4]

She had lost one set of boys—the NLD's student members—and now she was about to lose the other ones: her family. They had a full month together after the beginning of her house arrest. Michael's visa was about to expire but the authorities agreed to extend it so he and his sons could return to Britain together. "Suu recovered her weight and strength in the days ahead," he wrote. "The boys learned martial arts from the guards. We put the house in order."[5] Then, September 2nd rolled around, school beckoned, and the three of them departed—never to be reunited as a family again.

Suu has always been very reluctant to say much about the personal, emotional costs of her choices, and about the ill effect of those choices on her children she has said next to nothing. "As a mother," she told

Alan Clements, "the greater sacrifice was giving up my sons"—but then added immediately what is always the corollary: "I was always aware of the fact that others had sacrificed more than me."[6] Coaxed by Clements to say a little more, she added, "When I first entered politics, my family happened to be here with me tending to my mother. So it was not a case of my suddenly leaving them, or they leaving me. It was a more gradual transition which gave us an opportunity to adjust."

There will be readers to whom those words may seem unacceptably hard-hearted. But Suu was weighing them carefully. In her long war of wills with the regime, all of this was ammunition. The last thing she wanted to do was give her jailors the idea that she or her family were suffering intolerably, that the slow torture of separation was working.

As has been mentioned earlier in this book, the unique aspect of Suu Kyi's long ordeal—one which marks it off sharply from the otherwise comparable experiences of people like Soviet dissident Sakharov or Nelson Mandela—was that, as the regime made amply clear to her, she could have brought it to an end by agreeing to leave the country for ever.

One of the things that made it psychologically bearable to remain cooped up alone while her family was on the other side of the world was the thought of them coming out to see her in the school holidays. But the regime was canny and cruel enough to see that, and to sever that heart-string now. Soon after Michael and the boys got back to Oxford, they learned that this would be their last trip to see Suu—or at least the last one they could bank on. The Burmese Embassy informed Michael drily that the boys' Burmese passports were now invalid because they were no longer entitled—on what grounds was not explained—to Burmese citizenship. "Very obviously," Aris wrote, "the plan was to break Suu's spirit by separating her from her children in the hope she would accept permanent exile." Until 1988, the longest time Suu and her children had been separated was a month. Now it was to be more than two years before they would see each other again.

*

In the flower-scented tranquility of University Avenue, Michael, Alexander and Kim had watched Suu shrink and dwindle and fade, then, once agreement with the authorities was reached, return to her normal state. But meanwhile outside in the city's streets the State Law and Order Restoration Council set about killing off the democracy movement once and for all.

Suu's apprehensions about the treatment of her party comrades, the motivation for her hunger strike, were not in the least fanciful. In the year since the crackdown of September 18, 1988, three thousand alleged activists had been jailed; that number doubled in the four months between Suu's detention and November 1989, and included many of her colleagues in the party. They were summarily tried by the newly empowered military tribunals, but they were also frequently tortured: One month after Suu's detention began—three weeks after the end of her fast—a declassified American Embassy cable revealed that the torture of political prisoners included burns to the flesh by cigarettes, electric shocks to the genitals and beatings so severe that they caused permanent damage to eyes and ears and sometimes death.[7] Hundreds more such prisoners were also punished in a way that was to become routine as the small but brutal civil wars on the frontier dragged on. They were forced to work for the army fighting Shan insurgents in northern Shan State, either lugging the army's equipment as porters or forced to walk ahead of the troops as human mine-detectors: If they were not blown up, it was safe for the soldiers to follow.

The mobilization of millions of Burmese against the military regime in the past year and a half now elicited a terrible retribution. Suu has always insisted that simply being confined to her home she had far less to complain about than colleagues who lacked the protection of her name and fame, and she is right. "The military regime seeks not only to break down the identity of former political prisoners," said a report by the Assistance Association for Political Prisoners, reviewing thousands of cases of abuse since 1988, "but to make them walking advertisements for the consequences of speaking out against the regime. Many former political prisoners repeatedly explain that once they are a political prisoner they are always a political prisoner."

Some of Suu's most senior colleagues were silenced more or less permanently. Win Tin, the veteran dissident journalist on the NLD's Central Executive Committee, was sentenced to three years' hard labor on October 3rd, but his term was repeatedly extended until he was finally set free in 2008, after nineteen years in prison, most of it in solitary confinement. And two days after Win Tin was sent down, the man who had become one of Suu's first political mentors when she returned to Rangoon to nurse her mother, the writer and war hero Maung Thaw Ka, was given a twenty-year sentence which, given his frail condition, was in effect a sentence of death.

Maung Thaw Ka, his name almost unknown outside Burma, is a good symbol of the awakening that had occurred since the spring of 1988, and of how ruthlessly and vindictively it was now being trampled. It was he, the fifty-one-year-old naval officer-turned-writer, who had given Suu a tour of the places in Rangoon where troops had killed students in the early months of the revolt, long before she decided to offer her involvement; it was he, with his big ears and wedge of a nose and a paunch showing through his striped shirt, who shared the little podium with her when she gave her maiden political speech at Rangoon General Hospital.

Like Tin Oo, the former defense minister, his career spanned the heyday of Aung San as well as that of his daughter. He was serving in the Burmese Navy during the war when the British forces handed the ship on which he was serving, the *May Yu*, over to Aung San's command. It was he who led the guard of honor when Suu's father was piped aboard.

He went into the navy as an ordinary seaman, rising to the rank of lieutenant commander. In 1956 the ship he was serving on was wrecked, and he and twenty-six shipmates took to two life rafts. One of them sank, with the loss of all on board; seven of the men on the second raft also died but he and the others survived for twelve days on boiled sweets and rainwater before being rescued. The book he wrote about the ordeal, *Patrol Boat 103*, made him famous. When he retired from the navy in 1969 he quickly became one of Burma's best-loved writers: Unlike Win Tin, whose refusal to compromise in his journalism led to him being effectively silenced for many years before 1988, Maung Thaw Ka was editor in chief of a state-sponsored magazine under the socialist regime, and wrote witty and gently satirical pieces that were immensely popular. As a retired sailor he was expert at sailing close to the political wind without being capsized.

The Swedish journalist Bertil Lintner, who knew him as a friend, said, "He was a lovely man. Before 1988 he would travel around the country and give lectures on literature. Agents from Military Intelligence always occupied the front row of seats in the hall, but he was a war hero so it was very difficult to punish him."[8] He also wrote poetry, and translated much English poetry into Burmese, including Shakespeare sonnets and poems by Donne, Herrick, Shelley and Cowper. His English was fluent. Through the years of Burma's enforced seclusion he was one of the few who insisted on throwing open windows to the world.

With the uprising of 1988 he saw a chance of real change coming to Burma and seized it, befriending Suu and helping her to understand in detail how the movement was developing, cosigning a letter to the authorities in August 1988 protesting the brutal suppression of demonstrations, and joining the Central Executive Committee of the NLD when it was formed. But he went further than that: He also wrote an open letter to the Burmese Navy, exhorting the service to stand by the people in opposing the military junta.

He was fearless in defying the authorities. He ran a little photocopy shop in downtown Rangoon, and when *Outrage* was published, Bertil Lintner's blow-by-blow documentary account of the 1988 events, he obtained a copy and kept it in the shop, allowing customers he trusted to make Xeroxes but not to take it away.

But he was suffering from a muscle-wasting disease, and when SLORC came to get him he was already a sick man. He was sentenced to twenty years' jail for trying to foment an insurrection in the armed forces. "At the time he entered Insein Jail he was already suffering from a chronic disease that was laying his muscles to waste," Suu wrote later. "His movements were stiff and jerky, and everyday matters, such as bathing, dressing or eating, involved a series of maneuvers that could barely be completed without assistance."[9] Like Win Tin, he was locked up quite alone. For a man with an advanced degenerative disease, that was a way to torture him to death without the trouble of laying hands on him.

"He was thrown on a concrete floor," Lintner told me. "They didn't give him any medical treatment. It was punishment—because he was the one who dragged Suu Kyi onto the public stage." He subsequently died in hospital. Until then he kept writing in the cell. He had nothing, he wrote in one of his last poems, "Just One Matchstick." But one matchstick could change the world.

> When a little spark turns into a big flame, it will burn away
> all the dirt that exists in this world,
> together with the worthless, unprincipled people.
> In twenty years the ashes produced by the fire started from Maung Thaw
>   Ka's one matchstick
> will build a historical cenotaph for the future.[10]

He died in June 1991, aged sixty-five.

*

As the arrests, tortures and deaths mounted up—by November 1989 a hundred activists had been sentenced to death by the new tribunals—everyone who had ever waved a placard or shouted a slogan lived in fear that their turn could be next. Suu had spent more than half her life in Britain, in a society where people might fear poverty or crime or old age, but where fear—mortal fear—was rarely employed as an instrument of government policy. In Burma she discovered it was the fundamental agent of coercion. As she saw it, the fear with which Burma was saturated explained why its development was so stunted.

"It is not power that corrupts but fear," she wrote in the months before her detention, in an essay entitled "Freedom from Fear" that was published around the world in 1990. "Fear of losing power corrupts those who wield it and fear of the scourge of power corrupts those who are subject to it."

Fear, *bhaya* in Burmese, "destroys all sense of right and wrong," she went on, which is why it is at the root of corruption. "With so close a relationship between fear and corruption it is little wonder that in any society where fear is rife corruption in all forms becomes deeply entrenched."

It was not only economic distress that ignited the revolt of 1988, she wrote, but the disgust of young people at the way their lives were poisoned and deformed by fear. In Burma, the only relationship to authority that was permitted was one of complete passivity, where the people were no more self-assertive than "water in the cupped hands" of the rulers. "Law and order," a relatively neutral phrase in English, translates into Burmese as *nyein-wut-pi-pyar*; literally, "silent-crouched-crushed-flattened."[11] That was the attitude SLORC required of the Burmese, and that was what they rose up against.

The insurrectionists proposed a different model:

> Emerald cool we may be
> As water in cupped hands,

Suu wrote in that essay,

> But oh that we might be
> As splinters of glass
> In cupped hands.

"Glass splinters," Suu wrote, "the smallest with its sharp, glinting power to defend itself against hands that try to crush, could be seen as a vivid symbol of the spark of courage that is an essential attribute of those who would free themselves from the grip of oppression."[12]

But where and how to find courage, when the rulers have become accustomed to drinking up their people like water, and the people have grown used to being swallowed? International gestures such as the UN's Declaration of Human Rights were fine and important, as were the efforts by people like her old boss U Thant and his successors to give the UN a role in policing the behavior of states that flouted it. But so far such powers were painfully limited: The fact that Sadako Ogata was in the country and investigating human rights' abuses for the UN Human Rights Commission on the day that U Maung Ko, General Secretary of the Dockworkers' Union, became the first NLD activist to die in jail said plenty about the UN's impotence.

So courage, that glass splinter quality, was essential. Suu feared her foreign readers would not grasp the immensity of what she was proposing, because it is hard for anyone brought up in a free society to put themselves in the shoes of the Burmese. "The effort necessary to remain uncorrupted in an environment where fear is an integral part of everyday existence," she wrote, "is not immediately apparent to those fortunate enough to live in states governed by the rule of law."[13] But if Burma was to be transformed—and that was the task she and her colleagues had taken on—then a major effort would be required. Not an effort directed merely at changing policies and institutions or raising living standards; parroting about freedom, democracy and human rights would not in itself make the difference. What was needed for society to change was first for the people to change.

This might be difficult, but it was not inconceivable: After all, as she wrote, "It is his capacity for self-improvement and self-redemption which most distinguishes man from the mere brute." And self-improvement, self-redemption, was needed now. "The quintessential revolution," she wrote "is that of the spirit, born of an intellectual conviction of the need for change in those mental attitudes and values which shape the course of a nation's development . . . Without a revolution of the spirit, the forces which produced the iniquities of the old order would continue to be operative."[14]

These are fine words that resonate down the years and have become her clarion call. But they beg the question: In the face of the systematic brutality employed by SLORC, where was this "intellectual conviction" going to come from? And would it be sufficient to do the job? Suu was still at an early stage of her self-interrogation on these questions. "Saints, it has been said, are the sinners who go on trying," she wrote, "so free men are the oppressed who go on trying." And it was Michael, either prompted by her or on his own initiative, who provided one of the tools she needed in the quest.

While her sons were now barred from Burma indefinitely, her husband was allowed one more visit—presumably in the hope that he would find the words to persuade his wife to go home with him when he left. But if that was the hope, the regime was badly mistaken: "I had not even thought of doing this," he wrote.[15] Instead they enjoyed what he insisted, despite the unpromising circumstances, was an idyllic break: They were fully united and agreed in their understanding of what she was doing and why.

He flew into Rangoon on December 16, 1989—exactly four years after the family had been united in Japan, on the occasion when Noriko Ohtsu took them to visit the temple with the Burmese Buddha. "The days I spent alone with her that last time, completely isolated from the world, are among my happiest memories of our many years of marriage," he wrote. "It was wonderfully peaceful. Suu had established a strict regime of exercise, study and piano which I managed to disrupt. She was memorizing a number of Buddhist sutras. I produced Christmas presents I had brought one by one to spread them out over several days. We had all the time in the world to talk about many things. I did not suspect that this would be the last time we would be together for the foreseeable future." Like those of their sons, several of Michael's future visa applications would be turned down: Having failed to persuade his wife to leave, he guessed that the regime "realized that I was no longer useful to their purpose."

Part of Suu's "strict regime" that he disrupted involved meditation: Once her detention began she took to rising at 4:30 AM and starting the day with an hour of vipassana sitting meditation. But it was not easy. "I did not have a teacher," she wrote some years later, "and my early attempts were more than a little frustrating. There were days when I found my failure to discipline my mind . . . so infuriating I felt I was doing myself more harm than good."[16] But one of the Christmas parcels Michael brought contained a useful surprise: a paperback with on the cover a thorny tree, a rocky peak and an expanse of blue sky into which the morning sun is about to burst. The title was *In This Very Life: The Liberation Teachings of the Buddha*, by a Rangoon-based monk, Sayadaw U Pandita. The book was to open her mind, and provide her with a practical guide to sitting quietly, doing nothing.

Aung San Suu Kyi's generosity of spirit had been remarked on by her Oxford friend Ann Pasternak Slater. "It is Suu's kindness that is most sharply present to me now," she wrote. "One early morning I came to see my [elderly, ailing] mother, as I did every morning, and found Suu with her. She had discovered my mother wandering, half-dressed and confused, and brought her home. I will not forget the serious gentleness with which Suu talked to her, the grave concern with which she turned to me as she left."

Now Suu was to learn, or to relearn, that in her native religion, "much value is attached to liberality or generosity," as she later wrote: It was regarded as the most important of the "Ten Perfections of the Buddha" and the "Ten Duties of Kings."[17] But this should not be misunderstood, she warned: It was not to exalt "alms-giving based on canny calculation of possible benefits in the way of worldly prestige or other-worldly rewards." Rather, "it is a recognition of the crucial importance of the liberal, generous spirit as an effective antidote to greed as well as a fount of virtues which engender happiness and harmony." Suu already knew, instinctively, that for her morality was inseparable from politics. Now, thanks to Michael's gift, she was beginning to learn how to go deeper.

*

Their idyllic, surreal holiday came to an end. Michael went away. And finally she was almost alone.

Not entirely alone, of course. In the Orient, only the hermit monk in his mountain cave is ever really alone, and perhaps not even he.

There were the soldiers outside the gate of her compound and the others inside, fifteen of them, all armed, day and night. There were her faithful companions-cum-housekeepers Daw Khin Khin Win and her daughter Mee Ma Ma, and her maid Maria, all three sharing the terms of her detention. In the smaller house in the compound lived her aunt Daw Khin Gyi, where she had always lived, and free to come and go.

But that was all. She was more alone than she had ever been since the birth of Alexander, sixteen years before. From being the center of attention for months and months, the center of the Burmese universe and of interest and concern far beyond Burma, now it was as if she had vanished from the world. What was most striking was the contrast: the hubbub then and the silence now.

Eighteen months earlier the old family home had become her mother's sickbay when Suu brought Khin Kyi home from hospital. Silence reigned. Then, after Ne Win announced his resignation, it became almost overnight a teeming political laboratory. Twice during the following year troops had arrived in strength and put the house under siege. The second time, on July 20, 1989, the day after Martyrs' Day, all her party comrades were bundled into army lorries and driven off to prison. She was left there with her two sons and her three companions, guarded by a dozen soldiers, in a bizarre parody of normal home life. Michael flew in to join them in their solitude and the parody was complete.

But now her family had gone, too, back to school, back to work, back to the West. Leaving her—"This ruler of our kingdom, a pretty thing, a pretty little thing," as the Kachin grandmother had cooed to her babies— the queen of what exactly? The mistress of all she surveyed? Hardly: With fifteen armed soldiers watching her every move there was nothing she could command.

The queen of herself then, if nothing else. The way Daw Khin Kyi had taught her.

*

She had lost. That was the point. She had challenged the Old Man, Number One, General Ne Win, to a duel, cheered on by millions—but he had the gun and she had only flowers to throw and now she had lost the duel and they had locked her up and thrown away the key.

If we look at Aung San Suu Kyi's life as a conventional political narrative that is how it goes—very unsatisfactorily. The sudden challenge, the mass acclaim, the tireless campaigning, the nationwide crescendo of support—then nothing: the nothing of outright defeat. An election landslide win the following year, contemptuously ignored by the men with the guns. Fifteen years of solitary nothing, interspersed with a few years of trying to climb back on the bandwagon before being locked away again; finally released in 2010 because at last the generals have hit on a way to pen her up permanently in the margins, to confine her to a public space as niggardly and narrow as that of her home, thanks to the fake election and the fake parliament.

That, in an ugly nutshell, is how this second phase of Suu's political life looks. Even before her release in November 2010 some correspondents were speculating on her perhaps imminent retirement—she was sixty-five, after all, well into bus pass territory.[18] A reader's letter published by the *Financial Times* in 2011[19] wondered sadly if she was now no more than "Burma's Queen Mum," a rather pointless ornament to a regime that, to quote Burma authority Robert Taylor, could now be "on the cusp of normality."[20] Tragic is the word that springs to these writers' lips, tragic waste, tragic destiny; a story without the remotest hope of a happy end.

But to read Suu's political career in this register is to overlook the way her thinking developed during the years of house arrest, especially during the very harsh period with which her detention began, and the way this new thinking linked up with a movement that had very quietly been gathering force in Burma for fifty years, though largely unknown to the outside world. It is also to overlook the fact that, despite the failure to capitalize on the early success and change the system, and despite her many years of enforced absence from society, she still enjoys the allegiance of the great mass of Burmese people.

These two facts—her quiet emergence as a symbol and talisman of the underground movement, and her continuing mass support—are closely connected. They explain why, for example, the mass monks' revolt of September 2007, the so-called "Saffron Revolution," culminated in one deputation of monks making their way through the military road blocks to her gate. They explain why the generals continue even now to regard her as the number one domestic menace to their continued rule, despite the fact that they have systematically dismantled the national cult surrounding her father and have done everything they can think of to marginalize and demonize her.

*

It is necessary to chart the development of her thinking after she was detained.

For Suu, steeped in the literature of Britain and India as well as Burma, the challenge for Burma was not to ape the political forms of the West, nor to find the right balance of tyranny and license to allow the capitalists to storm in and take over as they had done in Bangkok. The deformation Burma had suffered under Ne Win was an offense and an insult, a prolonged abuse to the nation's soul. The challenge was to find a way out of the trap Ne Win had constructed, the bunker he had turned the country into. Democracy was part of that, to be sure, but the true challenge was a far greater one than swapping one political system for another. And it was during her house arrest that she identified the chink of light that she dared to hope could lead her and her country out of the trap, the bunker, the labyrinth.

In the long essay Suu researched and wrote during her year in Shimla in 1986, she celebrated what India had achieved thanks to Gandhi, the "Great Soul," and his contemporaries and forbears in the Indian Renaissance. "In India," she wrote, "political and intellectual leadership had often coincided. Moreover, there had been an uninterrupted stream of able leaders from the last years of the nineteenth century until independence. This provided a cohesive framework within which social and political movements could experiment and mature."[21] Such a framework was conspicuously absent in Burma—but that did not mean it could never exist: All it meant was that Burma's modern experience had been far too compressed for such an evolution to occur. She quoted a British scholar, J.S. Furnivall, founder of the Burma Research Society, who she felt was on the right track. He wrote in 1916:

We were looking for the human Burma, that mysterious entity of which each individual Burman . . . is on an infinitesimal scale a manifestation and a representative, which is a norm subsuming all their individual activities, and which represents all that is vital and enduring in this country as we know it; the partnership, as Burke puts it, between the dead, the living and those yet to be born . . .

For the Burma that we hope to assist in building is like some old pagoda recently unearthed and in course of restoration . . . [It is necessary] to clear away cartloads of rubbish. We have carefully to set in order the foundations and the whole building brick by brick, but I for one firmly believe that if the Burma of the future is to be a lasting fabric, it must be built up on the old foundations.[22]

Suu commented, "In such views can be seen the seeds of a renaissance: The urge to create a vital link between the past, the present and the future, the wish to clear away 'cartloads of rubbish' so that old foundations might become fit to hold up a new and lasting fabric. But it was a renaissance that did not really come to fruition."

Written shortly before her return to Burma in 1988, with her encounters with Burmese students in Japan and their hopes for her so fresh in her mind, it is clear that the essay was more than the dissection of some dusty old intellectual movements. Whether consciously or unconsciously or somewhere between the two, Suu was limning her own task and her challenge: what someone with her parentage, education and knowledge of the world might dream of achieving. It had culminated in the High Noon of Martyrs' Day, in calamitous defeat, detention, humiliation, dispersion. But beyond those awful experiences, and in a strange way *through* and *thanks to* those awful experiences, she glimpsed a way out. And it all began with meditation.

*

That intellectual and spiritual journey is a large part of the story of the past twenty years: how and why she remained relevant and inspiring to her people—and to millions more beyond Burma's borders—despite everything its rulers could do to render her irrelevant, alien and extraneous. In the process she has at least made a start on creating a new Burma "built on the old foundations" as Furnivall put it—one built on the truths of Buddhism, but not in the old, mechanical, reductive version for which Burma became notorious—"acquiring merit" to assure a more auspicious reincarnation—but living the religion's values in one's everyday life. "When people have been stripped of all their material supports," she wrote during her first years of detention, "there only remain to sustain them the values of their cultural and spiritual inheritance."[23] The generals had stripped "all their material supports" from the best and brightest in Burma, and reduced Suu herself to a walking shadow. Now the only way forward was back.

2
LANDSLIDE VICTORY

O N Sunday May 27, 1990, Aung San Suu Kyi, still under detention in her home, cast her vote in her country's first free general elections for thirty years. The ballot paper was put into an envelope which was sealed and taken from her home by a regime official.

To most foreign observers, it looked like a futile gesture. For weeks the international media had been scrutinizing Burma's upcoming poll and concluding that it was bound to be rigged.

The military junta had done everything in their power to ensure a good result—a win for the National Unity Party (NUP), the junta's tame proxy party, as the BSPP had been rebranded.

The top leadership of the NLD had been put out of action, with Aung San Suu Kyi under house arrest since July 20th. U Tin Oo, the retired general who was chairman of the party and who had been detained the same day, was sentenced to three years' hard labor in December and taken to Insein Jail. Most of their closest colleagues had been jailed and would not re-emerge for years. The party was now run by a skeleton staff of those who remained at liberty, led by U Kyi Maung, aged seventy-two, the tubby, wisecracking former colonel who had been one of the first people to join Suu two summers before.

In January the regime sought to neutralize the threat posed by Suu's personal popularity by barring her from standing as a candidate because of her marriage to a foreigner—a new rule. Her image was everywhere in the NLD's campaign, on banners, T-shirts, posters, badges and scarves; cassette tapes of her campaign speeches were sold from market stalls. But the lady herself was firmly locked away.

General Khin Nyunt, head of Military Intelligence (MI) and the second most powerful man in the junta, in two long speeches drove home the message that Suu's party was a menace to the country's future. On August 5th, he repeated the now-familiar claim that the NLD had been infiltrated by communists. The following month, at a press conference where he spoke for seven hours, he made the diametrically opposite allegation that Suu and her party were at the heart of an international rightist conspiracy involving powerful foreign countries. The speech was later published in a 300-page book with the catchy title *The Conspiracy of Treasonous Minions and Traitorous Cohorts*.

Emasculating the NLD, however, was only part of the task of manufacturing a good result. SLORC now set about tackling the remaining challenges with military thoroughness.

Other enemies of army rule were put under house arrest, including former prime minister U Nu.

The regime identified city neighborhoods with a high proportion of opposition supporters and broke them up. In the months leading up to the election at least half a million people around the country were forced to abandon their homes in the cities and move to crudely constructed and malaria-ridden new townships far away.

Practically all conventional forms of campaigning, including rallies, door-to-door lobbying and media interviews, were banned. Criticism of the military was a criminal offence. Gatherings of more than five people remained illegal under martial law rules, though each party of the ninety-three registered for the poll was allowed to hold a single rally, on condition that seven days' notice was given. Each was also permitted a single, pre-approved ten minute statement on state television, and fifteen minutes on state radio.

To make sure the heavens were on their side, the regime made sure to pick a good day: May 27th contained a plethora of lucky nines, two plus seven for the day itself, plus the fact that it fell in the fourth week of the fifth month.

An offer from the US to send election monitors was tartly rebuffed, and all foreigners were banned from the country for weeks before the election.

On the eve of polling, the generals could be well pleased with their handiwork: Myanmar, as she now was, had been through the wringer in the past twenty-four months since Ne Win's crass decision to demonetize the currency then throw a spanner into the constitutional arrangements by raising the possibility of multiparty elections. But since the locking up of "that woman" as Ne Win referred to Suu (he refused to pronounce her name), the situation had improved all round.

The socialist ideology which had conditioned policy for a generation was consigned to the waste bin along with the BSPP, and Burma reopened for business. Some Western countries may have found it awkward dealing on normal trade terms with a country that had slaughtered thousands of its unarmed citizens in cold blood, but Thailand, Singapore and South Korea had no such inhibitions, snapping up contracts to extract timber, jade, precious stones and seafood at bargain prices.

A South Korean company, Yukong, became the first foreign company to be allowed to explore for oil onshore, rapidly followed by Shell, Idemitsu, Petro-Canada, and finally the American oil firms Amoco and Unocal. When the army roared into downtown Rangoon on September 18, 1988, the nation's foreign exchange reserves had been less than $10 million. Now they were between $200 and $300 million.

Tight security prevented any significant demonstrations to mark the anniversaries of the great uprising of 8/8/88 or the military crackdown of the following month. Meanwhile, in a further sign of America's softening approach, the generals and Coca-Cola signed a deal to bottle its drinks in Burma. To demonstrate to the general public and the world at large that SLORC knew a thing or two about good governance, a major clean-up campaign was launched, reminiscent of the operation by Ne Win himself in 1958 under his caretaker government, and Rangoon's public buildings gleamed with fresh paint.

The governments of western Europe and the US remained dubious, unwilling to forget how SLORC had come to power. But an election run with military efficiency, producing a solid working majority for the NUP—or with the votes shared between such a plethora of parties that the army would be fully justified in retaining control—would surely bring them round.

*

The regime might have been more circumspect about the election—might have booted it far into the mists of the future, claiming that they needed to wait until true stability had been achieved—if they had seen what Suu saw as she traveled round the country with her party.

The concept of democracy had been much bandied about in Burma since Ne Win's momentous speech. But what did the Burmese really know about the subject? Those over the age of forty-four would have vague memories of the last free election in which they were entitled to vote, which U Nu had won with a large majority. But anyone under that age, brought up in a one-party dictatorship which shut the country off from the outside world, would be hazy about it.

Knowledge may have been thin, but as Suu went on the campaign trail in the first half of 1989 she found insatiable interest. "More than a quarter-century of narrow authoritarianism under which they had been fed a pabulum of shallow, negative dogma had not blunted the percep-tiveness or political alertness of the Burmese," she wrote in an essay during campaigning:

> On the contrary . . . their appetite for discussion and debate, for uncen-sored information and objective analysis, seemed to have been sharpened.
>
> There was widespread and intelligent speculation on the nature of democracy as a social system . . . a spontaneous interpretative response to such basic ideas as representative government, human rights and the rule of law.
>
> The people of Burma view democracy not merely as a form of government but as an integrated social and ideological system based on respect for the individual.[1]

The state media might scorn imported concepts such as democracy and human rights as somehow "inimical to indigenous values," but Suu maintained that they cohered fully with the faith system which was at the root of Burmese culture. "Buddhism . . . places the greatest value on man . . . Each man has in him the potential to realize the truth through his own will and endeavour and to help others to realize it . . . The proposition that the Burmese are not fit to enjoy as many rights and privileges as the citizens of democratic countries is insulting."

But with all the top leaders now out of action and the party facing heavy intimidation by the junta, getting the NLD's message about its program to the voters was complicated: Grassroots party workers had to go about their work like drug dealers, sidling up to potential supporters and discussing what was on offer under their breath. But at least they had a manifesto to work from.[2]

It was a resoundingly reasonable document. Burma today lacked a constitution, it pointed out. The new one would be written in collaboration with all the other parties whose representatives won seats in the *Pyitthu Hluttaw* or "national assembly," as the parliament was called. The powers of executive, legislature and judiciary would be separated. National sovereignty would be vested in the parliament, to which all other organs of state, including crucially the army, would become accountable. The conflicts that had raged around Burma's borders for decades would be ended by giving the "ethnic nationalities" greater autonomy than the 1947 constitution allowed them, including "the right to self-determination with respect to . . . politics, administration and economic management in accordance with the law." Education, health care and social welfare, so brutally cut back under army rule, would be given far greater attention than before. The economic liberalization that SLORC had started to introduce would be pursued, though the interests of Burma's farmers would be protected.

*

And pigs would fly: The NLD might dream and scheme all they liked behind their prison bars, but it seems with hindsight that the military had no intention of ceding power, whatever the election result. And they were confident that the people, *their* people, so used to being "water in the cupped hands" of the army, comfortably familiar with the forms and foibles of the old BSPP, now the NUP, would in the privacy of the polling booth turn their backs on dangerous novelty and show due gratitude to the force that had kept them safe from foreign machinations all these years.

So confident were the generals that they began to relax a little. They admitted a handful of foreign journalists and television news crews to watch the Burmese line up and vote. As polling day approached, martial law restrictions were partially lifted. The soldiers thronging Suu's villa were temporarily replaced by police in plain clothes. Army and uniformed police disappeared from the streets. It was the usual Burmese vanishing trick, as seen on the day of Suu's mother's funeral, another manifestation of the "zero-sum" attitude to power, where the army is either overwhelmingly present or totally absent—but even if absent, everyone knows they are not far away. The NLD took advantage of the pull-back to take to the streets in their pick-up trucks, imploring the people of Rangoon to be sure to give them their vote.

In the end the people needed no imploring. The lines began forming outside schools and government offices where voting was to take place early on the morning of May 27th. The army was again conspicuous by its absence: The voting was overseen by civilians, as if Burma's conversion to civilian rule had happened by magic, overnight. People put on their Sunday best to perform this important and extremely rare civic duty. As in India, every registered party was symbolized by an icon depicted on the voting slip. These included a beach ball, a comb, a tennis racket and an umbrella. Powerfully evocative symbols such as the peacock were banned, but the NLD had cannily chosen the *kamauk*, the farmer's straw hat, to symbolize their party—making it easy for their supporters to indicate their preference while appearing to wear normal rustic costume.

Nationwide, more than twenty million people were eligible to vote. In seven constituencies where the army was fighting insurgents, polling was cancelled altogether; in many other border areas, only a fraction of registered voters managed to vote because of the violence. But in most of the country the turnout was heavy, with some 72 percent casting their votes in total.

The most glaring anomaly about the election was that it was held in a constitutional vacuum, the old 1974 constitution having been dissolved in the so-called "coup" that brought SLORC into being in September 1988, and not replaced. It was assumed by the NLD and other parties that the first, vital task of the winning parties would be to draft a constitution. But how that would happen had not been spelled out.

Late on the night of polling the Chinese news service, Xinhua, was the first foreign news agency to report the first result of Burma's first election for thirty years: The NLD candidate for Seikan Township in Yangondaw, a woman called San San, obtained over half the votes cast.

That result was followed by a flood more. And to the shock and horror of the military, the overwhelming majority of results went the same way. Voters did not care for the Evergreen Young Men's Association, the National Peace and Comfort Party, U Nu's League for Democracy and

Peace, nor for the army's favorite, the NUP. Aung San Suu Kyi's party was sweeping the board.

Results continued to dribble in over the coming days, and practically all of them tended the same way. The junta had said it would take three weeks for all results to be known, but it became clear within twenty-four hours that Suu's party, all of whose top leaders were in jail or detained in their homes, had won a landslide victory. And nobody knew what to do next.

This, according to Bertil Lintner, following events as closely as he could from Bangkok, was when the NLD missed its best opportunity to change Burma for ever—without a shot being fired in anger. "At the last minute the regime had allowed the foreign media in," he pointed out—and this gave the NLD a rare and precious weapon, one which they totally failed to use.

> This was before electronic media and so on, but nevertheless the world media came in, including television networks, for the actual election day. Once they had seen the way things were going the government searched for ways to delay and delay and delay the counting of the votes, saying, oh, we have to bring the ballot boxes to Rangoon and count them here and things like that, and it would take a long time. But it was already clear that the NLD had won.
>
> What the NLD should have done at that point [before all votes were counted but when it was clear that they had won] was to declare victory: to hold a press conference at the party headquarters in Rangoon, invite the entire media, and say, we've won the election and therefore it is ridiculous that our leader is under house arrest. At three o'clock this afternoon we are going to go and liberate her. And then they could have sent out a lot of speaker vans around Rangoon to tell everyone to go to University Avenue at three o'clock. And millions of people would have shown up. They could have lifted off the gates and carried her off to the television station and she could have been put in charge and called for calm and the loyalty of the armed forces and all the rest of it. It would have been all over in forty-eight hours.[3]

But nothing of the sort happened: the reason being, Lintner, says, that the party was now essentially leaderless.

> The NLD mishandled it. When Suu Kyi was placed under house arrest, the party was decapitated. They were all arrested, Ma Thanegi, U Win Tin, all the smart people in the leadership. So the initiative went to the second

rung in the party, people like U Kyi Maung, a nice old man, a retired army colonel. Kyi Maung was strong enough to keep the whole thing together and lead it through the election to victory. But then he said, now the military has shown some goodwill by letting the election happen and making sure the vote goes fairly, so we have to show some goodwill too and not push things.

They didn't lose their nerve, they just miscalculated. By saying okay, they've shown some goodwill, we have to show some goodwill, they gave enough time for the military to re-group and strike back.

Instead of marching en masse to University Avenue and setting their leader free, the NLD erected a large blackboard outside its headquarters to keep the public abreast of what was happening—a homely version of the vote-athon apparatus of modern TV news channels. It stood there for weeks as the results continued to arrive from distant corners of the country. Every time a new result came in it was chalked up on the board. In the early days the crowds watching the board spilled from the pavement onto the road, hundreds strong, and every time a fresh NLD win was written up, they sent up a cheer of approval.

But then after a few days, with many seats left to declare but with the NLD on track for an overwhelming victory, the novelty wore off and the numbers began to dwindle. It was all very fine, people said to each other—but what did it mean exactly? What was supposed to happen next?

In mid-June, more than two weeks after polling, SLORC admitted that, with many constituencies still to declare results, the NLD had already won an absolute majority. In the end they won 392 of the seats they contested, slightly more than 80 percent of the total. But in fact the scale of their victory was even greater than that: Their allies in the ethnic states, running under the umbrella of the United Nationalities League for Democracy, the UNLD, won 65 seats. Their ally in the Shan States, the Shan Nationalities League for Democracy, became the second biggest winner nationwide, with 23 seats. Overall the NLD and its allies won more than 94 percent of the seats. The United Nationals Democratic Party of U Aung Gyi, the former general who had been Suu's colleague at the head of the NLD before turning on it, won a single seat. The NUP, despite (or rather because of) its backing by the army and its decades in power under the BSPP avatar, won a mere 10 seats.

Compounding the shock for SLORC and adding an extra element of paranoid unease was the fact that several constituencies where serving soldiers constituted the majority of voters, such as Dagon township in Rangoon, had elected NLD MPs.

The political landscape of Burma was turned inside out, and even the army could not deny that something had happened. But in mid-June they clearly had no idea what to do next, frozen in the headlights of hostile public opinion.

"The final result is expected within the next week," reported Terry McCarthy and Yuli Ismartono in the *Independent* on June 15, 1990.

> But the military has so far refused to be drawn on how power will be transferred to a civilian government, when this might happen, or when they intend to release Aung San Suu Kyi . . .
>
> The military, confident up to a week before the elections that there would be no clear winner and that it would easily be able to manipulate the Assembly, is now left without a master plan, and the old paranoia is starting to creep back in.[4]

A spokesman for the regime, asked about SLORC's plans, sounded as if he was discussing the aftermath of a nasty ambush in guerrilla country rather than a victory for democracy in the sight of the world. "We don't know who is our enemy and who is not," he told the *Independent*, "so we have to tread very carefully."[5] Asked whether SLORC would be dissolved after a transfer of power, the spokesman, Colonel Ye Htut, told the paper, "Yes, but as you know, SLORC is the army itself. SLORC will be dissolved, but the army will continue to exist . . ."

It was not until July that SLORC was ready with a coordinated response. It was a textbook example of the tendency of authoritarian regimes, following Orwell, to say that two plus two equals five. The elections were not, as the foreign press had mischievously reported, for the purpose of electing a government, they said. All that was a misunderstanding. There was no constitution, so how could there be a government? First there must be a constitution, then a government. So what those 485 people—or a fraction of them, to be selected by SLORC, plus a supplement (in the event it turned out to be a very large supplement, 600 percent of the elected quota) of army officers to advise them—had been elected to do was write a constitution. Only after the constitution had been written and ratified could a civilian government take office. Until then—SLORC remained in charge.

It was not an entirely new theme. At the beginning of May, McCarthy had reported, "The army is indicating that the elected body will not be a national assembly from which a government will be chosen, but rather a constituent assembly, empowered to write a new constitution for the country."[6] The need for such an assembly before power was handed over had in fact been repeatedly voiced by Khin Nyunt, the ambitious heir apparent, the man "who breathes through Ne Win's nostrils" as the Burmese put it.[7]

But Khin Nyunt had been contradicted repeatedly by General Saw Maung, the head of the junta, who had said after the crackdown of September 1988 that he would "throw flowers in the path of the government" and that the sole task of SLORC was to pave the way for the new, elected government. On January 9, 1990, he reiterated, "It is our duty to hold an election so that a government can be formed. Once the election is over, it will not be the Defense Forces' responsibility to see that a government is formed . . . "[8] On polling day itself he said it once again: As the *Economist* reported on June 2nd, "While he was casting his vote, General Saw Maung, the leader of the State Council, told a journalist that he would hand over power to whichever party was victorious. Various spokesmen from the army and the foreign ministry have said that a newly elected government could 'move as quickly as it likes to take power.'"

But that was then. Once the NLD had flattened all contenders, it was plain to see that two and two made five.

*

The claim that on May 27, 1990, Burma voted not for a government but for a constitutional convention became the junta's mantra for the next eighteen years, its perennial alibi for hanging on to power, justifying endless procrastination on the road to democracy. Today the claim has attained the status of holy writ among apologists for the regime. In February 2011, Burma scholar Michael Aung-Thwin, professor of Asian Studies at the University of Hawaii, wrote in a newspaper article, "Virtually every credible scholar of Burma has demonstrated that both the

NLD and Suu Kyi knew at the time that these were constituent assembly elections, not national elections."[9]

The claim was certainly helpful in justifying SLORC's hanging on to power. But as veteran Burma-watcher Lintner pointed out, it makes no sense. "The election was held to elect the *Pyitthu Hluttaw*, the national assembly," said Lintner, who at the time of the election was Burma correspondent of the *Far Eastern Economic Review*:

> The new *Pyitthu Hluttaw* was to have the same number of MPs as the *Pyitthu Hluttaw* in the old one-party BSPP set-up, but with more parties represented. No one suggested before polling day that, of those 485 MPs-elect, 100 would be selected to sit with 600 other people selected by the military to draft a new constitution. That announcement came two months after the election, in July. It was clear that there would have to be a new constitution but that would be up to the parliament to decide, not the military. What's the point in electing 485 people if you are then going to hand-pick 100 of them? It didn't make sense at all.
>
> In 1990 the wrong party won. If in 1990 the National Unity Party had won, would they have been arrested and forced into exile? Of course not: There would have been a new government within weeks. They would have been in parliament right away, the military would have said okay, now you can write the constitution! The wrong party won and that's the bottom line. The military didn't expect it.[10]

*

Aung San Suu Kyi's own thoughts about the election and its strange aftermath were a matter for conjecture. Although she was able to follow events on radio and television, she was forbidden to make any public comments.

And her isolation was about to become even more drastic. Up until July 1990 she had received letters from her family, sent to the British Embassy in Rangoon and brought to her door by SLORC. In fact Khin Nyunt boasted about the fact. At a news conference on July 13th, he said:

> We have been very lenient [towards her] . . . [She] is permitted to move about freely . . . We assisted in repairs to her compound and her residence and have been providing weekly medical care and treatment. We even

provided orthodontic care at her request to correct her uneven teeth. Her spouse, Dr. Michael Aris, and her sons have been sending her letters, foodstuffs, goods, books and documents from Britain through the British Embassy in Rangoon. We accept responsibility of delivering these letters, goods and foodstuffs to Daw Aung San Suu Kyi without exception . . .[11]

But when she heard of Khin Nyunt's boast, she decided to accept none of these "favors" any more: If she could not, as she had demanded, go to Insein Jail with her colleagues, she would certainly not allow herself, locked up in her home, to be portrayed as a pampered beneficiary of army rule. She said later:

[SLORC] seemed to think they were doing me a tremendous favor by letting me communicate with my family. It was in fact my right. I've never accepted anything as a favor. So I would not accept any favors from them. Also, I did not think that they had a right to keep me under house arrest for longer than a year. In fact they had no right to arrest all those NLD [members] who had been successful in the elections. So it was a form of protest against injustices they were perpetrating as well as an indication that I would accept no favors from them.[12]

The flow of letters, goods and services into her home abruptly ceased. And her solitary life became very much harder.

The regime refused to give any estimation of when she might be let out—let alone entertain the idea that she should play a role in the new government. In the same speech in which he vaunted SLORC's provision of dental care, etcetera, Khin Nyunt addressed that question.

The NLD openly declared that Daw Aung San Suu Kyi must play a leading role in establishing a new democratic state and that Daw Aung San Suu Kyi must lead in the talks with the SLORC . . . Which is more important: obtaining power and the release of Daw Aung San Suu Kyi, or the long-term interests of the country and the people? . . . I believe this is not the time for an individual approach or for a personality cult in insisting that a specific person be included in working for the long-term interests of the state.

Meanwhile, a new phase in Burma's political game was about to begin: the manhunt for the winning candidates.

3

LONG LIVE HOLINESS

JUST as it is untrue that Burma has never enjoyed an era of freedom—it lasted twenty-six days in August and September 1988—neither is it true that the elections of May 1990 did not produce a government. But instead of being sworn in at Rangoon with all the dignity at the Burmese state's disposal, it was formed in a malarial camp in the jungle close to the border with Thailand, under constant threat of bombardment by the Burmese Army.

In her short but seminal essay on the role played by fear in authoritarian societies, "Freedom from Fear," Suu was careful to point out how the behavior of the oppressors as well as the oppressed is twisted by fear. "Fear of losing power corrupts those who wield it," she wrote. ". . . fear of being surpassed, humiliated or injured in some way can provide the impetus for ill will." She wrote the essay before being put in detention; but now that her party and its allies had won the election, the fear of those who had terrorized their nation for decades—the fear of confronting the vengeful fury of their victims—undermined any hope of power changing hands. "The army leaders are paralyzed by fear," said a Western diplomat in Rangoon, "fear of the revenge of the people. It's the Nuremberg syndrome which held up political reform in Argentina and Chile for so long."

First SLORC spent six weeks issuing the election results in dribs and drabs. Then, when the NLD's landslide victory was beyond dispute, they announced a two-month moratorium to allow claims of abuse and misconduct by defeated candidates to be investigated. The NLD's acting leader Kyi Maung, the most senior of those who remained at liberty, judging that it would be a mistake to pile on pressure, allowed the junta to play for time, but finally summoned the party's winning candidates—its MPs-elect—to a mass meeting at the Gandhi Hall in central Rangoon on July 28th and 29th.

At the meeting's conclusion they issued a statement, the "Gandhi Declaration," condemning the continuing delays as "shameful," and rejecting SLORC's plans for a constitutional convention as irrelevant. "It is against political nature," they declared, "that the League, which has overwhelmingly won enough seats in parliament to form a government, has been prohibited from minimum democratic rights." They gave the junta a deadline of September 30th to transfer power.

But the endgame was approaching. Even before the MPs could meet, SLORC announced a decree, number 1/90, refusing in advance any demands they might come up with. The MPs might have been elected to the *Pyitthu Hluttaw*, but now nobody inside the regime was talking about convening it. Before that happened, they said, a National Convention would have to be set up—it was the first anyone had heard of such a body—to draw up the guidelines for the new constitution; only after that could the Assembly convene to write its own draft constitution, which would then have to be approved by SLORC—and so on indefinitely into the future. No time frame was proposed, and participation in the Convention was not the right of the new MPs: Instead SLORC would pick the delegates it fancied. And just to make sure they stuck to this agreement, MPs-elect were obliged to sign a "1/90 declaration," renouncing any right to form a government.

But all these pseudo-judicial measures were not sufficient to staunch the fears of the junta's leaders, of whom it appeared that Ne Win was still the unchallenged boss. There was no real substitute for the medieval measures employed by the kings of old (and indeed the British colonialists)—to feel really secure you needed bodies in firmly locked cells.

Thus on September 6th, three weeks before the NLD's deadline to the junta, SLORC targeted the last vestiges of robust NLD leadership, arresting Kyi Maung and his deputy and sentencing them to ten years' jail for treason. Eighteen members of the NLD's central executive committee out of twenty-two were now in detention. At the same time SLORC tackled the party's foot soldiers, arresting more than forty MPs, allegedly for refusing to sign the 1/90 declaration. Two of them died in jail soon after their arrest, apparently under torture. And what of Aung San Suu Kyi herself? SLORC told foreign diplomats in Rangoon that she would only be freed if she agreed to give up politics and leave the country for ever.

Hope of reaching any sort of accommodation with the junta was now dead. The country had come full circle since Ne Win's "multiparty democracy" declaration of July 1988 and was back exactly where it started—with the same psychopathic tyrant in charge.

The men and women who had been voted into power by their fellow-countrymen were all now in grave peril, and some of the most promising and well-qualified new MPs decided that there was nothing to be gained by hanging around in Rangoon waiting to be arrested. Eight of them, led by a cousin of Suu called Dr. Sein Win, the newly elected MP for Paukkaung, 125 miles north of Rangoon, and Western-educated like her, trekked through the mountains in the east of the country, finally arriving at a place called Manerplaw: the jungle camp which was the headquarters of the Democratic Alliance of Burma (DAB), a coalition of the insurgent forces that had been fighting the Burmese Army for many years.

First the MPs declared a ceasefire with the Alliance, then they announced that they were forming a government. Claiming the support of more than 250 elected MPs, they explained that their efforts to form a government, first in a monastery in Mandalay, then in a foreign embassy in Rangoon, had been foiled. So instead they were setting up what they called the National Coalition Government of the Union of Burma (NCGUB) here in Manerplaw, with Sein Win as prime minister.

And it was there, a few months later, that I caught up with them.

*

As you would expect of a camp that had managed to hold out against everything the Burmese Army threw at it, Manerplaw was not easy to reach. For some fifteen years it had been the command center of the most stubborn and enduring of Burma's ethnic armies, the Karen National Liberation Army. GIVE US LIBERTY OR GIVE US DEATH read the sign over the camp's entrance. The settlement had survived because it occupied a narrow shelf between the Moei river on the east and steep mountains that climbed straight out of the grassy parade ground on the west. Beyond those mountains was another, more daunting range before the descent towards the Salween river and the positions held by the Burmese Army.

The only practicable way for a foreigner to approach Manerplaw was from the Thai side.[1] Commissioned to write a magazine piece about

Manerplaw and its residents, I took a bus to the Thai border town of Mae Sariang with the photographer Greg Girard, and persuaded the owner of our little hotel to take us closer to our destination.

The tarmac road soon gave way to rutted mud and we bumped down it for hours, fording streams and winding through wooded mountains. When our driver's pick-up truck died on us he flagged down a lorry which took us the rest of the way to the riverside village of Mae Sam Leb: no more than a dirt road lined with little eateries and stores selling chains and spare parts for outboard engines, ending at a dice gambling den on the shore of the Salween river.

We had arrived in the war zone. Directly across the river but out of sight was a Burmese Army post. The bamboo shops of Mae Sam Leb were as new as they were flimsy: A year before the village had been wiped out by Burmese Army bombs. In the weeks before our arrival in early April the army had been pounding Karen villages in the area.

At the river we found a long-tailed boat going our way, with a boy who looked about ten at the helm. When it was crammed full of passengers we set off, a cool breeze in our faces and the water slapping against the sides. We turned into the Moei River heading southeast, with Thailand and its denuded mountains on the east bank, the richer forests of Burma on the west, and the grey forms of steep conical peaks looming ahead. We puttered along for several hours. Finally the boat nosed on to a gravel shore on the west side and we had arrived.

It was the hottest time of day in the hottest period of the year, during the weeks before the monsoon arrives, and Manerplaw snoozed in the baking heat. In long barracks on stilts thatched with leaves, young rebel soldiers sprawled inertly. Chickens and ducks clucked and quacked in the shadows.

But the impression of somnolent ease was deceptive. Every day for the past ten days the Burmese Army had attacked Karen strongholds, withdrawing a week before our arrival. They shelled and bombed nine Karen villages, destroying several, killing two villagers, wounding many more and driving about three thousand to take shelter in the forest or in refugee camps on the Thai side. Mortars were fired at Manerplaw from the Salween river. And four times a day the planes came over: Every day the sound of exploding bombs drew closer. Burmese Army troops had seized a hilltop position not far away, increasing pressure on the insurgents, who the previous year had lost six riverside camps further south. Manerplaw was now one of the last few strongholds that the rebels still held.

*

The stubborn struggle of the Karen, first for independence and latterly for self-government, was one of the fundamental reasons why the "Union of Burma" has never been more than a form of words. "The first thing colonial rule denies a people is their history," Martin Smith wrote in his classic book on Burma's insurgencies. "The new Republic of Burma which came into being on January 4, 1948, bore little resemblance to any nation or state from the historic past."[2]

The mountains and rivers that hemmed Manerplaw were the southerly extensions of north–south ranges that girdle Burma's central plains and that have conditioned the way the country we call Burma has developed since prehistoric times; "the natural routes of migration," as Smith writes, "to a constant flow of peoples from the high plateaus of Central Asia."[3] The mountains and rivers were a formidable obstacle to potential invaders, but they were also a barrier to anyone within the land that the mountains enclosed who sought to unify it.

Dozens of ethnic groups, "an anthropologist's paradise," settled in Burma over the centuries and met and commingled ceaselessly, but dominion never went unchallenged for long. Power spread out from city-states founded variously by the Mon, Burman, Arakanese and Shan groups, but the natural barriers ensured that it oscillated frequently between their valley kingdoms.

The great city of Pagan on the Irrawaddy, for example, marked Burman ascendancy in the eleventh century under the Burman king Anawrahta, but its glory was short-lived. In the fourteenth and fifteenth centuries it was the Shan, cousins of the Thais, who predominated, overtaken in the sixteenth centuries by the Mon kings of Pegu. The Burmans of the central plains returned to preeminence under King Alaunghpaya in the eighteenth century, but their final conquest of the Mon and Arakanese kingdoms, carving out a kingdom roughly equivalent to present-day Burma, was only achieved on the eve of the first incursion by the British.

Less than half a century later, the dynasty Alaunghpaya had founded, the Konbaung, came crashing down.

The Burmans, who may account for about two-thirds of the total population, have thus dominated the country that bears their name for some centuries, but the long history of contention between the different ethnic groups lives on. The perceived injustice of Burman tyranny is explained and lamented in their folk tales. "When Yuwa [God] created the world he took three handfuls of earth and threw them round about him," goes the Karen creation myth, as retold by George Scott. "From one sprang the Burmans, from another the Karens, and from the third the Kalas, the foreigners. The Karens were very talkative and made much more noise than all the others, and so the Creator believed that there were too many of them, and he threw another half handful to the Burmans, who thus gained such a supremacy that they soon overcame the Karens, and have oppressed them ever since."[4]

The men from the plains tried to conquer the hill tribes, and failing that to steal their land and their women, to tax and raise levies from them and to carry them away as slaves, and the animosity accumulated over the centuries. But it reached a new pitch with the Japanese invasion.

Today around two million Karen live in the border area, and two or three million more in the delta area near Rangoon. When the British took their third and final bite out of Burma in 1886, annexing lower Burma and gaining mastery of the whole country, the Burmans were subjected to direct British rule, but minorities including the Karen were given a degree of control over their own affairs. The Karen population was a mixture of Buddhists and animists; Christian missionaries who poured into the region found the animists ripe for conversion.

When the Japanese invaded in 1942, the Karen troops remained loyal to the British, and in retribution both the Japanese and their Burman allies under Aung San committed atrocities against the Karen that have never been forgiven or forgotten. As a Karen leader, Saw Tha Din, said to Martin Smith in 1985, "How could anyone expect the Karen people to trust the Burmans after what happened during the war—the murder and slaughter of so many Karen people and the robbing of so many Karen villages? After all this, how could anyone seriously expect us to trust any Burman government in Rangoon?"[5]

During independence negotiations the Karen held out for their own homeland; they alone of the largest ethnic groups on the borders refused to sign Aung San's famous Panglong Agreement, granting the "races" full internal autonomy within a Union of Burma.[6] Instead they took up arms against the Burmese state, and have been fighting ever since. The camp at Manerplaw was now the front line of that endless guerrilla war.

But with the decimation of anti-regime protesters in the Burmese heartland that had been under way since mid-1988, Manerplaw had acquired a new meaning. Now it had also become the last bolt-hole within Burma for those committed to democratic change.

*

It was in the summer of 1988, after the first massacres in Rangoon and elsewhere and when it became clear that the army was serious about punishing those who had risen up in protest, that political refugees began arriving in Karen. Burmese Army propaganda claimed that these hills were full of bandits and savages, but when the first Rangoon and Mandalay students came out of the woods the Karen fighters made them feel at home. "They welcomed us and took care of us like their own children," said Thaung Htun, a former student in Rangoon who was one of the early arrivals.[7] By the time the newly elected MPs arrived, Manerplaw was already home to a substantial community of internal exiles.

Early in the morning, when the weather was still tolerably cool, Greg the Canadian photographer and I visited each group in turn. Cocks crowed; mist hung low over the river and snagged in the trees on the mountainside. Down by the river the freedom fighters of the Central Committee of the All-Burma Students' Democratic Front were washing their clothes and brushing their teeth and plunging in for a cool bath. They swept the dusty paths in the village of bamboo and rattan they had built in the north of the settlement, sweeping the dead leaves into piles and setting them alight. A medical graduate who was the Committee's Foreign Secretary did the rounds of the huts of students suffering from malaria. No one who spent more than a few weeks in Manerplaw escaped the debilitating illness.

On a hillock not far away was the campus of the bravely named Federal University, throbbing to the pulse of Thai pop music. It was a university only in aspiration: There were two volunteer teachers, Janette from England and Jennifer from Canada, who taught English, Economics, History, Music and other subjects to several dozen refugee students from all parts of the country. The classrooms were huts, and books were in short supply, but the students worked hard, with lectures and tutorials carrying on late into the night by paraffin lamps and candles.

The Democratic Alliance of Burma, which coordinated the different groups, was based in a long house in the woods. There I met Khaing Saw Tun, a lawyer and democracy activist from Arakan in the far west of Burma, who had been a student leader in Rangoon in the 1960s. The changes made to the judicial system under Ne Win had made the lawyer's job almost impossible, he told me: After 1974, trained judges were relegated to the role of technical staff, with no say in the running of trials, which were in the hands of friends of the generals. "People no longer chose a lawyer who knew the law, but a lawyer who knew a judge, or they went straight to the township councils, or delivered a petition direct to Ne Win," he said. "There is no law in Burma now. We Rangoon lawyers are supermen: We practice law where there is no law."

When the NCGUB arrived it set up home alongside these groups and others, all seven MPs moving into a solid teak house set at some distance from the rest of the settlement, whose population was now about five thousand. Prime minister Sein Win was away during our visit, but his Foreign Minister, Peter Limbin, had just returned from a canter around Europe and was full of good news: Planning only to attend a session of the UN's sub-Commission on Human Rights in Geneva, he had been inundated with invitations and expressions of goodwill from European governments.

He anticipated the obvious question. "I didn't even ask them to recognize our government," he said. "Only a fool would do that now. First we have to make friends. They have to find out who we are, they have to trust us. And we have much to learn—about federal systems of government, for example. I went to Europe to learn, and to make friends." Dr. Sein Win had the same message: His coalition government was only an interim body, which would dissolve once the *Pyitthu Hluttaw*, the national assembly, had been allowed to meet and a full government established. Given the obvious impossibility of doing any sort of real work inside Burma, their most urgent task, in tandem with an associated group based in Mae Sot, on the Thai side of the border, called NLD-Liberated Areas (NLD-LA), was to build bridges to the outside world.

*

Alongside the MPs, lawyers, students, teachers and Karen fighters, Manerplaw also hosted a community of monks, living in the half-built headquarters of the All Burma Young Monks' Union under a sign that read LONG LIVE HOLINESS. Because, although the generals were all traditional Burman Buddhists, and had for many years gone through the conventional motions of Buddhist piety, since the uprising of 1988 a gap had opened up between the monks and the junta, and was widening all the time.

Suu and her colleagues had established good relations with the sangha, as the community of monks is known, from the beginning of their campaign. During the campaign trips of late 1988 and the first six months of 1989 they had frequently been given hospitality in monasteries around the country and participated in pagoda ceremonies. At the same time Suu's surging popularity among the Burmese masses reflected the fact that she was increasingly seen not only as a political leader but also as a religious figure: as a *bodhisattva*, a holy person dedicated to relieving the sufferings of others, or as a sort of angel or spirit, a *nat-thana* in Burmese, a contemporary equivalent of historical figures who had met unhappy deaths, often at the hands of the authorities.[8] Visiting Burma in 1990, Kei Nemoto, a Japanese scholar, observed, "There seems to be a big discrepancy between Burmese people's expectations of Suu Kyi and her own image of the future, democratic Burma. The ordinary supporters of Aung San Suu Kyi tend to worship her as the goddess [*nat-thami*] of . . . suffering Burma. If Suu Kyi herself is content with this personality worship, there will be little unhappiness between them. But she is not."[9]

Yet although Suu has always decried efforts to depict her as some kind of a goddess and to worship her, she was clear from the outset of her political career that moral and ethical concerns were at the heart of her message. On this she has never wavered. So the support and solidarity of monks who, like the rest of the population, had labored for decades under the brutish and incompetent rule of the generals, was hardly a surprise.

These two themes—her saintly resonance with the superstitious masses, and her appeal to the hearts and minds of the nation as the leader who had dared to defy the generals and launch a political revolution—came together in the summer of 1990 as it slowly dawned on the Burmese that their mass endorsement of the NLD in the privacy of the polling booth was being betrayed.

In a phenomenon analogous to the bloody tears supposedly wept by images of the Virgin Mary in devoutly Roman Catholic countries, in the months after the election people around Burma began claiming that the left breasts of Buddha images in their local temples were swelling and weeping. "This story was believed even by people living in big cities like Rangoon or Taunggyi," reported Professor Nemoto.[10] The "miracle" was seen by many as a good omen for Aung San Suu Kyi—the swelling left breast symbolizing a mother's nurture, and indicating that her power would grow and that she would succeed in saving Burma from suffering.

And in a related development occurring at the same time, the monks themselves—the incarnation, one might say, of Burma's collective conscience—began for the first time since independence to demonstrate their anger at the impiety of the rulers.

Burma loves anniversaries, especially ones of great political moment, so when August 8th—the second anniversary of the brutal army crackdown against the 8/8/88 uprising—rolled around with the generals no closer than ever to convening parliament, some kind of protest was inevitable. What was interesting and new—and, for the generals, extremely unsettling—was that among the brushfires of anger that broke out on that day, the most significant was a protest not by students but monks.

On the day of the anniversary, several hundred monks left their monastery in Mandalay before dawn with their begging bowls. There was nothing unusual about that: It was the unchanging ritual of the monks to give laypeople living and working near the monasteries an opportunity to gain merit by offering them food every morning of the year. What was different this time was that the monks carried their bowls upside down, symbolizing a boycott, a temporary excommunication, of the military regime: the exclusion of the army from the spiritual benefits it was in the exclusive power of the sangha to confer. Their march was joined by thousands of laypeople.

The military had already been deployed around the city in anticipation of trouble. The soldiers ordered the demonstrators to halt, and when they refused the soldiers opened fire, killing at least four people, two of them monks.

In response to the bloodshed, the sangha announced that their boycott of the regime would go on indefinitely. It spread rapidly from Mandalay to the rest of the country. By October, when the regime ordered the monks to end the boycott or face the forcible disbanding of their orders, around fifteen thousand monks in 160 monasteries in Rangoon—one-quarter of the capital's total—were on strike. In Mandalay, the religious capital of the country, the number was about twenty thousand.

When students and workers had protested en masse in 1988, the army's response was straightforward brutality, with thousands mowed down in cold blood. But this time around, because the protests were led by and overwhelmingly composed of monks—acting, as they were to do again seventeen years later in the Saffron Revolution, when it became obvious that for non-monks to protest would invite bloody mayhem—the junta's response was deeply conflicted.

On the one hand they threatened to dissolve hostile monasteries and force protesting monks back into ordinary life; and these threats were eventually acted upon when three monastic sects were dissolved. And the army garrisoned Mandalay to stop the protests recurring.

"The military has raided more than a dozen monasteries," the *Washington Post* reported,

> . . . and seized a variety of prohibited items ranging from political tracts to slingshots . . . This former Burmese capital has the look of an occupied city. But instead of foreign invaders, like the British who captured Mandalay in 1885, today's occupiers are members of Myanmar's own Tatmadaw, as the army is called. Helmeted troops armed with automatic weapons and grenade launchers patrol neighborhoods on foot and in trucks, man barbed-wire roadblocks on downtown streets and guard key intersections and installa-tions. As the 11 PM curfew approached one night this week, soldiers cradling German-designed G3 assault rifles set out in single file through a residential neighborhood like a combat patrol through enemy territory . . .[11]

But at the same time as purging the sangha, a quite different approach was tried: Some generals responded to the monks' demand for an apology for the killings in August by getting down on their knees and begging forgiveness. "The military stepped up efforts to appease senior Buddhist abbots," the *Washington Post*'s report continued, "by staging televised appearances in which the generals knelt before them . . . The generals . . . were filmed giving the monks such nontraditional offerings as color television sets and bottles of imported soft drinks."

*

SLORC's split response betrayed the fact that the monks' challenge, coming on top of the drubbing the regime-sponsored NUP had suffered at the ballot box, was a powerful assault on their claims to legitimacy.

Legitimacy in postcolonial states is a fragile and fissiparous commodity. In the first forty years of Burma's history, legitimacy boiled down to a single name: Aung San, the saintly father of the Burmese Army, the new nation's founding hero. Prime minister U Nu had been the Bogyoke's close comrade-in-arms, and ruled in the martyr's place, following the plans for government which Aung San was developing when he died, with a broadly socialist program and with the ethnic minorities linked to the center in a loose federal structure.

When Ne Win's military junta seized power in 1962, Aung San's name was again invoked at every opportunity. And this time authority was found in Aung San's writings for the dramatically anti-democratic change of direction dictated by Ne Win.[12] In 1957, in the run-up to the coup, Ne Win's pet scholar, Dr. Maung Maung (who became a short-lived President of the Union in 1988), published in the *Guardian*, the Rangoon-based newspaper he edited, an essay entitled "Blue Print," which was purportedly Aung San's vision of Burma's future. In the essay, written in early 1941 when he was in Japan, the future Burmese leader denigrated parliamentary government which "fosters the spirit of individualism," advocated a "strong state administration as exemplified [in the 1930s] in Germany and Italy," and declared that "there shall be only one nation, one party, one leader" and "no parliamentary opposition, no nonsense about individualism. Everyone must submit to the State which is supreme over the individual."

This was nothing like the sort of democratic model of governance advocated by Aung San after the defeat of the Japanese and his alliance with the returning British, the sort of policy adopted by Burma when it became independent. And although the "Blue Print" has for many years been routinely listed among Aung San's other literary works, Gustaaf Houtman, the Burma scholar, has uncovered persuasive evidence to indicate that it was probably not written by Aung San at all, but dictated to him by his Japanese military patrons, reflecting their own fascist priorities. But because Maung Maung depicted this prescription for authoritarian rule as the work of the sainted national founder, Ne Win was able to maintain the national Aung San cult without a hiccup.

All that changed dramatically with the ascent of Aung San Suu Kyi. As we have seen in previous chapters, the embrace by Suu of forces hostile to military rule led to the junta quietly and progressively dismantling the Aung San cult—casting themselves off from the one figure who for decades had given them his blessing from beyond the grave.

Where to turn instead for authorization? On coming to power, General Saw Maung had insisted that SLORC had no intention of hanging on to power for long, but planned to hand over to a multiparty democracy—civilian rule—as quickly as possible. But now that "that woman" had won the election hands down, a quick handover was out of the question. SLORC would have to remain in power indefinitely—but on what basis?

With Aung San no longer available, the regime cast further back, to the line of kings abruptly amputated by the British in 1885. Renaming the country Myanmar, discarding "Burma" as a colonial invention (although the word "Bama" has been in use for centuries by the Burmese themselves) was a first step. But that was for foreign consumption. If the generals were to be accepted on the same terms as the people had accepted their kings, they would have to start behaving more like kings. And fundamental to Burmese kingship for a thousand years had been the king's relationship to the sangha.

When the Buddha and his successors endorsed the right of a particular monarch to rule, that legitimized the king in the eyes of the people; and the monks performed the ceremonies of purification and so on which kept the palace on the right track, karmically speaking. It was a symbiotic relationship, because the king in turn was the patron of the sangha, giving robes and food to the monks in person and spending a large part of his fortune building them monasteries and pagodas for the greater glory of the Buddhist faith. The king was also the ultimate authority, with the right to de-recognize parts of the sangha if particular groups of monks went off in strange directions.

It was this relationship which SLORC, and General Saw Maung in particular, now needed to buy into to obtain legitimacy in the eyes of the people—the more urgently because Aung San's daughter had gained an overwhelming popular mandate to replace them. But now, at the military's moment of greatest need, the monks were voting with their feet and their bowls—for the other side. No wonder the generals were deeply divided over how to respond, with the followers of the tough Ne Win line urging a fierce crackdown, while the more pragmatic and/or superstitious were desperate to find a compromise, even if it involved going down on their knees and giving the monks Coca-Cola.

It is perhaps not surprising that General Saw Maung, the titular head of the junta, a mediocre, ill-educated career soldier like most of the officers with whom Ne Win surrounded himself, should have proved unequal to the strain caused by these rebuffs by both the people and monks. The first public sign that he was facing an insurrection within his brain as well as on the streets came in a long and rambling speech he gave in November 1990, a month after crushing the monks' uprising.

"If we look at the efforts for independence," he told an audience of local administrators in the town of Prome, in a speech monitored by the BBC,

> . . . if we choose a certain outstanding period to speak about that, we will have to say it is the time of the Thirty Comrades . . . If we are to assume that Burma gained independence because of the Thirty Comrades, then the Thirty Comrades is the core force of Burma. The Defense Services were born from that core force and continue to exist until today. In other words, the Defense Services have always been there. They were there throughout efforts for independence and also after independence, protecting the nation from the perils that emerged from time to time . . .

Through the rambling emerges his compulsion to plot himself in the line of heroes who created the independent nation—in other words, in the line of Aung San, whose name he cannot bring himself to utter.

Next he turned to the 1988 uprising—and he is unable to dissemble his sense of guilt for what happened.

A similar situation arose again in 1988 and everybody knows that the Defense Services had to control the situation. The year 1988 was not so long ago and whatever happened then cannot be forgotten. Whatever I have done was done so that there is no blemish either in the nation's history or in my own personal history.

The Defense Services are the core force of the nation, and they in turn are born from the people. It is essential to understand this . . . I understand that we cannot be divorced from the people. We are also constantly teaching the Defense Services personnel so that they understand this also . . .

And what of himself? This general with the people's and monks' blood on his hands? How was he to convince himself that he possessed any worth at all? "I am a person who never lies," he slurred. "I have never once lied throughout my career. I work with discipline and abide by rules. I never lie to the others and I hate anyone lying to me . . . How long am I going to be lied to?"

Within a year, Saw Maung had gone off the rails completely. During a golf tournament for top army officers in Rangoon on December 21, 1991, he brandished his revolver and threatened to shoot onlookers, declaring himself to be the reincarnation of King Kyansittha, one of Burma's greatest, and most peaceable, early monarchs. Four months after that, in April 1992, it was baldly announced that Saw Maung had resigned due to ill health.

*

What is legitimacy and how is it obtained? According to the German sociologist Max Weber, it means that if you issue a command, it is probable that it will be obeyed, perhaps out of fear but for other reasons, too: "affective" reasons, that is emotional reasons, and "ideal" reasons, having to do with beliefs and thoughts. Weber thus picks up the themes of the Scottish philosopher David Hume, who argued that the authority of government rests on opinion—opinions of interest, corresponding to fear and the hope of advantage—but also opinions of right: At least some subjects must be convinced that it is right to obey before the ruler can muster enough force to persuade those who are not.

But in the aftermath of Burma's election, and SLORC's decision to ignore the result, the junta's stock of legitimacy was desperately low. An army of occupation can keep a territory subdued, as the British did in Burma following their three nineteenth-century wars there—but that is not legitimacy. And SLORC was now in a very similar position: ruling by fear alone.

After visiting Manerplaw in the spring of 1991 I traveled through mainland Burma in the only way permitted at the time, on a guided tour. In the cities people were too terrified to say anything to a foreigner. I brought a letter from the lawyer I had met in Manerplaw, Khaing Saw Thun, to deliver to Daw Myint Myint Khin, the female head of the Bar Association who was also a member of the NLD's Central Executive Committee. I hoped she would give me a good interview and introduce me to some other important people. But it was not to be.

Her office was on the first floor of an old building in the congested and chaotic commercial heart of Rangoon. She received me with frigid courtesy: Standing behind her desk she read Khaing Saw Thun's letter, then handed it back and asked me to leave at once. "As soon as you have gone," she said, "Military Intelligence will come up those stairs. They will want to know what you were doing here and if you gave me anything. So please take the letter away." The following month she was arrested and sentenced to twenty-five years in prison. I have no way of knowing whether my intrusion was partly responsible.

That was what rule by fear was like—but it was fear alone; there was no element of grudging respect, no concession that the army was perhaps within its rights to act like this. Once we were in our tour bus, safely away from possible spies, our guides were uninhibited in their expressions of loathing and disgust for SLORC. They pointed out roads that had been constructed by forced labor, and miserable new shanty towns built for those bulldozed out of the city center. In the ancient city of Pagan—once I had quietly revealed to the guide that I was a journalist—I was loaned a bicycle and given a special one-man tour of the sad new township where the lacquerware-makers of the city had been decanted by the regime in their efforts to tart up the city for foreign tourists. The ordinary people of

Burma, in the aftermath of the election, were the subjects of a regime that they regarded as both brutal and illegitimate.

Gustaaf Houtman draws an important distinction between two Burmese terms that both translate roughly as "power": *ana*, which he renders as "the naked power of the state," and *awza*, the primary meaning of which is "nutrition" and which conveys the idea of giving strength, as in "rich soil." Houtman translates *awza* as "influence."

"Ana and awza, just like authority and influence, blend into one another," he writes. "One who is greatly influential is often given authority, and one who is in a position of authority is also able to influence."[13] A great leader like Aung San, and like a very few Burmese kings (including Kyansittha), possessed both ana and awza—which explains their magnetic hold on the emotions of the people. But in the aftermath of the 1990 election, SLORC found its last residue of awza used up. "The army," he writes, "used to holding the reins of power since 1962, knows that their authoritarian (ana) instruments have failed to create enduring structures of state, and they now fear the invisible, fluid, and unbounded trickling throughout the country of influential (awza) and popular personalities . . . They fear these individuals might just succeed in snatching away their privileges."

The generals could console themselves that the one personality above all others who embodied awza, Aung San Suu Kyi, was locked away from the people and completely incommunicado, her ample resources of awza unable to be expressed. But if they had known how she was spending her time while bottled up in University Avenue, even that comfort would have been denied them.

*

Although Aung San Suu Kyi has spent more than fifteen years in detention, the first years were the hardest to bear. She has said as much on numerous occasions. Soon after she was released in November 2010 she told BBC reporter John Simpson, "the first years were the worst . . . they threw me in at the deep end."

Every human consolation had been taken from her, one by one: Her party colleagues, her friends, her children, her husband. She had no telephone to compensate. She still had her family's letters and parcels with books and tasty items of food that would remind her of home. But in the run-up to the election, Khin Nyunt tried to obtain a little of the *awza* that Suu possessed in such ample quantities by telling the press that the junta was doing her the favor of passing on all these luxury goods that would turn the average Burmese pale with envy. One of the parcels addressed to her was opened and the contents photographed for the *New Light of Myanmar*: a Jane Fonda work-out video, the *Encyclopaedia Britannica*, novels, food in tins and jars, laid out for the cameras.

After that, Suu declined to accept any more letters or parcels until her release in 1995. It was a refusal that has been attacked as obdurate and harsh, particularly for its effect on her children, who had no contact with her at all for about two years. But given her desire to live in full solidarity with her imprisoned party colleagues, it is understandable. Receiving mail should be a detainee's right; instead it was presented as a favor, and she refused all favors that accorded her special status.

Her isolation deepened. She had no visitors, either from elsewhere in Burma or from abroad. To maintain solidarity with her comrades in jail, who would have starved without relatives to provide food for them, she refused to accept food from the regime. Instead, as she had no access to money, she instructed her guards to remove furniture from the house and sell it to buy her food. They went along with the charade—though in fact the furniture was stored in an army warehouse. But the money the fictitious sales yielded was barely enough to keep her alive. She later told an interviewer:

> Sometimes I didn't have enough money to eat. I became so weak from malnourishment that my hair fell out, and I couldn't get out of bed. I was afraid that I had damaged my heart. Every time I moved my heart went thump-thump-thump and it was hard to breathe. I fell to nearly 90 pounds from my normal weight of 106. I thought to myself that I'd die of heart failure, not of starvation . . . Then my eyes started to go bad. I developed spondylosis, which is a degeneration of the spinal column.[14]

She paused, then told the interviewer, putting a finger to her head: "But they never got me up here."

Sometimes she would wake at night in the dilapidated old house, and then her father's spirit would keep her company, she said. "I would come down at night," she told another reporter, "and walk around and look up at his photograph, and feel very close to him. I would say to him then, 'It's you and me, father, against them,' and I felt very comforted by his presence. I felt at times as if he was there with me."[15]

Suu had already known plenty of sorrow in her life, from the assassination of Aung San to the death of her brother six years later. But she had never been tested like this before. It commanded all her inner resources.

When, years later, she was awarded an honorary degree by the University of Natal—"the equivalent," she responded appreciatively, "of a cohort of legendary heroes coming to the aid of our cause"—her speech of thanks, delivered by Michael on her behalf, dwelt on the lessons she had learned in those terrible days.[16]

"Those who have to tread the long and weary path of a life that sometimes seems to promise little beyond suffering and yet more suffering need to develop the capacity to draw strength from the very hardships that trouble their existence," she wrote. "It is from hardship rather than from ease that we gather wisdom. During my years under house arrest I learned my most precious lesson from a poem by Rabindranath Tagore, many of whose verses, even in unsatisfactory translation, reach out to that innermost, elusive land of the spirit that we are not always capable of exploring by ourselves. The title of the poem, 'Walk Alone,' is bleak and its message is equally bleak."

> If they answer not your call, walk alone.
> If they are afraid and cower mutely facing the wall,
> O thou of evil luck,
> Open thy mind and speak out alone.
>
> If they turn away and desert you when crossing the wilderness,
> O thou of evil luck,
> Trample the thorns under thy tread,
> And along the blood-lined track travel alone.
>
> If they do not hold up the light when the night is troubled by storm,
> O thou of evil luck,
> With the thunder-flame of pain ignite thine own heart,
> And let it burn alone.

Suu went on, "It is not a poem that offers heart's ease, but it teaches that you can draw strength from your harshest experience, that a citadel of endurance can be built on a foundation of anguish. How can anyone who has learnt to ignite his heart with the thunder-flame of his own pain ever know defeat? Victory is ensured to those who are capable of learning the hardest lessons that life has to offer."

But what is the nature of the "victory" that these hard lessons ensure? It cannot mean that the generals are going to cave in, simply because a woman has suffered. So what *does* it mean?

*

Once in detention, the habits of discipline instilled by her mother came to Suu's help. "I started off on the basis that I would have to be very disciplined and keep to a strict timetable," she said later. "I thought that I must not waste time and let myself go to seed . . . I would get up at 4:30 and meditate for an hour . . ."[17]

This was new. It was a practice that began with her detention, more or less: In the time when she suddenly went from being the busiest, most in-demand person in Burma to having all the time in the world, and no one to share it with.

Before this her Buddhist practice had been conventional. In 1987 she had put her sons through the shinbyu ceremony, like every Burman mother in the country. The year before that in the Japanese countryside she had shown sudden devotion before a Burmese shrine. And once a week she told her Buddhist rosary. On the campaign trail, Ma Thanegi wrote in her diary about the mantra Suu recited every week on Tuesday, the day of the week when she was born—when she remembered to do so:

> Lights out and I said to Suu thank God it's not Tuesday. Suu asked why and laughed when I said because on Tuesday she must tell her beads for 45 rounds. I think at the time she was 44 and every Tuesday which is her birthday she would recite a prayer and tell the 108 beads for 45 rounds. She said she only managed 15 at Nyamdu on April 4th—sacrilegious but I deliberately forgot to remind her on subsequent Tuesdays. I don't believe that charms and sutras and beads can change one's fate, only *metta* [loving-kindness] can, and she has the love and prayers of millions.

That was in April 1989. But the terrifying dramas of the subsequent months culminated in Suu's total isolation. And now she needed something deeper than merely repeating some old words.

Buddhists would say that the teaching you need appears when you need it. "Not long before my house arrest in 1989," Suu wrote later, "I was granted an audience with the venerable U Pandita, an exceptional teacher in the best tradition of great spiritual mentors whose words act constantly as an aid to a better existence."[18]

U Pandita, who is based at a meditation center in Rangoon's Golden Valley, not far from Suu's house, is a world-famous teacher of insight meditation. Face to face and in his writings he teaches practical Buddhism with the simplicity and directness of someone teaching cabinet-making or gardening.

"We do not practice meditation to gain admiration from anyone," he wrote in his book, *In This Very Life*, which Michael gave Suu at Christmas. "Rather, we practice to contribute to peace in the world. We try to follow the teachings of the Buddha and to take the instructions of trustworthy teachers, in hopes that we too can reach the Buddha's state of purity. Having realized this purity within ourselves, we can inspire others and share this Dhamma, this truth."

Before Burma began selling off its oil and gas, meditation was the nation's most important export. But although the teachings of U Pandita and his late master, Mahasi Sayadaw, closely reflect the dharma of the Buddha, they are revolutionary.

Until about sixty years ago, meditation was something the monks did. Everyone was born, it was believed, with their karmic account book in a better or worse state, depending on their previous incarnations. Those impelled to become monks for life were by definition those closer to the goal of *nibbana* or liberation; men and women who spent their lives as farmers or shopkeepers were by definition further away from the goal.[19]

Monks meditated to purify themselves, and to inspire others with Buddha's truth. Laypeople did not need to bother with such strenuous non-activity. Instead, in order to acquire merit, they gave monks food and clothing. If they were wealthy they could acquire even more merit by building pagodas. Thus emerged the stereotype satirized in Orwell's

Burmese Days of the venal Burmese businessman who, after a life of greed and corruption, hopes to redeem himself by splashing out his ill-gotten money on pagodas.[20]

Yet even as Orwell was writing, this stereotype was becoming outdated.

When the British abolished the Burmese monarchy in 1885, they did away with a spiritual hierarchy that had survived every other upheaval for a thousand years. The monks lost their royal patrons, which is why monks were at the forefront of every revolt against British rule. Who was to keep them in robes and bowls now? Who was to become their partner in a symbiosis of patronage and sanctification like that which they had enjoyed with the kings?

This vacuum produced a revolutionary idea, which one could define as spiritual republicanism: The people could be the new patrons, the new kings. Individually they might be poor, but en masse they were rich. The revolutionary idea at the heart of this new movement is found in the title of U Pandita's book: *In This Very Life*. Laymen did not have to look forward to hundreds more reincarnations before coming to realization. If they behaved like monks—above all, devoting hours every day to meditation—they too could "realize this purity" in a single lifetime. At the same time they would also gain the other benefits of meditation. In particular they could improve morally. "Morality can be looked on as a manifestation of our sense of oneness with other beings," U Pandita wrote.

This revolutionary idea became the seed of a mass movement, Burma's mass lay-meditation movement.[21] This is the movement which has sent Burmese insight meditation around the world, while inside the country around a million people of all ages and classes and both sexes—twice as many as serve in the Burmese Army and around twice the number of full-time monks—come together under teachers like U Pandita, committed to meditation practice which for them is not only a quest for personal purity but a way of purifying society.

These organizations, like the one based at Panditarama, U Pandita's center in Rangoon, are now rich and powerful, owning large properties in the best parts of the cities, with the allegiance of huge numbers of people, including many professionals and indeed many army officers.

Because these organizations are centered around revered teachers, and have scrupulously avoided overt involvement in political activity, the junta cannot touch them. Intellectually and socially, they are the closest thing to liberated areas the country possesses: the only places people can discuss and reminisce without fear of being spied upon. Through all the violence of 1988 and 1989 and the wild political lurchings of the regime in the years that followed—through the abject failure of the junta in the past fifty years to foster any state institutions worthy of the name—they remained as solid and stable as befits organizations where all the members spend many hours every week cultivating mindfulness. And although, to repeat, they have never taken any political initiatives, in their solidity, wealth and freedom from the otherwise all-pervasive corruption, they retain a potential to influence future change in Burma: an abiding presence for good.

By listening humbly to U Pandita in the summer of 1989, by reading his book and getting up every morning to meditate, Suu herself became a part of that movement. In July 1988 she had made her great exordium with her maiden speech at the Shwedagon. One year later, in the silence and solitude of her home, she took a step that was, from the point of view of consolidating her identity as a modern Burmese, perhaps even more significant.

U Tin Oo, the former Minister of Defense who was the chairman of her party, meditated; indeed he had spent years as a monk after his dismissal by Ne Win. U Kyi Maung, the party's acting leader, was also an avid meditator, and in conversation with Alan Clements succeeded in putting the benefits of the practice in a nutshell. "You were quite surprised when I told you how much we laughed together on the day of Suu's arrest," he said, referring to her house arrest. He continued:

> It can be explained by the fact that the narrator had no regrets at all for what had happened in the past. The "I" and the "me" of the past are dead and gone. By the same token, the narrator of the present is not worried about what might happen to "him" of the future. In fact, "he" is not status-conscious at all. What I strive for is to live a life of complete awareness from moment to moment and to provide the best service I possibly can to all living beings without discrimination and with a detached mind. Does religion serve politics? I do not speculate. I just try to do my best.[22]

Now Suu had joined them. "Like many of my Buddhist colleagues, I decided to put my time under detention to good use by practicing meditation," she wrote. "It was not an easy process."[23] But after getting hold of U Pandita's book, she improved. ". . . There were times when I did more meditation because I was getting better at it," she said. ". . . Once you have discovered the joys of meditation . . . you do tend to spend longer periods at it."[24]

What she learned from her teachers and from her hours every day on the cushions was, more than any other influence, to determine her political trajectory in the years ahead. "We want a better democracy, a fuller democracy with compassion and loving kindness," she was to say years later. "We should not be ashamed about talking about loving kindness and compassion in political terms. Values like love and compassion should be part of politics because justice must always be tempered by mercy. We prefer the word 'compassion.' That is warmer and more tender than 'mercy.'"[25]

In particular, the special vehemence with which she had condemned Ne Win was a tone she would not use again.

"General Ne Win," she had said in June 1989, ". . . was responsible for alienating the army from the people, fashioning the military into a body answerable only to him . . . U Ne Win is still creating all the problems in this country . . . [He] caused this nation to suffer for twenty-six years."[26]

Those were the tough, hurtful, uncompassionate words that had led directly to her detention. "U Pandita spoke of the importance of *samma-vaca* or right speech," she wrote years later of her audience with the teacher in 1989. "Not only should one speak only the truth, one's speech should lead to harmony among beings, it should be kind and pleasant and it should be beneficial."[27]

If she had listened to U Pandita before making that speech, those harsh words against the tyrant might have gone unsaid. In which case, could she have escaped being locked up? It is another of Burma's haunting "ifs."

4

THE PEACE PRIZE

On July 10, 1995, after 2,180 days in detention, Aung San Suu Kyi was suddenly set free. She emerged a changed woman into a dramatically different world.

The day after her release she met the press in Rangoon and read a statement about her hopes for the future. In photographs taken at that press conference she looks a different person. The flesh is taut on her cheekbones, demonstrating how austerely she has lived in her six years alone, but emphasizing her striking beauty, which the privations of detention have done nothing to undermine—no wrinkles, no shadow of fear or self-pity. In the moist heat of July her black fringe is damp on her brow, her cheeks and eyelids ruddy. She has always looked much younger than her years, and that is still true now, three weeks after her fiftieth birthday. But there is a maturity in her face not seen before. It is strange to speak of a fifty-year-old wife and mother-of-two attaining maturity, but that is the impression one gets, comparing this face with her face on the campaign trail in 1989. Then she was a girl on an amazing trip. Now she was a survivor who had emerged from a severe trial not merely alive but purified, as her meditation teacher had promised.

"When I knew I was going to be free, I didn't know what to think," she said a few days later. "But once I met my colleagues I was very very happy. The first person I saw after I was free was U Kyi Maung, who led our party to victory in 1990, and his wife, and the moment I saw them, then I was really happy. But before that I didn't know what to think. I thought, I'm going to be free—that means I'm going to have to work a lot harder!"[1]

Greeting her release—which made news all over the world—Archbishop Desmond Tutu exulted, "Aung San Suu Kyi is free! How wonderful—quite unbelievable. It is so very like when Nelson Mandela walked out of prison on that February day in 1990 and strode with so much dignity into freedom. And the world thrilled at the sight."[2]

In her words to the press, Suu also evoked South Africa. "During the years that I spent under house arrest, many parts of the world have undergone almost unbelievable change, and all changes for the better were brought about through dialogue . . . Once bitter enemies in South Africa are now working together for the betterment of the people. Why can't we look forward to a similar process?"[3]

But if she put her hopes of dialogue in the form of a plaintive question rather than an affirmation, it was for good reason. Her counterparts in the freedom struggles that had gripped the world during her years locked in her home—Mandela, Tutu, Havel, Walesa and the rest—were now major players, some of them already in power. But Suu's release had been so sudden and unexpected—for herself as much as for the rest of the world—that she could only guess what it might lead to.

*

Freedom meant she could get together with those of her colleagues in the party's Central Executive Committee who had also been released, return with them to the NLD's decrepit office and get down to work, putting back together the pieces of the party which had been shattered by SLORC since the election. "What I need," she said, one month after her release, "is a proper office for our democracy party. All I've got is a single old typewriter."[4] It also meant she was besieged by requests for interviews. Before her house arrest she had been a figure of sympathetic concern to the rather small number of people around the world interested in Burma. But in her years away she had become a superstar.

It all started modestly enough. "Dear Suu," read the letter from Rachel Trickett, sent to her care of her husband two weeks after Burma's election in 1990, "It gives me great pleasure to inform you that the Governing Body of St. Hugh's College . . . voted to elect you to an Honorary Fellowship."[5] A woman given to bitterness might have raised an eyebrow at this accolade from a college that had twice prevented her from changing subjects then cursed her with a third-class degree, before barring her from undertaking a second BA. However, as Suu was by this time no longer receiving letters, it is unlikely that she heard of the honor till the middle of 1992, when it would have been buried under weightier tidings.

Not long after her college's announcement came the news that the European Parliament had decided to award her the Sakharov Prize for Freedom of Thought, named after the Soviet Union's most famous dissident when he was still internally exiled in Siberia. The same year she was given the Thorolf Rafto Prize for Human Rights. But an award of even greater moment was in the offing.

It was set in train in December 1989 when John Finnis, professor of Law and Legal Philosophy at Oxford, sent the nomination off to Oslo. Others backed her as well: Václav Havel, one of her most important and eloquent supporters down the years, eventually became her sponsor. Then on October 14, 1991, the committee in Oslo announced that Suu was the new winner of the Nobel Peace Prize.

To suppose that the announcement might have induced SLORC to change their ideas and initiate negotiations is to misunderstand their psychology. But the generals were not unaware of its significance: It was a major declaration of international support, at the very moment when they were doing everything they could think of to make the world forget her. It is said that General Saw Maung, chairman of SLORC at the time, took the award as a personal humiliation, and never recovered. It was two months later that he had an attack of mania on the golf course. Four months after that he was forcibly retired.

As Suu was unable to receive the award in person, Alexander and Kim accepted it for her at the ceremony held in Oslo on December 10, 1991. Explaining why Suu had been chosen, the chairman of the committee, Professor Francis Sejersted, gave a speech that was both subtle and strongly felt.

The occasion, he said, "gives rise to many and partly conflicting emotions. The Peace Prize Laureate is unable to be here herself. The great work we are acknowledging has yet to be concluded. She is still fighting the good fight . . . Her absence fills us with fear and anxiety . . ."

Lacking power and even the faintest prospect of power, what sort of function did a figure of her evident courage and resolution fulfill? "In the good fight for peace and reconciliation," Sejersted went on, "we are dependent on persons who set examples, persons who can symbolize what we are seeking and mobilize the best in us. Aung San Suu Kyi is such a person. She unites deep commitment with a vision in which the end and the means form a single unit . . ."

He noted how strongly she had been inspired by her father and Mahatma Gandhi. And he made the difficult but essential point that, for visionaries as courageous as these, success was not necessarily to be measured in the terms that worldly politics admits. "Aung San was shot in the midst of his struggle," he reminded the audience. "But if those who arranged his assassination thought it would remove him from Burmese politics, they were wrong. He became the unifying symbol of a free Burma and an inspiration to those who are now fighting for a free society . . . His example and inspiration . . . over forty years after his death, gave Aung San Suu Kyi the political point of departure she needed."

It is the profoundest thing that can be said about her struggle, and the one that confounds all those who demand to know, even today, what are her chances of gaining power. To figures like Gandhi, Aung San and his daughter, the categories of life and death are only of relative importance.

Professor Sejersted also addressed any possible charges that by awarding her the Nobel Prize, Norway was somehow claiming her for the West. "In its most basic form the concept of human rights is not just a Western idea, but one common to all major cultures," he said. And he quoted favorite lines of Suu's, expressing the preeminence of moral values in terms peculiarly well-suited to the Burmese heat:

> The shade of a tree is cool indeed
> The shade of parents is cooler
> The shade of teachers is cooler still
> The shade of the ruler is yet more cool
> But coolest of all is the shade of the Buddha's teachings.

Alexander, now eighteen, stood up to speak in his mother's place. It was an intensely moving moment, given the cruel manner in which Suu's destiny had forced the family apart, with untold emotional consequences for him and his fourteen-year-old brother. In his speech, Alexander showed a keen understanding of why his mother had made the choices she had. "Although my mother is often described as a political dissident," he said, "we should remember that her quest is basically spiritual. As she

54 University Avenue, Rangoon, the family home where Suu was detained for more than fifteen years.

Suu and some of her "boys," student members of the NLD who were her loyal bodyguards during campaign tours. The blazing smiles reflect the optimism of the party's heady first months in 1988 and '89.

General Ne Win, known as "the Old Man" or "Number One."

Sein Lwin, "the Butcher," who briefly replaced Ne Win as head of state in 1988, until forced from power by mass protests.

General Than Shwe, who ruled Burma for eighteen years.

General Saw Maung, the ruling general purged in 1992 after he became mentally unstable.

Khin Nyunt as Prime Minister in 2004, shortly before he was purged.

General Maung Aye, who shared power with Than Shwe after Khin Nyunt was purged. An "obdurate and unimaginative" soldier according to a British diplomat.

Nyo Ohn Myint: As a young history professor at Rangoon University, in August 1988, he was one of the first intellectuals to urge Suu to seize the opportunity to lead the democracy movement.

U Win Tin, founding member of the NLD, during his nineteen years in jail.

The journalist, poet, and political activist Maung Thaw Ka, standing to Suu's left.

Suu with NLD cofounder U Kyi Maung, addressing a crowd of supporters at the entrance to her home in 1996.

Above: A video grab of Suu speaking at Monywa, hours before her attempted assassination.

Left: Monks on the march in Rangoon, September 2007.

Below: A monk covers his eyes against smoke during the uprising.

Left: Suu with President Thein Sein after their historic meeting on August 19, 2011. They stand under a portrait of Suu's father Aung San in a moment of symbolic reconciliation, which opened the door to rapid reform.

Below: Suu welcomes Hillary Clinton to her home on December 2, 2011, during the first visit to Burma by a US Secretary of State since 1955.

Left: Suu, addressing Burma's parliament as a newly elected MP on July 25, 2012, demands legal protection for Burma's ethnic minorities.

Below: Suu, pictured in her upstairs office in the NLD's Rangoon headquarters during her meeting with the author in March 2011.

In November 2012, Suu visits monks wounded in a government crackdown on protesters against a copper mine in Monywa, northwest of Mandalay.

Houses burned to the ground during ethnic clashes between Buddhists and Muslim Rohingyas in Arakan state, in Burma's far west, are guarded by a soldier in November 2012.

In the company of, from left, former First Lady Laura Bush, House Minority Leader Nancy Pelosi, former Secretary of State Hillary Clinton, and Senate Minority Leader Mitch McConnell, Suu receives the Congressional Gold Medal from House Speaker John Boehner on September 19, 2012, during her first visit to the US in twenty years.

Burma old and new: The reforms have thrown the contrast between the traditional Burmese lifestyle and newly imported trends into high relief.

has said, 'the quintessential revolution is that of the spirit' . . . 'To live the full life,' she says, 'one must have the courage to bear the responsibility of the needs of others . . . one must *want* to bear this responsibility . . .'"

His words cast us back to the moment described by Ma Thanegi when Suu returned to the tiny cabin the two women shared on a riverboat in the midst of one campaign trip, and Suu, patching the tattered shirts of her student bodyguards, said how at home in Oxford, in another life, she had sewn name tags on her sons' school shirts—and then her eyes filled with tears.

Bertil Lintner was in the audience to see the prize awarded. "Alexander was extraordinary," he said. "The whole audience was spellbound. There was a standing ovation afterwards which never seemed to end. And everyone was looking at each other and saying, who is this kid? And I asked Michael afterwards, 'Did you write that speech for him?' And he said, 'Yes, I wrote something but he changed all of it.' And he was very impressive. People on the Nobel Prize committee said they had never heard a speech like that."[6]

*

If it was indeed the Nobel Committee's choice that pushed Saw Maung over the edge into insanity, Oslo can claim the credit for the most significant development in Burmese politics since the birth of SLORC—though sadly not one that has helped turn Burma into a more civilized country.

In the short term, however, the ascent of General Than Shwe to the chairmanship of SLORC in Saw Maung's place was a boon for Suu and her family.[7] Than Shwe's career is an object lesson in how, in paranoid military dictatorships, it is often the most mediocre and unpromising candidates who get to the top.

Born in 1933 in the central Burmese town of Kyaukse, which was for months the bloody front line between Allied and Japanese forces in the last months of the war, Than Shwe quietly rose through the ranks despite laying claim to no striking military successes, until he was appointed Deputy Defense Minister in July 1988, at the party congress where Ne Win dangled the promise of multiparty democracy before his people. After Saw Maung had put himself out of contention, the role of *generalissimo* became a contest between Than Shwe and military intel-ligence chief Khin Nyunt.

The latter, he of the seven-hour press conferences, the movie star manqué who led the regime's chorus of slander and abuse against Suu Kyi, was the most articulate, wily and ambitious of Burma's top generals. He had been very close to Ne Win, and was friendly and approachable with foreign diplomats. His English was weak—at the end of one of his interminable harangues to the press he barked, "Any answers?" when he meant, "Any questions?"—but that didn't stop him trying to speak it. But despite all these attributes, Khin Nyunt had two handicaps: As head of Military Intelligence he knew where all the bodies were buried—an asset in turf wars against his peers until it became a dreadful liability; and he had no battlefield experience from fighting insurgencies on the country's borders, which put him at a grave disadvantage compared with those who did have it. Even those as unappetizing as General Than Shwe.

Than Shwe's rise is also another proof of Suu's insight that fear corrupts those who wield power quite as much as those who are subject to it. Only in a system dominated by fear could a man like Than Shwe rise to the top and stay there: Throughout his career he gave the impression of being so unimpeachably mediocre as to be without ambition or hope of success. He was a man incapable of provoking fear—until suddenly he was at the top of the tree.

The comments of those who had dealings with him are uniformly unflat-tering. "Short and fat with not a strong voice," says one. "Relatively boring," says another. "No evident personality." "Our leader is a very uneducated man." "There were many intelligent soldiers but he was not one of them . . . a bit of a thug." "You feel that he's got there by accident . . ." The closest Than Shwe gets to being complimented is in the description of a former World Bank official. "He is such an old fox," he said.[8]

Burma was now ruled by a military triumvirate consisting of Than Shwe, Khin Nyunt and General Maung Aye, this last another "obdurate and unimaginative" soldier according to a retired British diplomat, who "kept on making the most idiotic decisions about export licenses and the like—he really didn't understand economics."[9] The aging Ne Win remained a shadowy figure in the background, and in the absence of any kiss-and-tell military memoirs or top-level defectors it is impossible to say how far he influenced events. But between them, the new rulers clearly felt it was necessary to turn over a new leaf.

Accordingly, once Than Shwe was in office he agreed to the repatriation of 250,000 Muslim Rohingya refugees from Bangladesh, whence they had fled to escape waves of brutal sectarian persecution by the Burmese Army;[10] and he released hundreds of political prisoners, including former prime minister U Nu. He ordered a cosmetic relaunch of the *Working People's Daily*, which was now titled the *New Light of Myanmar*, though the contents remained as turgid and one-sided as before.

Most significantly of all, in 1993 he set up an organization called the Union Solidarity and Development Association (USDA). Although not a political party, the USDA was a bid to claw back the civilian support that the regime had ceded so disastrously to the NLD. In form it was a sort of giant social organization. State employees were required to join it or lose their jobs; once they were inside it offered everything from courses in computers, sports, art, music and Buddhism to subsidies for farmers. It worked to wean members away from the NLD, exerted close control over all other social organizations in the country and incubated a militia force that the army was to use repeatedly to do its dirty work.

The USDA was to prove the regime's most effective tool for combating its massive post-election unpopularity: By a mixture of bribery and coercion, millions of Burmese were induced to come over to the army's side, at least superficially, providing the regime with the legitimacy— "opinion of interest," in Hume's terms, but also to an extent "opinion of right"—that it so painfully lacked in the aftermath of the election. Its patronage by the army was so generous that within fifteen years it had swelled to embrace more than half the population.

Aung San Suu Kyi was also on Than Shwe's "to do" list, but not because he had any interest in opening a dialogue with the hated NLD. In 1992, Japan, Burma's biggest donor of foreign aid and its closest ally ever since bailing out its stricken economy with war reparations in 1955, had, under American pressure, signed the official Development Assistance Charter, which required donors to pay attention to the state of human rights and democracy in the countries they helped. Japan was now the world's second largest economy after its hectic years of growth in the 1980s, but it remained susceptible to moral pressure from the United States, and had shocked the junta by suspending all aid to Burma in January 1989. Japan had, however, also been one of the first to recognize SLORC as legitimate, just the next month; both Burma and Japan were keen to do business together again, and now Japan impressed on the generals the need to overcome this human rights hurdle.

The obvious way was to do as the whole Western world demanded and let that woman out. But the regime's stinging humiliation in the elections was still too fresh in their minds. So Than Shwe temporized. He announced that he would hold talks with the NLD, but took no steps towards doing so. And in the meantime, for the first time in more than two years, he granted Suu's family permission to visit.

Michael came first, in May 1992. He stayed for two weeks, banned as before from having contact with anyone outside her house—essentially sharing her conditions of detention. On his return to Bangkok he told a press conference that Suu was "in good health, but not particularly robust" and committed to staying in Burma. "Things have not been easy for her," he went on, "but in the days we spent together she repeatedly pointed out to me that others have suffered much more than she has."

It was an acutely political statement: giving little hint of the health scares, the weight loss and hair loss, the outright poverty of her solitary life once she had resolved to refuse all offers of help from the regime, but at the same time underscoring that she was far from the pampered poster child of the West depicted in the state's propaganda. "Hers is an austere and disciplined life," he said. Under house arrest Suu spent her time "reading politics, philosophy, literature, Buddhist writings and listening to the radio." She had also "with her own hands" sewn curtains for every room in the house. Regarding the government's intentions, he said, she had "an open mind."

Of course the mind of the government itself was anything but open: The only satisfactory solution for the generals was for Suu to disappear— without leaving any blood on their hands. In March 1991, while General Saw Maung was still in charge, the Burmese Embassy in London had called Michael in and proposed that he write to her and ask her to come home. He turned them down flat, saying he knew well what her response would be.

SLORC did not give up there. They had clearly learned from their numerous in situ spies that Suu had taken up meditation, and was in general showing more signs of Buddhist piety than in the past. So in the same year they prevailed on a senior Buddhist monk called U Rewata Dhamma to visit Suu and request her on the regime's behalf to leave the country.

The choice of this divine was not random: The connections between U Rewata Dhamma and Suu's family went back decades. They had first got to know him in Rangoon, then when they moved to Delhi the acquaintance was renewed: The monk had gone to India's Varanasi University to study Sanskrit and Hindi, as well as to learn more about Mahayana Buddhism. And when Suu settled down in Oxford with Michael and their first child, it so happened that Rewata Dhamma moved to England to set up the Birmingham Buddhist Vihara. The strong karmic connection was revived.

Apart from her husband, therefore, the regime could not have picked a more influential person to try to persuade Suu to leave. And it is a reflection of the great respect in which Suu held the monk that she did not turn him down flat. Instead she agreed that she would indeed do as he proposed and leave Burma—on four conditions: the transfer of power to civilians; the release of all political prisoners; fifty minutes of broadcast time on government-run TV and radio stations; and, finally, to be allowed to walk to the airport, a distance of more than ten miles.[11]

In the depths of the toughest period of her detention, with a regime billboard outside her house that screamed, in Burmese and English, CRUSH EVERY DISRUPTIVE ELEMENT, Suu had not lost her sense of humor.

*

U Rewata Dhamma did not give up there. He realized the futility of trying to get her to depart, but understood the urgent need to get Suu and the regime talking. And it was thanks to pressure from him, as well as pressure from Japan and the world at large, that the two sides finally met, for the first time since the funeral of Suu's mother in January 1989.

There were two encounters, the first on September 20, 1994, with both Than Shwe and Khin Nyunt present, the second with Khin Nyunt and two other generals. This second meeting, on October 28th, was splashed across the front page of the following day's *New Light of Myanmar*. Senior General Than Shwe got the top spot in that day's paper, with a short piece in which it was reported that he had sent "felicitations to the Republic of Turkey" on its national day. Other senior junta figures also made it onto the front page: We learn of deputy-prime minister Vice Admiral Maung Maung Khin meeting Japanese businessmen to discuss investment, the American chargé d'affaires calling on the Minister for Forestry, and the Minister of Transport receiving the Ambassador of Pakistan.

But readers were left in no doubt about the day's top story: "Dialogue between the State Law and Order Restoration Council Secretary-1, Lt-Gen Khin Nyunt and Daw Aung San Suu Kyi" as the headline put it. It was immortalized in no fewer than three front-page photographs, in the largest of which they beam at each other across an oversize bowl of flowers. No background was given, no mention of Suu's role in her party—no mention of the party at all, in fact—and no mention of the fact that she had spent five years and more detained at the regime's pleasure. But here it was, at last: "Dialogue" according to the headline.

"The discussions, which were frank and cordial," ran the report, "covered the current political and economic situation of the country, the political and economic reforms . . . and steps that should be taken with a view to the long-term welfare of the nation." The absence of grammatical errors suggests that Suu may have looked over the draft.

And that was it. After the talks finished she was driven back to University Avenue and house arrest. It was the closest she would come to negotiating with Burma's military rulers for the next eight years, and they went precisely nowhere. When rumors began to circulate that the two parties had reached an undisclosed agreement—the first step towards her release and an ongoing dialogue—she smuggled out a statement denying it. "There has not been and there will not be any secret deal with regard to either my release or to any other issue," she insisted.

Both the empty "dialogue" and Suu's release nine months later reveal the importance of Japan's influence on the regime.[12] The Japanese ambassador's residence is within sight of Suu's house; on July 10, 1995, Japanese diplomats were the first foreigners to be tipped off about what was unfolding, and witnessed the white car carrying the chief of police pull into 54 University Avenue at 4 PM to inform Suu that she was free. The Japanese government then did as it had promised, welcoming her release, and indicating that aid to Burma would soon be resumed.

Although Japan's wartime control of Burma ended in disaster, the two countries for many years enjoyed a unique bilateral relationship. Not only had Aung San, Ne Win and other young anti-imperialists trained there, but many Burmese students were given scholarships to study in Japan during the war years, and formed an influential cadre of leadership afterwards. As the first Asian country to modernize and challenge the West, Japan felt under an avuncular obligation to help Burma as it took its first faltering steps as an independent nation.

Burma's generals learned much from the Japanese approach to dealing with the West. Japan's brutal experience during and after the Pacific War had taught it that the bullying demands of the West could not be ignored, but did not have to dictate the way the state behaved. They must be honored in form, but the substance was another matter. Japan was always urging the regime to do as Japan did after its surrender and erect a decorous constitutional facade, one which was acceptable to the United States in particular. For the same reason, they tried to get the regime to understand the importance of releasing Aung San Suu Kyi—not as a first step to negotiating with her, let alone ceding power to the NLD, but as a sop to the West. What mattered was to concede the symbolic demand. By doing the minimum necessary, the generals could carry on ruling and doing business just as before.

The junta eventually went along with Japan's ideas. Yet in the long run such diplomacy of gestures brings only grief. The gesture—in this case, the release of Suu—seems to contain the promise of further development, yet on further examination proves empty. What has been presented as promising proves to be treacherous, and what has been claimed to be a demonstration of sincerity turns out to be the opposite.

The straight-talking American ambassador to the UN, Madeleine Albright, was to make that clear to the generals very soon. Visiting Rangoon in September 1995, two months after Suu's release, the highest-ranking American to meet the regime since 1988 told Khin Nyunt that merely releasing Suu was not nearly enough to persuade the world that it was making progress towards democracy. She urged other countries including Japan to hold back on investing in Burma until more serious steps were seen.

Far from signalling a thaw in American–Burmese relations, Albright's visit saw them go into the deep freeze, with President Clinton agreeing to Congress's demand for the first American commercial sanctions against Burma since the ban on arms sales back in 1988.

*

One reason SLORC felt able to free Suu was because they had convinced themselves that she no longer mattered: The election result was a flash in the pan, six years is a long time, the demonising efforts of state propaganda had done their job—and besides, she was a woman! It was the same cocktail of wishful thinking and male chauvinism that had led them down the garden path in 1990. And it was to make them look just as foolish very quickly.

Suu never planned to give impromptu talks from the slightly undignified position of her front gate, teetering on a table and hanging on to the spikes; it just happened that way. On the day of her release, as the news raced through Rangoon, people began making their way to University Avenue. Inside, Suu had been joined by U Tin Oo and U Kyi Maung, two of her most senior colleagues, released from jail a few months earlier, and U Aung Shwe, who had been acting leader of the party while the rest were out of action. Soon her former student bodyguards and office assistants, many of whom had spent years in jail, were also streaming back along the road to sign up for duty again. Ma Thanegi, her personal assistant during the campaigning months, had told her before they parted in 1989 that she wanted to go back to painting full time and would not be available to help any more. But after Suu's release in 1995 Ma Thanegi was asked if she could help out for a few days until Suu found someone else. She agreed, and turned up the next day.

And the ordinary people of Rangoon came too. By July 11th, the day after her release, thousands were milling around the gates of Suu's house, hoping for a glimpse of her. Her first instinct was to go and mingle with them, but Tin Oo and Kyi Maung discouraged it: She was still frail after her years of austerity, and some crackpot, or regime agent, could take advantage of her proximity to do her harm. So instead a table was taken out of the house and pressed up against the steel gate and, to the delight of those gathered on the other side, suddenly her head appeared above it, flanked by her lieutenants. They clapped and roared their welcome.

She spoke for ten minutes, telling them that democracy could still be achieved, that patience was required, and that she and her party hoped soon to be in dialogue with the regime. Then she got down again. But if the Military Intelligence agents in their pressed white shirts and sunglasses, beadily observing the goings-on, imagined that that would be the end of it, they were soon to be disabused. Some of the crowd went away but more arrived. They stayed all night. By the morning there were even more. Out of simple politeness, Suu got up on her table and spoke again. And still they didn't go home. A microphone and loudspeakers were rigged up so it was more like a proper meeting. They were still there the following day, so she addressed them again. And so on.

This went on for an entire week and still the crowds did not disperse. Finally Suu and her colleagues realized that no work was going to get done if this continued, so instead of daily meetings they persuaded people to come only at the weekends, when she and her top colleagues would take it in turns to talk.

The weekend chats quickly became the hottest ticket in Rangoon— metaphorically speaking, because attendance was free. By September they had become a fixture of the city's week. "Tourists are making a beeline for 54 University Avenue," Agence France-Press reported on September 12, 1995, "just for a glimpse of Aung San Suu Kyi . . . Typical of the tourists is a young woman who told AFP she was a law student who traveled all the way from the United States to see Burma's Nobel Peace Laureate. 'Ever since I read her book *Freedom from Fear*'—the collection of essays by and about her first published in 1991—'I had this burning desire to meet Aung San Suu Kyi personally,' she said."

But the tourists—Suu sometimes tossed them a few words in English— were a small minority. Most who came were the same ordinary citizens who had flocked to her election campaign meetings. "Hundreds gather in the street to hear her preach reconciliation and exchange banter with the crowd," the *Economist* reported on November 4th. "The gatherings are more organized now than when she was first freed. An atmosphere of happy spontaneity persists, but in front of her, like bouncers at a pop concert, stands a row of young men in grey T-shirts emblazoned with her portrait."

A British diplomat who served in Rangoon from 1996 said that SLORC's generals weren't the only ones still in denial about Suu's popularity. "I was constantly being told by my ASEAN [Association of Southeast Asian Nations] colleagues that Suu was a complete busted flush, yesterday's person, that people hadn't really heard about her anymore," he recalled. Yet these claims didn't survive a reality check. "When we traveled around, I was often approached by Burmese villagers who said, 'It's great what you are doing for Suu, we all love her, keep it up . . .'"[13]

*

The frozen détente between Suu and the regime could not last. She demanded dialogue, and got silence. They wanted her silence, and got adoring crowds listening to her speeches. Finally, they wanted her party's compliance in what they called the National Convention—and the party decided fairly quickly that it would not give it.

The National Convention, set up in 1993 after Than Shwe had taken charge of SLORC, was the junta's answer to the problem of what to do about 1990's election result. But as months turned into years and the Convention made no discernible progress, it became clear that it was essentially a way to postpone the whole question of multiparty democracy indefinitely.

The Convention's task was to draft the principles of a new constitution—the necessary preliminary, the dogma now went, to a handover to a democratically elected government. It consisted of slightly less than a hundred MPs-elect, plus six hundred appointees of the junta, overwhelmingly military men. The NLD had signed up to the Convention while Suu and her top colleagues were in detention. But as soon as she and her old colleagues were able to take a good look at it, they realized it was a device to put a legalistic gloss on the military's refusal to acknowledge the election result, and to legitimise their rule.

"The military's primary provision from the inception of the process," wrote David Steinberg, "was that the military would play the primary role in the society."[14] Chapter I, 6 (f) of the draft constitution which the body was set up to rubber-stamp referred to "enabling the Defense services to be able to participate in the National political leadership of the State." It was, in other words, a way to enshrine and perpetuate the status quo. And in November 1995, Suu, Tin Oo and Kyi Maung announced that the party was pulling out.

*

If the National Convention was, in the NLD's view, the wrong way to go, what was the right way? What would a well-governed Burma look like?

Suu's first excursion outside Rangoon after her release was to the town of Thamanya in the province of Pa'an, a day's car ride out of the capital to the southeast. Various explanations have been floated as to why it was important for her to go there. One put forward by Gustaaf Houtman is that, given the flat refusal of the junta to agree to start negotiating, it was in search of an intermediary—another Rewata Dhamma, the man who had brought about her first meetings with the generals. "Aung San Suu Kyi's initial intention," he wrote, "appeared to have been to visit a monk greatly respected by both the people and the members of the regime, with the aim of working towards reconciliation. Some even speculated that she met with some high-ranking military officials at Thamanya in preparation for future dialogue."[15]

If that was the plan, it came to nothing—on her return from the visit she invited Ne Win to a ceremony to mark the end of "Buddhist Lent" but he did not show up. But in any case there were other good reasons to pay respects to the aged monk who lived in a hut in the monastery at the top of the hill.

The hill of Thamanya, as Suu wrote in the first of her "Letters from Burma," published in Tokyo's *Mainichi Daily News*, "is known throughout Burma as a famous place of pilgrimage, a sanctuary ruled by the metta of the Hsayadaw, the holy teacher, U Vinaya."

In Burmese Buddhism, metta is one of the "Brahmavihara," the "Divine Abidings," along with compassion, sympathetic joy, and equanimity—one of the divine qualities which the cultivation of the mind through meditation brings to fruition. "In contrast to the aggressive, destructive quality of hatred," wrote Sayadaw U Pandita, "metta, loving-kindness, wishes the welfare and happiness of others. When one has tasted the flavor of the Dhamma . . . you want others to have the same experience."[16]

As Suu's Buddhist studies progressed in the solitude of house arrest, metta became for her the most important of the attributes which she felt must be encouraged for Burma to "be built up on the old foundations" (as J.P. Furnivall had put it in 1916 in the *Journal of the Burma Research Society*). Her stress on the concept gives insight into the way her political thought was developing—how she was knitting together ancient spiritual virtues with ideas about the way people must learn to behave at the social and political level.

What is the NLD's founding principle? she asked delegates to the party conference held in May 1996.

> It is metta. Rest assured that if we should lose this metta, the whole democratic party would disintegrate. Metta is not only to be applied to those that are connected with you. It should also be applied to those who are against you. Metta means sympathy for others. Not doing unto others what one does not want done to oneself . . . So our League does not wish to harm anyone. Let me be frank: We don't even want to harm SLORC.
>
> . . . Power comes with responsibility and I believe that anyone who understands that cannot be power-crazy. I know how much responsibility goes with a democracy. That is why we are not power-crazy people. We are only an organization that wants to do its utmost for the people and the country. We are an organization that is free from grudge and puts metta to the fore.[17]

Pie in the sky, you might say: the sort of talk that only an enthusiastic ingénue could come out with, still enthusiastic after all these years alone. But in her reflections on her visit to Thamanya, Suu offered an example of how metta was to be applied in the political life of the country.

On October 4, 1995, Suu, along with three cars full of party colleagues, made one of those predawn starts so familiar from her campaigning period and set off towards the Hill of Thamanya—to visit a corner of Burma where metta ruled.

"There is a special charm to journeys undertaken before daybreak in hot lands," she wrote. "The air is soft and cool and the coming of dawn reveals a landscape fresh from the night dew." Then dawn broke. "In the distance could be seen the white triangle of a stupa wreathed in morning mist, tipped with a metal 'umbrella' that glinted reddish gold in the glow of the morning sun."[18]

Suu's joy at finally breaking free from the city after so many years cooped up illuminates the piece—but countering that is the dire condition of the roads. "The road had become worse as we traveled further and further away from Rangoon," she wrote. "In compensation the landscape became more beautiful. Our eyes rejoiced at rural Burma in all its natural glory even though our bones were jolted as our car struggled to negotiate the dips and craters in the road."[19]

Towards evening they neared their destination.

As we approached Thamanya, the quiet seemed to deepen . . . Suddenly it occurred to us that the quietness and ease had to do with something more than the beauties of nature or our state of mind. We realized that the road had become less rough. Our vehicle was no longer leaping from crater to rut and we were no longer rolling around the car likes peas in a basin.

As soon as we passed under the archway that marked the beginning of the domain of Thamanya, the road became even better: a smooth, well-kept black ribbon winding into the distance . . . The road had been built and maintained by the Hsayadaw for the convenience of the villagers who lived around the hill and of the pilgrims who came in their tens of thousands each year. It was far superior to many a highway to be found in Rangoon.[20]

What is the connection between a modern, well-maintained road and loving-kindness? In the Burmese context the analogy is vivid. Metta permeates both the mentality of the man who plans the road to benefit his visitors, and of those who contribute their labor to build and look after it. The contrast to the rest of the country, where roads are carelessly planned by disaffected engineers, built by villagers forced to leave their fields and work for nothing, then left to fall apart because of the pervasive corruption, could not be more stark. That, for Suu, was the contrast between a country where metta is cultivated and one where it is not.

"No project could be successfully implemented without the willing cooperation of those concerned," she concluded.

People will contribute hard work and money cheerfully if they are handled with kindness and care and if they are convinced that their contributions will truly benefit the public.

   . . . Some have questioned the appropriateness of talking about such matters as metta and thissa (truth) in the political context. But politics is about people and what we have seen in Thamanya proved that love and truth can move people more strongly than any form of coercion.[21]

But could love and truth move the stony heart of SLORC? Suu, as Gustaaf Houtman sees it, gave the regime two choices. It could continue to play the part of Devadatta, the cousin of the Buddha who became his disciple but was then plagued by feelings of jealousy and ill-will and plotted to kill the Blessed One. Or it could instead take the role of Angulimala, the serial killer who wore a necklace of his victims' fingers around his neck, but who on meeting the Buddha renounced his evil ways and became a monk.[22]

But SLORC's ruling generals showed no sign of being impressed with the analogy. As far as they were concerned, they were the heirs of the kings. And all they required was submission.

5

HEROES AND TRAITORS

THE generals dismissed Aung San Suu Kyi as an alien and an agent of the West: The Nobel Peace Prize Committee had made the award to "a follower they [i.e. the West] had raised," they said, but SLORC would "never accept the leadership of a person under foreign influence who will dance to the tune of a foreign power."[1]

In one sense they were perhaps right. Suu was a believer in progress. She wanted to see her society improve, with better education, better standards of living, better roads, happier people, and she did not see such improvements as inconsistent with their Buddhist faith. They were perhaps right in seeing themselves as faithful to Myanmar tradition, where a king's duty was to win wars, build pagodas, feed monks and bask in glory; where it was accepted by the people that rulers were one of the "five evils" and if the rains came on time and the king's tax farmers left one with enough to eat, that was about the best one could hope for. "Stagnation" is a term of criticism when applied to governments in the West; in Burma it means business as usual.

The seven years between 1995 and 2002 were for Burma in general and Suu in particular a long lacuna, a "melancholy, long, withdrawing roar," during which the brave but vague promise of her release was followed by nothing but disappointment, exploitation, abuse, persecution and loss.[2] The junta shelved attempts to write a new constitution, changed its name, cut ceasefire deals with most of the ethnic groups on its borders, conducted a fire sale of teak, jade, oil and gas, joined the Association of Southeast Asian Nations (ASEAN) and played sad, absurdist games of cat and mouse with Aung San Suu Kyi. The brave hopes that had brought Suu worldwide fame and the Nobel Peace Prize threatened to curdle completely.

*

When Suu and her colleagues in the NLD announced in November 1995 that they were pulling their handful of MPs-elect out of the National

Convention, the structure set up to draft a new constitution for Burma, it soon became clear that they had crossed an invisible line. Whatever SLORC had expected from Suu when they released her, it wasn't that. Perhaps they imagined that she and her colleagues had been so cowed by their years in prison, or so grateful for their release, or both, that they would now be prepared to toe the line. But by ordering a walkout from the Convention, Suu gave them clear warning that she was going to be just as difficult to manage this time around as last.

The junta retorted that, on the contrary, it was the NLD that had been expelled. The departure from the Convention of much the most important political party in the country gave them the excuse to put the process on ice, and the Convention remained in suspension for most of the following eight years. And in the meantime SLORC again took up the task of limiting the damage "that woman" could do.

Khin Nyunt is often seen—partly on account of that grinning front page he shared with Suu after their "dialogue" in 1994—as the relatively tender face of SLORC, but while she was in detention he had warned of the danger she posed because (according to a fifteenth-century treatise from which he quoted) if a female were to take power "the country will be in ruins."[3] And now it was clear that Suu and her party's brief and uncon-summated honeymoon with SLORC was over.

In November Alan Clements, a former Buddhist monk hoping to conduct a series of interviews with Suu, was in Rangoon, waiting for an appointment. "For six weeks I had been holed up in a hotel room in Rangoon waiting for a telephone call from Aung San Suu Kyi's office," he wrote.[4] At their preliminary meeting, Suu had told him, "Our situation is unpredictable under the SLORC, so please be patient . . . My father used to say, 'Hope for the best but prepare for the worst.' I think this is always the best approach."

Towards the end of that month it began to look as if the interviews would never happen because Suu would be back under lock and key. By late November, Clements went on, Suu and her party colleagues "came under increasing attack in . . . the *New Light of Myanmar* . . . Almost daily half-page editorials denounced Aung San Suu Kyi and her colleagues in violent terms. The military promised to 'annihilate' those 'destructionists' who disrupted the 'tranquility of the nation.'"

On November 30th, Clements went to visit U Tin Oo, the party's chairman, whom he had known when they were both monks in the same Burmese monastery. But when he rang the bell, the former general's wife came to the door with a grim look on her face and told him, "He's upstairs gathering medicines and a few belongings. I'll get him for you."[5]

Tin Oo was getting ready for the authorities to come and take him off to jail again. When he came down, he said to the American, "Don't worry. You shouldn't be here. Daw Aung San Suu Kyi is preparing to be re-arrested too . . ."

In the event it was a false alarm. But it marked the beginning of an ugly new phase.

*

Months before Suu's release, the junta had begun touting 1995 as "Visit Myanmar Year": Khin Nyunt's favorite theme was attracting foreign investment, and he alone of the top three generals dreamed of emulating Thailand's success as a tourist destination. It was a proposal that went against the grain of a regime always tempted to withdraw into its shell at the first sign of foreign trouble; the Ne Win approach, marshalling tourists in groups and flying them around the more famous sights then showing them the door, was much more their way of doing things. But the promise of tourist dollars got the better of their prudence.

By releasing Suu, Khin Nyunt cleared away the most glaring obstacle to a successful tourist drive, which was postponed for a year and renamed "Visit Myanmar Year 1996." But of course Suu free meant Suu at liberty to talk to her foreign friends. And in March 1996 she told the world exactly what she thought of Khin Nyunt's stunt. Suu, reported Harriet O'Brien in the *Independent* on March 17, 1996, "had previously taken the attitude that some foreign investment and tourism would help to ease the military's grip on the country, but she has changed her mind. [She said,] 'Make 1996 a year for *not* visiting Burma.'"

In Burma's best-known beauty spots, new hotels were already being thrown up in readiness for the hoped-for tourist influx, O'Brien reported— but here was the world's most famous Burmese telling everyone not to bother.

"Burma will always be here," Ms. Suu Kyi said, announcing the boycott. "Visitors should come later." She went on, "Most materials for hotels are imported. The result is that each hotel signifies a lot of money, but really only for overseas suppliers. Some construction companies have even been bringing in workers from abroad. Within the country there's really only one privileged group making money."

The previous month, in one of her "Letters from Burma" in Tokyo's *Mainichi Daily News*, Suu had argued that it was "not yet time to invest" in Burma.[6] And in the *Independent* interview she made a more wide-ranging attack on foreign investment, condemning a recent visit by a British trade delegation. "It's not right for the British government to do all it can to support human rights here and then to promote trade with Burma against democracy," she said. "The sort of involvement being suggested won't help to bring about sustained economic and social development."

The issue of investment and sanctions has continued to provoke fierce debate ever since. In the spring of 2011, Suu's declaration that she was still opposed to the lifting of sanctions provoked the *New Light of Myanmar* to warn that she and her party "will meet their tragic ends" if they continued in this vein. It was the first threat to her since her release in 2010: proof that, even though sanctions have not achieved their goal of inducing the regime to negotiate, they remain a very touchy subject.

Ma Thanegi, Suu's friend and companion who kept the intimate diary of their campaign travels in 1989, claims that the permanent rift that opened up between the two women was caused by their conflicting views on sanctions. Freed from Insein Jail in 1992, Ma Thanegi had gone round to greet Suu when she emerged from detention, and resumed helping out in the party's office a couple of days a week. But soon, she said, she found herself in disagreement with Suu's policy pronouncements.

"When she began telling foreign investors to stay away, I told her that it would hurt the people, who need jobs. She replied, 'People will just have to tighten their belts.' I said, 'There are no more notches.' I insisted on this issue but she said, 'It's not true.'" And there the discussion ended.[7]

Ma Thanegi claimed that this was another case in which Suu's instincts for moderation were trumped by the more hard-line demands of others in the party—the same process, she says, that happened before Suu's house arrest, when young party members opposed U Kyi Maung's suggestion that they try to negotiate with SLORC and Suu agreed to adopt their tougher approach. She also maintains that Suu naively read too much into Madeleine Albright's vigorous statements of support after her visit in September 1995. Ma Thanegi noted in her diary:

> The first two or three days when she spoke from her gate she talked of reconciliation, and I heard through a US Embassy official who was the CIA Chief that his Burmese MI contacts said SLORC was pleased, but still had a "let's wait and see" attitude. Some NLD members were angry with her for being "soft" and asked her if she were "surrendering." Her speeches turned hard-line. I told her she should not openly criticize [SLORC] but should wait to discuss these things when she meets them. She said she must be honest. I told her some people do not deserve honesty.
>
> Madeleine Albright . . . came and said we are behind you all the way, and not being a political person, Ma Suu doesn't see that "behind you all the way" is just politics, just happy talk—they are not going to send in the Marines to shoot the military down and impose democracy.

Since 1995 Ma Thanegi has repeated her attack on Suu's line on sanctions and the tourism boycott many times and very publicly, perhaps most damagingly for the NLD's cause in the pages of *Lonely Planet's* controversial Burma guide book. "Ma Thanegi . . . told us many NLD members have always been against the [tourism] boycott," the guide's editors wrote in the 2009 edition. "Many people around Aung San Suu Kyi tried to dissuade her on the boycott," they quoted her as saying. "In '96, '97, '98, '99. I gave up trying around then."

Suu may at first have regarded Ma Thanegi's opinions as worthy of her attention but not necessarily more than that: After all, the two of them had become friendly during the campaign tours, but Ma Thanegi was not even a member of the party, let alone of its Central Executive Committee. But when Ma Thanegi began repeating them to any foreign journalist willing to listen—the "no more notches" line has been recycled many times over the years—she must have considered the possibility that her closest companion, the one to whom she had given soap, toothpaste and a good pair of sandals before she was taken to jail, had to all intents and purposes gone over to the other side.

The point of no return came when the Indian writer Amitav Ghosh quoted the "no more notches" line in a piece about Burma published by the *New Yorker* in August 1996.[8] After that, communication between the two women ceased.

"I didn't want to really quarrel with [Suu]," Ma Thanegi told me, "so I stopped going to see her. Then after the *New Yorker* article came out Michael [Aris] wrote me a letter accusing me of disloyalty." Ma Thanegi became *persona non grata* for the party: She must have done a deal with the devil.

As her diaries on Suu's campaign trail make clear, Ma Thanegi is a very robust, self-confident, plain-spoken woman, never one to hide her views for fear of causing offence: One of the reasons she made such a good companion for Suu was that she was incapable of flattering her. On the other hand she admitted to me that she had been subjected to several periods of interrogation during her time in jail, including at least one that went on all night. Given the importance to the regime of weakening Suu's prestige abroad, transforming her most sophisticated Burmese friend into a highly articulate enemy would be a goal worth pursuing.

Ma Thanegi denies that she was acting on the orders of SLORC in attacking Suu. "They did not try to put any words into my mouth," she told me. "They knew they couldn't influence me at all. I knew that if I stopped being involved in politics my life would be okay."

But her frequent and uniformly anti-NLD comments to foreign media show that she has by no means "stopped being involved in politics." A former friend said he knew that Ma Thanegi had been "turned" by MI in prison, and even knew the person responsible. "Khin Nyunt's man worked on Ma Thanegi successfully," he said. "Colonel Hla Min was her main contact as he was one of the most polished, by the military's standards, and US-high schooled."[9] This information was confirmed by Aung Lynn Htut, a former senior officer in Military Intelligence and number two in the Burmese Embassy in Washington, who sought political asylum in the United States in 2005, after the fall of Khin Nyunt, his boss. "All political matters were under the control of Counter-Intelligence Department," he wrote in an e-mail. "Khin Nyunt allowed Colonel Hla Min to keep in touch with Ma Thanegi."[10]

Why would she succumb? In return MI would have promised to leave her in peace, the former friend suggested. "Being left alone is no small reward if you are an artist, a writer, who has many foreign visitors. You'd be surprised how weak-kneed professionals and intellectuals get in these situations, especially if there is both pressure and the seduction of access to power. Picking up the phone and talking to an MI agent and getting one's Internet line fixed is a huge privilege, and a concrete allure of being in the good books of the regime." He said the 2006 film about informers in communist East Germany, *The Lives of Others*, gives a good idea of the Burmese situation.

Ma Thanegi denied having been given any material inducements to attack her old friend. "I have a comfortable living because of my inheritance," she said, "I'm fine, I don't need to live in a huge house." But Ma Thanegi has never had any political aspirations of her own, so what possible reason could there be to attack Suu and her ideas so publicly if not to weaken her standing and improve that of the regime? If she remained as fond of Suu as she evidently was throughout the trips they took together but felt that she had recently taken some wrong turnings, surely she would have taken care to make her views known only to the close circle of people in the party who were in a position to influence her? Going public with her denunciations appears to be the clearest possible declaration of enmity.

The larger question is: Was Ma Thanegi right? Was Suu justified in supporting sanctions which could further damage the already miserable living standards of ordinary Burmese? By yielding (as Ma Thanegi claims Suu did) to the demands of her more hot-headed colleagues, was she not backing a policy that would only antagonize the regime while condemning her people to unrelenting poverty? Should she not have been prepared to sacrifice her revolution for the sake of her people's prosperity?

But Suu's insight was that, under this regime, economic liberalization could not be expected to produce any significant degree of freedom or democracy—or even more generalized affluence. SLORC's most significant reform was to allow foreign companies to invest in Burma, but from the outset they ensured that all the investment was done through them personally or through cronies in their control: No foreigner was allowed to get an independent toehold in the country. Profits went straight into the generals' pockets and any sign of independence was promptly punished.

Suu only began speaking out in favor of sanctions once the faint hopes of dialogue after her release had come to nothing and her party had pulled out of the National Convention. By speaking out now she was putting in play the one tool that guaranteed her a hearing and a standing both in Rangoon and the world outside. Had she opposed sanctions she would have gained nothing, and there would have been little besides moral squeamishness to prevent the rest of the world forming an orderly queue at the border to do business with SLORC: After all, Western businessmen do business with plenty of other vile regimes around the world. But if Burma had gone the way of Indonesia under Suharto, the Philippines under Marcos, Zaire under Mobutu or Libya under Gaddafi *with her blessing*— what would have been the point of her entering politics in the first place?

In the *New Yorker* piece where Ma Thanegi ventilated her opposition to sanctions, Amitav Ghosh noted how Suu's manner had changed since her release. In their first interview, soon after she emerged from house arrest, they had laughed and joked together; in the second, nearly a year later, she rebuffed his arguments bluntly. For example, she refused to accept that the governments of ASEAN should be condemned for launching a policy of "constructive engagement" with Burma. "Just because [these governments] have decided on a policy of constructive engagement, there is no need for us to think of them as our enemies," she told him.

"I was witnessing, I realized, Suu the tactician," he wrote. "She was choosing her words with such care because she wanted to ensure that she did not alienate the leaders of nations who might otherwise think of her as a threat.

". . . She now seemed much more the politician. Suu now had a party line."[11]

Ghosh gives the impression of being rather upset by the change—as a fellow Oxford graduate and an old acquaintance he seems to think he deserved something rather more intimate and, dare we say, feminine in the way of conversation than what he got the second time around.

But within the very narrow scope the regime had left her, Suu was learning the ropes.

*

The other issue Suu raised in her interview with Harriet O'Brien has been just as hotly debated as trade sanctions: the question of whether or not tourists should visit Burma. Since Ne Win's coup in 1962, the vast majority of Burmese have been isolated from the rest of the world, which has left them ill-informed, culturally impoverished, and at the mercy of the state's propaganda. By opposing tourism, it was argued, Suu exacerbated that isolating effect, helping to keep her people mentally shackled in a country that has become a prison for them, closing off valuable sources of free information. At the same time she put a moral obstacle in the way of non-Burmese learning more about her country at first hand.

Suu's supporters countered that most tourists who visit tropical destinations have no real interest in what is going on in the places they visit and have no significantly beneficial effect on the lives of the people they come in contact with. In Burma they travel on roads built by forced labor and stay in hotels built on land obtained by bulldozing the villages of the poor. And because of the generals' stranglehold on the economy, most of the money they spend ends up in the regime's pockets.

Suu and her party's opposition to tourism, amplified in the West by the Burma Campaign UK and the US Campaign for Burma, has certainly helped to keep the growth of Burma's tourism sector in check: It remains minuscule compared with that of neighboring Thailand—Burma gets only 1.4 percent of the number of tourists who visit Thailand, 200,000 compared with its neighbor's fourteen million[12]—but the regime's failure to create a modern tourist infrastructure and an environment in which foreign businesses can work without fear of having their assets stolen are probably more significant factors than the boycott.

In November 2010, in the run-up to Suu's release, the NLD announced a U-turn on tourism. Win Tin, the veteran journalist and member of the party's Central Executive Committee who had served nineteen years in prison, said in an interview that the NLD had changed its policy. "We want people to come to Burma," he said, "not to help the junta but to help the people by understanding the situation . . . For the outside world to see, to know our situation, that can help our cause a lot."[13] Later Suu herself endorsed the change. While not encouraging package tours and cruises, she said, she believes that "individuals coming in to see the country, to study the situation in the country, might be a good idea."[14] And in June 2011 the NLD formally reversed its policy on the issue.

However this does not mean the floodgates are about to open: Lonely Planet will continue to enjoy a near-monopoly of the market for guide-books. Rough Guides' publishing director Clare Currie said she hoped that Suu's release "will ultimately help open Burma to travelers. However, we think it is too soon for a complete change of mind. We are not currently planning to publish a guidebook to Burma—such a guide would really depend upon sustained improvements in the political situation as well as on a proven and robust travel infrastructure."[15]

*

Suu's declarations on trade and tourism were her response to the regime's failure to make good on their promise of talks. She had tried being accom-modating; now she tried exerting a little pressure. But that did not work any better: The regime quickly gave notice that the change in leadership four years before had not made it any more yielding. In May 1996, when the NLD summoned party members to the capital to attend a National Convention, SLORC struck preemptively, arresting 258 party members, 238 of them elected MPs. Suu and her colleagues went ahead with the conference anyway, attended by fourteen delegates. Its final commu-niqué warned that if the regime did not release all political prisoners and convene the parliament elected in 1990, the party would go ahead and draft a constitution itself.

Suu now found herself in a war of attrition with the regime. SLORC responded to the party's constitution initiative by issuing a new law, threatening anyone who spoke or acted against the (so-far undrafted) constitution with long prison terms. The crowds attending her weekend talks continued to swell, even when SLORC threatened those who attended with twenty years' jail. To close them down, in September they put a barricade across the road—so Suu and her colleagues went out to nearby street corners and held the meetings there. SLORC reacted to that by rolling out their thuggish new weapon, the delinquent fringe of the Union Solidarity and Defense Association (USDA), the mass, regime-sponsored organization launched in 1993 by SLORC's chairman, Senior General Than Shwe; in a nasty incident in November 1996, a 200-strong mob of USDA thugs attacked the cars of Suu and her colleagues when they drove from her house, smashing the windows of one with a bar.

Suu's reply to the intimidation was one of those statements that have helped turn her into a legend. "If the army really wants to kill me, they can do it without any problems at all, so there is no point in making elaborate security arrangements," she told the *Times* of London. "It is not bravado or anything like that. I suppose I am just rather down to earth and I just don't see the point to this worry."[16]

Remarks like this make it more rather than less difficult for non-Burmese to appreciate the climate of fear that passes for normality in Burma. If Suu can be so nonchalant about her personal safety, people think, how bad can things really be? An Australian social anthropologist called Monique Skidmore, who was doing research in Rangoon during those months of late 1996, provided a corrective: "The refusal to allow Aung San Suu Kyi to hold roadside talks . . . meant that a great tension settled upon Rangoon in the latter part of 1996," she wrote. "Young people, especially students, festered with impotence."[17]

She related the story of a diplomatic friend who drove to University Avenue to photograph the road blocks around Suu's house. When he returned home later that night he found his dog lying dead in front of the house, with its eyes burned out. "It took several weeks to become caught up in the fear that engulfed the city," she wrote. "I began unconsciously to stay indoors, seeking refuge from the military gaze."[18]

But the safety of interiors was illusory. She wrote:

> The Generals are not content to control only the flow of information in the public domain, they seek to dominate, reconstruct and regulate urban space in a ceaseless breaking down of barriers that previously signaled sanctuary. The experience of fear occurs in these "open" and regulated spaces as people . . . shuffle from one sanctuary to another . . . When terror becomes a means to enforce domination, violence becomes the primary force that maps social space . . .[19]

Suu defied the terror and shrugged off the threats of violence; if she was traumatized by the way the regime had violated her domestic space during the previous six years, she took care never to show it or talk about it. But the regime had not given up its quest for ways to hurt her.

One of her family's oldest friends in Rangoon was an aging businessman called Leo Nichols, part-Scottish, part-Greek, part-Armenian, part-Burmese, "Uncle Leo" to his many friends, and perhaps the only expatriate businessman to have survived the Ice Age of capitalism ushered in by Ne Win. It was Uncle Leo who had phoned Suu in Oxford at the end of March 1988 to inform her of her mother's illness.

A Roman Catholic and the son of the owner of a Rangoon-based shipping company, he had returned to Burma after the Japanese defeat in the Second World War. In 1972, as the prospects for foreigners in the country crumbled, his family emigrated to Australia, but he insisted on staying on in "the only place he could ever regard as home," as Michael Aris later put it.[20] He was appointed honorary consul to the Scandinavian countries, which gave him a degree of diplomatic protection. While he was forced to sell off his treasured collection of vintage cars, he buried his favorite Bugatti at Pagan—or so he claimed.

Nichols had had his run-ins with the regime in the past: During the uprising of 1988 he had frequently offered Suu advice and practical help, for which he was later subjected to a severe interrogation. After she was released from house arrest in 1995 he met her every Friday for breakfast and resumed his role as helper and adviser, finding a gardener to redeem her ruined garden, for example, and workmen to repair her house, while continuing to support her political campaign. One practical way he helped out was by sending her "Letters from Burma" to the *Mainichi Daily News* in Tokyo from his fax machine.

And that was how the regime nailed him. He owned two fax machines, one of them registered but the other one not. Possession of a fax machine without a license is a criminal offence in Burma, carrying a maximum sentence of five years. In April Nichols was arrested, interrogated over many days and sentenced to three years' jail.

Like the sentence given in 1989 to another of Suu's friends and protectors, the writer and war hero Maung Thaw Ka, it was in effect a sentence of death: He was confined to Insein Jail without the medicines for his heart condition and diabetes. Two months later he fell ill and was taken to Rangoon General Hospital where he died soon afterwards, aged sixty-five, perhaps of a heart attack or a stroke.

Nichols' death and the betrayal by Ma Thanegi and other friends and colleagues were the occasion for one of Suu's most painful and strongly felt essays.

In her writing as much as in her interviews, Suu is generally at pains to put on her best, most cheerful face. That is an Asian reflex, encountered everywhere from Rangoon to Tokyo, but in Suu's situation it was also sound tactics: If she had shown any hint of anger or misery, the regime could have congratulated itself that its campaign to damage her morale was working. But in "Letter from Burma No. 33, A Friend in Need," the mask of equanimity slipped.

It is an essay about how persecution subjects friendship to the toughest test of all, pitilessly exposing one's friends' true qualities. The process yields surprises. Those one might have considered weak reveal their strengths. But others who seemed infinitely dependable give up the struggle with shocking ease.

Thanks to what she calls "the full force of state persuasion," concepts previously confined to the covers of books—"villainy and honor, cowardice and heroism"—become the stuff of everyday life. "The glaring light of adversity," she writes, "reveals all the rainbow hues of the human character and brings out the true colors of people, particularly of those who purport to be your friends."[21]

Some, like Nichols, emerge from the test with greater stature than before. "The man stripped of all props except that of his spirit is . . . testing the heights that he can scale," she wrote. But others shrivel and collapse. "The kiss of Judas is no longer just a metaphor, it is the repeated touch of cool perfidy on one's own cheek. Those held in trust and esteem show themselves capable of infinite self-deception as they seek to deceive others. Spines ostensibly made of steel soften and bend like wax . . ."

Suu had been brought up with high moral standards, in emulation of her father. In the England of the Sixties, comfortable and prosperous, that didn't seem to matter very much: Her loud championing of virginity before marriage and her insistence that children strictly obey the rules of party games were regarded as marks of risible eccentricity rather than anything more important.

But in the testing fire of Burma, those standards were the difference between honor and shame, between hope and despair. To be Suu's friend and supporter in London or Oxford or Washington, DC, is easy. To be her friend in Rangoon or Mandalay is one of the toughest decisions you can ake. True friendship, as she pointed out in the same essay, demands the highest moral qualities: "According to the teachings of Buddhism, a good friend is one who gives things hard to give, does what is hard, bears hard words, tells you his secrets, guards your secrets assiduously, does not forsake you in times of want and does not condemn you when you are ruined. With such friends, one can travel the roughest road."[22]

Suu did not want for such friends: It is one of the paradoxes of brutal societies that they inculcate great virtue in those who defy their brutality. But by turning Ma Thanegi and others, and killing Nichols, the Burmese regime discovered in what way and to what extent Suu was vulnerable. And they had an even crueler trick up their sleeve.

*

Throughout the 1990s, Michael Aris plays a shadowy but at the same time a central role in Suu's story. If ever there was a case of true friendship being tried in the fire of adversity it was their marriage. During their decades as man and wife there were the frictions and irritations that come up in all marriages: Suu disliked his smoking and nagged him to stop, complained to her friends that he was too easygoing to fulfill his potential at university and too tolerant of English social hypocrisy. In family snaps from those years she frequently looks as if she would rather be anywhere on the planet than north Oxford.

Family life certainly had its trials, yet when the real tests came Michael was magnificent. If Suu was born to do what she found herself doing in Burma, Michael was born to be her perfect foil, her perfect other half.

That statement requires immediate qualification: For their sons he could never replace their mother, nor even be a very satisfactory substitute. He knew how to cook an omelette, but it was a great relief for the whole family when he found a pair of Burmese Christian nuns to come and live with them in Oxford and take care of the housekeeping. (SLORC eventually found a way to terminate that arrangement, forcing the nuns to return to Burma.) Nor could he begin to compensate emotionally for Suu's absence. That was an unfillable void.

But from the start Michael understood the path she had gone down, understood why it was for her an unavoidable decision, and realized that as a result the family's life had entered an utterly new phase. Never did he show any hint of bafflement, resentment, doubt or hostility, emotions that would be quite understandable for an ambitious man whose career and indeed whose whole life had been thrown out of kilter by his partner flying off at a dangerous, extraordinary tangent.

Instead, without a blip, he became her other half in the world outside: marshalling support, passing on news, giving interviews and then, as Suu's defiance became a global phenomenon, traveling tirelessly as her personal envoy to collect awards and pass on messages. He was "her knight in shining armor," said one friend, "the one who was defending and fighting for her and trying to slay the dragon for her."[23] It was at Michael's suggestion that Ma Thanegi kept her campaign trail diary in 1989; it was Michael who, seven years later, wrote to Ma Thanegi terminating the relationship after she began launching public attacks on Suu and the NLD.

Peter Carey commented:

In the first twenty years of their marriage [Suu] was the north Oxford housewife, but after 1988 that completely turned on its axis and it was not Michael who was the focus any longer, it was Suu, and Michael was there to provide the support, to bring up the children, to drive them to school, to make the meals.

In the 1990s the reality began to dawn: He was a single father in Park Town . . . looking after his children, being as good a father as possible, the tides of Burma lapping to the door—faxes and messages and requests for interviews, press releases.[24]

Carey quotes a Javanese saying about the qualities required to be a good wife: "'To follow behind and serve as a good woman should'—I think that was the role that Michael adopted, he was following behind and serving but in an incredibly discreet and subtle and effective fashion."

In photographs and videos Michael always looks much the same: tall, gentle, reflective, a little untidy; perhaps somewhat stern and sad but always calm and composed. But there was a more volatile side to his character that the camera did not see. "Michael stayed with me once in

Bangkok after the house arrest started," said Terry McCarthy, who at the time was the *Independent*'s correspondent in Bangkok.

> We were friends, we got along very well, and I remember him shouting down the phone to the people in the Burma immigration office, his eyebrows going mad . . . He looks very affable and calm in the photographs but he had a fiery side too, and he found the behavior of the generals so irrational that it drove him mad. Suu on the other hand knew where they were coming from, she knew why she had infuriated them so . . . Although he supported her fully, it was very tough for him. That's why he was so angry with the generals: He blamed them for taking his wife away from him.[25]

He may also have had an unrealiztic view of Suu's hopes of coming to power. Soon after her release from detention in the summer of 1995, he and Kim were granted visas—he could not have known that it was the last Burma visa he would receive in his life—and flew to Rangoon. Ma Thanegi said that when she met him there she felt he had convinced himself that power was about to drop into his wife's hands:

> Once in late June or early July 1995, Dr. Aris and I sat on the stairs in the NLD office—there were too many people downstairs and no chairs left— talking about the situation. He was very excited and sure that NLD would soon be in power. He kept saying, the regime *must* learn to change, they *must* learn to change. I said, they're not going to, they're not going to. We went around in circles like this for about five minutes. I could not penetrate his wild expectations.

Another old friend, Bertil Lintner, found a different flaw in him: excess of prudence:

> He was overly cautious. When he and the boys flew from Rangoon to Bangkok in late August 1989, everybody knew they were coming but nobody knew what they looked like: Very few people in Bangkok had met Michael and the kids. And we Bangkok-based reporters were there to meet them and it was sort of agreed that I would identify Michael as I was the only one who knew him. So when he and the boys came out I said, "Hello, Michael!" and he said, "Not you!" So I said all right, and stepped aside.

In the evening he rang me and said, "I'm sorry about that, let's get together tonight"—he had brought out a load of stuff he wanted me to have. But he didn't want people to know I even recognized him. It was silly.[26]

Yet Michael had excellent reason to be very careful: The regime saw Suu's marriage to him as one of the main chinks in her armor, and never missed an opportunity to insult her for her supposed "treachery" to Burma in marrying a foreigner. Michael was a treasure for her, but in her dealings with her co-nationals he was always a liability.

"The *Bogadaw* [a term for the wife of a European] has lost her right to inherit her father's name, Aung San," the *New Light of Myanmar* declared in a typically venomous piece on May 9, 1997. "She should be called Daw Michael Aris or Mrs. Michael Aris . . ." Why had she lost the right? Because the English, the writer claimed (in defiance of the historical record) had been behind Aung San's assassination, and because she had failed to "safeguard [her] own race," sullying her blood by mixing it with a foreigner's. For the regime's propagandists, her marriage to Michael was all the proof they needed that Suu was an agent of foreign powers.

As a result Michael was discreet to the point of invisibility in supporting Suu, and demanded that Alexander and Kim behave likewise. Yet although he continued to work in his beloved Tibetan studies, publishing several specialist books and finally succeeding, with the warm encouragement of the Prince of Wales and the generous support of the Rausing family, of Tetrapak fame, in setting up Britain's first Tibetan and Himalayan Studies Center at Oxford, no one close to him doubted that it was around Suu and her struggle that his life revolved.[27]

His sister Lucinda estimates that he spent at least half his time working on Suu's behalf, and says he had a secretary who worked exclusively on Burmese matters. "I don't think Suu ever realized how much he did," she said.[28] But as the years passed and every visa application after 1995 was turned down, the strain began to tell. Lintner recalled:

He was offered this teaching fellowship in Sanskrit at Harvard. It suited him perfectly well and Suu was happy with it too. He had this small studio flat in Cambridge, Massachusetts, I visited him there, I went to see him in his room. He was still afraid of Burmese spies: He didn't want to meet in public.

It was tragic to see that room. There were pictures of Suu on all the walls. And ashtrays with cigarette butts towering up . . .[29]

The strain of the years of enforced separation was now telling on him fatally. In the summer of 1998 he suffered appalling backache, which is often associated with some forms of cancer. Tests that he took in September proved negative, but in January 1999 he sent Suu a letter via the daughter of a Rangoon-based friend with the news that he had been diagnosed with prostate cancer.

Soon it became clear that his condition was deteriorating quickly, and his attempts to persuade the Burmese regime to give him a visa took on a sudden urgency. All his eminent connections and those of his family were pressed into service: Prince Charles and Countess Mountbatten were only two of the great and good who sent letters to Senior General Than Shwe, pleading with him to issue the dying man a visa so that he and Suu could meet one more time before he died.

It was perhaps inevitable, given the extremely narrow view the regime has always taken of its interests, that they would interpret Suu's emotional emergency in the cruelest and most stupidly calculating way conceivable: as the best opportunity yet to get her to leave the country.

A Western diplomat who was close to Suu remembers this harrowing period vividly. "They not only said no to these appeals—in fact they never replied—but they cynically used it in psychological warfare," he recalled. "Towards the very end they started printing stuff saying, of course any time Suu Kyi wants to leave she can go to her dying husband, it's the duty of every proper wife to go and be at the bed of the dying husband rather than the other way around, etcetera, etcetera. I was so sickened by the way they dealt with this thing that I refused to shake the foreign minister's hand any more. I thought he was very, very craven in going along with this despicable tactic."[30]

Michael was failing fast, and friends of the couple in Rangoon witnessed their tragedy at close quarters. One of them recalled:

> Towards the very end Michael was extremely, falsely optimistic—about the visa, about himself: Sure, he said, I shall be getting better soon, the visa will be coming through soon. He may genuinely not have realized how quickly this disease was going to carry him off. It was one of the most ghastly trials that Suu has ever had to face, and she did it with enormous dignity and courage.

Another friend added:

> Her bravery in such an appallingly difficult time was testimony to her being an exceptional person. Ultimately I think her strong Buddhist faith sustained her.

Back in England, Suu and Michael's old friend Sir Robin Christopher, at the time the British ambassador to Indonesia, visited Michael in hospital. Both Suu and Michael had always been keenly aware that if she ever left Burma that would be the end of the story—her passport would be cancelled and she would never be readmitted. Now, however, they began to discuss the possibility again in earnest. But the conclusion they reached was the same as before.

Michael Aris died on March 27, 1999, his fifty-third birthday, less than three months after learning that he had the disease. Christopher flew to see Suu in Rangoon soon afterwards. "I arrived as a memorial ceremony to Michael was in progress," he said. "There were probably about 300 people there in the garden, monks chanting, Suu listening to them." When it was all over he and Suu talked things over at length. Christopher recalled:

> At the end it was tragic that he was not allowed to see her. She talked about it a lot, and how they had discussed it. They both understood that there were an awful lot of her followers in Burma whose livelihoods depended on her being there: If she wasn't there they would be rounded up and either killed or imprisoned. And a number of families existed on the meager support that she was able to pull together. Food and freedom were the issues: food for the families of those that were imprisoned, who would have completely gone under without her help, while she felt her closest followers would almost certainly have been arrested once she was out of the way. So in other words an awful lot of lives depended on her staying where she was. Michael was going to die anyway. They shared the decision. It was a very strong relationship.
>
> She was grieving. But fundamentally this had not destroyed her. She had seen it coming, they had communicated a lot, she was wracked by the issue of whether she should go back or whether she shouldn't. But she was consoled by the fact that Michael had said, don't come. Don't come. He entirely understood the situation.[31]

"I am so fortunate to have had such a wonderful husband who always understood my needs," Suu wrote on the day of his death. "Nothing can take that away from me."

The military regime, which in 1997, on the advice of an American public relations consultancy, had changed its name, to the State Peace and Development Council or SPDC, had run out of ideas. They had succeeded in confining Suu to Rangoon: Every time she had tried to travel since 1998 they had blocked her at the capital's outskirts. Her refusal to turn back had led to a series of stand-offs that had their farcical elements, but each time the regime eventually got its way.

But they could not induce her to leave the country. They had tried every trick they could think of, to no avail. Their attempt to exploit her love and grief to get her to fly to Michael's deathbed was the last throw of the dice.

Eighteen months after his death, on September 21, 2000, she made her most determined attempt yet to break out of the army's grip, but again she was stymied on the city's outskirts. For nine days she stayed in her car in the suburb of Dala, to the south of the capital, refusing the regime's demand that she return home. Eventually, on September 2nd, a 200-strong detachment of Lon Htein (riot police) turned up and forced her to go back. On reaching University Avenue she was once again put under house arrest.

PART FIVE
THE ROAD MAP

1

MEETING SUU

ON the evening of Tuesday, May 7, 2002, I flew into Rangoon for the second time in my life, the first time in eleven years. That same day Suu had again been released from house arrest. With a tourist visa for Myanmar, obtained the previous week after the usual anxious wait, I left Delhi and flew to Bangkok in the hope of becoming one of the first British reporters to interview her. At Bangkok airport I bought a ticket to Rangoon and boarded the half-empty plane.

You take off from the concrete megalopolis of Bangkok, its Buddhist heart practically entombed in cement, and although you are flying from one Asian capital to another—from the capital of one Asian country to its neighbor which is actually substantially larger, and which once held Siam in thrall—it's like going from a real city to a country town. Bangkok disappears into its own smog. Within half an hour, as you begin to descend, the waters of the delta are grey and turbid under the plane's lights; the few, faint lights of Rangoon and its suburbs wink dimly, a civilization away from the blazing furnace of Thailand. A few vehicles crawl along the narrow roads. There are no traffic jams.

Yet although still the country cousin, it was soon clear that Rangoon was a different city from the one I had visited before. Mingaladon Airport had a new international terminal which looked like an airport terminal in any country in the world, made of concrete, glass and marble, well lit and with none of the dinginess and betel juice-stained corners of the old building. The taxis waiting outside were the same beaten-up 1970s Nissans and Toyotas as before, but the hotel I had been recommended, the Sofitel Plaza, was new: a bland, shiny, gilded multistory palace with uniformed doormen, obsequious reception staff and swift, hissing lifts. It cost $40 a night with breakfast—next to nothing.

Burma had clearly been going through some changes. I had been the South Asia correspondent of the *Independent* for nearly five years but Burma had been so quiet compared with the rest of the region that I had found no occasion to come before. The last occasion I had written about it was in 2000, during Suu's nine-day stand-off with the army, which culminated in her return to detention.

That story had made it sound as if nothing significant had changed since the last time I was here in 1991; it was still stuck in the mud of confrontation and repression. But all this modernity was something new. And now Suu free again—what was the story? What was going on?

As I did the rounds of Western diplomats, aid agency staff and Burmese insiders willing to talk to me, it became clear that Suu's release this time was different from that of 1995. The first time was a stunt: an attempt to prod the Japanese into resuming aid, perhaps a genuine misunderstanding by the regime of what a "gesture" was, and that a gesture with no substance behind it would yield very limited results. Back then neither Suu nor anyone else had been given advance warning of her release; it was preceded by very little diplomatic activity, and after it happened all Suu's requests for dialogue with the regime were met with stony silence.

"In 1995 the country was booming," Leon de Riedmatten, an international mediator, head of the Center for Humanitarian Dialogue and right-hand man of UN envoy Razali Ismail, explained soon after I arrived. "The generals thought they would succeed economically, so they had no need to deal with the opposition."

That was the period, with Military Intelligence chief Khin Nyunt making his presence felt, when the smart new airport building and hotels like the Sofitel and the even swankier Traders were built, when the ceasefire deals were cut with the insurgent groups, when the doors were thrown open to tourists for Visit Myanmar Year, when Burma was given observer status in ASEAN—when it must have seemed to SLORC that they were on the brink of being accepted by the rest of the world on their own terms. Releasing Suu was the icing on the gingerbread, a sop to the West and one which would not require any follow-up because—as the generals must have assured each other, still sealed into their impregnable conceit—the people had forgotten all about her anyway. In the *New Light of Myanmar* they depicted her in cartoons as a gap-toothed crone, boring Rangoon street urchins to death with her interminable rants—and that was what they really thought of her. The Achilles heel of regimes such as this is the reluctance of junior officers, who are in touch with reality, to tell their superiors uncomfortable truths.

But after Suu's release in 1995, any hopes SLORC may have entertained of pain-free international integration rapidly unraveled. Suu's charisma proved as powerful as ever, and her message no less disagreeable. Generals brought up in Burma's closed socialist system struggled to make sense of the rules of international capitalism and fiercely resisted the loss of control which they brought with them: Burma remained an impossible working environment for foreign businesses. Rangoon and the other towns and cities on the tourist route were smartened up for Visit Myanmar Year, but then in 1997 the Asian financial crisis struck and Burma's frail recovery was hit along with the far more robust economies of its neighbors. The flashy new hotels were now half-empty most of the time.

De Riedmatten, who had first begun brokering talks between Suu and the regime in June 2001, explained to me his view of the country's political prospects. "There is no other choice than cooperation between the NLD and the regime," he said. "The first priority is how to improve the living conditions of the people. Then they should start talking about the future of the country. Today the situation is completely different from '95: Now they have to cooperate, both sides need the other."

Yet as our conversation progressed it became clear that there was still a long way to go before anyone could start claiming results. "They [Suu and the regime] have talked, but they have not yet agreed to do things together," he admitted. "Until last Monday"—when Suu was still in detention—"they talked to each other, and found some understanding, some room; now it's the test. They say: Let's see if, when she's out, [her actions] correspond to what we thought. On her side she wants to see how far she can do what she wants."

But then the optimism came steaming back into his voice. "I think the process is irreversible," he said, "the question now is the pace . . . They all need to go quite fast."

It was clear that I had arrived in Rangoon at an interesting moment. Change was bursting out all over. For thirty years, ever since Ne Win closed down the free press after his coup, Burmese newspapers had been as dreary, mendacious and slavish as any in the world. But even that seemed to be changing: A bald, blunt-mannered Australian called Ross Dunkley who had spent seven years building up the *Vietnam Investment*

Review in Ho Chi Minh City, arrived to launch an English language weekly, Burma's first, called the *Myanmar Times*.

In the paper's newsroom—"the biggest in the country" he boasted— Dunkley explained to me how he had reached this point. "I sold the Vietnam paper to James Packer, the son of Kerry [Packer, the media and cricket tycoon]," he said. "In '99 I started to think what I was going to do next, I had Myanmar in mind anyway, I came for a week in '99 to have a look around. It's a virgin market."

On holiday in California, Dunkley chanced to meet a Burmese expatriate called Sonny Swe, the son of Brigadier General Thein Swe, a high official in Military Intelligence, which was of course headed by Khin Nyunt. Dunkley had been knocking around Asia long enough to know the value of a well-placed patron, and Sonny seemed the ideal person to help him break into Burma. "Coming into a market like this you have to have a political umbrella," he pointed out. "Our general is a diplomatic assistant to Khin Nyunt."

The *Myanmar Times* was quite unlike any other Burmese paper on the market. The front page was not dominated by a picture of a general handing out an award or inspecting something, the editors clearly under- stood the difference between a news story and a hole in the head, the headlines encouraged you to read on, and one got the impression that some of the reporting might even be true. I asked Dunkley, "What about censorship?" He replied: "I said [to Sonny] I will refuse to submit to press censorship. Sonny assured me it wouldn't happen." Then, a little later in the conversation: "It's a question of how to put the right spin on things." And later still: "Now it's a new ball game. We have to think about the right to press freedom or we cannot move forward. It's one of the fundamental rights. I see the *Myanmar Times* as a litmus test to determine how fast [the country is] moving forward. We're the first paper in the country to talk about the NLD, the first to talk about HIV/AIDS . . ."

And if his generals were purged or Sonny went missing—did Dunkley have an exit strategy, a plan for extracting himself from Burma and getting back to Perth with the loot? "I've got no exit strategy," he said. "I see this as my family business."

*

I met Dunkley on the morning of Thursday, May 9, 2002 and when the interview was over I took a taxi from his office a couple of miles to a shabby-looking two-story house with an overhanging roof on a broad and busy main road near the Shwedagon pagoda, the headquarters of the NDL. The entrance was crowded with party members: students, grizzled political veterans, women on their haunches with babies, all flapping fans and chatting in the pre-monsoon heat and waiting for a particular event. I had a pretty good idea what it was.

Inside the long dingy oblong of the ground floor the scene was no less busy, with an impromptu English class under way in one corner, party women running up peacock flags on treadle sewing machines in another, the librarian shelving battered paperbacks in her small collection. A few foreign journalists were sitting on the sidelines, waiting for the main event.

In my notebook I recorded Suu's arrival at the office:

1 PM: She's approaching. Staff pull themselves into shape, pin on red arm bands, line up either side of door, staring out watchfully, drumming fingers, gulping water from water pot. One electric fan going is the only sound.

1:10: No action. There is a poster of Suu next to Aung San on the wall behind the grill of a Post Office type desk at the entrance.

1:23: Everyone suddenly re-mustered—she comes striding in at the head of a group of four, quick, definite, unhesitating, arms swinging like a soldier, smiling lightly, and vanishes up the stairs.

After waiting most of the afternoon it was eventually my turn to go up the stairs.

"The door to the long, shabby, boiling hot committee room squeaks open," I wrote in the *Independent* on May 13, 2002,

and the famous lady in the blue Burmese jacket and longyi is discovered sitting at one corner of a long table.

She rises: a firm handshake, very long fingers; a head rather large for the slim, fragile-looking frame—some say she has lost weight since she was last seen in public, and she is certainly ashy pale. But the gaze of her large brown eyes is bold and steady. "I'm sorry to have kept you waiting such a long time," she says in her cut-glass Oxford accent. "Please give my regards to all our old friends at the *Independent*."

I mentioned how struck I was by the amount Rangoon had changed since my last visit. Did she feel that Burma was finally on the move? "I've always said I'm a cautious optimist," she said. "So in one sense I agree with people when they say that. At least we're somewhere new where we have not been and I would cautiously say that where we are is better than where we have ever been. But I think the more important thing is where we're going to, and how quickly."

De Riedmatten, Suu's go-between with the regime, made the same point during our meeting: Speed was important, her release had put some momentum back into the relationship but for trust to build there must be a follow-up, and soon.

There were some in Rangoon, supposedly well informed, who were sure it was coming. De Riedmatten put me on to one of them, a retired Burmese professor, "a political observer-cum-analyst" as he asked me to describe him, who invited me to his home and told me with serene confidence,

> Aung San Suu Kyi has made concessions to the government and they will move towards some kind of democracy on Suharto regime lines, with 25 percent of seats reserved for the military. The government is prepared to go along with recognition of the results of the 1990 election, but will retain veto powers. They are not going to give up all power right away. I believe a lot of details have been agreed. They are now putting finishing touches to the agreement.

As evidence for progress, he pointed to the low profile Suu had maintained in the days since her release. "I don't think she would have agreed not to hold mass meetings without concessions on the part of the government," he said.

Suu confirmed that she had been lying rather low, despite her liberty. "I've been to see one or two people," she said, "an old aunt of mine; I went to pay my respects to an abbot who has been very kind to us—but nothing much, because there hasn't been time." She confirmed that her party was not going to be dogmatic about 1990—demanding that the military simply relinquish power, which had been the NLD's theme song in the past. "We are not holding on to the 1990 elections in the sense of using it to gain power," she insisted. "What we are concerned about is the democratic principle, not so much the question of who holds power. Which means there is obviously room for negotiations as to how they choose to honor the results of the 1990 election." I pointed out that twelve years had passed since that triumph, so if anyone questioned her party's claim to represent the views of the Burmese people today they would have a point. "It's fair to say that," she conceded. "But who's to say we won't get a bigger majority this time?"

But belying the confidence of the "political observer" I had met that agreement was right around the corner, Suu sounded a much more cautious note. In fact she gave me no reason to think that substantive talks had even begun. She had agreed not to hold impromptu meetings at her front gate, as she had done in 1995; the regime had agreed to let her out of her house. As far as I could tell that was the extent of their accord so far.

Suu hinted that she was impatient for things to start. "I believe that in an official statement the authorities said something about turning a new page," she told me, "and I certainly don't want the page to remain blank for a long time—blank until it turns grubby. What we want is for the page to be filled up, quickly, with a lot of useful and desirable stuff. The confidence-building stage is over, and it has to be over, you can't keep on at that stage forever, it becomes counterproductive."

Did she mean, I pressed, that she was waiting for the regime to make the next move? "I don't think I would put it like that," she replied. "I think if it is the right time, either side should be prepared to make the right move. It's not a question of you first or me first."

Yet clearly that is what she *was* waiting for: It was up to the holders of power to give an indication that they were prepared to do more than merely restore her freedom of movement. That meant their taking a first, irreversible step to acknowledging her as an interlocutor, as a person with a just claim to discussing issues of immense moment with them on a basis of something like equality. There is no indication that they had ever taken that step in the past, if you ignore the meaningless "Dialogue" splashed across the *New Light of Myanmar* eight years before, nor that they had taken it now.

Much has been made down the years of Suu's alleged stubbornness, her inflexibility, her refusal to concede the slightest thing in the interests of starting a dialogue. Ma Thanegi, whom I met for the first time a couple of days after seeing Suu, made that point. "I think she should be more compromising," she told me. "She should set up a good relationship with the government. She should talk to them privately and not scold them." But regardless of whether Suu used sweet words to describe her captors or blasted them to hell, the ball was and would remain in their court. Diplomats, mediators, the UN Envoy, "political analysts," journalists, all of us could enthuse, encourage, cajole, remonstrate until we were blue in the face. But until a certain general grasped this particular nettle, nothing would happen.

"We have both kept our sides of the bargain," Suu told me. "I have not been stopped from going wherever I pleased, and they have not followed us, they have not made problems for some of our supporters . . . I think we've kept our side of the bargain because we've made it clear to our people that we don't want them to come here and turn every day into a political rally."

Suu had kept her side: Her supporters, the thousands and thousands who had crowded around her garden gate seven years before, did as she requested and stayed well away. Now it was up to the generals to take the whole thing a step further. But amid the atmosphere of heady optimism, there were more somber voices. "Is it a developing situation?" a British diplomat queried, not impressed by the excitement. "Nothing concrete has been achieved. There are no easy answers here. The regime have dug themselves a very deep hole. Coming out of that hole is going to be difficult."

His gloomy words turned out to be prescient. After a week I went home to Delhi, having given the *Independent*'s readers what I hoped was a pleasant jolt with the news that (as the headline ran) "Burmese junta hints at power-sharing deal with Suu Kyi." But there was no follow-up, no hint from the generals that talks were planned or under way, no rumors of progress on the diplomatic grapevine. I might have made the whole thing up.

*

The Rangoon-based experts who had stoked hopes of progress were not, however, living in fantasy land: Eight years later, after she emerged from her third spell of house arrest on November 13, 2010, Suu herself revealed, in an interview with a local journalist, that she had had a series of talks with Brigadier General Than Tun, the officer appointed by the regime to liaise with the NLD—the first and only negotiations in more than twenty years to go beyond preliminaries. "We were almost there," she said. But these talks were a long time starting, and in the end, through no fault of Suu's, they were aborted before anything could be achieved.

Both the proximity of success and the eventual failure were caused by the particular strengths and weaknesses of Khin Nyunt.

By the time Suu emerged from detention in May 2002, Burma's Ne Win period was over. The old tyrant Ne Win was still alive, but in the months before Suu's release two of his children had been accused of plotting a coup and arrested, and he himself had been put under house arrest. He was to die in December, lonely and little-mourned and still in detention. Khin Nyunt's rise to the top had been facilitated by his patron Ne Win, the man "through whose nostrils" he breathed, as the Burmese said, and Ne Win's disgrace and death left the protégé exposed. Khin Nyunt held two key jobs—head of Military Intelligence and Secretary-1 of SPDC, the ruling council—and it was he who had rescued the state from bankruptcy by dropping Ne Win's disastrous economic policies and approving oil and gas deals with foreign companies. He was likewise the force behind the signing of ceasefire agreements with most of the warring groups on Burma's frontiers, the opening up of the tourism market and the drive to build new hotels: cautiously starting to align the country with its Southeast Asian neighbors, taking some tentative bites out of Burma's image as a hermit state.

If he was interested in converting Burma from a military autocracy into a democracy, it was a very well-kept secret. On the contrary, all the evidence indicates that what he was really interested in doing—like Burma's other military rulers before and since—was concentrating as much power and wealth as possible in his own hands. The difference between him and Ne Win or Than Shwe was that Khin Nyunt showed rather more intelligence and imagination in the way he went about it.

Robert Gordon, Britain's ambassador to Rangoon in the late 1990s, remembers him as the only senior figure in the regime he could really communicate with.

"He was a fascinating figure," he said, "much more approachable than the other top generals."[1] Not only was he, at the peak of his career, uniquely powerful, but he was also the closest thing to an acceptable face that the regime possessed. "Often key visitors would be introduced to him, and he would make efforts to speak English—badly but intelligibly." On one occasion, Gordon recalled his young son squirting the general in the face with a water pistol: Khin Nyunt laughed it off, and both father and son lived to tell the tale.

"With Khin Nyunt," he went on, "I always felt there was a very subtle mind, but too subtle for its own good. Endless amounts of effort would be expended on trying to bring Khin Nyunt and Suu together, and you'd have to go back crab-like through several intermediaries."

Ingrid Jordt is an American anthropologist, whose unusually deep and close familiarity with Burma began with her taking the Buddhist precepts as a nun in a Burmese monastery in the mid-1980s. She subsequently returned to the United States and followed a career as an academic, writing the first and so far only book in English about Burma's mass lay meditation movement. As an "old yogi," a veteran meditator, she makes regular return visits to the country.

As Jordt sees it, Khin Nyunt was the key figure in the regime's attempts to claw back the religious legitimacy which Ne Win had sacrificed back in the 1960s when he adopted a rigorously secular political structure and deprived the sangha of state patronage.

"Khin Nyunt was the main force behind the revitalization of religion during the 1990s," she said. "It was during this period that we saw the regime tie its legitimacy ever more closely to the *sangha* and to religion. His efforts need to be seen as a reaction to the mostly hands-off approach to religion by the military regime during the Ne Win period."[2]

In changing the country's name from Burma to Myanmar in 1989, the military regime was seeking to align its rule with that of the precolonial kings. Part of that effort involved undoing the secularizing tendencies of Ne Win and once again knitting the monks into the nation's political structure. As Jordt sees it, Khin Nyunt was the driving force behind this tendency, and was frequently shown in the state media feeding monks, visiting religious sites and supervising the restoration of old pagodas and the building of new ones.

The culmination of these efforts was the restoration of the Shwedagon, the most important religious building in the country, in 1999. It was an undertaking fraught with karmic promise and peril, and the placing of the *hti*, the delicate golden "umbrella," on the topmost tip of the stupa was the most tense moment of all: the moment when, if the ruler performing the sacred ceremony was morally unworthy, nature could be expected to rebel. A taxi driver told Jordt that when the Shwedagon's hti was being put up, everyone was frightened that there would be earthquakes and storms, because they knew the regime was not good. But when the hti was successfully hoisted and nature had made no calamitous objections, everyone felt disheartened, because it meant that these rulers were legitimate—which rendered Burma's situation even worse. It meant that they were stuck with this government.

"In Burmese thinking, political legitimacy is not based solely on regime performance," she said, "but is based on the idea of whether rulers have accumulated the spiritual potency—*hpoun* in Burmese—that sustains power, even if rulers are cruel and oppressive. But eventually a bad king's store of merit runs out and a virtuous king takes his place, thanks to having a larger store of merit-based hpoun."

As his Shwedagon project shows, Khin Nyunt was a risk-taker, in contrast to his fanatically cautious colleagues at the head of the junta. And just as he was prepared to risk all by hoisting the Shwedagon's hti, he was also prepared to talk to Suu. With his rough but workable English, his university education and his trips abroad, he saw clearly that she and her party were the most important obstacles on the road to the junta's acceptance by the international community. If some kind of accommodation could be reached with them, the rewards in terms of removing sanctions, the inflow of new business and the approval of the West could change the nation's prospects dramatically.

With his once all-powerful patron finally out of the picture, Khin Nyunt had to move stealthily: hence the elaborate complications involved in bringing him and Suu together. But indirectly the negotiations appeared to be grinding slowly forward. Razali Ismail, the career diplomat from Malaysia who had become the UN Secretary General's special envoy for Burma, flew in and out of Rangoon frequently, paying at least a dozen visits during this period and always saw both Suu and Khin Nyunt when he did: Coming from a country respected by the junta for President Mahatir's Look East policy, he enjoyed more prestige and had more leverage than any other UN envoy before or since.

But before any breakthrough could be achieved, the whole process was derailed in the most violent assault on Suu and her colleagues since the party's creation.

*

Aung San Suu Kyi's claim to significance rested on two facts: her party's overwhelming victory in 1990, and her and her party's continuing popularity with the Burmese masses. While the first fact could not be denied even by the junta, the second might fluctuate as political and social conditions within the country evolved: Suu could not take it for granted, given the regime's relentless persecution of the NLD's officers and members around the country. Her rapport with ordinary people all over the country had been the great transforming event of the 1989 election campaign. After the years of isolation she needed to meet them again, to reassure them that even though the revolution had not yet succeeded she was still dedicated to the cause. That is why, on regaining her freedom, it was an urgent priority for her to pick up where she had left off in May 1989 and go back on the road.

But it was an equally urgent priority for the junta to prevent this happening. With the much-touted new constitution still undrafted, and the National Convention that had been given the job of drafting it in suspension for years, no new elections were in view. But the generals had a visceral fear of Suu's massive popularity and the mandate to rule which it implied, the mandate they had long since betrayed.

Their slogan against Suu was that she "relied on external forces"—that she was a puppet of the West. And it was very disagreeable for them to be presented with new evidence that, on the contrary, what she relied on was internal forces—the overwhelming weight of popular opinion inside the country.

During her last spell of liberty, in the late-1990s, Suu had repeatedly tried to resume her tours of the country but had repeatedly had her car blocked by the military close to Rangoon, resulting in deadlocks which on several occasions lasted for days. For the regime the drawback to this tactic was that, because of the proximity to the capital, these confrontations were quickly picked up by the foreign media. They succeeded in bottling her up, but at the cost each time of conceding another propaganda goal.

The time was ripe for a radically different approach. So now, while Khin Nyunt and his colleagues were creeping in their crab-like fashion towards some kind of an agreement with Suu, his main rival in the ruling triumvirate, Senior General Than Shwe, was developing a very different strategy for dealing with Aung San Suu Kyi's popularity once and for all. He would have her eliminated.

2

NIGHTMARE

WITHIN a few weeks of her release in May 2002, Suu put to the test the agreement UN envoy Razali Ismail had prized from the junta, granting her not merely the right to leave her home but perfect liberty to go wherever she chose. She took her democracy show back on the road.

And it was as if she had never been away, as if nothing had happened in the thirteen years since her last election campaign trip in May 1989. If anyone supposed—and some of the most powerful men in the country apparently did suppose—that the Burmese masses had forgotten all about their heroine in the intervening years, it was a rude awakening. As videos shot during her meetings attest, everywhere she went the crowds were again vast and vastly good-humored. Her tours in 1989 had been the most dramatic political manifestations in Burma's independent history, the most vivid demonstrations, nationwide, of the strength of opposition to the junta and the strength of support for her. The reruns in 2002 and 2003, despite the passing of the years, were no less so.

But this time around there was a sinister new element. One of the initiatives taken by Than Shwe soon after supplanting Saw Maung at the head of the junta in 1992 (as described in Part Four) was the creation of a mass organization to counter the influence of the NLD. The Union Solidarity and Development Association (USDA), which has since mutated into the Union Solidarity and Development Party (USDP), now Burma's notional ruling party, is the military's civilian proxy: its means of securing the allegiance of millions of ordinary Burmese at every level of society by giving them favorable access to services and facilities, ranging from paved roads to courses in computing, from which the masses of those who don't belong are excluded.

That is the relatively respectable face of the organization. But there is another side to the USDA which is not respectable at all. When occasion demands, it provides hoodlums, thieves, drunks, drug addicts and other men with nothing to lose with the weapons and training to do the dirty jobs which the regime does not care to sully the military's fair name by entrusting to soldiers. The USDA can rapidly mutate into a force of mercenary vigilantes, given a vicious edge by opening the gates of the jails, offering drink, drugs, crude weapons and meager bribes to the inmates, then sitting back and watching the mayhem.

Suu had long experience of their tactics. "The USDA has become a very dangerous organization," she said in 1996. "It is now being used in the way Hitler used his Brownshirts . . . [it] is being used to crush the democratic movement."[1] The same year, when Suu and her colleagues were driving from her house in University Avenue to address a meeting nearby, a USDA gang attacked the car and smashed the windows; two years later other thugs from the organization forced her car off the road. And during her new tours of the country, this shadowy militia dogged Suu and her colleagues every step of the way.

The new calendar of visits, submitted to and approved by the military authorities in advance, covered much the same ground as the earlier ones. The journeys began in June 2002; Suu traveled in a new Toyota Land Cruiser, and to counter the USDA threat her team included a significantly larger number of student bodyguards than previously.

They visited Mon state, to the east of Rangoon, where Ma Thanegi had noted in 1989 that the crowds were the biggest in the country; the watery land of the Irrawaddy Delta west and north of Rangoon, where Suu was born and where, in February 1989 in the village of Danubyu, she had narrowly avoided being shot dead. They went southeast to Karen state, bordering Thailand, where she paid a second visit to U Vinaya in the town of Thamanya, the celebrated anti-regime monk, now ninety-two and increasingly frail, whom she had first met after her release in 1995 and whose work in creating a town animated by metta she had described in her "Letters from Burma."

They visited Arakan state on the border with Bangladesh, Chin state, bordering India in the northwest, Shan state to the northeast, site of her father's agreement with Burma's ethnic races in 1947, and many places in between—some ninety-five townships altogether, as the regime later recorded.

On May 6, 2003, she arrived in Mandalay, Burma's old capital, for the second time since her release, and made a number of sorties into the surrounding countryside, the last of which began on May 29th and would take her west to the town of Monywa.

The journey was planned as carefully as a military manoeuver—which in a sense it resembled, despite the authorities' formal approval of the itinerary. Suu had warned her companions that if they were attacked by the USDA, they were not to retaliate. So their only hope of safety was in careful planning, and in numbers.

Wunna Maung, one of her bodyguards, said later in testimony to the US Congress:

> Before our journey we heard many rumors that local officials of the military regime were training their troops with blunt weapons, including clubs, spears and iron spikes. For this reason, Daw Suu advised us to absolutely avoid any words or behavior that might lead to confrontation with any members of the military. She told us that if we were attacked we must not fight back. Even if we are struck or killed, she said, we should absolutely not fight back.[2]

Suu was well aware of the potential danger they faced. During one of the most tense periods of her previous spell of freedom, in November 1996, the secretary of the USDA, U Win Sein, who was also Minister of Transport, had told a meeting of villagers near Mandalay that killing Aung San Suu Kyi was their duty. Daw Aung San Suu Kyi, "the creator of internal political disturbances" must be "eradicated," he said. "Do you understand what is meant by eradicated?" he asked them. "Eradicated means to kill. Dare you kill Daw Suu Kyi?" Villagers within earshot later testified that he repeated the question five or six times but received no reply.

Given this high-level interest in her elimination, Suu was taking no chances. At 9 AM on May 29th, seven NLD cars and twenty motorcycles rolled out of Mandalay on the road west. In the lead, a few hundred yards ahead of the rest, was a scout car; next came Suu's dark green Toyota, driven by a law student called Kyaw Soe Lin, one of the party's legal staff, followed by two other cars filled with senior NLD figures, including party vice-chairman U Tin Oo, then the cars of local supporters. The group consisted of about a hundred people in all.

The trouble that awaited them had been carefully prepared. Starting six days earlier, the military authorities in the area, under the command of plump, pasty-faced Lieutenant Colonel Than Han, had mustered local USDA members from townships around the town of Shwebo, sixty miles north of Mandalay, a total it is claimed of about 5,000 men, and brought them to the grounds of Depayin High School along with more than fifty lorries and ten pickup trucks, to train them for the assault. On the day of the attack they were issued with their weapons: bamboo staves, baseball bats, sharpened iron rods, and similar crude implements, many of them specially made by a local blacksmith.

Less than two hours after the NLD party's departure, as they approached the town of Sagaing, hundreds of USDA members were waiting for them. "Before entering Sagaing," said Wunna Maung, "we witnessed about six hundred people holding signs that read, 'We don't want people who don't support the USDA.'" They were chanting the same slogan, as if they had learned it by rote. But their numbers were dwarfed by thousands of townspeople behind them, who were drowning them out with cries of "Long Live Daw Aung San Suu Kyi."

More USDA members had massed at another stop the party reached in midafternoon, but again their numbers were swamped by Suu's supporters and their action came to nothing. Suu and her colleagues carried out their prearranged program, reopening local NLD offices closed years before by the authorities, hanging up signboards outside them, making speeches to large crowds, then moving on to the next stop. All the time they were closely observed and filmed by local police and agents from Military Intelligence.

By 6 PM the NLD entourage reached Monywa. The military made them welcome by cutting off the town's electricity supply—or so Suu's supporters charge, though it may just have been one of the regular power cuts. They also made sure that the abbot of a local monastery whom Suu intended to visit was away on official business. None of this inhibited the local people from turning out in huge numbers to greet the visitors, and the next morning, after spending the night at a supporter's home in the town, Suu addressed them from the balcony of a building in the town center. No one present could have known that this would be her last speech before a Burmese crowd for more than seven years.

She began talking soon after 8:30 AM. Early May, before the rains break, is the hottest time of the year in upper Burma, and even at this hour of the morning her listeners were fanning themselves to keep cool. But the heat had not discouraged them from turning up: Practically the entire population of the town was there, packing the square in front of the building, spilling back into the streets and lanes leading away from it, standing in solemn silence in the full sunshine—only one umbrella was visible—then breaking into raucous applause when she said something they liked. There might have been twenty thousand people packed into that roasting hot public space. A few of them drifted away before she finished, but of the state-sponsored critics who had turned out to abuse her the day before there was no sign.

Suu wore a sky-blue silk htamein and a large cluster of yellow jasmine flowers in her hair, and her heavy fringe flopped down over her eyebrows.[3] Lines under her eyes betrayed the fatigue of the trip, which had already lasted nearly a month, her longest outing since her release, but as usual she spoke vigorously, fluently and without notes. When the audience clapped and cheered, she smiled and wobbled her head from side to side appreciatively, a charming, unconscious gesture she had perhaps picked up during her teenage years in Delhi.

She was recognizably the same woman who had galvanized a million listeners—even those who could not hear a word she said—in the grounds of the Shwedagon pagoda nearly fifteen years before. But she was not the stern, girlish, shouting figure of that occasion. Here was a mature leader, familiar with the rigors as well as the pleasures of being a public figure; familiar also and apparently quite relaxed about being the unique focus of the hatred of the most powerful men in the country. It was a burden she had grown accustomed to; now, with her husband gone and her sons grown up, bearing it had become her life.

She began, as so often before, with a reference to her father. He had visited the town in 1947, when he was "quite tired," she said, and came to Monywa for a rest; he had commented that he found the people "very prudent." "I have to say," she went on, "that [for me] Monywa is strong and firm rather than prudent. . . . In 1988 Monywa was extraordinarily firm, and I feel that it is now even stronger." The place went wild.

"The reason for this," she pursued, ". . . is because the people don't like injustice. They don't like bullying." But during her trips around Mandalay earlier in the month, she said, "members of the USDA tried every method to destroy our works by means of bullying. We had to be very patient."

Now she chose her words carefully. "We believe that everyone has the right to demonstrate," she went on. ". . . But they are not staging true demonstrations. They forced some people to join them."

It was clear that the USDA's persistent intimidation had become the dominant theme of the tour, one it was impossible to avoid. So, in her characteristic way, she met it head on.

"We do not react to them," she said. "We only report them to the authorities. But the authorities are taking no action . . . because they argue that they are doing things within legal boundaries. As the authorities are taking no action, the members of the USDA are becoming more daring." She told the crowd that at several villages in previous days,

> they threatened our supporters with sticks, machetes and catapults. But we didn't react to them. We only reported the case to the police station. The next day they increased the harassment . . . When we came to Monywa we heard about the one-sided bullying [here], we heard how the USDA was mobilizing its members . . . We also saw them do it along the way: There were cars with many [USDA] demonstrators. Other people are banned from using cars, are not allowed to hire cars, but they have many cars . . .

Yet the size and warmth of the crowds that came out to greet her gave her heart, she said. Everywhere she went, "The people have been supporting us in massive numbers. I believe they support us because they can't stand bullying and injustice . . ."

The speech over and the ceremonies of reopening the town's NLD office concluded, the party set off again, bound for Shwebo district, thirty miles to the northeast. As usual, they had obtained full authorization for this journey in advance, but as the jabs and taunts of their enemies intensified, they must have felt like an army patrol traveling through hostile guerrilla country: never sure when the next attack would come or what form it would take.

And now, as they headed towards Depayin township, the army joined in the harassment. "When Daw Aung San Suu Kyi arrived near Zeedaw village," an eyewitness later testified, "military authorities from the Northern Command headquarters stopped the convoy including the cars

of the people of Monywa who had come to see them off." Suu and her
party were permitted to proceed, but when her supporters returned later
to the same village on their way back to Monywa, "the police waiting in
readiness beat them up and put them under arrest."

Unaware of this, Suu and her team drove on to the town of Butalin,
where she once again performed the ceremonial reopening of the
local party office. They were now deep into the flat paddy fields of the
countryside, far from any sizeable town and even further from the gaze
of foreign diplomats and journalists. They stopped at the little town of
Saingpyin, where Suu had an emotional encounter with the family of the
local NLD MP-elect, who was still serving a jail sentence. Meanwhile her
minders sent a car on to scout the road ahead. Ominously, it failed to
return. Motorcycles were sent to find out what had happened to it, but
they too disappeared.

Still miles from their destination, with darkness closing in, Suu and her
team were driving blind into *terra incognita*, with a hostile army presence
behind them and no way of knowing what lay ahead.

By the time they arrived at the little village of Kyi it was pitch-dark.
They had not planned to stop here, but a little way beyond the village
the headlights of Suu's car picked up two elderly monks sitting on the
roadside, who hailed them as they approached.

"They asked if Suu could address a gathering," Kyaw Soe Lin, her
driver, recalled. "I told Daw Daw"—"aunty" Suu—"that we shouldn't stop
as we usually get harassed around dusk. But the monks said they had been
waiting for Suu Kyi since the evening before and requested that she give a
speech and greet them." To turn down such a request from two old monks
would be the height of bad manners, whatever the circumstances. Suu fell
into the trap. According to Kyaw Soe Lin, "Daw Daw said we should stop
for them."

But the old men were not monks at all but imposters from the USDA.
And as the convoy halted on the road while Suu decided how best to
accede to their request, the full fury of the USDA fell upon them.

Four vehicles which had been tailing them, two lorries and two pickup
trucks, now roared up alongside the convoy and armed men poured out,
shouting anti-Suu slogans. When the local villagers, who had come out of
their houses to see what was going on, started shouting back at them, the

USDA thugs attacked them with iron rods, bamboo staves and baseball bats. One of the USDA lorries took a run at the villagers in its headlights, and the villagers scattered in terror—whereupon a much larger USDA force—four thousand according to some eye-witnesses, though the figure is impossible to verify—who had been waiting to ambush the convoy poured from the sides of the road and attacked the NLD cars and their motorcycle outriders and local supporters.

"We watched helplessly and tried to show courage," said Wunna Maung, the bodyguard.

> Because we had been told to never use violence, we tried to protect Suu's car by surrounding [it] with our bodies in two layers. As we waited, all the cars behind us were being attacked, and the USDA members beat the NLD members mercilessly. The attackers appeared to be either on drugs or drunk.
>
> The USDA members struck down everyone, including youths and women. They used the iron rods to strike inside the cars. I saw the attackers beat [NLD vice-chairman] U Tin Oo and hit him on the head before they dragged him away. He had a wound on his head and was bleeding.
>
> The attackers beat women and pulled off their longyi and their blouses. When victims, covered in blood, fell to the ground, the attackers grabbed their hair and pounded their heads on the pavement until their bodies stopped moving. The whole time the attackers were screaming the words, "Die, die, die . . ." There was so much blood. I still cannot get rid of the sight of people, covered in blood, being beaten mercilessly to death.[4]

What saved Suu's life, according to Aung Lynn Htut, the senior MI officer who later defected to the United States, was that the officers in charge of the attack had not expected her car to be at the front—which was why the initial attack was concentrated on the cars in the middle and the rear. But it was not long before they realized their mistake.

"As the USDA members approached Daw Suu's car, we braced ourselves for the attacks," Wunna Maung recalled. "The attackers first beat the outer ring of my colleagues on the left side of Daw Suu's car, and smashed the window . . . As my colleagues collapsed one by one, the attackers then started beating the inner ring of security. The attackers hit my colleagues ferociously, because they knew we would not fight back."

Wunna Maung was only saved because he was on the right side of the car, while the attacks were concentrated on the left.

Inside the car Suu's driver pleaded with the attackers, telling them who exactly he was carrying in the back—but that only inflamed them further. "My anger exploded," he admitted, "I wanted to run them over." He put the vehicle into reverse, stamped on the accelerator and the car hurtled back; the assailants reacted by raining blows on the car, breaking the windows both in the front and the back, where Suu was traveling, as well as the wing mirrors and the headlights, and battering the car's bodywork.

Over his shoulder as he roared backwards Kyaw Soe Lin saw wounded colleagues sprawled across the road, in his path; frightened that he might run them over, he again reversed direction—but now the road ahead was blocked by trucks.

Pulling over to the verge he succeeded in squeezing past them, but then found himself faced by dozens more trucks, their lights illuminating more attackers—two to three hundred was his estimate—"there were so many of them," he said—some of them holding banners with anti-NLD slogans.

The USDA men looked on "in surprise," he said, as he hurtled towards them. Some of his party's bodyguards were clinging to the outside of the vehicle, hanging on for dear life. "I was worried that the attackers might pull them off if we got too close," he said, "so I drove straight at them, pretending I was going to run into them, and they scattered. Then I pulled the car back onto the road and kept on driving."

In the murk ahead he saw more road blocks, but resolved to get through them without stopping. "I realized that all of us, including Daw Daw, would die if we didn't get out of this place, so I kept on driving." As he roared through the hostile mob they threw objects at the car, smashing the remaining windows and one of them striking him.

"Daw Daw asked me if I was okay. I said I was fine and kept on driving. I knew that if I stopped at the road blocks they would beat us to death." He kept driving as fast as he could, weaving through another barricade of trucks and past a line of police with their guns pointed at the road, and other figures with guns who looked like soldiers. "I drove through them but didn't hit anyone as they jumped out of the way," he recalled. "Daw Daw said we should only stop when we reached Depayin."

But they didn't make it that far. As they entered the town of Yea U, armed guards forced them to stop, demanded to know who was in the car, and made them wait. Half an hour later a large contingent of soldiers turned up. "One officer, apparently a battalion commander, arrived and put a gun to my temple and ordered us to go with them," Kyaw Soe Lin said. "Daw Daw nodded at me, so I did as they said. We were taken to Yea U Jail." Suu's year of freedom—her year of living more dangerously than ever before—was over.

*

Suu survived the Depayin massacre without serious injury thanks to the courage and skill of her driver, but it cost the lives of about seventy of her supporters. For the outside world, and for most people in Burma, too, it was seen as another disastrous setback for the cause of Burmese democracy. But in the highest, most secretive echelons of the junta, a different story was being played out. Depayin was the worst, bloodiest and most perilous moment in Suu's career, indeed in her entire life. Yet paradoxically the months that followed brought her and her party closer to a political breakthrough than they have ever been before or since—one which only now, nearly a decade later, is coming to light.

The aftermath of Depayin reveals two things about the Burmese junta. One is the extraordinary brutishness of Senior General Than Shwe, who soon afterwards admitted ordering the massacre, with the aim of "eradicating" Aung San Suu Kyi. The other is the total disarray within the ruling triumvirate. However, as the negative consequences of the massacre unfolded, it was Than Shwe's rival Khin Nyunt who, against the odds, found himself back in the ascendant. And his longstanding ambition of reaching agreement with Suu and her party finally began to bear fruit.

*

In the days after the attack, Suu was locked up in Insein Jail, all her senior colleagues in the party were put in jail or under house arrest, and party offices throughout the country, including the ones she had been busy reopening in the days leading up to the attack, were closed down again. The brave if vague hopes raised by her release, which had led the insiders

I interviewed in May 2002 to predict a power-sharing agreement between her and the junta, were dashed.

The international community, which had been expecting to see results from Suu's liberation, was shocked. The United States and the European Union tightened economic sanctions, the United States banning most imports (although Burma's three main exports, gas, gems and timber, continued to get through the net), and Japan, as ever a bellwether for what the junta could get away with, suspended economic aid. Even the flaccid councils of ASEAN were bounced into reacting by the United States, demanding Suu's release for the first time ever.

For UN envoy Razali Ismail, the massacre killed off all the hopes that had been raised during many months of painstaking negotiations. He flew into Rangoon a few days after the massacre, when Suu's condition and even her whereabouts were still unknown, and demanded to see her. "I was taken in a car with darkened windows, and we changed cars along the way," he recalled. "Finally we arrived at Insein Prison and I was totally shocked. They had never told me she was in jail: Khin Nyunt had simply told me he had rescued her from the mob."[5]

Despite everything that had happened, Suu told the Malaysian diplomat that she was still willing to "turn the page" and use the situation as an opportunity for dialogue. But Ismail could see no redeeming elements in the situation: Instead he anticipated all too clearly the outside world's reaction. "I came out very angry," he said. "I told Khin Nyunt, 'What are you doing? Do you know if I go out and tell the world that Aung San Suu Kyi is in Insein Prison what will happen? What are your intentions? Why are you keeping her like this? Why is she looking so bedraggled?' The next day she was given clean clothes, better food, and within two weeks she was out." Suu was taken straight from the prison to her home, where she was once again put under detention.

Yet although Khin Nyunt was the target of Ismail's anger—his only interlocutor within the junta—Khin Nyunt was just as livid himself.

It was he who had been the junta's representative in the talks with Suu and Ismail that had begun well before her release from detention; it was he who saw her integration into Burma's governing structure as the key to his country's international rehabilitation. And now his plans, like Ismail's, were in ruins.

Khin Nyunt and Brigadier General Than Tun, his subordinate who had the job of liaising with Suu, had warned her that it was risky to tour the country so soon after her release, but they had no prior knowledge of what was planned at Depayin. That was because of the intense distrust between the three men at the head of the junta, all of whom had climbed to the top by different routes. Khin Nyunt was a university graduate who had gone on to the Officers' Training School in Rangoon, Maung Aye was a product of the Defense Academy in Maymyo, the old British hill station near Mandalay, while Than Shwe had no such elite training but had come up through the ranks. Each had their own culture, their own entourage and their own views of Burma's future, and they guarded their secrets jealously.

In the immediate aftermath of the massacre, the regime tried to claim that what had happened at Depayin was a minor incident provoked by youths and monks who supported the NLD. In a press conference on June 6th, Deputy Foreign Minister U Khin Maung Win said that Suu's motorcade "attempted to plough through" a crowd of "townspeople protesting against her visit," causing injuries to people in the crowd and provoking "clashes between the townspeople and the motorcade" that resulted in four people dying and fifty being hospitalized.

But it was not long before the truth emerged. Soon after the massacre, according to the defector Aung Lynn Htut, "Maung Aye and Khin Nyunt approached Than Shwe and asked him whether he had ordered the assassination of Aung San Suu Kyi. He admitted yes, he had ordered the attack to kill her."[6]

Than Shwe, whose ruthlessness is matched by an amazing unawareness of the effect his orders can have on the outside world, later repeated the admission to a larger audience. In a letter to Asian governments, he justified the attack by claiming that Suu and her party had been "conspiring to create an anarchic situation . . . with a view to attaining power" by Suu's birthday on June 19th. He maintained that he was faced with "a threat to national security by this militant group," and was compelled to take firm measures "to prevent the country from sliding down the road to anarchy and disintegration."

But within a month of the attack, as the scale of the outside world's reaction became clear, Than Shwe was forced onto the defensive. In June, as the true culprits were exposed and the US Congress's Subcommittee on

International Terrorism, Nonproliferation and Human Rights mounted an investigation, he ordered the closure of USDA offices around the country. It was a sham—none of them stayed closed for long, and soon the organization was once again prospering—but it was a sign that his attempt to bluster his way out of the crisis had failed.

Than Shwe is an intensely superstitious man, like his predecessors, and it is possible that he saw in Suu's survival of this concerted and well-planned attempt to kill her further proof of her supernatural powers. With the careful work of rebuilding Burma's prestige now in tatters, he was forced to accept that a new policy was required. And the only man to provide it was Khin Nyunt. The only English speaker at the summit of the junta, the only man willing and able to talk to foreign diplomats, he was put in charge of cleaning up Than Shwe's mess. And in August, less than three months later, Than Shwe named him prime minister in place of himself, retaining his own positions as head of state and chairman of the State Peace and Development Council.

"Khin Nyunt's power had been on the wane in the months leading up to the Depayin massacre," said Dr. Maung Zarni, "but the failure of Depayin, which was intended to get rid of Aung San Suu Kyi, and the negative international reaction to it, put him back in the game: His men were the most polished in the Ministry of Defense and within SPDC as a whole. It was his team's trouble-shooting prowess that gave Khin Nyunt greater scope."

Five days after his promotion, in response to the new sanctions, Khin Nyunt announced the plan that has dominated political discourse in the country ever since: the Seven-Point Road Map to Democracy.

It was an attempt to tackle the bogey of legitimacy which had bedeviled the junta ever since the army crackdown of September 18, 1988. When the newly named SLORC took the place of the old socialist one-party system designed by Ne Win, it was presented as a stopgap to deal with the emergency caused by the popular rising, which would melt away once a new government had been elected.

When the elections were won by the NLD, that plan was aborted and SLORC, later renamed SPDC, clung to power, but still with the understanding that it was a provisional arrangement that would last only until a permanent constitutional framework could be agreed on. But with the NLD's walkout from the torpid, regimented and pre-cooked National

Convention in 1996, all efforts to build that framework were suspended, along with the Convention itself. Khin Nyunt's road map was an attempt to get the whole process started again.

The first step, as he told his colleagues in the highest levels of the junta at Rangoon's People's Assembly Building at 9:30 AM on August 30, 2003, "is to reconvene the National Convention that has been adjourned since 1996." Subsequent steps would involve the drafting of a constitution by the National Convention, the submission of the constitution to a referendum, the holding of new elections under the constitution and the convening of parliament, followed by the building of "a modern, developed and democratic nation." This, he told his colleagues, would be the "road map" to "a disciplined democratic system."

Khin Nyunt only mentioned Suu directly once in the speech, referring to the fact that his senior colleague Than Shwe had "with magnanimity" met her—nine years before plotting her violent death—to try to "find ways to smooth out the differences." Elsewhere he refers to her obliquely as "an individual" and "a preferred individual," but her problematic person dominates his discourse. The National Convention had been suspended because her party, overwhelmingly the most important one, had walked out of it; the only way to reconstitute the Convention and gain the credibility of the outside world, in particular of the "big nations" which are "unfairly pressuring our country"—a clear reference to the new sanctions imposed after the Depayin massacre—was to persuade the NLD to sign up for it again. And although no mention was made of this in his speech, and few hints of it were picked up by the foreign press, this was now his urgent priority.

Days after Depayin, Suu had told Razali Ismail that, despite all that had happened, she was prepared to "turn the page." If, despite everything, she could bring herself to do that, then Khin Nyunt's road map might actually lead somewhere.

*

The talks went on in the weeks and months after August 2003. It is clear that both protagonists were committed to making real progress. Khin Nyunt was still under the thumb of Than Shwe, but as prime minister he now had greater scope than before to make the concessions Suu required if she was to persuade her party to sign up for some kind of power-sharing arrangement.

Than Shwe had been bruised and weakened by the Depayin outrage, but it remained a perilous undertaking. The senior general's loathing of Suu had by no means diminished after the failure of his plot to assassinate her. For him she would always and only be "that woman" and, as Razali Ismail attested, he could and did terminate meetings if her name was mentioned. Everyone knew how important she was to the outside world, and (in their view) how arrogant, obstinate and difficult to deal with, even though under house arrest. Somehow, though, she and her party would have to be smuggled into the road map, almost without Than Shwe's knowledge.

We don't know where or when the talks occurred or how many there were; all that is certain is that they took place, that Suu's main interlocutor was Than Tun—and that, as Suu revealed cryptically for the first time in 2010, "we were almost there."

That revelation came out of the blue, in November 2010. A journalist for the regime-friendly Burmese magazine the *Voice*, harping on Suu's proverbial obstinacy in an interview with her soon after her release from detention, asked why she had refused to negotiate with the regime. "But we did," she replied. "And we were almost there. And the people who were leading these negotiations are still alive. But I can't reveal anything more." It was the first time that the existence of the negotiations had been made public. "Than Tun met her many times, sometimes openly, sometimes secretly," a senior Burmese journalist told me in Rangoon in March 2011, on condition of anonymity.

According to the defector Aung Lynn Htut, the agreement was finally drafted in May 2004 and envisaged the NLD rejoining the National Convention that it had walked out of in 1996. But when Khin Nyunt presented the agreement to Than Shwe, the latter got cold feet: He realized that it would change the status quo, and that the prestige of Khin Nyunt would rise while his own position, as Suu's failed assassin, would inevitably decline. So he simply rejected it, and there was nothing that Khin Nyunt or anyone else could do to get him to change his mind.

"Than Tun had to go back to Aung San Suu Kyi and tell her the deal was off," an insider said. "She was furious. 'You all ought to wear htamein!' she exploded, using a favorite (sexist) Burmese insult, implying that the negotiators were as 'untrustworthy as women.'" The long-simmering power struggle between Khin Nyunt and Than Shwe now came to a climax, and Than Shwe deployed his superior forces and the well-founded fears that MI and its secret archives engendered among his colleagues to bring his rival down. Military Intelligence was always a thorn in the side of the rest of the army: One of Khin Nyunt's predecessors during the Ne Win years had been purged just as abruptly when his colleagues decided that he knew too much. Than Shwe, Maung Aye and their cronies have corruptly amassed billions of dollars in kickbacks over the years, so the activities of Khin Nyunt's agents always posed a potential threat to them.

In July 2004, while Khin Nyunt was away in Singapore, they struck preemptively: A raid on an MI depot in Shan State by officers of a parallel intelligence network set up by Maung Aye found evidence that Khin Nyunt's network was involved in illicit trade. On his return Khin Nyunt in retaliation angrily ordered his underlings to compile incriminating dossiers on the other top men in the junta, but before he could find an opportunity to blackmail them, he was brought down: On October 18, 2004, he was arrested while on a trip to Mandalay. The following day the state media carried a single-sentence announcement signed by Than Shwe which said that Khin Nyunt, now sixty-four, had been "permitted to retire on health grounds." This was soon proved to be nonsense when he was put on trial, charged with corruption, and sentenced to forty-four years in jail. The prison sentence was commuted to house arrest, but Than Tun, who had refused to reveal any details of his talks with Suu despite being tortured, was sentenced to 130 years. He is still being held in one of Burma's most remote jails, in the far north.

A collateral victim of the purge of Khin Nyunt was General Thein Swe, the father of Sonny Swe, who was the friend and patron of the Australian journalist Ross Dunkley. The General, a senior member of Khin Nyunt's Military Intelligence team, was sentenced to 149 years in prison. As a result, all Dunkley's dogged brown-nosing over the course of the decade came to nothing. Lacking a reliable protector within the regime, he was painfully exposed, and on February 13, 2011, the inevitable finally occurred when he was arrested at Rangoon airport on returning from abroad. He was remanded in custody in Insein Jail, accused of assaulting a prostitute. Within three weeks, a crony of the regime called Dr. Tin Tun Oo had prized the company from his grasp, taking over as Chief Executive while Dunkley remained in jail, awaiting trial.

The Australian was duly convicted but treated with unusual leniency by Burmese standards: On June 30, 2011, he was sentenced to one month in jail and released because of the time he had already served. He told reporters he would appeal against the conviction.

Khin Nyunt's weakness was his strength, as mentioned earlier, and his strength was his weakness. As head of MI, a desk-bound officer with no military achievements to boast of, he was at a permanent disadvantage when it came to obtaining the support of the army at large. He had sought to compensate for this by fashioning the most intrusive and ubiquitous domestic intelligence network the world has ever seen, Orwell's *1984* brought to life; by pacifying, by whatever means necessary, much of the wartorn border, signing ceasefire deals with more than twenty armed groups; and finally, by trying to cut a deal with Suu.

But Than Shwe, alarmed by the prospect of Suu finally dividing the army and taking the spoils, applied brute force and brought the process to an end. As Suu had written many years before, "It is not power that corrupts but fear. Fear of losing power corrupts those who wield it . . ."[7]

3

THE SAFFRON REVOLUTION

AUNG SAN SUU KYI disappeared from view on May 30, 2003, the same day she had made the speech in Monywa, and reappeared nearly seven and a half years later, on November 13, 2010.

For most of that period her human contacts were restricted to the mother and daughter who now kept house for her, and her doctor who paid occasional visits. Every so often the UN's latest envoy, a Nigerian called Ibrahim Gambari who was Under-Secretary General to Kofi Annan, was given permission to meet her; later, when she was charged with a criminal offence, she was given access to a lawyer, a colleague in her party.

But that was about all. She had no telephone line, let alone a computer with Internet access, no way of talking to her colleagues in the NLD, and she received no mail. As during previous periods of detention, her most important and valuable companion was the radio, which she listened to for many hours every day. But despite everything the BBC World Service and Voice of America could tell her, she emerged in November 2010 like Rip Van Winkle, amazed by the sight of ordinary Burmese talking into mobile phones—a device she had never used—dazzled by the profusion of Internet cafes in Rangoon, and tantalized by the possibilities offered by such unheard-of facilities as Facebook and Twitter.

Given the length of her latest spell of detention and the completeness of her isolation, it was surprising to hear her say, in one of her first post-liberation interviews, that it was not these years but her first years of house arrest—from 1989 to 1995—that were the worst. Perhaps she had simply grown used to the solitude, the simplicity, the regularity; the lake beyond the ragged garden shimmering in the sun; the monsoon rain dripping through the holes in the roof. "For some years," she wrote in a column for the *Mainichi Daily News* after her release in 2010, "I had spent the monsoon months moving my bed, bowls, basins and buckets around my bedroom like pieces in an intricate game of chess, trying to catch the leaks and to prevent the mattress (and myself, if I happened to be on it) from getting soaked."

The roof leaked because her estranged brother Aung San Oo had filed a court case in 2000 claiming that by rights half the house belonged to him—and blocking repairs on the basis that they would "damage" his property. The lawsuit dragged on until the last year of her detention, when, to the surprise of those who despaired of Burmese justice, the court found in her favor.

In her absence the years from 2004 to 2010 marked a great improvement in the regime's luck, or its strategic skills, or perhaps both. Perhaps it was the purging of Khin Nyunt that made the difference: Always tugging against the will of his more conservative colleagues, he was the force behind Suu's release both in 1995 and 2002, convinced that the only way to deal with Suu and her party was to incorporate them into the junta's machinery rather than leaving them outside to make mischief.

Suu's failed assassin Than Shwe felt no such compulsion. He had perhaps been persuaded that she could not, in fact, be done away with, but he was determined to lock her out of the country's new political arrangements permanently. It took time and stolid determination to do so, but in the end the effort paid off.

At seventy-seven, the age Ne Win was in the crisis year of 1988, Than Shwe crowned his career with the engineering of a comprehensively rigged general election which left Suu and her party—not the "opposition" as so often described in the foreign press but the runaway winners of Burma's only genuine election in modern times—out in the cold. He (or his clever advisers) then contrived to distract the world's attention from his outrageous election scam by setting Suu free the following week. She emerged, to the jubilation of thousands of her supporters and the relief of the world, into a new landscape where she had no role. Is that the end of the story?

*

Democracy has had scant opportunity to sink roots in Burma's soil. When Suu and her colleagues traveled around the country in 1989, one of her main tasks was to explain what this thing democracy was. She reported that people received it with great enthusiasm. Not surprising: Almost any political novelty would be preferable to the existing regime. But a generation of military dictatorship, which followed little more than a decade, and a chaotic decade at that, of democratic experiment, meant that Burmese democracy was very much a work-in-progress when Suu was put under house arrest for the first time. Since then the regime has done everything in its considerable power to kill it off.

If we try to assess Aung San Suu Kyi's success and importance on the basis of the strength and the achievements of her party, therefore, we will come away with a poor result. Like the AFPFL, which her father headed, the NLD has always been more a "united front" than a party, a bundle of aspiring politicians with different ideas and backgrounds, bound together by the desire to end military rule and by belief in Suu and her charisma. It had little of the ideological glue that defines a party in much of the world, and but for her it would surely have broken into several warring factions long ago. After the watershed of July 20, 1989, when she was locked up for the first time, the junta declared open season on the party, jailing practically the entire top leadership; when it went on to win the election anyway, the persecution proceeded apace, with many MPs-elect in jail, many more in exile, and those that remained in the country living furtive existences. Similar persecution continued for the next twenty years, culminating in the de-registering—essentially the outlawing—of the party and the closure of all but one of its offices by 2007.

So to judge Suu on her success in implanting democracy in her country is to invite the retort: She has failed. An honorable failure, certainly, in the circumstances, but a pretty total one. The travesty of democracy on display in 2010's election, with the largest party conjured into existence practically overnight by the simple device of taking the USDA and replacing the A with a P, shows how far democratic Burma has yet to travel.

But Suu's impact on Burma is only partly reflected in the development, or lack of it, of democracy.

Her appeal to the people of Burma at the outset was nothing to do with her principles or democracy and everything to do with her name. Then there was her courage, the courage of this "pretty little thing" to defy the anger of Ne Win as no one had defied him for twenty-six years. There was her fragile beauty, and the charisma of all these things together. There was her commitment to nonviolence, about which she was adamant from the beginning, and her steady adoption—a little hazily at first, but gaining in confidence as she became an experienced meditator during her years of house arrest—of the Buddhist wisdom that has always underpinned Burma's notions of morality, both private and public. Then, as the cord that bound all these qualities together, there was her steadfastness: her willingness to undergo bitter personal suffering for her cause, and her refusal, year after year, to give in.

This is why, of all the political figures to whom she has been compared, Gandhi is the only adequate comparison. A leader of the Indian National Congress, he was never contained by the conventional expectations of the political life, but burst those bonds time after time. He was a democrat inside the party, but he was seen by his millions of devotees as far more than a politician: as a sage, an embodiment of the Indian soul, and, in his clothing, his adoptive poverty and his devotion to the spinning wheel, as the apotheosis of the Indian peasant.

Suu is sometimes compared unfavorably with Gandhi in terms of strategic skill, and it may be true that nothing in her career matches the genius of his march to the Gujarati coast to make salt, in defiance of the Raj's taxation laws. But the idea that it was Gandhi who forced the British out of India is a myth. By the time Britain pulled out—to a timetable dictated by postwar British austerity and the hostility to British imperialism of the United States quite as much as by the power of the Congress—Gandhi was already lamenting the failure of his movement to yield a united nation. The last decade and more of his life, as the independence movement he symbolized was finally producing results, was a succession of failures. Yet while he lived Gandhi incarnated not merely the democratic hopes of India but its pride, its courage, its community-transcending solidarity, its will to shake off centuries of tyranny and reinvent itself. Those achievements dwarfed his failures on the petty political plane.

Something very similar is true of Aung San Suu Kyi, and explains why, despite her absence from the scene from 2003 to 2010, and despite the near-death of the NLD during those years, her influence continued to be the single most important counterweight to the brutal might of the army.

During these years, Burma's history consists of two parallel stories: the official one, which shows the steady and now almost unresisted consolidation of power by the SPDC; and the buried, underground history of the Burma which Suu represented and which like an underground stream was hidden from view most of the time, having no longer any legally permissible ways to show itself—but which then surged out, when the time was ripe, as an astonishing torrent.

*

The official story is best summarized in a series of dates. On May 30, 2003, as we have seen, Suu survived her assassination attempt but was taken into custody; she was later put in a purpose-built shack inside Insein Prison with a view of the gallows. She remained in jail for more than three months. In September it was rumored that she had gone on hunger strike—but it was untrue. She had been taken to hospital suffering from a gynecological complaint, which was operated on; there has been speculation that she had a hysterectomy. Afterwards she was not sent back to Insein but put in detention again in her home. The first photographs of her since her speech in Monywa in May 2003, taken with Ibrahim Gambari in November 2006—UN envoys had been refused visas for the previous two years—show her looking noticeably older, and very pale and thin.

Meanwhile the Seven-Point Road Map to Democracy announced in August 2003 was being put into effect. Khin Nyunt was now also in detention along with his family members, many of his subordinates were in jail, and his entire military intelligence apparatus had been dismantled. But where Than Shwe demonstrated great cunning was in retaining the road map even after he had sacked its architect. Without Khin Nyunt, and without Suu, it could still serve a useful purpose: In fact the absence of those troublemakers made it potentially much more useful to him.

The first requirement of the road map was for the National Convention to be reconvened, and so it came to pass, without the participation of the NLD. Almost unnoticed by the outside world with the exception of Beijing's punctilious Xinhua News Service, the National Convention met several times: from December 2005 to the end of January 2006, from October to December of the same year, and from July to early September

2007. At each of these sessions, leaders of the regime-sponsored NUP and other regime-friendly politicians sat down with representatives of the ethnic "nations" on the borders which had cut ceasefire deals with the regime, and the SPDC's bureaucrats coached them through the constitutional scheme they had concocted.

The result of their work, published in September 2007, was only the bare bones of a constitution, but its thrust was quite clear: to legalize and render permanent and indissoluble the preeminent power of the military over Burma's political life. The constitution was put to the people in a referendum in May 2008, just as the poor farmers of the Irrawaddy Delta were struggling to recover from a cyclone in which more than 130,000 of them died. The referendum sailed through, thanks to strong-arm tactics at polling stations throughout the country, setting the scene for the nation's long-delayed return to multiparty democracy—of a sort.

This constitutional cavalcade was interrupted in 2005 by the stunning news that the site on which builders had been working at a place called Pyinmana, four hours' drive north of Rangoon, for the past few years was not another—or not just another—military cantonment but Myanmar's new capital: Naypyidaw, "Abode of Kings," located at the spot where Aung San, having switched sides, launched his offensive against the Japanese Army.

With a constitutional settlement under way, relative peace on the borders (though the army continued its war against the Karenni and the Shan, and its scorched earth policy against the Karen forced tens of thousands of Karen refugees into Thailand) and with the democrats well and truly gagged, the regime began to look more comfortable than it had in many years.

The much-ballyhooed Western sanctions were porous at best; the UN's finger-wagging was so laughably ineffective that it could safely be ignored; the ongoing plundering of the country's resources brought the dollars pouring in. And the regime had become adroit at playing its two giant neighbors, China and India, off against each other. Both were eager for minerals and for strategic regional advantage, and were happy to overlook almost anything to obtain them. India in particular, for a long time highly critical of the regime and its abuses, had learned to keep its mouth shut. "[The generals] are feeling feisty," a Western diplomat told the *Financial*

Times in May 2006. "They have never been in as comfortable a position internationally as they are today."

*

There is, however, an alternative history of Burma during these years, an underground history.

One man whose career embodies that history is a small, feline Burmese monk called Asshin Issariya. He has taken the nickname, or *nom de paix*, of King Zero, because, he explains, Burma no longer has any rulers worthy of the name. I met him in the Thai border town of Mae Sot.

In this most traditional of Buddhist countries, the monks lost much of their central role as teachers after the British introduced secular education, but they retain vast importance as a moral force. According to Theravada belief, it is the devout life of the monk that helps the layman progress towards nirvana. The layman feeds the monk and the monk rewards the layman with merit. It is a symbiosis.

At his monastic university in Rangoon, Asshin Issariya learned to take the educational duties of the monk seriously. "My first teacher was very interested in politics," he said. "This was a great advantage for me. As he always listened to the BBC, I could also hear it every day. In this way I learned about the situation of our country . . . I felt strongly that when I graduated I would need to do something strong for our country."[1]

In 2000 he set up a small library in the university. In the same year he and some other monks went into the delta region where Suu had been blockaded during one of her attempts to travel into the countryside. "We went with the hope of being able to ask her advice about what we should do," he said.

They were unable to meet her, but when they went back to Rangoon, Military Intelligence sent the university authority a report on their trip with a warning. "The university decided to close our library," he said. "They said that if we continued to operate our library the regime would close the entire university. So I decided to leave the university because I could not run my library."

But the library bug had bitten him. Not by chance, setting up a chain of public libraries was Suu's dream before she became involved in politics.

Anybody who seeks to change Burma soon runs up against the fact that the first thing to change is the level of ignorance. He said:

> I left the university and moved the library to the village in Rangoon division where I was born and raised. I organized for a lot of people to read the books.
>
> Then I went to Mandalay and met another monk at the Buddhist University there, and we started teaching English, Japanese, French and computers. We also opened three libraries in Mandalay as well as a library in the university. By 2004 we had opened a total of fourteen libraries, all in monks' organizations. The library itself is open but within each library there is a section of political books that is kept secret.

While the National Convention slowly worked through its agenda, in the real world inhabited by the Burmese masses life was becoming harder than ever. In late 2006 the price of rice, eggs and cooking oil shot up by 30 to 40 percent. Burmese monks are closely in touch with the cost of living of the ordinary people: Tightening circumstances are soon reflected in the amount of food they receive in their alms bowls. So effective had been the terror tactics used by the regime in 1988 that very few people had dared to protest openly in the intervening years, and it had been around a decade since the last mass demonstrations. But so unacceptable were the price rises that in February 2007 a small protest against them was held in Rangoon. The authorities stamped on it hard, jailing nine of those involved.

Laymen knew they could anticipate swift and brutal repression when they took to the streets in protest, but the rules were different for monks: There is a powerful religious taboo against harming them. That is why King Zero and some of his brothers conceived the idea of a "peace walk": not a conventional protest but a religious procession, consisting solely of monks, chanting sutras, "for the poor," as he put it. "Two other monks and I from Mandalay and Yangon met secretly in Thailand to discuss how to do the peace walk and we planned it in detail, we told the foreign media about it. The idea was to do a peace walk because the people in our country are very poor," he explained. "We put up stickers all over the cities."

But the initiative was overtaken by events.

As we have seen, the final meeting of the National Convention was held from July to September 2007. It was the crowning session of a constitution-writing process that had begun fourteen years earlier. But in mid-August 2007, acting with the same arrogant dispatch as Ne Win when he demonetized high value banknotes in 1987, Than Shwe removed at a stroke the government subsidy from fuel. This caused the price of petrol and diesel to rise immediately by 66 percent, while the price of Compressed Natural Gas, used by buses, went up 500 percent in a week. Immediately the cost of travel went through the roof, adding another intolerable burden to the lives of the poor.

Protests against the cuts began in Rangoon on August 19th, led by a small group of activists, members of the "88 Generation Students," those blooded in the events of that year, several of whom had recently been released from jail. Prominent was Min Ko Naing, the leader of Rangoon's students nineteen years before. But repression was swift and violent, and thirteen of the protesters, including Min Ko Naing himself, were beaten and arrested. The regime was quick to suspect a revolutionary conspiracy behind this tiny protest. The civil unrest, according to the *New Light of Myanmar*, was "aimed at undermining peace and security of the State and disrupting the ongoing National Convention."

On September 1st, King Zero and his colleagues met to discuss the situation. Four days later, a small demonstration in the town of Pakokku, on the Irrawaddy River near Pagan, which included monks, was broken up by troops; in the process some monks were beaten up and tied to trees and at least one disappeared. The next day young monks from the town took to the streets again and demanded that the regime apologize for the attack on their brothers, giving a deadline of September 17th.

No apology was forthcoming, so the Peace Walk, led by King Zero, U Gambira and others in the newly-formed All Burma Monks' Alliance, began in earnest. First in Rangoon then in Mandalay and subsequently in other towns, the sangha began to walk through the streets, sometimes empty-handed, sometimes with their bowls turned upside down to indicate their repudiation of the military.

The processions began small but grew day by day: On September 24th the march in Rangoon consisted of 30,000 to 100,000 monks, making it much the largest show of popular strength since 1988. It stretched through the city for nearly a mile. To the extent that anybody had noticed it in the first place, the concluding session of the National Convention earlier in the month, the crowning triumph of Than Shwe's rule, disappeared under this tsunami of indignation: the unprecedented sight—flashed around the world on satellite television—of tens of thousands of barefoot monks padding down Rangoon's imperial boulevards in the driving rain.

Under the monsoon downpours they walked at the steady pace of Buddhist monks everywhere: neither pounding nor ambling, not marching in lockstep like soldiers but clearly a body of people, a corps on the move, saturated with rain, bare feet slapping on the slick tarmac.

If it was a political event it was of the most minimal kind: no banners, no slogans, no speeches, no protection, no masks, no helmets, no weapons. No shoes, even. They only carried flags, the multicolored flag of Buddhists.

Until the bloody days of the crackdown they faced no resistance: no police, not even one, no soldiers, not even a hint of control; just these irresistible human rivers swelling with endless new tributaries and streams. Marching, they chanted over and over the Metta Sutta:

> *Sukhino va khemino horitu, sabbasatta bhavantu sukhitatta, ye keci panab-hutatthi, tasa va thavara va-navasesa; digha va ye va mahanta, majjhima rassaka anukathula . . .*

"May all sentient beings be cheerful and endowed with a happy life," they chanted. "Whatever breathing beings there may be, frail or firm, tall or stout, short or medium-sized, thin or fat, those which are seen and those unseen, those dwelling far off and near, those already born and those still seeking to become, may all beings be endowed with a happy life . . . As a mother protects her baby, her only child, even so towards all beings let us cultivate the boundless spirit of love . . ."

Everywhere they marched, the cameras of undercover Burmese video journalists, working for an independent Burmese news organization based in Norway, the Democratic Voice of Burma (DVB), captured them and the images went round the world.

In the West the mobilization of the monks was soon being called "the Saffron Revolution," to be set alongside all the other "color" revolutions, Orange, Green and so on, that had changed the political face of Eastern Europe. But it made an uneasy fit: The monks had no banners, no apparent leaders, they shouted no slogans and made no speeches. They just chanted and walked.

Ingrid Jordt, the American anthropologist and former Buddhist nun, was frustrated by Western misunderstandings of the phenomenon, misunderstandings which she feared could put the monks' lives in danger.

> I got a call from Seth Mydans of the *New York Times* who said, "I'm writing an article about the militant monks, I just need a few quotes from you." I told him, you're not going to get any because you've got it all wrong. If the *New York Times* writes that Burma has militant monks, then you have given carte blanche to the regime to crack down on those monks tomorrow, because that would mean they are playing politics. And he didn't use that phrase in his piece, and the uprising went on for twenty days or something, because they couldn't crack down on monks when they were just being moral admonishers.[2]

As the monks' movement gathered momentum, I returned to the region to report it. At Mae Sot on the Thai border one refugee monk explained to me why monks take to the streets.

"To play a violent role would be far from our beliefs," he said. "But we can have a mediating role. When Lord Buddha was alive he mediated between one particular king and the people who were rebelling against him, in a peaceful way. We monks are Buddha's sons and so we try to follow in our father's footsteps."

In the same town I met Dr. Naing Aung, one of the student leaders in the uprising of 1988 who had fled into exile after the massacre that brought that rebellion to an end and who was still a leader of the democratic movement outside Burma. He explained to me what had changed between 1988 and 2007:

> The big difference is that when we came out of Burma we were preparing for the armed struggle to overthrow the regime. We came out and began training to fight alongside the ethnic armies that were fighting the regime.
>
> But now the protesters inside Burma are for the unarmed struggle. They want to win it by winning people's hearts. It requires more courage because they are facing fully armed soldiers and they have no weapons. But they say, anyway we can't compete against the army in armed power—but we can compete in terms of the support of the masses, in terms of truth and justice. They have been taking up Gandhian methods, what we call political defiance: demonstrations, boycotts, refusing to have religious communication with the regime . . .

The scenario sketched by Naing Aung was of a nation, estranged from its rulers for more than a generation, which far from giving up the struggle for freedom had discovered new resources for the fight in its traditional faith, and new ways to carry on that fight—of which the monks' uprising was the first sign. And in choosing these means and this new nonviolent vanguard, people were also falling in with the woman for whose party they had voted in overwhelming numbers. Aung San Suu Kyi had written:

> In Burma we look upon members of the sangha as teachers. Good teachers do not merely give scholarly sermons, they show us how we should conduct our daily lives . . . In my political work I have been strengthed by the teachings of members of the sangha . . . Keep in mind the hermit Sumedha, who sacrificed the possibility of early liberation for himself that he might save others from suffering. So must you be prepared to strive for as long as might be necessary to achieve good and justice . . . [3]

The fact that the monks' protest had erupted so soon after the conclusion of the National Convention may have been a coincidence, but it was instructive. Than Shwe had sought to correct one of Burma's glaring anomalies, the fact that it lacked a national constitution and was ruled ad hoc by soldiers and emergency decrees. By this means he hoped to persuade his people, and the world, that Burma was back on a good course. But nothing he did could remedy the moral decay and corruption of which that anomaly was only one of many signs.

The climax of the uprising—captured only by a mobile phone camera—came on October 24th, when the barricades parted and one column of chanting monks was allowed to come almost to the gate of Suu's home. Suu came out of the gate and saluted them with tears in her eyes as they continued chanting.

The crackdown began the next day: The regime threatened violence if the marches did not cease. Soldiers surrounded the Shwedagon, the mustering point for Rangoon's marches, and on the night of September 26th began raiding monasteries, beating, arresting, forcibly defrocking and killing monks. When monks and members of the public defied the overnight repression to march again in Rangoon, troops opened fire, killing at least nine including Kenji Nagai, a Japanese video journalist, shot dead in cold blood. The murder was recorded by *Democratic Voice of Burma's* brave undercover cameramen and the shocking images sent around the world.

"This popular uprising marked a new era in post-Independence Burmese politics," says Jordt. "Burma had finally entered the age of information." For the first time the Burmese people were able to see political reality—protest and violent repression—played out in real time on their televisions.

In an open-air coffee shop in the town of Kaw Thaung, in the far south of Burma, where I was reporting the uprising—the closest I could get to the action, Rangoon being under lockdown—one large television was tuned to a Japanese samurai drama, the other to CNN. During those days, much of the American channel's news coverage was devoted to "the Saffron Revolution" with shots of tens of thousands of marching monks intercut with clashes on the streets, lorries full of troops and trashed monasteries. The customers in the coffee shop watched round-eyed and in silence.

According to Jordt, Than Shwe's violent suppression of the protests, which millions of Burmese saw with their own eyes on television or the Internet, put him in a special category of vileness.

In suppressing the monks' uprising, Than Shwe claimed in the state-run press that he was merely acting as a "good king" and punishing what he claimed were "bogus monks" who were betraying their cloth by turning political. "But that claim simply did not stand up in light of the images of monks being violently abused and beaten, of monks' corpses floating in the rivers," she said. "These were horrific images that shocked the devout nation of Buddhists. Than Shwe was seen as nothing more than a monk killer. The regime's claim that these were only bogus monks was dismissed, as were the claims that the monks were playing politics."

The Burmese were in no doubt, says Jordt: They expected any day that Than Shwe would "descend head first into the hell realms," unless his astrologers and sorcerers were clever enough to come up with some black magic—*yadaya* in Burmese—to keep that fate at bay.[4]

Where did that leave Aung San Suu Kyi, locked up in her home throughout these events?

"She is seen as a witness, a moral compass for her country," says Jordt. "Where she has the greatest traction is in her role as moral exemplar."

It is a role analogous to that of the monks: They shape the morality of individuals by exemplifying morally ideal behavior, while Aung San Suu Kyi plays a similar role in the political realm. "Her virtue-based politics . . . contrasts starkly with the ruling generals' oppressive and cruel reign," Jordt said.

> Her power lies in being a witness to the process of moral degradation and violent oppression by the military regime. She inspires the populace to recall or imagine a different kind of social contract between ruler and ruled based on the highest human aspirations of compassion, loving-kindness, sympathetic joy and equanimity: the four sublime states of mind.
>
> When the file of monks was permitted to walk down University Avenue and stop at the gate of her home, this performance evoked the way in which the sangha traditionally conferred its moral endorsement on an aspiring ruler, sanctifying their claim through recognizing their virtue.

She thereby became, to invoke a Burmese notion of political legitimacy, the "rightful pretender to the throne."

The Burmese believe that evil acts provoke reactions in nature. Eight months after the violent suppression of the monks, in May 2008, the regime announced the referendum to endorse the new constitution that had been rubber-stamped by the National Convention—the fourth step on the road map. But days before the referendum could be held, a violent cyclone struck the country, killing 138,000 people, mostly poor farmers in the Irrawaddy Delta, rendering 2.4 million more homeless and causing billions of dollars in damage.

Jordt says that popular opinion in Burma was in no doubt that the disaster had been provoked by Than Shwe's abuse of the monks. "Cyclone Nargis was taken as a sign that the regime was illegitimate and that the country was being punished as a whole for the rulers' bad actions against the monks," she said. "A little poem was secretly circulated through the population, encapsulating their dire expectations":

> Mandalay will be a pile of ashes
> Rangoon will be a pile of trash
> Naypyidaw will be a pile of bones.

4

THE PEACOCK EFFECT

JOHN WILLIAM YETTAW, who lives in a small mobile home in the Ozark Mountains, Missouri, is a four-times married Vietnam War veteran and a devout Mormon; a man who believes that God speaks to him and sends him on urgent missions.[1]

One of his three ex-wives has said he suffers from post-traumatic stress disorder. NLD sources have referred to him, not without reason, as "a nutty fellow" and "that wretched man."[2] What is also true, however, is that under the compulsion of God, or trauma, or plain nuttiness, he did what even the most enterprising journalists had not bothered to attempt—neither I nor Kenneth Denby nor even John Simpson, during the many years of Aung San Suu Kyi's detention: He made his way to her home, under the noses of her many guards, not once but twice.[3]

He didn't get an interview, but then that was not what he was after. His mission was to warn her that terrorists planned to assassinate her, then pin the blame on the junta.

His first visit came during a twenty-six day trip to Burma in November 2008. During her years of detention, as well as the mother and daughter who kept house for her, there were numerous guards both at the razor-wire barricaded gate, and inside the house. The first time Yettaw made his way to her home—swimming across Inya Lake with the help of home-made wooden flippers—he failed to meet her: He was stopped at the shore and eventually sent on his way, after leaving a copy of the Book of Mormon for Suu as his visiting card. Acting no doubt on information from one of the people who had intercepted him in the grounds of her home, he did not swim back across the lake but took the easy way out, walking along the lake shore then through a drainage pipe which brought him out near the American Embassy.

The following year Yettaw, now fifty-three, still apparently obsessed with Suu and determined to warn her in person, made his second attempt. He arrived in Rangoon on May 2, 2009, and checked into a small downtown

hotel. The following evening he took a taxi to the spot near the American
Embassy where he had emerged from the drain the previous year, and
followed the route he had taken then in reverse: walking through the
drainpipe and along the lake shore to the back entrance to 54 University
Avenue. And this time, oddly enough, despite all the security, he had no
trouble meeting Suu.

She reportedly pleaded with him to leave at once; he refused, complaining
of exhaustion and cramp (even though, contrary to newspaper reports but
according to the court record, he had not at that point done any swimming
that night). He stayed two nights in the house, eating at least two meals,
and leaving various unexplained items there, including two chadors. He
was said to have spent a lot of the time praying. He eventually left at around
midnight on May 5th, swimming across the lake with the aid of his famous
flippers and two empty five-liter water bottles.

He was arrested five and a half hours later while swimming in the lake
close to the home of the American chargé d'affaires on Pyi Road, at the
opposite end of the lake to Suu's house. He admitted having come from
Suu's house. How he had spent the intervening five and a half hours has
never been clarified—and Yettaw has yet to agree to be interviewed at any
length.

This story begs several questions. As he was apprehended during his
first visit, and was clearly breaking several Burmese laws, why was he
not arrested there and then? How was he able to pay a second visit to
her home? After meeting Suu in May 2009 on this second visit—just two
weeks before she was due to be released from house arrest—why did he
not return to his hotel by the far more convenient land route? And how
did he pass the hours between bidding Suu farewell and being arrested?

Yettaw's visitation was bad news for Suu. Her latest and longest spell
of detention had begun in 2003, and was renewed every six months after
that, year after year. But under the law used to confine her, the "Law
to safeguard the state against the dangers of those desiring to cause
subversive acts," which was passed in 1974 after the U Thant uprising,
five years was the maximum term allowed. In 2008 the regime extended
her house arrest for another year; the UN's working group on arbitrary
detention ruled that this final extension was illegal under both Burmese
and international law.

Unless it wanted to incur more of the same sort of opprobrium, the regime would have to release the nation's hottest political prisoner into the blinding glare of international publicity at the end of May 2009—a year or more ahead of the general election which was intended to crown Senior General Than Shwe's constitutional marathon, step six of the famous road map.

With the "Saffron Revolution" and the popular anger it had channeled less than two years in the past, Suu at large would present the regime with a serious problem. Yet to keep her detained in defiance of its own laws would be to put all its budding claims to be a legitimate, constitutional force in jeopardy.

It was thus highly satisfactory for the regime that Suu was caught in the act of committing what, by their lights, was a criminal offence.

Indeed, it was so satisfactory that it is very hard to believe that the incident was not craftily set up. There is of course no proof either way, but the whole incident reeks. A Western diplomat, who requested anonymity, was quoted by *Newsweek* as saying that when Yettaw was in Thailand, before his second visit, two agents of Burmese Military Intelligence—in its new, post-Khin Nyunt incarnation—approached him posing as members of the NLD and told him the Lady was ready to receive him.

The main charge against Suu was that she had violated the terms of her detention by allowing a visitor to stay at her home overnight. In the old days Burma had no hotels because hospitality was freely offered to travelers, even those with no claim of family or friendship. It is typical of the way military rule has corroded the traditional morality and practices of the country that what was once a basic rule of life is now a crime.

Both Yettaw and Suu and her companions were put on trial for the alleged offences. Yettaw was charged with entering a restricted zone and breaking immigration laws. The trial was held inside Insein Prison, where Suu and her companions were remanded for its duration, Suu in prison officers' quarters. Foreign journalists were as usual refused visas that would have allowed them to attend, but fifty-one ambassadors and other foreign diplomats attended some of the hearings, along with a couple of dozen local journalists.

Suu pleaded not guilty to the charges, blaming Yettaw's appearance at her home on a failure of security. British ambassador Mark Canning, who was in court to hear her testify, said, "She made it clear that the whole thing had been thrust upon her. When pressed about why [Yettaw] did it, she said they should ask him." In answer to questions, she said she did not tell the military authorities about his intrusion. "I allowed him to have temporary shelter," she said.[4]

"Mr. Yettaw's antics are a gift for Burma's military junta," Phoebe Kennedy wrote in the *Independent* on May 27, 2009, "which can use them as a pretext to keep the popular figurehead of peaceful resistance locked up during and beyond elections due next year."[5] A senior figure in the regime, Brigadier General Myint Thein, claimed the authorities had considered freeing her at the expiration of her detention order, but the situation had "regretfully" changed on account of Mr. Yettaw.

Yettaw was sentenced to seven years jail, and Suu and her companions to three years each. A coup de théâtre was provided before the verdict when a message came from Senior General Than Shwe in person, remitting half of the sentences of the three women: Suu's detention would be extended "only" by eighteen months, to November 2010. This act of leniency, it was explained, was on account of Suu "being the daughter of Bogyoke Aung San who sacrificed his life for the independence of Myanmar, viewing that peace, tranquility and stability will prevail, that no malice be held against each other, that there be no obstruction to the path to democracy."[6]

There was no such mercy for Mr. Yettaw, but after three months in jail he was sent back to the Ozarks, his release having been secured by American Senator Jim Webb, who repaid the junta by giving numerous interviews calling for the repeal of sanctions.

*

John Yettaw is Everyman: The whole world wants a part of Suu, wants to warn her, award her, co-opt her, write about her, possess her, exploit her, empathize with her, love her, be loved by her. The brave, frail beauty locked up year after year like some princess in a dismal fairy story has taken possession of our collective unconscious, in defiance of the remoteness of her country and the obscurity of its politics.

Suu is one with brave fellow Nobel Peace Prizewinners Shirin Ebadi and Mairead Maguire, and in the courage she has shown in overcoming great obstacles is comparable to Malalai Joya, the woman Afghan MP, and the indomitable Pakistani lawyer Asma Jahangir—but just to list those names is to appreciate the chasm between them and Suu. She is in a league of her own, far more famous than any of them. Which car-maker would dream of using any of the other women on that list to sell their cars, as Chrysler and Lancia have done with Suu? What manufacturer of designer lamps would use the image of another of these women in their advertisements year after year, as the Italian firm Artemide has made use of Suu—"There is a light on earth" runs the copy—without even feeling the need to print her name?

Despite her instinctive hostility to the idea, Suu has become an A-list international celebrity; but again she cannot be compared with any other star because it is her inaccessibility that keeps her celebrity voltage so high. Yes, she will accept the role of Guest Director of the Brighton Festival in the UK; she will humbly accept the latest of the sixty-six honorary degrees (and similar) and fifty-seven international prizes (and other miscellaneous tributes) that, at the time of writing, have been showered on her. And though she will never turn up to receive them in person, for more than twenty years she has had the best alibi in the world.

The upside of Suu's fame is that it gives Burma's democracy struggle a prominence in newsrooms around the world that, in her absence, it would absolutely lack. The Dalai Lama has had a comparable importance for Tibet's struggle against China. The downside is that, unlike the Dalai Lama, for many years she has had no direct control over how her name and image are used.

Campaigners have been understandably eager to use her smiling or troubled face to lend heft to their appeals, but in trying to grab one minute of the attention of American teenagers, for example, the realities of Burma have on occasion been buried under a "fight the evil ones" rhetoric more appropriate to *Star Wars*. Exploited in this way, Suu risks being reduced to a cipher of Western self-righteousness, graphic shorthand for how great it makes us feel to empathize with a beautiful woman horribly put-upon by bullies in uniform. She is the love interest in our *Rambo* version of the Burmese democracy struggle. The result is a rising tide of cynicism about such campaigns and the real economic interests they often further. Look at the difference between the economic profiles of Bangkok and that of Rangoon, and imagine how much money remains to be made once the latter is fully wrenched open. The Chrysler ad featuring Suu climaxes with the car they are trying to sell smashing down a wall. The subtext is not hard to fathom.[7]

Because for many years she had no control over how her name and image were exploited, Suu finds herself at the center of debates over Burma for reasons that have everything to do with her image but nothing to do with her. In April 2011, for example, Andrew Marshall, a Bangkok-based journalist, picked up on Suu's celebrity status to write in *Time* magazine, "In our celebrity-obsessed age, it is perhaps inevitable that a nation's struggle for democracy is re-cast as a one-woman reality show . . . Realpolitik, though, is no match for romance." Celebrity, reality show, romance: By singling out the meretricious ways in which Suu's persona is sometimes exploited, Marshall sought to undermine her importance.

He was taking his cue from a new report on Burma by the International Crisis Group (ICG): An indication of Suu's relative insignificance, he suggested, was in the fact that her name "appears just six times" in the twenty-one page ICG report which concluded that the time was ripe, after November 2010's election, for the world to start re-engaging with Burma. All that stands between us and that sensible objective, Marshall suggests, is our trivial, immature obsession with a beautiful celeb.

A more craven way of playing into the Burmese regime's hands is hard to imagine. As discussed in the last chapter, the road map to what is sometimes translated as "discipline-flourishing democracy" and which led to 2011's elections was the most substantial political achievement of the regime since 1990. But it was also fraudulent through and through. The regime's success in holding elections and obtaining the result it needed is very far from indicating that Suu and her party have become irrelevant. In fact the truth is exactly the opposite.

In the past the generals have repeatedly behaved as if they believed that all they had to do to make the Burmese forget about Suu was to lock her away. After having this wishful thinking punctured repeatedly over the space of fifteen years, they finally realized the bitter truth that Suu remains central to mass resistance to their rule, no matter how long they lock her up for.

Digesting this unwelcome fact, they saw that the only way their proxies could win an election was if it was comprehensively fixed; with the NLD and Suu in particular not only out of the way but out of the running. And that, with a degree of care and finesse unusual for them, is what they then contrived.

The ICG conclusion quoted by Marshall is that Burma's election presents the West with "a critical opportunity to encourage [Burma's] leaders down a path of greater openness and reform."[8] But this is simply to do the regime's bidding and accept the illusion of change for the real thing. It is to accept the bank robber's claim that he earned his fortune honestly as good grounds for investing in his company—even though you watched him while he robbed the bank. The only reason for doing that is because you have for many years been looking for even the flimsiest excuse to do business with these people. And sadly that is true of the ICG, a lavishly financed think tank which fulfills a useful function in some countries but which has been unreliable about Burma for a decade.

What else has the Burmese regime done, either before or after its civilian makeover, to persuade the world that it is interested in going down "a path of greater openness and reform"? Have they released any political prisoners? Done anything to bring a just peace to borders ravaged by war for half a century? Taken a single step to reforming a judiciary which has for half a century merely done the military's bidding? Done anything about investing in health and education, where Burma has long been close to the lowest levels in the world? They have done none of these things. They have fixed a referendum, fixed an election, and set up an impotent, purely decorative parliament—because that's the way, they have been told, to make the West believe they are moving in the right direction.

*

Aung San Suu Kyi's great gift to her country was that she threw open the windows to the outside world. At the same time she also opened the windows of the world to Burma. And more than twenty years after her return home, the message with which she galvanized her people is still reverberating, far from Burma's shores.

When Suu disappeared into detention in July 1989, it seemed that Burma's democracy struggle had run its course. Thousands had died, thousands more had been driven into exile, thousands were in jail; tens of millions, the mass of the Burmese, returned to their former lives of poverty and fear. There were to be no more mass protests for nearly twenty years.

Yet the seeds that Suu had planted on August 26, 1988, at the Shwedagon, the seeds she had scattered far and wide in the first six months of 1989, were not all strangled by thorns. Actions, Buddhists believe, have consequences: That is the meaning of the word "karma." "My actions," says the Vietnamese Zen monk Thich Nhat Hanh, "are my only true belongings." By insisting that the Burmese could shake off their fear and lead lives of dignity, and that immoral power, incarnated in the army, could be defeated by nonviolent resistance, and by persuading tens of millions of Burmese to vote for her party, she changed something profoundly. She did not lead her revolution to triumph, but she changed the world.

Aung San Suu Kyi's life tends to be described in a one-dimensional manner, as the story of a courageous woman who challenged a military junta and lost. It has been my intention in this book to show that the real story is much more complex and interesting than that. Suu's ambition went far beyond the narrowly political, and despite the failure and marginalization of her and her party on the political plane, her impact on her society has been enormously rich and important. Whatever happens or does not happen between now and her death, Burma will never be the same again.

That is a story that I believe has been missed by her previous biographers, perhaps blinded by the million-watt glare of her fame. But there is another story which is even more extraordinary, and that has never previously been told. Suu changed Burma by throwing open the windows of her stale and stagnant homeland and letting the winds of the world blow in. What is not appreciated is how, in the process, she also changed the world.

The key element was her insistence, from the first days of her involvement in the uprising of 1988, on nonviolence. Without her insisting on it, it is probable that the Burmese revolution would have taken a very different course. Already when she stood up at the Shwedagon in August 1988, students were counterattacking the riot police and the army with Molotov cocktails and other crude weapons, as they had done during the U Thant funeral riots in 1974, and suspected spies were being lynched in the streets. But Suu was adamant from the start that all that had to stop. And she got her way. The NLD's rallies, wherever they were held, were uniformly peaceable. Her colleagues and escorts were uniformly self-disciplined in the face of great provocation, from Danubyu to Depayin.

Many in the democracy movement in 1988 saw her insistence on nonviolence as a grave handicap, ensuring their defeat. After she was put in detention in July 1989, thousands of activists fled to the borders to train with the ethnic armies, so that instead of meeting the Burmese Army's aggression with nonviolence they would, next time around, be better equipped to fight back.

But those who fled to Manerplaw, the Karen Independence Army's camp on the Thai border, to train with the Karen guerrillas, were in for a surprise. When they got there they came face to face with foreign experts telling them that, far from being a fatal weakness, Suu's insistence on nonviolence, developed with sufficient creativity, could be the key to victory.

*

It was in the early 1980s that Burma and its problems got under the skin of a US Army officer called Robert Helvey, the United States military attaché from 1983 to 1985. He saw how the Ne Win tyranny held the people in its grip. "Burma has a special place in my heart," he said.

> As defense attaché in Rangoon, two years living in Rangoon and getting around the country, I really had an opportunity to see firsthand what happens when a people are oppressed to the point that they are absolutely terrorized. When people would talk to me—and it required a bit of courage to talk to a foreigner—sometimes they would place their hands over their mouths because they were afraid someone was watching and they could read their lips. That's how paranoid they became.[9]

It wasn't that the dictatorship was not opposed: People on the borders had been resisting the Burmese dictatorship militarily for decades. But as a military man, Helvey saw that their efforts were doomed to fail. He said:

> There was a struggle for democracy going on but it was an armed struggle on the periphery of the country, in the border regions. And it was very clear that the armed struggle was never going to succeed.

So when I got back [to the US], I kept Burma in the back of my mind. Here was a people that really wanted democracy, really wanted political reform, but the only option they had was armed struggle. And that was really a non-starter, so there was really a sense of helplessness.

Helvey returned to the United States and was appointed senior fellow at the Harvard Center for International Affairs in Cambridge, Massachusetts. He was there in 1988 when Burma blew up, and he was watching keenly. And it was around this time, as the revolt was gathering force, that this military man had an encounter with nonviolence that changed his life.

"When I was up at Cambridge one day," Helvey recalled in an interview, "I saw a little poster saying 'Program for Nonviolent sanctions.' I didn't have anything to do that afternoon so I went up to the seminar . . . Primarily, I guess, being an army officer, I was going to find out who these people are, you know, these pacifists and things like that— troublemakers. Just trying to get an understanding of it."[10]

The man giving the seminar was a maverick American academic called Gene Sharp. Helvey recalled, "[Sharp] started out the seminar by saying, 'Strategic nonviolent struggle is all about political power. How to seize political power and how to deny it to others.' And I thought, 'Boy, this guy's talking my language.'"[11]

One of the main charges laid against Suu over the years has been futility: Nonviolence, people say, may have worked for Gandhi and the Congress, but they were up against the Raj with its tender conscience, a long way from home. Challenging the Burmese Army was a different matter. "Resorting to nonviolence tactics," wrote Thant Myint-U, "she tried to provoke the government . . . But she wasn't facing the Raj of the 1930s or the Johnson administration of the 1960s. These were tough men who played a very different game . . . Unlike the British, Burma's generals were never ready to quit Burma."[12]

As a career army officer, one would expect Colonel Helvey to feel the same way about Suu's nonviolent approach. But Burma had opened his mind.

Listening to Gene Sharp, Helvey said, "I saw immediately that there may be an opportunity here for the Burmese. You know, if you only have a hammer in your toolbox, every problem looks like a nail. So maybe if they had another tool in their toolbox, they could at least examine the potential of strategic nonviolent struggle. So that's how I got interested in it."

It so happened that Dr. Gene Sharp was, and remains, the world's leading authority on nonviolent struggle. His involvement had begun with working with the Norwegian resistance to Nazi/Quisling rule in the Second World War. For more than thirty years he held a research appointment at Harvard's Center for International Affairs. His books include *The Politics of Nonviolent Action* and *Gandhi as a Political Strategist*.

After the seminar, Helvey introduced himself. "We met for coffee and for lunch, and our conversations kept expanding because there's so much overlap. If you think strategically about nonviolent conflict, you use some tools used by the military. You think about the environment in which the conflict is waged. About the rules of engagement. About problem-solving methodologies. About strategic estimates. About operational planning."

Under Sharp's influence, Helvey set about beating his sword into a ploughshare. "After I retired from the military," he said, "I continued my interest in nonviolent conflict and began teaching and consulting." And after the democratic uprising was killed off in September 1988 he went back to Burma to take another look.

Instead of going to Rangoon, though, he went to Manerplaw, the jungle camp on the Thailand–Burma border which I described earlier, where the Karen guerrillas who had been fighting the Burmese since independence had been joined by students, monks and intellectuals fleeing army persecution. And he tried to win over the hard-boiled leader of the Karen Independence Army, General Bo Mya, to his ideas.

"I went into his office and gave him a short pitch—the sources of power, and how the focus of the strategic nonviolent conflict is to undermine the organizations and institutions that hold up the government . . . I explained how with that theoretical understanding you could purposely undermine these pillars of support and train people to resist and defy.

"There was a big grunt and he just turned around and walked away. No thank you, no nothing." When Helvey told a friendly Karen in the camp what had happened, he advised him to try again—leaving out the word "nonviolence."

"So we came up with the term 'political defiance' instead of 'nonviolence.' It sounded more courageous." The word change worked: Bo Mya ordered

Helvey to run introductory courses on "political defiance" for everybody in Manerplaw—Karens, students, monks, everyone.

Helvey persuaded his original mentor, Gene Sharp, to come over and join him. Bo Mya "never converted," Helvey admitted. "He felt that people who participated in nonviolent actions were probably cowards, but he was pleased that Gene and I were able to provide opportunities for cowards to participate in the struggle . . ."

Helvey and Sharp found themselves face to face with student politicians who, until the army takeover on September 18, 1988, had believed they were on the brink of seizing power; with elected NLD MPs whose only reward for their commitment to democracy was to be hunted down like vermin; with monks deeply estranged from a regime which paid lip service to Buddhism while committing atrocities and practicing black magic. They were all Suu's "sons," the great new family she had embraced on her return to Burma; but now that she was under indefinite detention they were more like orphans.

All of them confronted the same conundrum. No one doubted the massive support that Suu and her party enjoyed—the support, as the election had proved, of the overwhelming majority of the people. But in the face of the army's refusal to yield an inch, how could you get there—into power—from here?

Helvey and Sharp endorsed Suu's own conviction, the rule she had imposed fiercely on her party, that every temptation to go down the way of violence should be resisted. Equally vital, and umbilically linked to it, was the need to retain the moral high ground.

Nonviolent struggle, Helvey says, "is a form of warfare. And you've got to think of it in terms of a war." But at the same time the commitment to keeping it nonviolent is vital. Violence, he said:

> is a contaminant to a nonviolent struggle . . . the greatest contaminant. I use the example of gasoline. If you get a little bit of moisture in your gas tank, the engine will still run—not real smooth—but it'll still run. But when the moisture level reaches a certain point, the engine doesn't run at all . . . Once violence becomes a policy or accepted, then it becomes a major contaminant—so major that you're going to lose the moral high ground . . . And the other thing is, you are meeting your opponent where he is strongest. And that's dumb. Why would you invite the enemy to fight you on his terms?[13]

Gene Sharp's involvement in the Burmese struggle did not stop at Manerplaw. At the request of an exiled Burmese dissident journalist based in Bangkok called U Tin Maung Win he wrote a series of articles on the nuts and bolts of nonviolence and how to practice it, which were published in Burmese in the magazine Tin Maung Win edited, *Khit Pyaing* (*New Era Journal*). "I could not write an analysis that had a focus only on Burma," Sharp later wrote, "as I did not know Burma well. Therefore, I had to write a generic analysis." Subsequently the articles were gathered together into a booklet and published in both Burmese and English. The English title was *From Dictatorship to Democracy—A Conceptual Framework for Liberation.*

Little known in the United States or Britain, the booklet has been translated into twenty-eight languages. As Sharp himself concedes, his booklet, though less than ninety pages long, "is a heavy analysis and is not easy reading." It concerns a subject, nonviolent resistance, that is still widely written off by mainstream opinion as something that only works for a Gandhi or a Martin Luther King, Jr., when you are pushing at an open door; the choice of cowards, in General Bo Mya's robust view, of *bien pensant* liberals too delicate to face up to life's ugly realities. But very quietly and surreptitiously, unnoticed by most of the media, nonviolent resistance has been changing the face of the world.

"In recent years," Sharp writes in the book's recently updated first chapter, with a hint of pride,

> Various dictatorships . . . have collapsed . . . when confronted by defiant, mobilized people. Often seen as firmly entrenched and impregnable, some of [them] proved unable to withstand the concerted political, economic and social defiance of the people.
>
> Since 1980 dictatorships have collapsed under nonviolent opposition in Estonia, Latvia, Lithuania, Poland, East Germany, Czechoslovakia, Slovenia, Madagascar, Mali, Bolivia and the Philippines. Nonviolent resistance has furthered the movement towards democratization in Nepal, Zambia, South Korea, Chile, Argentina, Haiti, Brazil, Uruguay, Malawi, Thailand, Bulgaria, Hungary, Nigeria and various parts of the Soviet Union.[14]

The little book that was begotten in Manerplaw went on to inspire an organization of Serbian activists who called themselves Otpor, the Serb word for resistance, and who in turn invented a raft of brilliant, startling, nonviolent tactics to undermine the tyrannical rule of Slobodan Milošević, leading directly to his downfall in October 2000. That revolution, as one journalist wrote "became a textbook standard for nonviolent, peaceful struggle" and prompted the creation of a group called Canvas, run by two Serb veterans of the victory, which "works with activists from nearly fifty other countries," including Iran, Zimbabwe, Tunisia and Egypt.

Nobody, we are told, saw the largely bloodless Tunisian and Egyptian revolutions coming: The West was convinced that violent jihad was the only sort of revolution the Muslim world was interested in. But from Tehran to Algiers, intelligent Muslims saw the disasters that fundamentalism brought in its train; they looked around the world for a better approach, and the ideas incubated by Sharp and Helvey helped them to identify it.

Arriving on the Burmese border when Suu was in her first years of detention, Helvey and Sharp brought a much-needed element of rigor and analysis to the nonviolent struggle as Suu had preached and practiced it. "For all her wonderful qualities," Sharp said in an interview with the *Irrawaddy* in March 2011, "and her heroism and inspiration for those who believe in democratic rights and the rights of the Burmese people, [Aung San Suu Kyi] is not a strategist, she is a moral leader. That is not sufficient to plan a strategy." Clearly both qualities, the strategic and the moral, are required for success. It is also true that, with its army so willing (unlike, say, Serbia's or Egypt's) to massacre unarmed demonstrators, Burma is one of the toughest schools of revolution in the world. But without Suu's "heroism and inspiration," Helvey and Sharp would never have made that trek to Manerplaw; and *From Dictatorship to Democracy* would not have been written.

The so-called "butterfly effect" identified by Edward Lorenz, by which the flapping of a butterfly's wings in Brazil can cause a hurricane on the other side of the world, is perhaps the most vivid contemporary elaboration of the workings of karma. But the flashing of the peacock's fan has been no less consequential.

AFTERWORD

THIS book was conceived in 2006, when Suu was under house arrest with no end in sight: Her detention was routinely extended year after year and she was isolated from the entire world, including her sons and other close relatives. There was therefore no possibility of informing her about the project, let alone seeking her cooperation. Four biographies of her had already been published, one in Japanese, one in French and two in English, and the following year a more substantial one, Justin Wintle's, appeared. But when the uprising of the monks erupted, which culminated with a group of them paying their respects at her gate, it was clear to me that she was still a figure of immense importance and influence, despite her isolation. This was not the sad story of a lost cause: Suu was still at the heart of the Burmese revolution.

Today, her centrality is acknowledged by all, and the revolution is well under way, at a speed that nobody foresaw. In the previous chapter, I quoted Gene Sharp as saying of her, "She is not a strategist; she is a moral leader. That is not sufficient to plan a strategy." Today, that judgement has a patronizing ring. And while she has not yet reached her strategic goal, she is much further advanced upon that road than one would expect of one who was "merely" a moral leader. While many have their doubts about her chances of transforming her nation root and branch, she has already shown that she has the determination, energy and ambition to lead it.

Surveying her progress over the two years since her release, one is reminded of how deeply she has meditated on the career of her father. Aung San steered a course which has the appearance of rank opportunism: sailing to China to seek the backing of the communists, accepting instead the support of the Japanese Fascists, finally deserting them when they began to lose and siding with the hated British instead. Yet all the time he was true to his single and simple goal: make his nation free.

Suu has shown herself equally agile—as free from "attachments," to put it in Buddhist terms—as her father. During her years of house arrest and provisional liberty, the generals and their mouthpieces frequently complained that she was "stubborn." It was a charge that filtered through to the West and still crops up from time to time in negative comments about her.[1] But it was rooted in the generals' preconceptions of how a Burmese woman ought to behave. What the generals really meant was that she should have submitted to their will but consistently refused to do so.

Suu has of course been extremely single-minded over the past two and a half decades, but that's a different thing from mere mulishness. In fact, from her very first political initiative, her proposal for a "People's Consultative Committee," designed with the intention "to present the aspirations of the people in a peaceful manner,"[2] she showed a willingness to try anything and everything—everything non-violent—to bring democratic change. Likewise there was nothing narrowly doctrinaire about her party, which was from the outset a huge church, perhaps too broad for its own good. Despite the harrowing treatment meted out to her and her colleagues during the grimmest years, she was always looking for ways to start a dialogue with the generals, and she met them several times. When in 2004 it seemed that they meant business, she agreed to work with them. That process eventually failed, but not because of her. It was not she who was stubborn and capricious but the generals themselves.

Finally, however—there is something of the fairy story or the miracle about it—a leader emerged from the ranks of senior officers who was not personally corrupt, and who had a more ample vision of Burma's possible future, and a clear understanding of how badly the nation compared with its neighbours. He did not fear or loathe Suu; rather, he grasped how she could be his key to unlock the world. And the whole game changed, remarkably fast.

*

I paid my sixth visit to Burma in 2010, intending to report the elections and then stay on to interview Suu again on her release. Unfortunately, Military Intelligence caught up with me the day after I had lunch with Ma Thanegi, and so eight days before Suu's release I was expelled. I was baffled as to how they had tracked me down: Another undercover British correspondent, a friend of mine, was never touched, even though we had interviewed the same high-profile NLD leader a few days before, had been in touch with the same NLD foot soldiers, and were staying at the same hotel.

Months later, back in Europe, I woke up one morning convinced that it was Ma Thanegi who had told MI about me and got me thrown out. She was friendly when we met in November, and gave me a fascinating, highly opinionated interview over lunch in a smart cafe near Bogyoke Aung San Market in central Rangoon, but less than twenty-four hours later I was being grilled by officers of the immigration police in the lobby of my hotel.

When I shared my suspicion with Burmese acquaintances, some of them agreed that it was quite likely. By reporting my presence, she would have killed two birds with one stone, reassuring her MI minders that she was still of use to them, while at the same time preventing me from meeting Suu on her release. After all, I now knew more about Ma Thanegi's relationship with Suu than anyone else on earth. It might well have occurred to me to ask Suu what had gone wrong between her and her acid-tongued aristocratic friend.

Whether or not it was Ma Thanegi's doing, I therefore found myself back in Bangkok far sooner than I had intended. I immediately applied for another visa with my second passport, but was refused. I was now on Burma's black list.

Five months later, however, with a different identity and a substantially altered appearance, I did succeed in returning to Rangoon, and met Suu again. This was in March 2011, and already the cautious process of building trust was under way. She had yet to start traveling again, but people were permitted to come to her. She gave interviews, met visiting politicians, including John McCain, and was reunited with members of her family, many of whom she had not seen for a decade or more. Her younger son Kim visited, bringing with him Michelle Yeoh, the Chinese film star who plays Suu in Luc Besson's film, *The Lady*. The week I was in Rangoon, NLD members from all over the country streamed through the party HQ for pep talks from Suu and her senior colleagues. MI agents lurking at the entrance kept tabs on everyone who came and went, but this ramshackle bastion of freedom was still in business.

At the end of March, a couple of weeks after my visit, a man called U Thein Sein, the leader of the Union Solidarity and Development Party, was inaugurated as Burma's president under the new constitution. It was not an event that stirred any interest in the world at large. This sixty-five year old retired general was severely tainted by his years of service to Than Shwe: He had been prime minister during the Saffron Revolution, had chaired the National Convention that cooked up the new constitution, and had been in charge of the regime's disgracefully inadequate response to Cyclone Nargis. He was, by all appearances, a machine man. With his pebble glasses and his palpable absence of charisma, his elevation aroused little excitement.

Yet right from the start he called for reform. While he attacked western sanctions in his inauguration speech, he also made plain his dissatisfaction with the state of the nation. He called for workers' rights and an end to corruption, and he appealed to experts from abroad for help in getting the country out of its mess. He even broke the taboo about not mentioning Burma's endless civil wars: The nation's minorities had, he said, been subjected to "a hell of untold miseries."[3]

One reason for this bold start was that power in Burma can be an ephemeral commodity. Than Shwe could do pretty much whatever he wanted as long as he was Senior General Than Shwe—the top man. Once he was gone, however, his influence faded as fast as the tropical twilight. Thein Sein, timid and inoffensive-looking with his bowed shoulders and shy smile, a man long remarked upon in Rangoon and then Naypyidaw for his refusal to accept bribes, stepped briskly out of his patron's shadow, and it was as if the patron no longer existed. What Than Shwe may think of the changes that his protégé has unleashed on Burma in the past two years, we can only guess.

The other factor, underestimated in the cynical world outside, was that in taking off his military trousers and tying on his longyi— in assuming the mantle of democratically-elected head of state—Thein Sein interpreted his new role in democratic terms. As Aung Min, his old friend and right hand man, the minister who accompanied Suu Kyi during her tour of the US in September 2012, explained to *The New Yorker* writer Evan Osnos, "He understands that he can't run the government the way it used to be run by the previous government, that this government is elected by the people. If you don't do what the people want, you won't survive." It was a novel notion for Burma, but one which the president grasped.

Despite his opening blast on the trumpet, it took a while for things to begin to change. In the meantime, the NLD remained in a perilous state of limbo: outside the registry of parties, unrepresented in parliament, little better than a pariah—a status underlined by Home Affairs Minister Lieutenant General Ko Ko at the end of June, when he warned Suu's party to halt all political activities. A ripple of anxiety ran through her supporters around the world: Could this latest spell of freedom, too, come to a cruel end?

The moment passed, and instead the initiative was seized by Thein Sein's reform-minded subordinates. Aung Kyi, a retired major-general who had been given the job of consulting with Suu Kyi after the crushing of the Saffron Revolution in 2007, and who was now a minister, sought her out once more. They held two meetings. No details were disclosed, but something reassuring must have been said, because in July Suu went on holiday.

It was the first time she had done so for well over twenty-three years. Emphasizing the fact that this was pleasure rather than work, Kim returned for a second visit, this time to join her on her vacation, and brought her a puppy. In Burma, their trip to Bagan, a magical, pagoda-dotted former capital, was described as a pilgrimage. She gave no speeches and did nothing that could be construed as political, but they were met by large, rapturous crowds everywhere they went.

Then on August 14, she was on the move again, heading for Bago, 50 miles north of Rangoon, for her first political date outside the city since 2003. And then, within less than a week, she got the breakthrough of her political life.

*

When Aung San Suu Kyi disappeared from public view in 2003, Naypyidaw did not even exist. As I described on page 372, the news that Burma's capital had shifted overnight to a greenfield site 200 miles to the north broke without warning in 2005; the state's unlucky bureaucrats were shipped north with no indication of where they were headed or why. So when Suu flew there from Rangoon on Friday, August 19, 2011, it was her first visit. She was received at the Presidential Palace by Thein Sein, a man she had never met before. Their meeting lasted nearly an hour; state television reported that they had held "frank and friendly discussions" to find ways and means of cooperation.[5] A government official said the meeting was "significant." The official photograph released afterwards shows them standing side by side, Suu appearing uncharacteristically tense and looking into the middle distance, the president by contrast smiling quizzically; the most significant detail, to those of us who have tracked the fluctuations in Burmese politics over the years, was the framed photograph of Aung San on the wall behind them. The attempts by Thein Sein's predecessors to weaken Suu by erasing her father from the nation's memory (see pages 148-9) were overturned at a stroke.

After the official meeting, Thein Sein invited Suu to his modest home in the capital, where his wife cooked them dinner. For the first time since her entry into Burmese politics, Suu was not only in the favors of the country's rulers, but in those of the top man's wife, too. Gossipy Burmese in years gone by were glad to regale foreign visitors with tales of how fiercely the wives of the top generals hated Suu, and how they would get together and do the Burmese equivalent of sticking pins in a voodoo doll to hurt her. Those days were gone.

This cordial meeting was followed by a flurry of reforms, including the legalization of trade unions and the setting up of a human rights commission. The release of some political prisoners was not a surprise—Than Shwe had done no less in 1992, soon after taking the top job—but when Thein Sein announced that work on a highly controversial dam on the Irrawaddy was to be suspended because it was "against the will of the people," it was clear that Burma was moving into uncharted territory. The dam was being built by the Chinese, and 90 percent of the energy it produced was earmarked for export straight back to China; suddenly it seemed permissible to thwart the plans of Burma's giant neighbour when they conflicted with the opinions of ordinary Burmese. This was extraordinary.[7]

Although Thein Sein had come to power through a grotesquely fixed election, it gradually emerged that he was very different from his predecessors: He was serious about bringing real reforms to his country, and he believed that it would be possible to do so in conjunction with Aung San Suu Kyi. He did not see her as a menace, a subversive, or an agent of foreign powers, but as a person whose unwavering commitment to democracy had given her unrivalled influence both at home and abroad.

He had the intelligence and the courage to see her not as an enemy to be destroyed but, potentially at least, as a vital ally.

The feeling was reciprocated. During the twenty-plus years that she had been back in Burma, Suu had never had anything good to say about its rulers. But Thein Sein was different, as Suu was quick to appreciate. On her return to Rangoon she told U Tin Oo, her party's deputy leader, "I have the feeling that I can work with him."[8] Subsequently, she never missed an opportunity to tell foreign interviewers that he was "a good listener" and that she trusted him.[9]

More than an ally, he was shaping up to be her partner. When Suu announced her intention to run for parliament in the by-elections scheduled for April 1, 2012, Thein Sein responded, in his first-ever interview with a foreign newspaper, the *Washington Post*, by floating the idea that she might be appointed a minister in his government.[10] The fact that such an idea was no longer inconceivable is a measure of how far Burma had travelled since Suu's release.

This was the good news that Burma had waited two decades to hear. Now the reforms came thick and fast, and even if many of them were superficial—the reform of censorship, for example, left intact the machinery of government that scrutinizes every word that gets into print—they changed the tenor of life. Suddenly, after two decades during which they had been taboo, Suu's image and words were everywhere. The first release of political prisoners was followed by two more, the second of which included Min Ko Naing, the most important student leader in 1988, and U Gambira, one of the monks who led the Saffron Revolution. And two days before that, the government announced its first-ever ceasefire with the Karen National Union, raising the prospect of an end to the civil war that had been raging since 1949.

Initiatives like these were enough to persuade Hillary Clinton that President Obama's policy of engagement with Burma was finally paying dividends—Obama himself said he detected "flickers of hope"—and in December 2011 she became the first U.S. Secretary of State to visit since John Foster Dulles in 1955. Her meetings with Thein Sein were complemented by two warm encounters with Suu. And in January 2012, Suu finally began travelling again in earnest. The huge crowds that came out to cheer her in Pakkoku, the town where the Saffron Revolution started, and everywhere else she went were proof that her popular appeal was undiminished. The NLD was allowed to register as a party again, former political prisoners were permitted to run for office, and in the April by-elections, the party's first electoral test since 1990, it swept the board, winning 43 of the 45 seats contested. The single seat won by the USDP, the ruling party, came as a result of the NLD candidate being disqualified. Suu herself stood as a candidate in the impoverished constitutency of Kawhmu, on the outskirts of Rangoon, and won by a huge majority. Any lingering doubts about whether her popularity with the Burmese masses had survived her years of confinement were answered. In her first address to parliament she called for an end to Burma's civil wars.

*

Burma had gone through dramatic changes in the first year of Thein Sein's presidency, but the reforms that meant so much to Western diplomats and journalists had so far had little impact on the lives of the ordinary people. Burma remained by far the poorest country in Southeast Asia, with indices of health, education, per capita income and living standards that were closer to the weaker states of sub-Saharan Africa than anywhere else in the neighbourhood.[11]

In the view of Kurt Campbell, President Obama's Assistant Secretary of State for East Asian and Pacific Affairs, it was this stark contrast with Burma's neighbours that may have impelled Thein Sein down the road of reform.

"His role as prime minister [before becoming president] and designated face to the outside world brought him to regional capitals that decades earlier appeared as poor cousins to cosmopolitan Rangoon," Campbell wrote in an article published in the Myanmar Times, "but now were thriving hubs of modernity. Burma's failure must have been manifest and its status as a pariah state . . . would have been painful to defend."[12]

The basic reason for Burma's stagnation was an opaque, totally corrupt business environment which discouraged all but the most reckless foreigners from getting involved.[13] Economic sanctions first applied by the US and the EU after the massacres of 1988, and steadily tightened in the years since, only strengthened the arguments for leaving Burma alone. The Chinese treated much of the country like a backward Chinese province, setting up mines and other businesses and buying up land and property on their own terms. Other Southeast Asians piled in to plunder Burma's remaining resources of timber, jade, and minerals. But apart from the opportunity to work in slave labor conditions in a Chinese mine, ordinary Burmese gained very little benefit from any of this activity.[14]

The enactment of fundamental reforms and the election of Suu and her party colleagues to parliament were enough to transform the situation. American and European businesses that had long renounced all thought of doing business in Burma began to think again.

One week after Suu's election victory, British Prime Minister David Cameron flew in and used his appearance before the international media in the garden of Suu's home to introduce the way this was going to be done. Sanctions would be suspended, he said, on condition of good behavior. Hillary Clinton had made a similar announcement in New York a few days before; the European Union fell into line two weeks later. And Suu, standing next to Cameron and sounding slightly arm-twisted, gave her approval. "I support the idea of suspension," she told journalists at the joint press conference with Cameron, adding that if those against reform refused to cooperate, "then sanctions could come back."

*

When Suu left her home in Oxford on April 1, 1988 and flew to Rangoon to nurse her stricken mother, she had no idea that decades would pass before she would see England—her home for more than twenty years—again. In the early months of 2011, the prospect of her being able to revisit that beloved landscape, so closely entwined with her memories of university and marriage and family life, still seemed distant. She had never left Burma because she feared that she would not be allowed to come back, that she would be forced into exile. But now that she was finally a public figure in her homeland, an MP, and on good terms with the president, that long-locked door swung open.

Thailand, just an hour away, was the dry run: In a chaotic four-day foray she braved huge, excited crowds in Bangkok and in a camp for

Burmese refugees near the border, and she made a speech to the World Economic Forum.[15]

Then, in early June, she finally returned to Europe, where she addressed an International Labour Organization conference in Geneva, collected her Nobel Prize in Oslo, and flew to London and drove to Oxford to be awarded, many years late, an honorary doctorate, and to be feted by her old college, St. Hugh's. In London she became the first woman, the first Asian, and the first non–head of state to address a joint session of parliament. On the last day of her British tour, she spent a morning with Britain's large Burmese community, where she was introduced by the comedian Zarganar and the artist Thein Lin, both of whom had spent years in jail as political prisoners.

She carried off the whole packed program with style and grace and fully lived up to her billing, often addressing these august assemblies without notes and with disarming informality. Five months later, in November, she repeated the performance at greater length, and covering much greater distances, in the US: collecting more honors awarded to her years before, including, most significantly, the Congressional Medal, and meeting Secretary of State Clinton again, President Obama in the Oval Office, and President Thein Sein on the fringes of the UN General Assembly. She also visited Burmese expatriate communities on the East and West Coasts and in Indiana.

Yet throughout these triumphal tours, during which she repeated over and over her calls for "democracy-friendly and human rights-friendly investment," a new shadow—the shadow of an unexpected and unwelcome political controversy—trailed her. It is one which, at the time of writing, she has not yet succeeded in shaking off.

The timing was uncanny, and some believe it was more than a coincidence.[16] As Suu was taking her first steps in Thailand, rumors began circulating that a Buddhist nun in the state of Arakan, in the far west, near the border with Bangladesh, had been raped and murdered. Arakan state is home to a mixed population of Buddhists and Muslims, some 800,000 of the latter of whom are known as Rohingyas, a dark-skinned community with some resemblance to the Bengali Muslims of Bangladesh.

Racial prejudice is no stranger to Burma: After Ne Win took over in 1962, he expelled hundreds of thousands of ethnic Indians, many of whom had been settled in Rangoon for generations, and though he did not try to do the same to the Rohingyas, who claim to have been living in Burma for centuries, and whose presence is mentioned in a British document going back more than 200 years, he refused to grant them citizenship.[17]

The community has been living in limbo ever since, and there have been frequent eruptions of violence between Rohingyas and their Arakanese Buddhist neighbors, with the Rohingyas routinely on the losing end: Tens of thousands have been forced into squalid camps. Refused entry by Bangladesh, and unwanted in Burma, they have been described as one of the most oppressed racial minorities in the world.

Now, as Suu began her travels, this old wound was viciously reopened: The majority community took revenge for the alleged murder of the nun, stopping a bus and killing ten Muslims on board while the police and army stood by. Both communities erupted in fury; dozens were killed and more than 100,000, overwhelmingly Muslims, were driven from their homes, many of which were burned down. On June 10, Thein Sein declared an emergency in Arakan state and sent in the army to restore order—but then in September, as Suu was again packing her bags, this time to fly to the US, violence flared again, even worse than before, with whole communities of Muslims driven from their homes and many killed. Rohingya organizations outside Burma described it as an attempt to ethnically cleanse Arakan state. Even more worryingly, the anti-Muslim violence found sympathetic echoes around Burma, with protests outside a (non-Rohingya) mosque in Rangoon and the largest demonstrations by Buddhist monks in Mandalay since the Saffron Revolution. There were even distant echoes in Britain: At the event at London's Royal Festival Hall in June where different Burmese "races" performed their local folk dances, the loudest applause was reserved for the Arakanese troupe— representing the Buddhists of Arakan. No one doubted the reason for the special acclaim.

Suu faced calls from far and wide to condemn the violence and offer her solidarity to the embattled and persecuted Rohingyas. The International Crisis Group commented that there was "an expectation… for her to break through partisanship and speak much more strongly and clearly against extremist rhetoric and violence."[18] This she has yet to do, at least in the strong and unequivocal terms that the world expects from a woman who has long been seen as an embodiment of the struggle for human rights.

Various explanations are offered. Could she be racially or religiously prejudiced, like the monks demonstrating in Mandalay? It seemed unlikely—her first serious boyfriend at Oxford was a Pakistani Muslim; twenty-four years later, one of the people chiefly responsible for persuading her to go into politics was Maung Thaw Ka, the Muslim author and poet. Steeped in the secular, anti-sectarian atmosphere of modern Britain, it is almost unthinkable that she should nurse such bigoted thoughts.

Maung Zarni, the Burmese activist-turned-academic, believes the explanation for Suu's reticence on this issue is simple: She is now a politician, aiming for a clean sweep in the general elections of 2015 followed (if she can change the clause in the constitution which bars the spouse of a foreigner from eligibility) by a possible term as president. "Politically [she] has absolutely nothing to gain from opening her mouth on this," he said. "She is no longer a political dissident trying to stick to her principles. She's a politician and her eyes are fixed on the prize, which is the 2015 Buddhist majority vote."[19]

That is one explanation, but nothing in her prior résumé prepares us to think of Suu as capable of such hard-nosed, cynical calculation. But there are two other factors.

While the Rohingyas have undoubtedly been settled on Burmese soil for a long time, their population has grown rapidly by comparison with their Buddhist neighbours, and the Burmese claim that illegal immigration is one of the reasons. They may well be right: the same phenomenon is found in the Indian state of Assam, where illegal immigration from Bangladesh has been an explosive political issue for more than thirty years. Bangladesh, with its large delta region, highly fertile but ever vulnerable to floods and other disasters, is one of the poorest and most densely populated countries in the world; it is not surprising that many should seek marginally better lives across the country's borders—nor is it surprising that their arrival in large numbers should provoke angry responses. In her meticulous way, Suu is bound to consider all these factors. During her visit to India in November, she described the violence in Arakan as a "huge international tragedy," adding, "We have to put a stop to [illegal immigration]. Otherwise, there will never be an end to the problem . . .Violence has been committed by both sides, this is why I prefer not to take sides and [why] I want to work towards reconciliation." (This analysis was quickly rejected by Bangladesh.)

Another reason is party collegiality: As just one of her party's leaders, even if she had wanted to condemn the violence more forcefully, she is obliged to consider the views of her colleagues. U Win Tin, one of her oldest party colleagues, has denounced the Rohingyas, and even some of the political radicals outside her party have been vehement in their expressions of hostility.

Given her intense moral seriousness, there can be no doubt that Suu is thinking about the issue long and hard: In November, she rather plaintively told journalists in Naypyidaw, "People want me to take one side or the other, so both sides are displeased because I will not take a stand with them."[20]

Throughout her adult life, Suu's moral scrupulousness has been one of her outstanding attributes. Her old Oxford friend Robin Christopher told me, "She would not do anything that she considered was wrong. She just wouldn't!" There is no reason to believe she has changed in that respect, and every reason to suppose that we have not yet heard her last word on this agonizing subject.

In March 2012, at the Women in the World conference in New York, Hillary Clinton spoke eloquently of the challenges of changing from a political icon—a term Suu says she hates—to a practicing politician. "I know that route," she told the conference, "and how hard it is to balance one's ideals and aspirations." Aung San Suu Kyi has been identified with her ideals for so long that it is unthinkable that she would now cold-bloodedly betray them. But how is she to bring them to realization, negotiating all the perils of practical politics? A master of Zen Buddhism in Japan used to tell students who had tasted enlightenment that they had merely taken "the first step on an iron road ten thousand miles long." That's much like the road the Lady of Burma faces now.

NOTES

PROLOGUE

1. "A voter can choose not to vote," one such homily noted: *New Light of Myanmar*, October 2010.

2. 94 percent of the seats: NLD won 392 seats out of 447, about 80 percent; its ethnic ally the Shan State NLD won 23 seats; other ethnic NLDs won another 7 seats, giving a grand total of 94.4 percent.

3. State employees and others were dragooned: interview with expatriate aid worker in Rangoon, November 2010.

4. We discussed how to take advance votes from members of thirty civil societies in Rangoon: *Irrawaddy* website, November 2010.

5. We have won about 80 percent of the seats: Agence-France Presse wire, November 8, 2010.

6. NLD-Liberated Areas: Burmese political parties are barred by law from having branches overseas, hence the name of this party, staffed by exiles from Burma and loyal to the NLD in Burma.

7. There is no legal basis for detaining her any longer: Agence-France Presse wire, November 13, 2010.

8. Soldiers armed with rifles and tear-gas launchers pushed aside the barbed-wire barriers blocking University Avenue: *Los Angeles Times*, November 14, 2010.

9. The previous week an NLD veteran, one of the party's founders, released from prison after nineteen years, had told me: U Win Tin, interviewed by the author in November 2010. Daw Aung San Suu Kyi: Daw is the honorific prefix used for women of middle age and above; "Ma" for younger women.

PART ONE

1. insisted on being described as a housewife: on her visa application for Japan in 1986; interview with Noriko Ohtsu.

2. Thant Myint-U, grandson of U Thant, in his book, *The River of Lost Footsteps*, casts Suu as little more than a footnote: "She wasn't facing the Raj . . . These were tough men who played a very different game" in Thant Myint-U, *The River of Lost Footsteps*, Farrar, Straus and Giroux (2006) p.337.

3. Michael W. Charney, in his *History of Modern Burma*: see "Aung San Suu Kyi's personal connections to the West . . ." in Michael Charney, *A History of Modern Burma*, Cambridge University Press, 2009, p.169. Her positive role for the mass of Burmese is disposed of in the phrase: "ASSK was . . . becoming a permanent symbol of popular opposition to the government," p.177.

4. A previous biographer, Justin Wintle, comes to the eccentric conclusion: Justin Wintle, *Perfect Hostage*, Hutchinson, 2007, pp.419–20.

5. Aung San was a boy from the provinces, shy, a poor speaker, with abrupt manners, and prone to long unexplained silences : Aung San Suu Kyi, *Aung San*, 1984.

6. But the Burmese experience was very different: see "Intellectual Life in Burma and India under Colonialism" in Aung San Suu Kyi, *Freedom from Fear*, Penguin Books, 1995.

7. In lower Burma the British had refused to accept the authority of the *thathanabaing*, the senior monk authorized by the king: cf. Donald Eugene Smith, *Religion and Politics in Burma*, Princeton University Press, 1965.

8. big enough to scare away the crows: tour guide in Mandalay to author, March 2008.

9. They "proclaimed the birthright of the Burmese to be their own masters": Aung San Suu Kyi in her short biography of her father, included as "My Father" in *Freedom from Fear*.

10. Burmans and Indian Muslims: Burman refers to the ethnic group, who have been dominant and the majority for some centuries.

11. the Japanese *tatemae*, what appeared on the surface, might speak of Burmese independence, but the *honne*, the unspoken reality, would be that "mighty Nippon" remained firmly in charge behind the scenes: cf. Takeo Doi, *The Anatomy of Dependence*, Kodansha International, Tokyo, 1973.

12. William Slim, the British general: see Field Marshal Viscount Slim, *Defeat into Victory*, Pan, 2009 (first published 1956), p.594.

13. He told journalists that he wanted "complete independence": Aung San Suu Kyi, "My Father," op cit.

14. Aung San Suu Kyi was two years old when her father died, "too young," as she put it, "to remember him": Aung San Suu Kyi, Preface in *Aung San*, p.xiii.

15. how a great civilization, which had been under the thumb of the imperialists for far longer than Burma, had not lost its soul: cf. "Intellectual Life in Burma and India under Colonialism" in Aung San Suu Kyi, *Freedom from Fear*.

16. A Burman to all outward appearances, but entirely out of harmony with his surroundings: cf. ibid, p.113.

17. Rammohun Roy set the tone for the Indian Renaissance: ibid.

18. General Ne Win: the head of the army; information from author's interview with Bertil Lintner and others.

19. From her earliest childhood: Michael Aris, Introduction, *Freedom from Fear*, p.xviii.

20. Again and again she expressed her worry that her family and people might misinterpret our marriage and see it as a lessening of her devotion to them: ibid.

PART TWO, CHAPTER 1: LATE CALL

1. sewing, embroidery: cf. interviews with Alan Clements, Aung San Suu Kyi, *The Voice of Hope*, Rider, 1997.

2. *shinbyu*: the coming of age ceremony which all Burmese Buddhist boys undergo: cf. Donald Eugene Smith, *Religion and Politics in Burma* and George Scott (aka Shway Yoe), *The Burman, His Life and Notions*, Macmillan,1882. (George Scott published his book under the pen name of Shway Yoe, leaving the impression that the author was Burmese.)

3. MPhil: author interview with Anna Allott.

4. Michael and Suu were about to turn in for the night: on March 31, 1988.

5. In Burma health care is ostensibly provided free of charge: Aung San Suu Kyi, *Letters from Burma*, Penguin, 2010, no. 44, Uncivil Service (2).

6. Outside on the city streets, the mood was dark and growing darker: the main source for my detailed description of the events of 1988 and 1989 is *Outrage* by Bertil Lintner, Review Publishing, 1989.

7. It emerged in April that the regime had sought and obtained from the UN the humiliating status of "least-developed nation": cf. David I. Steinberg, *Burma/Myanmar: What Everyone Needs to Know*, OUP USA, 2010, p.77.

8. Rather than soothing the already inflamed temper: Bertil Lintner, *Outrage*, p.71.

9. Sir, may I request you . . . not to get involved or you will regret it: quoted in *Outrage*, p.72.

10. We held a big meeting on the Prome Road campus [north of the city center] on June 21st: quoted in *Outrage*, p.75.

11. The word 'monsoon' has always sounded beautiful to me: *Letters from Burma*, no. 29.

12. In a letter to her parents-in-law: private information.

13. an island of peace and order: Michael Aris, Introduction, *Freedom from Fear*, p.xvii.

14. "When we first arrived," Michael wrote: unpublished letter from Michael Aris to Anthony Aris, August 5, 1988.

15. Dear delegates: quoted in Bertil Lintner, *Outrage*, pp.83–4.

16. "The atmosphere," Michael wrote: unpublished letter from Michael Aris to Anthony Aris, August 5, 1988.

17. "The nation," wrote Bertil Lintner, "and possibly even more so the diplomatic community in Rangoon, was flabbergasted": Bertil Lintner, *Outrage*, p.85.

18. Sein Lwin's takeover: unpublished letter from Michael Aris to Anthony Aris, August 5, 1988.

19. "Dissatisfaction among the public gave way to hatred," wrote Lintner. "'That man is not going to be the ruler of Burma": Lintner quoting an unnamed Western diplomat in *Outrage*, p.90.

20. During the uprising of 1988 he sent messages of solidarity to Burmese students in Tokyo: author interview with Dr. Maung Zarni, who also provided the subsequent analysis of the operation of the dynastic principle in Burma.

21. She, like the whole country, was electrified: Michael Aris, Introduction, *Freedom from Fear*, p.xviii.

22. Suu's house quickly became the main center of political activity in the country and the scene of such continuous comings and goings as the curfew allowed: ibid., p.xx.

PART TWO, CHAPTER 2: DEBUT

1. She must also have known the truth behind the rumor: this story came from a Burmese source who requested anonymity.

2. Ne Win himself was among the people she invited over for lunch: information from Aung San Suu Kyi, reported orally to Ma Thanegi and recorded in the latter's diary. All quotes from Ma Thanegi come from unpublished diaries and other writings in the author's possession, used with her permission.

3. Perhaps he had noticed the flag flying at her gate: the diaries of Ma Thanegi.

4. I replied that I would never do anything from abroad, and that if I were to engage in any political movement I would do so from within the country: Aung San Suu Kyi, "Belief in Burma's Future" in *Independent*, September 12, 1988.

5. U Kyi Maung, a colonel in the army who had been imprisoned for years for opposing Ne Win's coup: cf. Alan Clements, Aung San Suu Kyi, *The Voice of Hope*, interview with U Kyi Maung, p.x.

6. He met her first, he said, "by chance, at the home of a mutual friend here in Rangoon. It was back in 1986": quoted in *The Voice of Hope*, p.236.

7. A Burmese Muslim whose tall figure and craggy face betrayed his roots in the subcontinent: interview with Bertil Lintner, Burmese sources.

8. "He took her round Rangoon," said Lintner, who subsequently got to know him: interview with author.

9. "My impression when I arrived was that the situation was extremely tense," he said later: quoted in Bertil Lintner, *Outrage*, p.91.

10. The first serious demonstration actually occurred on the afternoon of August 3: Dominic Faulder, "Memories of 8.8.88" on *Irrawaddy* website.

11. A fifteen-year-old schoolboy called Ko Ko took to the streets of central Rangoon on August 6th along with thousands of others: interview with author, Rangoon, November 2010.

12. "Despite its overwhelming superiority of force, the regime is today under siege by its people," Seth Mydans wrote in the *New York Times*: Seth Mydans, "Uprising in Burma" in *New York Times*, August 12, 1988.

13. "The euphoric atmosphere prevailed all day," wrote Bertil Lintner: *Outrage*, p.97.

14. The tanks roared at top speed past [Sule] pagoda, followed by armored cars and twenty-four truckloads of soldiers: Mydans, op cit.

15. staff at the hospital where her mother had once worked believed the army had killed 3,000 civilians in cold blood: quoted in *Los Angeles Times*, August 17, 1988.

16. Aung San Suu Kyi played no part in the demonstrations: interview with Indian journalist Karan Thapar in July 1988.

17. As Bo Kyi, one of the leaders of the students, put it, "When we staged demonstrations in 1988, in March, April, May": author interview with Bo Kyi, Mae Sot, November 2010.

18. But Maung Maung had lost whatever intellectual respectability he might once have claimed when he wrote the official hagiography of Number One: Gustaaf Houtman, "Aung San's *lan-zin*, the Blue Print, and the Japanese occupation of Burma" in *Reconsidering the Japanese Military Occupation of Burma (1942–45)*, edited by Kei Nemoto, ILCAA, Tokyo 2007; Patricia Herbert, Obituary of Dr. Maung Maung in *Guardian*, July 13, 1994.

19. "I was twenty-six," Nyo Ohn Myint remembered: interview with author, Chiang Mai, November 2010.

20. I appealed to her to meet the student movement. She said no [...] Aung San's bravery—everything: interview with author.

21. On August 15th, she and Hwe Myint, one of her earliest political allies, wrote to the Council of State: xerox of original document courtesy of Martin Morland.

22. nursing her gravely ill mother, keeping her sons up to the mark with their studies: private information.

23. U Win Tin, a stubbornly contrarian journalist who had been silenced for years by Ne Win . . . Three groups formed around her, he explained: interview with author, Rangoon, November 2010.

24. Despite his communist background and the help he was providing to Suu, Thakin Tin Mya, her gatekeeper, was a member of the ruling BSPP: cf. Thierry Falise, *Aung San Suu Kyi: Le Jasmin ou la lune*, Editions Florent Massot, Paris, 2007. Translated here by the author.

25. So please don't launch any attacks on him, and don't incite the people to do so, either: quoted in *Aung San Suu Kyi: Le Jasmin ou la lune*, p.73.

26. Ralph Fitch, an English merchant who saw the pagoda in 1586, called it "the fairest place, as I suppose, that is in the world": quoted in Norman Lewis, *Golden Earth*, Eland, 1983, p.272.

27. a misty dazzlement: quoted in Norman Lewis, *Golden Earth*, pp.272–4.

28. the focus during the 1920s and 1930s of the first mass demonstrations against British rule: see Gustaaf Houtman, *Mental Culture in Burmese Crisis Politics*, ILCAA, Tokyo (available on Google Books) for an illuminating account of the transgressive effect, for the ruling generals, of Suu's appearance at the national shrine.

29. Overnight thousands of leaflets were printed, stigmatizing Suu as the puppet of a foreign power: cf. Thierry Falise, *Aung San Suu Kyi: Le Jasmin ou la lune*.

30. One of her advisers urged her to don a bullet-proof vest for protection. "Why?" she retorted. "If I was afraid of being killed, I would never speak out against the government": Thierry Falise, *Aung San Suu Kyi: Le Jasmin ou la Lune*, p.78.

31. "We didn't go along the main road," Nyo Ohn Myint the lecturer recalled: interview with author.

32. In those days the population of Rangoon was about three million: interview with author.

33. It has been said with some authority that she read her speech from a prepared text: a full video of the speech can be found on YouTube. An English translation is published in *Freedom from Fear*.

34. "It was so direct and down to earth," said Bertil Lintner: interview with author.

35. "Reverend monks and people!" she shouted: *Freedom from Fear*, pp.192–8.

36. See note 15, Part Two, Chapter 2.

37. My first impression was that she was just another general's daughter: quoted in documentary *Aung San Suu Kyi—Lady of No Fear* directed by Anne Gyrithe Bonne, Kamoli Films, Denmark 2010.

PART TWO, CHAPTER 3: FREEDOM AND SLAUGHTER

1. And it was Aung San Suu Kyi—the "governess" as she has been labeled, the Burmese "Mary Poppins," the "Oxford housewife," the political ingénue: epithets favored by Justin Wintle.

2. one paper called *Phone Maw Journal*, named after the student whose killing by the army in March had ignited the revolution, informed its readers: cf. Lintner, *Outrage*.

3. "The Rangoon Bar Association took its courage in both hands and issued a signed protest calling for change," he recalled: Martin Morland, "Eight Minutes Past Eight, on the Eighth of the Eighth Month," unpublished essay.

4. a student recently returned from Rangoon called Pascal Khoo Thwe was caught up in the excitement: cf. Pascal Khoo Thwe, *From the Land of Green Ghosts*, Harper Collins, 2002.

5. A young woman called Hmwe Hmwe who had joined the democracy movement in Rangoon traveled to Mandalay: Lintner, *Outrage*, p.119.

6. In Mandalay, the young monks' organization. . . had resurfaced: ibid, pp.119–20.

7. The army evidently hoped that things would get so out of hand that the people would have had enough and beg the old regime to come back: Morland, "Eight Minutes Past Eight, on the Eighth of the Eighth Month," op cit.

8. On September 5th, four men and one woman were caught outside a children's hospital: Lintner, *Outrage*, pp.121–2.

9. the future of the people will be decided by the masses of the people: quoted in *Outrage*, p.126.

10. his pithy formulations of how to apply the simple truths of Buddhism to solitary confinement had a powerful influence on Suu herself: see Part Four, Chapter 3. .

11. "I thought to myself, let's see what this lady is up to," he said later. "Now is the time, a revolution is stirring: quoted in Alan Clements, Aung San Suu Kyi, *The Voice of Hope*, p.237.

12. From the age of seventeen until nearly fifty, my life was a struggle: ibid., p.279.

13. Two years later, accused of involvement in an abortive coup, he was sacked and jailed: cf. Thant Myint-U, *The River of Lost Footsteps*.

14. My [old army] colleagues urged me to address the public: quoted in Alan Clements, Aung San Suu Kyi, *The Voice of Hope*, p.275.

15. "We agreed that I would meet her," he remembered, "and that I would go alone": ibid., p.276.

16. "On September 16th," as Burma historian Michael Charney records, "the State Council announced that": Michael Charney, *A History of Modern Burma*, p.158.

17. sweep everything aside, bring everything down, rush in on human waves shouting their war cries to the cheers of outsiders, and establish their occupation: Michael Charney, *A History of Modern Burma*, p.157

18. Any high-ranking army officer who had taken an armed infantry unit into the capital and declared his support for the uprising would have become a national hero immediately: Lintner, *Outrage*, p.127.

19. The city of Rangoon, and indeed the whole country, ran disturbingly smoothly without Big Brother: Morland, "Eight Minutes past Eight, on the Eighth of the Eighth Month."

20. Nyo Ohn Myint recalled, "My first job was buying fried rice at the restaurant nearby . . .": interview with author.

21. In order to bring a timely halt to the deteriorating conditions on all sides all over the country: Lintner, *Outrage*, p.131.

22. It had started drizzling shortly after the brief radio announcement: Lintner, *Outrage*, p.132.

23. Walking through Rangoon was an eerie experience: Terry McCarthy, "Fragile Peace Settles on Rangoon" in *Independent*, September 21, 1988.

24. Some people began banging pots and pans inside their houses in a desperate show of defiance: Lintner, *Outrage*, p.132.

25. Through loudspeakers mounted on the military vehicles, the people were ordered to remove the barricades: Lintner, *Outrage*, p.132.

26. A spokesman for Tin Oo commented, "This is a coup d'état by another name. This ruins everything": quoted in Terry McCarthy, "Burmese Army Coup" in *Independent*, September 19, 1988.

27. All through the night we were kept awake by the noise of machine gun fire: interview with author.

28. "It is better that I should be taken off to prison," she told them: quoted in author's interview with Nyo Ohn Myint.

29. The machine gun was pointed straight at the front gate: interview with author.

30. At least 100 people—and perhaps four times that number—were shot dead in the streets of Rangoon yesterday: Terry McCarthy, "Burmese Army Coup" in *Independent*, September 19, 1988.

31. No one in the large column that marched down past the old meeting spot near the City Hall and Maha Bandoola Park saw the machine-gun nests: Lintner, *Outrage*, p.133.

32. The Burmese Red Cross was working furiously to gather the wounded and dead from the streets: Terry McCarthy, "Burmese Army Coup" in *Independent*, September 19, 1988.

33. police mingled with the crowds to observe us, having prudently abandoned their uniforms: Pascal Khoo Thwe, *From the Land of the Green Ghosts*, HarperCollins, 2002, p.173.

34. "We fled," he said, "because we realized that this time it was different": Lintner, *Outrage*, p.147.

35. Suppression associated with the coup led to between 8,000 and 10,000 deaths: Michael Charney, *A History of Modern Burma*, p.161.

36. I went up there with a couple of other journalists and we had a long chat in her living room looking over the lake: interview with author.

37. I would prefer not to remain in politics if I can avoid it: quoted in Terry McCarthy, "Burma Opposition will not Give in to Army Rule" in *Independent*, September 20, 1988.

38. "We do not wish to cling to state power long," he insisted. On the contrary, he spoke of "handing over power to the government which emerges after the free and fair general elections." "I am laying the path for the next government," he said, and "I will lay flowers in the path of the next government": quoted in Gustaaf Houtman, *Mental Culture in Burmese Crisis Politics*, p.44.

39. "It's going back to the 1962 formula," a man near the Sule pagoda in central Rangoon told McCarthy: Terry McCarthy, "Fragile Peace Settles on Rangoon" in *Independent*, September 21, 1988.

40. During the day he carries a revolver: quoted in Terry McCarthy, "Ne Win Still Fights for Control" in *Independent*, September 28, 1988.

41. someone who had spent nearly half her life in England, a country where the words "Glorious Revolution" refer to an event, exactly three hundred years before, in which no lives were lost and which set British democracy on such a big, fat keel that it has been gliding forward ever since: the overthrow of King James II by British parliamentarians, who invited the Protestant William of Orange to invade the country and replace him. The agreement between William and Parliament, resulting in the Bill of Rights of 1689, created the unwritten but still effective English Constitution and drastically reduced the risks of a return to an absolute monarchy.

PART TWO, CHAPTER 4: THE FUNERAL

1. he was "passionate about books": see later ref. to Ko Myint Swe, p.237.

2. All effort is now being put to establish the National League for Democracy: fax from Michael and Suu to relatives in England, St. Hugh's archive.

3. "the throne was painted over with representations of the peacock and the hare," according to George Scott: Shway Yoe (Scott's pen name), *The Burman, His Life and Notions*, pp.449–50.

4. I am working . . . to achieve the kind of democratic system: Aung San Suu Kyi, "Belief in Burma's Future" in *Independent*, September 12, 1988.

5. In 1874, King Thibaw's predecessor, King Mindon, informed that William Gladstone's Whigs had lost the general election in Britain, remarked, "Then poor Ga-la-sa-tong [Gladstone] is in prison I suppose. I am sorry for him. I don't think he was a bad fellow": quoted in Houtman, *Mental Culture . . .*, p.214. I am greatly indebted to Dr. Houtman for his book and for his conversation and insights into democracy in the Burmese context.

6. The Burman is the most calm and contented of mortals: Shway Yoe (George Scott), *The Burman*, p.65.

7. "Traditional Burmese education did not encourage speculation," she wrote: "Intellectual Life in Burma and India Under Colonialism" in Aung San Suu Kyi, *Freedom from Fear*, p.93.

8. emphatically rules by what is called in the Western kingdoms the right divine: Shway Yoe (Scott), *The Burman*, pp.454–5.

9. Gandhi was of a practical turn of mind that looked for ideas to suit the needs of situations: "Intellectual Life in Burma and India under Colonialism" in Aung San Suu Kyi, *Freedom from Fear*, p.108.

10. Let anybody appear who can be like such a leader, who *dares* to be like such a leader. We are waiting: in Donald Bishop, "Thinkers of the Indian Renaissance" and quoted in turn in "Intellectual Life in Burma and India under Colonialism" in Aung San Suu Kyi, *Freedom from Fear*, p.128.

11. a loose confederation of political parties and local influential leaders and strong men: Steinberg, *Burma/Myanmar: What Everyone Needs to Know*, p.53.

12. Gustaaf Houtman cites three reasons why the concept of "opposition" has failed to gain any traction in Burma: Houtman, *Mental Culture in Burmese Crisis Politics*, p.214.

13. "In Burma," writes Houtman, "those who declare themselves opponents to the regime are either extremely courageous or extremely foolish—there is little in between": Houtman, ibid.

14. "I went wrong," she told U Win Khet, one of her close assistants, privately, "but not without a reason": quoted in Wintle, *Perfect Hostage*, p.295.

15. He had left Rangoon in late September or early October, ostensibly for a "holiday in Maymyo," the British-built hill station northeast of Mandalay: Ma Thanegi papers.

16. Aung San Suu Kyi was "surrounded by communists" it was claimed; she was "going the same way as her uncle's Burma Communist Party": writers of opinion columns in the *Working People's Daily*, and Khin Nyunt.

17. General Saw Maung, visited University Avenue the evening before the funeral to sign the condolence: Steven Erlanger, "Burmese, Still Under Military Rule, Settle Into a Sullen Waiting" in *New York Times*, January 9, 1989.

18. I hope this occasion has been an eye-opener: Terry McCarthy, "Rangoon Peaceful for Funeral of Widow" in *Independent*, January 3, 1989.

PART TWO, CHAPTER 5: OPEN ROAD

1. She was coming to open a new NLD office in a suburb on the outskirts of Rangoon: interview with the author.

2. it was at the town of Panglong, in the far north of the region, in February 1947, that Suu's father signed a historic agreement: cf. Martin Smith's classic book on Burma's insurgencies, *Burma: Insurgency and the Politics of Ethnicity*, Zed Books, 1991.

3. It costs a lot to keep Gandhi poor: Sarojini Naidu, quoted by Jyotsna Kamat, "India's Freedom Struggle" on www.kamat.com.

4. she had not touched alcohol since experimentally sampling sherry with Indian friends in the ladies loo of Oxford's Bodleian Library, more than twenty years before: see Part Three, Chapter 3, p.197.

5. Boys very interested in traditional dress, esp. that of the Padaung women: "Padaung women" are the so-called "giraffe-necked women" who wear numerous brass rings around their necks.

PART TWO, CHAPTER 6: HER FATHER'S BLOOD

1. In a letter released internationally by his lawyers, the regime's former critic repeated his earlier accusation: Loktha Pyeithu Nezin, Rangoon, March 16, 1989, translated in BBC Summary of World Broadcasts, March 18, 1989.

2. "I don't believe in armed struggle," she told a journalist during these difficult days, "but I sympathize with the students who are engaged in armed struggle": quoted on BBC Summary of World Broadcasts, April 3, 1989.

3. by the spring of 1989, press estimates of membership ran as high as three million, in a total population of around 50 million: Terry McCarthy, *Independent*, April 19, 1989.

4. Two days later Erlanger returned to the subject in the long *New York Times* piece, which probably did more than anything else to put her on the world map: Steven Erlanger, "Rangoon: Journal: A Daughter of Burma, but can she be a symbol?" in *New York Times*, January 11, 1989.

5. The water festival of *Thingyan*, the Burmese New Year: in the original Indian myth, the King of Brahmas lost a wager with the King of Devas, Thagya-min, and was duly decapitated, but his head was too hot to be allowed to touch the ground and was passed from the hands of one goddess to another. As it was too hot to hold, it had to be cooled by the pouring on of water. A more generic explanation is that this is one of many traditional rain-making festivals. Cf. Scott, *The Burman, His Life and Notions*.

6. In front of me was a young man holding our NLD flag: Alan Clements, Aung San Suu Kyi, *The Voice of Hope*, p.52.

7. She explained that the captain's rejection of her proposal to walk at the side of the road struck her as "highly unreasonable": *The Voice of Hope*, p.52.

8. In a later interview she said of that split-second decision, "It seemed so much simpler to provide them with a single target": Fergal Keane, "The Lady Who Frightens Generals" in *You* magazine, July 14, 1996.

9. The fact that she had survived the army's attempt to kill her was proof positive of her high spiritual attainment: Houtman, *Mental Culture . . .*, p.328.

10. She was "a heroine like the mythical mother goddess of the earth," one admirer wrote three years later: Gustaaf Houtman, "Sacralizing or Demonizing Democracy" in *Burma at the Turn of the 20th Century*, ed. Monique Skidmore, University of Hawaii Press, 2005, p.140.

PART TWO, CHAPTER 7: DEFIANCE

1. Alas, your poor Suu is getting weather-beaten: "Dust and Sweat" in Aung San Suu Kyi, *Freedom from Fear*, p.225.

2. A joke current in Rangoon in those days went that Ne Win's favorite daughter Sanda had challenged Suu to a duel: Wintle, *Perfect Hostage*, p.319.

3. no water festival pandals: in India and Burma a pandal is a temporary shrine set up during a festival, usually made of wood, and the focus of festival revelry.

4. the happy highways where I went/ And cannot come again: lines from A.E. Housman, *A Shropshire Lad*.

5. fragrant *nakao* on their cheeks: Burmese women grind the bark of particular trees into creamy paste and apply it to their cheeks as a face cream. *Nakao* is a type of bark.

6. history did not in fact end after all: in *The End of History and the Last Man*, published in 1992, Francis Fukuyama argued that the revolutions that ended the Cold War signaled the end of ideology as a factor in the world's divisions.

7. "had such success making alliances between many political and ethnic groups, much like her father . . . that it looked as if she had the ability to unify the opposition in a manner that would leave no political role" for the army: Houtman, *Mental Culture . . .* , p.46.

8. when the regime introduced a newly designed one kyat note in 1989, the designer showed his anti-regime feelings in a very delicate manner: the fullest account of the one kyat note fiasco is in *Small Acts of Resistance* by Steve Crawshaw and John Jackson, Union Square Press, 2010.

9. give lectures on the meaning and achievement of the hero's life. But not this year, and not ever again: my account of the dismantling of the Aung San cult owes much to *Mental Culture in Burmese Crisis Politics* by Gustaaf Houtman.

10. On that date they set up a twenty-one-member "Commission of Enquiry into the True Naming of Myanmar Names": Michael Charney, *A History of Modern Burma*, pp.171, 173; Houtman, *Mental Culture . . .* , pp.43, 49.

11. Now, Suu announced, her party's defiance of the regime would be enshrined in all its literature, in a permanent call to nonviolent resistance: cf. Houtman, *Mental Culture . . .*

12. "General Ne Win," she declared, "[who is] still widely believed to control Burma behind the scenes, was responsible for alienating the army from the people": Houtman, *Mental Culture . . .*, p.17.

13. When the peace of his lakeside villa was disturbed by a Christmas party: Harriet O'Brien, *Forgotten Land*, Michael Joseph, 1991, pp.104–6.

14. "We don't have any intention to seek a confrontation," Suu insisted to the *New York Times*' Steven Erlanger: Steven Erlanger, "As Tensions Increase, Burma Fears Another Crackdown" in *New York Times*, July 18, 1989.

15. "Now it is obvious who is behind the recent bombing," said Khin Nyunt, "and plans to disrupt law and order": quoted in Keith B. Richburg, "Myanmar Moves on Opposition, 2 Leading Activists Under House Arrest" in *Washington Post*, July 22, 1989.

16. "I was picked up at my hotel at night on the 18th, after curfew, although I had a valid journalist visa," he recalled: quoted in Lintner, *Outrage*, p.174.

PART THREE, CHAPTER 1: GRIEF OF A CHILD

1. If the British sucked our blood, the Japanese ground our bones: quoted in William Slim, *Defeat into Victory*, p.590.

2. He became more and more disillusioned with the Japanese: ibid.

3. The arrival of Aung San, dressed in the near-Japanese uniform of a Major General, complete with sword: ibid., p.591.

4. He went on to say that, at first, he had hoped the Japanese would give real independence to Burma: ibid., p.593.

5. My father died when I was too young to remember him: Aung San Suu Kyi, *Freedom from Fear*, p.3.

6. "I have a memory of him picking me up every time he came home from work," she told Alan Clements: Alan Clements, Aung San Suu Kyi, *The Voice of Hope*, p.83.

7. I don't remember my father's death as such: ibid., p.75.

8. How long do national heroes last? Not long in this country; they have too many enemies: quoted in Wintle, *Perfect Hostage*, p.141.

9. I never felt the need for a dominant male figure: ibid., p.83.

10. She was such a dignified woman with a very distinctive voice: interview with author.

11. My mother was a very strong person: ibid., p.86.

12. There was a Buddhist shrine room at the top of the house: interview with author.

13. My mother was very good: ibid., p.196.

14. "I was very close to him," she said: ibid., pp.75–6.

15. It was not something that I couldn't cope with: ibid., pp.75–6.

16. "When I was young," she said, "I was a normal, naughty child": ibid., p.63.

17. "Ours was a mixed school," her friend Tin Tin remembered: interview with author.

18. This tightly planned section of the city was "imperial and rectilinear": Norman Lewis, *Golden Earth*, p.14.

19. These massive columns now rise with shabby dignity from the tangle of scavenging dogs and sprawling, ragged bodies at their base: ibid., pp.14–16.

20. The school was on Sule Pagoda Road in the middle of town, north of the pagoda: interview with author.

21. politics has always been linked to literature and literary men have often been involved with politics, especially the politics of independence: Alan Clements, Aung San Suu Kyi, *The Voice of Hope*, p.61.

22. When I was about twelve or thirteen I started reading the classics: ibid.

23. Before the coup Burma was the one country in Southeast Asia with a really good economy: interview with author.

24. At the weekend we had jam sessions: interview with author.

25. "The Burmese," writes Michael Charney, "had achieved independence without a revolution": Michael Charney, *History of Modern Burma*, p.72.

26. The last occasion when Burmese affairs had been strongly featured in the British press: Norman Lewis, *Golden Earth*, p.22.

27. His delusions did not last long. They were "stripped away: ibid., p.22.

PART THREE, CHAPTER 2: THE GANG OF FIVE

1. I soon hated my new school and till well into adulthood would avoid going anywhere near it: from *Bungalows,* bageechas *and the* babalog, in *Remembered Childhood—Essays in Honor of Andre Beteille,* eds. Malavika Karlekar and Rudrangshu Mukherjee, Oxford University Press New Delhi, 2009.

2. Delhi, characterized by much heat and disorder: Harriet O'Brien, *Forgotten Land*, p.57.

3. Her mother was shrewd, funny and generous: quoted in Edward Klein, "The Lady Triumphs" in *Vanity Fair*, October 1995.

4. She also met his daughter Indira, shortly to become prime minister herself, and her sons Sanjay and Rajiv: when Suu was visited in Rangoon by India's Foreign Secretary, Nirupama Rao, in June 2011, Suu recalled her friendship with Rajiv Gandhi and asked Ms. Rao to pass on her greetings to his widow, Sonia Gandhi.

5. always full of good gossip about the latest political intrigues which she dispatched with much wit and humor: ibid., pp.58–9.

6. In Delhi Suu learned, at an impressionable age, the ways of "the argumentative Indian": the title of a book (pub. 2005) by Amartya Sen, the Nobel Prize-winning Bengali economist.

7. Both in their different ways had a world outlook: quoted in Aung San Suu Kyi, *Freedom from Fear*, p.116.

8. In Delhi Suu was discovering the great cry of freedom, written in English, of Rabindranath Tagore: these lines from the poem "Walk Alone" by Tagore were quoted by Suu in her address to the University of Natal on April 23, 1997, on being given the honorary degree of Doctor of Laws. The address was read in her place by Michael Aris. "Many of [his] verses," she wrote, "even in unsatisfactory translation, reach out to that innermost, elusive land of the spirit that we are not always capable of exploring by ourselves."

PART THREE, CHAPTER 3: AN EXOTIC AT ST. HUGH'S

1. I was really annoyed!: interview with author.

2. Every male who met Suu had a little bit of a crush on her: interview with author.

3. She had strong views about her country, and about right and wrong: interview with author, London, 2010.

4. We got to know each other in Oxford, as freshwomen at St. Hugh's College, in 1964: Ann Pasternak Slater, "Suu Burmese," published in Aung San Suu Kyi, *Freedom from Fear*, pp.292–300.

5. When I first got to know her as a student I can remember her talking very proudly about her father: interview with author, Oxford, 2010.

6. my mother, who was another foreign oddity: Lydia Pasternak Slater, chemist, translator and poet and the youngest sister of Boris Pasternak.

7. four years after the Lady Chatterley trial and two years after the Beatles' first LP: "Sexual intercourse began/ In nineteen sixty-three/ (which was rather late for me)—/ Between the end of the Chatterley ban/ And the Beatles' first LP" from "Annus Mirabilis" by Philip Larkin. *Lady Chatterley's Lover* by D. H. Lawrence was first published by Penguin Books in 1960, more than thirty years after its original publication in Italy: its exculpation under Britain's new Obscene Publications Act on grounds of literary merit was a major cultural event.

8. "When we first arrived," Pasternak Slater's memoir continued: in *Freedom from Fear*, p.293.

9. he carried around one of the works of John Ruskin, and his social philosophy was based as much on primitive English socialism as on anything suggested by the Vedas: *Unto This Last* by Ruskin had a dramatic impact on Gandhi's social philosophy; he carried a copy of the book with him at all times, and in 1908 he translated it into his mother tongue, Gujarati.

10. Aung San Suu Kyi was, briefly, a pupil of mine when she was reading for the honors school of PPE: Mary Warnock in a review of *The Voice of Hope*, in the *Observer Review*, May 25, 1997.

11. She was curious to experience the European and the alien: Pasternak Slater in *Freedom from Fear*, p.294.

12. Suu set out, a determined solitary figure in the early morning haze: ibid., p.295.

13. She was curious to know what it was like: Pasternak Slater in *Freedom from Fear*, p.295.

14. She was more comfortable with Indians than with Brits to begin with: interview with author.

15. It wasn't a romance. It was an utterly genuine friendship: interview with author.

16. Suu "was much more interested in getting to meet Algerians and in what was happening in the country than in the many parties to which she was invited": Ma Than É, "A Flowering of the Spirit: Memories of Suu and her Family" in Aung San Suu Kyi, *Freedom from Fear*, pp.275–91.

17. She didn't want to be doing PPE: interview with author.

18. He was in Queen's College. We knew each other but were not chums: interview with author.

19. One university friend mentioned that she was still talking about him "at least a year after she left Oxford": private information.

20. Some of her Indian friends did not approve of Hyder. "He was a bit of a sleazeball," said one: university friend of Suu who requested anonymity.

21. She would discuss these things with me when she came to Burma: interview with author.

22. Aung Gyi had been a subordinate of Ne Win's in the 4th Burma Rifles during the war: cf. Michael Charney, *History of Modern Burma*, pp.120–1.

23. The only reliable classes were those who contributed to the material needs of society, such as the peasants and the industrial workers: ibid., p.122.

24. in a letter written years later: private information.

PART THREE, CHAPTER 4: CHOICES

1. Her Oxford friend Ann Pasternak Slater worried for her: Ann Pasternak Slater, "Suu Burmese" in Aung San Suu Kyi, *Freedom from Fear*, p.295.

2. "She called me Di Di," she remembered—the affectionate Indian equivalent of "aunty": author interview with Lady Gore-Booth, and quotes from documentary *Aung San Suu Kyi— Lady of No Fear.*

3. From a diplomatic point of view, we should have said "Go": interview with author.

4. He and his identical twin brother, Anthony, were born in Havana, the sons of an English father, John Aris, and a French-Canadian beauty, Josette Vaillancourt, whom he fell in love with and married while working as ADC to the Governor General of Canada, Lord Tweedsmuir (better known as the thriller writer John Buchan): thanks to Lucinda Phillips for details about her family.

5. He was smitten from the word go: Anthony Aris, interview with the author

6. as Norman Lewis put it, "through failure to spend a token period as a novice in a Buddhist monastery, the foreigner has never quite qualified as a human being": Lewis, *Golden Earth.*

7. While he was still at Durham: interview with author.

8. "Getting to and from New York University meant a long bus ride," Ma Than É wrote: Than É, "A Flowering of the Spirit" in Aung San Suu Kyi, *Freedom from Fear*, p.284.

9. "I see myself as a trier," Suu told Alan Clements: Alan Clements, Aung San Suu Kyi, *The Voice of Hope*, p.33.

10. A more believable explanation is that, within those few weeks, Suu discovered that Professor Trager was on friendly terms with high officials in the Ne Win regime: the true reason why Suu dropped out of Frank Trager's course was one of several questions I gave to Suu, in writing, during our meeting at her party's headquarters in March 2011, but she declined to answer them. A future biographer may be more lucky. Trager's friendship with Ne Win cronies is mentioned by Robert Taylor in "Finding the politics in Myanmar" in *Southeast Asian Affairs*, Institute of Southeast Asian Studies, June 2008.

11. U Thant "saw no reason why I should not go wherever I wished": Norman Lewis, *Golden Earth*, p.33.

12. U Thant said that the railway service from Rangoon to Mandalay was working: ibid., p.23.

13. "Thant's dream," wrote his grandson, Thant Myint-U, "had been to become a civil servant in the British Burma administration.": Than Myint-U, *The River of Lost Footsteps*, p.271. Much of the detail in this chapter is culled from this work.

14. "in real life no less dreadful than it sounds" according to Thant Myint-U: ibid., p.333.

15. a rambling seven-bedroom red-brick house: ibid., p.38.

16. "U Thant and his family would be warmly welcoming," Ma Than É remembered: quoted in Aung San Suu Kyi, *Freedom from Fear*, p.285.

17. We liked him and his wife and children: ibid.

18. "Some members of the [Burmese] delegation had said they would like to meet us, she wrote: ibid., p.286.

19. Suu's calm and composure were for me very reassuring: ibid.

20. Soon afterwards she was writing to thank her brother-in-law-to-be: private information.

21. Suu made a choice. She decided that a husband and children would be greatly preferable to a career in the UN, however brilliant it was promising to be: Aung San Suu Kyi, *Freedom from Fear*, pp.286–7.

22. With six months' more hard slog in a city she had learned to dislike: private information

23. Recently I read again the 187 letters she sent to me in Bhutan from New York: Michael Aris, Introduction in *Freedom from Fear*, p.xix.

PART THREE, CHAPTER 5: HEROES AND TRAITORS

1. It was a lovely ceremony: quoted on *Aung San Suu Kyi—Lady of No Fear* video.

2. the World's End and Gandalf's Garden: the World's End, a section of Chelsea close to the Gore-Booths' home, named after a local pub called the World's End, became one of the centers of London hippy culture in the 1960s and 1970s and home to an influential boutique called Granny Takes a Trip. Gandalf's Garden, named after the wizard in the Tolkien trilogy, *The Lord of the Rings*, was the home of a mystical community of that name which ran a shop in the World's End and published a magazine of the same name.

3. serious, sad, uncertain: Pasternak Slater in Aung San Suu Kyi, *Freedom from Fear*, p.295.

4. the local cuisine, in which pork fat and chilies played a dominant role, was largely inedible, she confided to a friend in Rangoon: recorded in Ma Thanegi's diaries.

5. she left 54 University Avenue once a year, for an annual medical check-up: Ma Thanegi's diaries.

6. "Never before," wrote Thant Myint-U, "had a call for the overthrow of a UN member state government been made from inside the UN": Thant Myint-U, *The River of Lost Footsteps*, p.311.

7. The Buddhist funeral service went as planned: ibid., p.313.

8. We put the coffin on a truck and thousands and thousands of us marched towards Rangoon University campus: interview with author in Rangoon, March 2011.

9. placed on a dais in the middle of the dilapidated Convention Hall, ceiling fans whirring overhead in the stifling heat: Thant Myint-U, *The River of Lost Footsteps*, p.313.

10. We took it to the site of the students' union building: former activist interviewed in Rangoon, March 2011, on condition of anonymity.

11. At about six that morning we were woken up at our hotel by a phone call: Thant Myint-U, *The River of Lost Footsteps* pp.314–15.

12. "The abiding image I have of the U Thant riots," wrote Harriet O'Brien: O'Brien, *Forgotten Land*, p.223.

13. officials of the government called Suu in and asked her if she planned to get involved in "anti-government activities": Aung San Suu Kyi, "Belief in Burma's future" in *Independent*, September 12, 1988.

14. "Uncle, I've heard that these days you are mostly looking after your grandchildren," she told him chidingly: Kyaw Zaw, *My Memoirs: From Hsai Su to Meng Hai*, Duwun Publishing, 2007. I am grateful to Dr. Maung Zarni for drawing my attention to this anecdote and translating it from Burmese.

15. a pretty but impractical house: Pasternak Slater in Aung San Suu Kyi, *Freedom from Fear*, p.296.

16. Memories of that time are still sunlit but with a sense of strain: ibid.

17. When I called in the afternoons with my own baby daughter: interview with author.

18. "Michael and Suu complemented each other, it was a marriage made in heaven," said Peter Carey: quoted in documentary *Aung San Suu Kyi—Lady of No Fear.*

19. "It was actually her husband Michael who I got to know first," Noriko said: there are two sources for Ms. Ohtsu's reminiscences in this chapter: a written account of her friendship with Suu, first published in the Japanese monthly magazine *Sansara* in November 1994, translated into English by the author and Junko Nakayama; and an interview with the author in Oxford in 2009.

20. She could be very critical and very disapproving—to me and certainly to Michael: interview with author.

21. It was Suu who gave the copy-book parties with all the traditional party games: Pasternak Slater in Aung San Suu Kyi, *Freedom from Fear*, p.297.

22. For the first fifteen years of the marriage it was all Michael: Carey quoted in documentary *Aung San Suu Kyi—Lady of No Fear.*

23. I think Suu thought that he could actually have pushed his way a bit more: interview with author.

24. "She was very much casting around for a role for herself," remembered Carey. "She said, is this my destiny to be a housewife, the partner of an Oxford don?": quoted in documentary *Aung San Suu Kyi—Lady of No Fear.*

25. Ann Pasternak Slater said, "She was becoming more serious, more focused, more determined, more ambitious": ibid.

26. a volume of essays: *Tibetan Studies in honor of Hugh Richardson*, edited by Michael Aris and Aung San Suu Kyi, published by Serindia Publications.

27. All those years spent as a full-time mother were most enjoyable: Suu TV interview, included in documentary *Aung San Suu Ky—Lady of No Fear.*

28. description of himself as a sickly, unwashed, gluttonous, thoroughly unprepossessing child: "My Father" in Aung San Suu Kyi, *Freedom from Fear*, p.4.

29. not so much to extremists as to the great majority of ordinary citizens: ibid., p.37.

30. It was on one of these visits that she struck up a friendship that was to prove important to her later on: Ko Myint Swe was wrongly identified by Justin Wintle in *Perfect Hostage* as U Tin Moe. The latter, a poet, is much older than Ko Myint Swe, who was a writer and member of the staff of Rangoon University Library. Ko Myint Swe was jailed in July 1989 with other NLD activists. I am indebted to Ma Thanegi for this information.

31. "We read several novels together," said Allott: interview with author.

32. In an interview years later, Suu said, "When I was young I could never separate my country from my father, because I was very small when he died and I'd always thought of him in connection with the country": Suu TV interview, included in *Aung San Suu Kyi—Lady of No Fear.*

33. a first *kikkake*: Japanese for a chance, an opportunity, a start, a beginning, a clue.

34. In Japan she had her first encounter with Burmese students: Yoshikazu Mikami, *Aung San Suu Kyi: Toraware no Kujaku*, translated by Junko Nakayama and the author, 1990. The title means "Captive Peacock."

PART FOUR, CHAPTER 1: ALONE

1. Suu told an American journalist: quoted in Edward Klein, "The Lady Triumphs," *Vanity Fair*, October 1995.

2. As the plane taxied to a halt: Michael Aris, Introduction to *Freedom from Fear*, p.xxiii.

3. The gates were opened and we drove in: ibid., p.xxiv.

4. A military officer came to give her his personal assurance: ibid., p.xxiv.

5. Suu recovered her weight and strength: ibid., p.xxv.

6. "As a mother," she told Alan Clements, "the greater sacrifice was giving up my sons": Alan Clements, Aung San Suu Kyi, *The Voice of Hope*, pp.140–1.

7. a declassified American embassy cable revealed that the torture of political prisoners included burns to the flesh by cigarettes: Lintner, *Outrage*, p.175.

8. He was a lovely man. Before 1988 he would travel around the country and give lectures on literature: interview with author, Chiang Mai, November 2010.

9. At the time he entered Insein Jail he was already suffering from a chronic disease: Aung San Suu Kyi, *Letters from Burma*, no. 39, Death in Custody (2).

10. When a little spark turns into a big flame, it will burn away all the dirt that exists in this world: many thanks to Khin Myint for this translation.

11. translates into Burmese as *nyein-wut-pi-pyar*; literally, "silent-crouched-crushed-flattened": in Houtman, *Mental Culture . . .*, p.377.

12. "Glass splinters," Suu wrote: "Freedom from Fear" in Aung San Suu Kyi, *Freedom from Fear*, p.182.

13. The effort necessary to remain uncorrupted in an environment where fear is an integral part of everyday existence: ibid., p.182.

14. It is his capacity for self-improvement and self-redemption which most distinguishes man from the mere brute: ibid., p.183.

15. I had not even thought of doing this: Michael Aris, Introduction, *Freedom from Fear*, p.xxv.

16. "I did not have a teacher," she wrote some years later, "and my early attempts were more than a little frustrating": Aung San Suu Kyi, *Letters from Burma*, no. 40, Teachers.

17. much value is attached to liberality or generosity: quoted in Houtman, *Mental Culture . . .*, p.355.

18. Even before her release in November 2010 some correspondents were speculating on her perhaps imminent retirement: CNN reporter, November 13, 2010.

19. A reader's letter published by the *Financial Times* in 2011: letter from Dr. Frank Peel, *Financial Times*, February 5, 2011. As quoted by the paper, he wrote that she would "soon have a position akin to a queen mother in the UK."

20. to quote Burma authority Robert Taylor, could now be "on the cusp of normality": Robert Taylor, "Myanmar in 2009: On the Cusp of Normality?" in *Southeast Asian Affairs*, 2010.

21. "In India," she wrote, "political and intellectual leadership had often coincided: "Intellectual Life in Burma and India under Colonialism" in Aung San Suu Kyi, *Freedom from Fear*, p.128.

22. We were looking for the human Burma: quoted in ibid., pp.119–20.

23. When people have been stripped of all their material supports: "Towards a True Refuge" in Aung San Suu Kyi, *Freedom from Fear*, p.247.

PART FOUR, CHAPTER 2: LANDSLIDE VICTORY

1. More than a quarter-century of narrow authoritarianism under which they had been fed a pabulum of shallow, negative dogma: "In Quest of Democracy" in ibid., page 168.

2. But at least they had a manifesto to work from: my thanks to Tom White, late of the British Council in Rangoon, for a copy of this document.

3. At the last minute the regime had allowed the foreign media in: interview with author.

4. But the military has so far refused to be drawn: Terry McCarthy and Yuli Ismartono, "Opposition Vote Leaves Burma's Rulers Stunned" in *Independent*, June 15, 1990.

5. We don't know who is our enemy and who is not: ibid.

6. The army is indicating that the elected body will not be a national assembly: Terry McCarthy, "EC to End Boycott of Burmese Junta" in *Independent*, June 15, 1990.

7. Khin Nyunt, the ambitious heir apparent, the man "who breathes through Ne Win's nostrils": epithet quoted by Roger Matthews in "A Beaten, Tortured People" in *Financial Times*, May 19, 1990.

8. It is our duty to hold an election so that a government can be formed: Saw Maung addresses meeting on "regional consolidation," BBC Summary of World Broadcasts, June 12, 1990.

9. Virtually every credible scholar of Burma has demonstrated: Michael Aung-Thwin, "Reality in Burma differs from myths" in *Honolulu Star-Advertiser*, February 4, 2011.

10. The election was held to elect the *Pyitthu Hluttaw*, the national assembly: interview with author. In a review of *Perfect Hostage* published by the *Far Eastern Economic Review* in June 2007, Bertil Lintner elaborated as follows: "In fact Khin Nyunt had said before foreign military attachés in Rangoon on September 22, 1988, 'Elections will be held as soon as law and order has been restored and the Defense Services would then systematically hand over power to the party which wins.' He didn't say a word about the need for a new constitution. And on May 31, 1989—a year before the election—the junta promulgated a *pyitthu hluttaw* election law. A *pyitthu hluttaw* in Burmese is a "people's assembly," i.e. a parliament, not a constituent assembly, which is a *thaing pyi pyitthu hluttaw*—a term never used before the 1990 election."

11. We have been very lenient [towards her]: Khin Nyunt responds to claims about the transfer of power, BBC Summary of World Broadcasts, July 16, 1990.

12. [SLORC] seemed to think they were doing me a tremendous favor by letting me communicate with my family: Aung San Suu Kyi, *The Voice of Hope*, p.146.

PART FOUR, CHAPTER 3: LONG LIVE HOLINESS

1. The only practicable way for a foreigner to approach Manerplaw was from the Thai side: my account of Manerplaw appeared in the *Independent* Magazine on May 25, 1991 under the headline "The Road to Manerplaw."

2. The first thing colonial rule denies a people is their history: Martin Smith, *Burma: Insurgency and the Politics of Ethnicity*, p.31.

3. the natural routes of migration: ibid., p.31.

4. "When Yuwa [God] created the world he took three handfuls of earth and threw them round about him," goes the Karen creation myth: Shway Yoe, *The Burman, His Life and Notions*, p.443.

5. How could anyone expect the Karen people to trust the Burmans: Martin Smith, *Burma: Insurgency and the Politics of Ethnicity*, p.62.

6. During independence negotiations the Karen held out for their own homeland: The fact that wars between the ethnic groups on Burma's borders and the Burmese Army have continued ever since independence enables the Burmese regime to claim that military rule has been the only way to keep Burma from breaking up. With the exception of the Karen, whose grievances are explained in this chapter, the truth is the opposite: As during long periods of military rule in Pakistan, it is the nation's alleged peril that justifies the army clinging to power—and thus prompts them to ensure that the embers of war never go out. Yet the Panglong Agreement prefigured a very different national arrangement. As Dr. Maung Zarni wrote in *Irrawaddy* in June 2011:

> While there are "natural" ethnic prejudices among Burma's "communities of difference" (in terms of religion, ethnicity, and ideology), these prejudices don't automatically evolve and deepen themselves into ethnic hatred and intractable conflicts. After all, Aung San Suu Kyi's father . . . was able to work out a multi-ethnic treaty on the eve of the country's independence.
>
> On the basis of ethnic and political equality, the country's minorities, with legitimate historical claims over their own ancestral regions, agreed to join the post-independent Union of Burma.
>
> This was no small achievement in the face of various attempts to mobilize ethnic grievances by local minorities and majority political elites . . .
>
> The country's conflicts regarding different ethnic communities are political because they are fundamentally rooted in the minorities' demands for, and the Burmese ruling classes' rejection of, the recognition that modern, post-independence Burma was the result of *the voluntary coming together of different ethnic groups which were all equally indigenous to the land.* "Ethnic Conflicts are the Generals' Golden Goose," (*Irrawaddy*, June 21, 2011 [italics added]).

A new Panglong Conference has been one of Aung San Suu Kyi's and the NLD's principal goals since her release from detention—one the regime seems determined to thwart.

7. They welcomed us and took care of us like their own children: quoted in Peter Popham, "The Road to Manerplaw" in *Independent Magazine*, May 25, 1991.

8. *bodhisattva*: in Burmese "bodhisatta" is "one who has vowed to become a Buddha" according to Sayadaw U Pandita. The term is more commonly used in Mahayana Buddhism than in the Theravada school found in Burma. "In Mahayana Buddhism, a bodhisattva is a being who seeks buddhahood . . . but renounces complete entry into nirvana until all beings are saved . . . A bodhisattva provides active help, is ready to take upon himself the suffering of all other beings, and to transfer his own karmic merit to other beings": *Entering the Stream: an Introduction to the Buddha and his Teachings*, eds. Samuel Bercholz and Sherab Chödzin, Rider, 1994, Glossary. But there is an analogous teaching in Theravada Buddhism, as Suu pointed out in *Letters from Burma*, no. 40, Teachers: "In Prome, a holy teacher told me to keep in mind the hermit Sumedha, who sacrificed the possibility of early liberation for himself alone and underwent many lives of striving that he might save others from suffering."

While Suu's admirers compare her to such figures, her detractors writing for Burma's state media often refer to her as a *nat* or spirit such as "Anauk Medaw," the Queen or Mother of the West. As Houtman points out, the interesting thing is that her enemies do not deny that she has supernatural characteristics, but claim that they are malignant ones. (cf. Houtman, "Sacralising or Demonising Democracy?" in *Burma at the Turn of the 21st Century*, pp.140–3.)

9. Visiting Burma in 1990, Kei Nemoto, a Japanese scholar, observed, "There seems to be a big discrepancy between Burmese people's expectations of Suu Kyi and her own image of the future, democratic Burma": Houtman, *Mental Culture . . .* , p.283, footnote.

10. This story was believed even by people living in big cities like Rangoon or Taunggyi: Professor Nemoto, "Aung San Suu Kyi, Her Dream and Reality," 1996, cited by Houtman in *Mental Culture . . .* , p.283, footnote.

11. "The military has raided more than a dozen monasteries," the *Washington Post* reported: William Branigin, "Myanmar Crushes Monks' Movement" in *Washington Post*, October 28, 1990.

12. authority was found in Aung San's writings for the dramatically anti-democratic change of direction dictated by Ne Win: Gustaaf Houtman: "Aung San's *lan-zin*, the Blue Print and the Japanese occupation of Burma" in *Reconsidering the Japanese Military Occupation of Burma*, ed. Kei Nemoto, Tokyo University of Foreign Studies, 2007. The discussion in this chapter owes much to Gustaaf Houtman's monograph *Mental Culture . . .*

13. *Ana* and *awza*, just like authority and influence, blend into one another: Houtman, *Mental Culture . . .* , p.169.

14. Sometimes I didn't have enough money to eat: quoted in Edward Klein, "The Lady Triumphs" in *Vanity Fair*, October.

15. "I would come down at night," she told another reporter: Fergal Keane, "The Lady Who Frightens Generals" in *You* magazine, July 14, 1996.

16. her speech of thanks, delivered by Michael on her behalf: speech given on April 23, 1997, text in St. Hugh's archive.

17. I started off on the basis that I would have to be very disciplined: Alan Clements, Aung San Suu Kyi, *The Voice of Hope*, p.143.

18. "Not long before my house arrest in 1989," Suu wrote later, "I was granted an audience with the venerable U Pandita": Aung San Suu Kyi, *Letters from Burma*, no. 40, Teachers.

19. those closer to the goal of *nibbana* or liberation: *nibbana* is the Burmese spelling of Nirvana.

20. the venal Burmese businessman: U Po Kyin.

21. This revolutionary idea became the seed of a mass movement, Burma's mass lay-meditation movement: exhaustively explained in Ingrid Jordt, *Burma's Mass Lay Meditation Movement: Buddhism and the Cultural Construction of Power*, Ohio University Research International Studies, 2007.

22. You were quite surprised when I told you how much we laughed together on the day of Suu's arrest: Alan Clements, Aung San Suu Kyi, *The Voice of Hope*, p.253.

23. Like many of my Buddhist colleagues, I decided to put my time under detention to good use by practicing meditation: Aung San Suu Kyi, *Letters from Burma*, no. 40.

24. "There were times when I did more meditation because I was getting better at it," she said: Alan Clements, Aung San Suu Kyi, *The Voice of Hope*, p.145.

25. "We want a better democracy, a fuller democracy with compassion and loving kindness," she was to say years later: Houtman, *Mental Culture . . .* , Appendix 2 (D18).

26. General Ne Win [...] ... was responsible for alienating the army from the people: quoted in Houtman, *Mental Culture . . .* , p.17. See also Part Two, Chapter 7, p.152.

27. U Pandita spoke of the importance of *samma-vaca* or right speech: Aung San Suu Kyi, *Letters from Burma*, no.40, p.159.

PART FOUR, CHAPTER 4: THE PEACE PRIZE

1. "When I knew I was going to be free, I didn't know what to think," she said a few days later: quoted in documentary *Aung San Suu Kyi—Lady of No Fear*.

2. Archbishop Desmond Tutu exulted: from Archbishop Desmond Tutu's Foreword to the second edition of *Freedom from Fear*, 1995, p.xv.

3. During the years that I spent under house arrest: ibid.

4. "What I need," she said, one month after her release, "is a proper office for our democracy party": Tim McGirk, "Suu Kyi Keeps Flame of Democracy Alight" in *Independent*, August 21, 1995.

5. "Dear Suu," read the letter from Rachel Trickett: St. Hugh's College archive.

6. "Alexander was extraordinary," he said: interview with author.

7. In the short term, however, the ascent of General Than Shwe to the chairmanship of SLORC in Saw Maung's place was a boon for Suu and her family: this discussion of Than Shwe is heavily indebted to Benedict Rogers, *Than Shwe: Unmasking Burma's Tyrant*, Silkworm Books, 2010.

8. The comments of those who had dealings with him are uniformly unflattering: quoted in Benedict Rogers, *Than Shwe: Unmasking the Tyrant*.

9. another "obdurate and unimaginative" soldier according to a retired British diplomat: the source of this quote requested anonymity.

10. whence they had fled to escape waves of brutal sectarian persecution by the Burmese Army: the Rohingya are the worst persecuted of all Burma's mistreated ethnic minorities, partly on account of their being Muslim rather than Buddhist. To escape persecution and seek a better life, many have crossed the border contiguous with Arakan state, where they are concentrated, into Bangladesh, but although Bangladesh is a majority Muslim state they have been treated like pariahs there as well, confined to improvised refugee camps in appalling conditions. Their sufferings continue today.

11. Instead she agreed that she would indeed do as he proposed and leave Burma—on four conditions: announced, with a sardonic twinkle in his eye, to a press conference by Michael Aris; see documentary *Aung San Suu Kyi—Lady of No Fear*.

12. Both the empty "dialogue" and Suu's release nine months later reveal the importance of Japan's influence on the regime: Gustaaf Houtman, in *Mental Culture. . .* and in conversation, contributed and clarified several ideas in this discussion.

13. A British diplomat who served in Rangoon from 1996: interview with author. The retired diplomat asked not to be named.

14. The military's primary provision from the inception of the process: Steinberg, *Burma/ Myanmar: What Everyone Needs to Know*, p.142.

15. "Aung San Suu Kyi's initial intention," he wrote, "appeared to have been to visit a monk greatly respected by both the people": Houtman, "Sacralising or Demonising Democracy" in *Burma at the Turn of the 21st Century*, p.148.

16. "In contrast to the aggressive, destructive quality of hatred," wrote Sayadaw U Pandita, "metta, loving-kindness, wishes the welfare and happiness of others": Sayadaw U Pandita, *In This Very Life*, Wisdom Publications, 2002, p.190.

17. It is metta. Rest assured that if we should lose this metta, the whole democratic party would disintegrate: Houtman, "Sacralising or Demonising Democracy," op. cit.

18. There is a special charm to journeys undertaken before daybreak in hot lands: Aung San Suu Kyi, *Letters from Burma*, no. 1: The Road to Thamanya (1).

19. The road had become worse as we traveled further and further away from Rangoon: ibid., p.4.

20. As we approached Thamanya, the quiet seemed to deepen: ibid., no. 2, p.17.

21. No project could be successfully implemented without the willing cooperation of those concerned: ibid., no.4, p.17.

22. Suu, as Houtman sees it, gave the regime two choices: Houtman, "Sacralizing or Demonizing Democracy," op. cit.

PART FOUR, CHAPTER 5: HEROES AND TRAITORS

1. "a follower they [i.e. the West] had raised," they said, but SLORC would "never accept the leadership of a person under foreign influence who will dance to the tune of a foreign power": "Voice of Myanmar" radio broadcast, January 27, 1992, quoted in Charney, p.176.

2. "melancholy, long, withdrawing roar": lines from Matthew Arnold, "Dover Beach."

3. the country will be in ruins: Khin Nyunt, quoted in BBC Summary of World Broadcasts, "Khin Nyunt addresses lawyers on their defects and why a woman should not lead," February 3, 1992.

4. For six weeks I had been holed up in a hotel room in Rangoon waiting for a telephone call from Aung San Suu Kyi's office: Alan Clements, Aung San Suu Kyi, *The Voice of Hope*, p.22.

5. He's upstairs gathering medicines: Alan Clements, Aung San Suu Kyi, *The Voice of Hope*, p.22.

6. Suu had argued that it was "not yet time to invest" in Burma: Aung San Suu Kyi, *Letters from Burma*, no. 11, A Note on Economic Policy.

7. When she began telling foreign investors to stay away, I told her that it would hurt the people, who need jobs. She replied, "People will just have to tighten their belts." I said, "There are no more notches": interview with author, March 2010.

8. The point of no return came when the Indian writer Amitav Ghosh quoted the "no more notches" line in a piece about Burma published by the *New Yorker* in August 1996: collected in Amitav Ghosh, *Incendiary Circumstances: A Chronicle of the Turmoil of Our Times*, p.183.

9. "Khin Nyunt's man worked on Ma Ma Thanegi successfully," he said: this Burmese source, who requested anonymity, has good contacts on both sides of Burma's political divide.

10. "All political matters were under the control of Counter-Intelligence Department," he wrote in an e-mail: e-mail correspondence with author, 2011.

11. Just because [these governments] have decided on a policy of constructive engagement, there is no need for us to think of them as our enemies: collected in Amitav Ghosh, *Incendiary Circumstances*, p.185.

12. Burma gets only 1.4 percent of the number of tourists who visit Thailand, 200,000 compared to its neighbor's 14 million: *Irrawaddy*, June 2011.

13. "We want people to come to Burma," he said: Kenneth Denby, "Let People See Our Suffering" in *The Times*, November 4, 2010.

14. individuals coming in to see the country, to study the situation in the country, might be a good idea: Phoebe Kennedy, "Welcome to Burma" in *Independent*, February 21, 2011.

15. will ultimately help open Burma to travelers: ibid.

16. "If the army really wants to kill me, they can do it without any problems at all, so there is no point in making elaborate security arrangements," she told *The Times*: quoted in Wintle, *Perfect Hostage*, p.382.

17. The refusal to allow Aung San Suu Kyi to hold roadside talks . . . meant that a great tension settled upon Rangoon in the latter part of 1996: Monique Skidmore, *Karaoke Fascism: Burma and the Politics of Fear*, University of Pennsylvania Press, 2004, p.7.

18. It took several weeks: quoted in ibid., p.9.

19. Generals are not content to control only the flow of information in the public domain: ibid., p.14.

20. he insisted on staying on in "the only place he could ever regard as home," as Michael Aris later put it: Dr. Michael Aris, "A Tribute to James Leander Nichols," St. Hugh's archive London, July 23, 1996.

21. The glaring light of adversity: Aung San Suu Kyi, *Letters from Burma*, no. 33, p.131.

22. According to the teachings of Buddhism: ibid, p.133.

23. He was "her knight in shining armor," said one friend, "the one who was defending and fighting for her and trying to slay the dragon for her": Suzanne Hoelgaard (quoted) in the documentary *Aung San Suu Kyi—Lady of No Fear*.

24. In the first twenty years of their marriage: Carey quoted in *Aung San Suu Kyi—Lady of No Fear*.

25. Michael stayed with me once in Bangkok after the house arrest started: interview with author.

26. He was overly cautious: interview with author.

27. the warm encouragement of the Prince of Wales: Prince Charles and Michael Aris became friends after the latter gave the Prince a detailed briefing on court etiquette and many other questions before the Prince's first visit to Bhutan. In the last weeks of Michael's illness Prince Charles invited him to Highgrove, where he agreed to become Patron of Michael's putative Foundation. Anthony Aris added, "The Rausing family secured the prosperity of Tibetan and Himalayan Studies at Oxford with a magnificent donation of $200,000 just before Michael's death."

28. "I don't think Suu ever realized how much he did," she said: interview with author.

29. He was offered this teaching fellowship in Sanskrit at Harvard: interview with author.

30. A western diplomat: the source of this quote wishes to remain anonymous.

31. I arrived as a memorial ceremony to Michael was in progress: interview with author.

PART FIVE, CHAPTER 1: MEETING SUU

1. "He was a fascinating figure," he said, "much more approachable than the other top generals": interview with author.

2. Khin Nyunt was the main force behind the revitalization of religion during the 1990s: interview and e-mail correspondence with author.

PART FIVE, CHAPTER 2: NIGHTMARE

1. "The USDA has become a very dangerous organization," she said in 1996: Houtman, *Mental Culture . . .*, page 119.

2. Wunna Maung, one of her bodyguards, said later in testimony to the US Congress: description of events up to, including and after Depayin massacre draws on the following sources: records of US Congress Ad Hoc Commission on Depayin Massacre, http://www.ibiblio.org/obl/docs/Depayin_Massacre.pdf; interviews with Suu's driver at Depayin by Democratic Voice of Burma, http://www.dvb.no/analysis/depayin-and-the-driver/12828; "Depayin considered as crime against humanity," Asian Legal Resource Center, http://www.article2.org/mainfile.php/0206/112/; detailed account of massacre on Ibiblio Public Library and Digital Archive, http://www.ibiblio.org/obl/docs/Yearbook2002-3/yearbooks/Depayin%20report.htm; Benedict Rogers, *Than Shwe*, op. cit.

3. Suu wore a sky-blue silk *htamein* (the female longyi) and a large cluster of yellow jasmine flowers in her hair, and her heavy fringe flopped down over her eyebrows: video of Monywa speech on YouTube; translation of transcript on World News Connection, May 30, 2003, via LexisNexis.

4. We watched helplessly and tried to show courage: report of Ad Hoc Commission on Depayin Massacre, Bangkok, July 4, 2003.

5. I was taken in a car with darkened windows, and we changed cars along the way: Benedict Rogers, *Than Shwe*, op. cit.

6. Maung Aye and Khin Nyunt approached Than Shwe: e-mail correspondence with Aung Lynn Heut.

7. It is not power that corrupts but fear: Aung San Suu Kyi, "Freedom from Fear" in *Freedom from Fear*, p.180.

PART FIVE, CHAPTER 3: THE SAFFRON REVOLUTION

1. My first teacher was very interested in politics: interview with author.

2. Ingrid Jordt, the American anthropologist and former Buddhist nun: I am greatly indebted to Ingrid for e-mails and conversations containing ideas and wisdom which illuminate the following pages.

3. In Burma we look upon members of the sangha as teachers: Aung San Suu Kyi, *Letters from Burma*, no. 40.

4. The Burmese were in no doubt, says Jordt: they expected any day that Than Shwe would "descend head first into the hell realms": when Burmese kings have committed such black acts as killing monks, the only way left for them to cling to power, Burmese believe, is by following the "dark arts," the so-called "lower path": praying to *nat* spirits, making use of alchemy, calling on the services of *weiksas* (wizards) and engaging in the practice of *yadaya*, which involves symbolically enacting events one dreads, to prevent them coming to pass. The

Thamanya Sayadaw, the much-esteemed monk visited by Aung San Suu Kyi in 1995 and 2002 (see above), died in 2003 at age ninety-three. His body was embalmed and placed in a specially built mausoleum near his temple, and became the focus of a large pilgrimage cult. On April 2, 2008, some six months after the suppression of the monks' revolt, however, fourteen armed men in military uniforms burst into the mausoleum, locked up the guards in a neighboring building, then stole the late abbott's embalmed body.

Ingrid Jordt explained, "Rumor immediately circulated that the military was performing lower path magic. It was said that Than Shwe's *bodaw* (teacher of the magical arts), in consultation with his astrologers, recommended that the monk's body be roasted and some of the flesh eaten in order to gain the power of the monk." When Cyclone Nargis struck Burma one month later, the popular explanation was that this was cosmic retribution for Than Shwe's impious act of cannibalism.

PART FIVE, CHAPTER 4: THE PEACOCK EFFECT

1. John William Yettaw, who lives in a small mobile home in the Ozark Mountains, Missouri, is a four-times married Vietnam War veteran: this account of Yettaw's misadventures is largely based on Robert Taylor's summary, from a translation of the records of the proceedings of the Rangoon court where Yettaw and Aung San Suu Kyi, were tried, in his article "Myanmar in 2009: On the Cusp of Normality?" in *Southeast Asian Affairs*, 2010.

2. NLD sources have referred to him, not without reason, as "a nutty fellow" and "that wretched man": however, Suu sent a private message to NLD colleagues saying that Yettaw was ill and telling her supporters not to attack him (private information).

3. neither I nor Kenneth Denby nor even John Simpson: Kenneth Denby is the *nom de plume* of *The Times*' intrepid correspondent in Burma. John Simpson is the veteran BBC foreign correspondent celebrated above all for single-handedly "liberating" Kabul from the Taliban in 2001.

4. British ambassador Mark Canning, who was to hear her testify: quoted in Phoebe Kennedy, "Suu Kyi testifies that she did not violate her house arrest" in *Independent*, May 27, 2009.

5. Phoebe Kennedy wrote: ibid.

6. being the daughter of Bogyoke Aung San: from Robert Taylor, "Myanmar in 2009: on the Cusp of Normality?" in *Southeast Asian Affairs*, 2010.

7. The Chrysler ad featuring Suu climaxes with the car they are trying to sell smashing down a wall. The subtext is not hard to fathom: the political frivolity of the car manufacturers who piously adopt Suu's image to sell their goods was brought home by one of the sequels to the Lancia ad: a new Italian campaign for Lancia's Ypsilon model starring French movie star Vincent Cassel and with the catchline "Il lusso è un diritto" ("Luxury is a right").

8. The ICG conclusion quoted by Marshall: International Crisis Group, Asia Briefing no. 118, *Myanmar's Post-Election Landscape*, March 7, 2011.

9. Burma has a special place in my heart: Helvey interview with Metta Spencer in *Peace Magazine*, vol. 24, no. 1, p.12.

10. When I was up at Cambridge one day: ibid.

11. [Sharp] started out the seminar by saying, "Strategic nonviolent struggle is all about political power. How to seize political power and how to deny it to others": Suu and Gene Sharp have never had the opportunity to meet, but if they did it is likely they would agree on the fundamental questions. In *The Voice of Hope*, Suu said, "We have chosen the way of nonviolence simply because we think it's politically better for the country in the long run to establish that you can bring about change without the use of arms . . . Here, we're not thinking about spiritual matters at all . . ." She reiterated the point when she responded by telephone to a question after her first Reith Lecture for the BBC in June 2011, saying, "I do not hold to nonviolence for moral reasons but practical and political reasons." She quoted Gandhi as saying that if he had to choose between violence and cowardice "he would choose violence any time."

But Suu protests too much when she disavows the moral arguments for nonviolence. She has always been vulnerable to attack by those in the movement who favor violence, and this is how she tries to deflect their criticisms: One recalls how, back in 1989, she told a journalist, "I don't believe in armed struggle but I sympathize with the students who are engaged in armed struggle." Yet, as this book indicates, her ideas about nonviolence and the "revolution of the spirit" are in fact rooted in her religious convictions.

12. "Resorting to nonviolence tactics," wrote Thant Myint-U: Thant Myint-U, *River of Lost Footsteps*, p.337.

13. a contaminant to a nonviolent struggle . . . the greatest contaminant: Helvey interview with Metta Spencer in *Peace Magazine*, vol. 24, no. 1, p.12.

14. "In recent years," Sharp writes in the book's recently updated first chapter: Gene Sharp, *From Dictatorship to Democracy*, The Albert Einstein Institution, p.1.

AFTERWORD

1."Stubborn," e.g., "Suu Kyi is very stubborn, she won't give way without a fight": former British ambassador to Thailand Derek Tonkin, quoted in "Suu Kyi refuses to use 'Myanmar' name," *Financial Times*, July 3, 2012.

2. See pp. 48–49.

3. Evan Osnos, "The Burmese Spring," *The New Yorker*, August 6, 2012, p. 56.

4. Ibid.

5. Myo Thant, "NLD says it's legal; not opposed to Parliament, government," *Mizzima News Agency*, June 30, 2011.

6. "Aung San Suu Kyi meets Burma's president Thein Sein," *Guardian*, August 19, 2011.

7. "Burma dam: Work halted on divisive Myitsone project," *BBC News*, September 30, 2011.

8. cf. Osnos, "The Burmese Spring," p.57.

9. BBC international development correspondent David Loyn, quoted in "Asean leaders approve Burma chairmanship bid," *BBC News*, November 17, 2011.

10. William Wan, "In exclusive interview, Burmese leader says lasting reform is coming," *Washington Post*, January 19, 2012.

11. In the UN Development Programme's Human Development Index 2011, Myanmar ranked between Angola and Cameroon among the nations of the world with the lowest indices of development.

12. Kurt Campbell, "Unlikely pair an inspiration to us all," *Myanmar Times*, December 3, 2012.

13. In Transparency International's Corruption Perception Index 2012, measuring perceived levels of public sector corruption around the world, Myanmar ranked 172 out of 176 countries, above only Sudan, Afghanistan, North Korea and Somalia.

14. Thomas Fuller, "Long Reliant on China, Myanmar Now Turns to Japan," *The New York Times*, October 10, 2012.

15. Thomas Fuller, "Amid Disorganization, Aung San Suu Kyi Visits Thailand," *The New York Times*, May 29, 2012.

16. Charlie Campbell, "Arakan Strife Poses Suu Kyi Political Problem," *The Irrawaddy*, June 13, 2012. Bertil Lintner, the veteran Burma-watcher, was quoted as saying of the eruption of anti-Rohingya violence in Arakan state, "The violence is clearly well-orchestrated and not as spontaneous as we are being led to believe. The answer is plain to see—the government is very worried about the support commanded by Suu Kyi. It wants to force her into a position where she has to make a pro-Rohingya public statement that could damage her popularity among Burma's Buddhists, where anti-Muslim sentiment runs high. On the other hand, if she remains silent she will disappoint those who support her firm stand on human rights." Whether or not Lintner's hunch about "orchestration" is correct, he precisely foresaw the dilemma in which the violence would place her.

17. Francis Buchanan, "A Comparative Vocabulary of Some of the Languages Spoken in the Burma Empire," *Asiatick Researches of Transactions of the Society Instituted in Bengal for Inquiry into the History and Antiquities, the Arts, Sciences and Literature of Asia*, Volume the Fifth, 1801, p. 223: "The Mahommedans settled at Arakan call the country Rovingaw."

18. "Myanmar: Storm Clouds on the Horizon," pp. 2-3, *International Crisis Group Asia Report* no. 238, November 12, 2012.

19. Colin Hinshelwood, "Can Suu Kyi Stay Silent?" *The Irrawaddy*, September 17, 2012.

20. Quoted in "Suu Kyi cannot back Rohingyas," *The News* (Pakistan), November 5, 2012.

GLOSSARY

aingyi—cotton blouse

anicca—Buddhist doctrine of impermanence

balachaung—pounded dried shrimp and fish paste deep-fried with sugar, chili and tamarind paste

baung-bi chut—"men-out-of-trousers," referring to soldiers-turned civilian politicians

bhaya—fear

bodaw—teacher of the magical arts

Daw—honorific prefix for middle-aged woman

Dharma—the teaching of the Buddha

gaung baung—sort of turban

honne—unspoken reality (Japanese)

hpoun—spiritual potency

htamein—ankle-length woman's longyi

kamauk—farmer's straw hat

kikkake—turning point (Japanese)

kyat—currency

longyi—Burmese sarong, long skirt-like garment for everyday use by both sexes

metta—loving-kindness

nakao—face cream made from a particular type of tree bark

nat-thana—powerful, persistent spirits that must be appeased

nibbana—Burmese for nirvana

samma-vaca—right speech

sangha—the collective of Buddhist monks

shinbyu—Buddhist coming-of-age ceremony for boys

tatemae—official reality (Japanese)

Tatmadaw—Burmese Army

thanaka—generic term for face cream made from tree bark

thathanabaing—senior monk

weiksa—wizard

yadaya—black magic

LIST OF NAMES

Note on Burmese names: Burmese do not have surnames, only given names which may number between one and four. Usually all given names are used when addressing someone, often preceded by an honorific, such as "U" (for an older man) or "Daw" (for an older woman).

Aung San Suu Kyi's family

ALEXANDER ARIS (Burmese name Myint San Aung): Suu and Michael's first son.

AUNG SAN: Suu's father, hero of Burmese independence struggle; often referred to as "Bogyoke" (pronounced "Bo-joke-e')—Burmese for "General."

AUNG SAN LIN: Suu's elder brother, drowned at age nine.

AUNG SAN OO: Aung San and Daw Khin Kyi's first-born son and Suu's eldest brother, emigrated to US, engineer.

DAW KHIN GYI: aunt who lived in Suu's University Avenue compound.

DAW KHIN KYI: Suu's mother, nurse-turned-diplomat.

DORA THAN É: celebrated prewar singer; not a relative but referred to by Suu as her "emergency aunt."

KIM ARIS (Burmese name Thein Lin): Suu and Michael's second son.

MICHAEL ARIS: Suu's husband.

THAKIN THAN TUN: brother of Daw Khin Kyi, leader of Burmese Communist Party.

National League for Democracy (NLD)

AUNG AUNG: son of Bo Min Lwin, Aung San's personal bodyguard; head of Suu's bodyguards during campaign tours.

AUNG GYI: retired general, leading figure in military regime before being purged; the first Chairman of NLD.

AUNG SHWE: head of NLD at time of Suu's release in 1995.

CHAN AYE: moderate member of NLD's central executive committee.

DAW MYINT MYINT KHIN: head of Rangoon Bar Association, member of NLD Central Executive Committee; jailed for many years.

DAW NWE: wife of Ko Myint Swe; ran party's PR operation with him.

HWE MYINT: one of Suu's earliest political allies.

KO AUNG: colleague of Ko Myint Swe in Suu's office.

KO MAW: colleague of Ko Myint Swe in Suu's office.

KO MYINT SWE: poet, Rangoon University librarian, party worker.

KYAW SOE LIN: party lawyer, Suu's heroic driver at Depayin.

KYI MAUNG: retired colonel, founder member of party.

MA THANEGI: painter, writer, Suu's personal assistant on tour although never NLD member.

MA THIDA: medical student and early member of party.

MAUNG THAW KA: naval hero-turned-writer and poet, advisor to Suu, died in jail.

MYO THEIN: Suu's driver on campaign tours, nicknamed "Tiger."

NYO OHN MYINT: university lecturer, early member of NLD, in exile in Thailand.

SEIN WIN: cousin of Suu's; Prime Minister of National Coalition Government of the Union of Burma NCGUB in exile.

THAKIN TIN MYA: communist; early collaborator with Suu.

TIN OO: retired general, vice chairman and cofounder of NLD, detained for many years.

U HLA PE: senior member of campaign touring group.

WIN KHET: personal assistant to Suu.

WIN THEIN: one of Suu's bodyguards on campaign.

WIN TIN: dissident journalist, founder member of NLD, jailed for nineteen years.

WUNNA MAUNG: Suu's bodyguard at Depayin.

The Regime

AUNG LYNN HTUT: former member of Khin Nyunt staff, diplomat in Burma's US embassy before defecting.

KHIN MAUNG WIN: deputy Foreign Minister, apologist for Depayin massacre.

LIEUTENANT GENERAL KHIN NYUNT: protégé of Ne Win; head of military intelligence.

GENERAL MAUNG AYE: third member of Than Shwe-Khin Nyunt triumvirate.

MAUNG MAUNG: President from August 1988 to Sep 1988, replacing Sein Lwin.

MAUNG TUN: major who countermanded Captain Myint U's order to fire on Suu and NLD at Danubyu, probably saving Suu's life.

BRIGADIER MYINT AUNG: fierce enemy of NLD at Danubyu.

MYINT U: captain at Danubyu who ordered troops to fire at Suu and NLD party.

NE WIN: general who seized power in coup in 1962; ex-comrade of General Aung San.

GENERAL SAW MAUNG: first Chairman of SLORC, supplanting Maung Maung as head of state.

SEIN LWIN: "the Butcher," briefly replaced Ne Win as President.

LIEUTENANT COLONEL THAN HAN: the military commander behind Depayin assault.

GENERAL THAN SHWE: Chairman of SLORC/SPDC, replacing Saw Maung in 1992; in power until 2010.

BRIGADIER GENERAL THAN TUN: member of Khin Nyunt staff; negotiated with Suu in 2004.

TIN AUNG HEIN: Minister of Justice under Ne Win.

TIN PE: the "Red Brigadier"; hard-liner in Ne Win regime.

U WIN SEIN: Secretary of USDA, Minister of Transport; urged "eradication" of Suu before Depayin.

Diplomats

IBRAHIM GAMBARI: UN Deputy Secretary-General in mid 1990s.

ROBERT GORDON: British ambassador in late 1990s.

RAZALI ISMAIL: UN envoy in early 1990s.

MARTIN MORLAND: British ambassador during 1988 uprising.

U THANT: third Secretary-General of the United Nations.

Historical Figures

BA MAW: Prime Minister between the wars.

BRIGADIER KYAW ZAW: one of Aung San's thirty comrades; chided by Suu for lack of involvement in political struggle.

SIR J.G. (GEORGE) SCOTT, aka Shway Yoe: British governor in Shan States; author of *The Burman*.

SUPAYALAT: Thibaw's queen, exiled with him in 1886.

THIBAW: last King of Burma, exiled by British in 1886.

U OTTAMA: Buddhist monk, anti-British activist.

Others

ASSHIN ISSARIYA, aka King Zero: Buddhist monk, leader of Saffron Revolution in 2007.

BO KYI: student leader in 1988; founder and head of Assistance Association for Political Prisoners.

GENERAL BO MYA: historic leader of Karen Independence Army.

KHAING SAW THUN: lawyer; refugee in Manerplaw camp, 1991.

DAW KHIN KHIN WIN: companion/housekeeper for Suu in detention.

KHIN MYINT: younger sister of Tin Tin, childhood friend of Suu's.

KITTY BA THAN: one of Ne Win's several wives.

LEO NICHOLS, "Uncle Leo": Anglo-Burmese businessman and family friend of Suu's.

MAUNG PHONE MAW: first victim of police violence, March 1988.

MAUNG ZARNI: sociologist and activist.

MEE MA MA: daughter of Khin Khin Win; fellow companion/housekeeper for Suu.

MIN KO NAING: student leader.

DR. NAING AUNG: student leader in 1988; now in exile in Thailand.

NITA YIN YIN MAY: information officer at British Embassy.

PASCAL KHOO THWE: former student leader, writer.

ROSS DUNKLEY: Australian entrepreneur and journalist, founder of the *Myanmar Times*.

SOE TINT: family friend of Suu's; escort of Daw Khin Kyi on Martyr's Day.

THANT MYINT-U: grandson of U Thant; writer.

TIN TIN: childhood friend of Suu's.

DR. TIN TUN OO: regime crony; Chief Executive of *Myanmar Times*.

U GAMBIRA: Buddhist monk; leader of Saffron Revolution.

U NU: elected Prime Minister; overthrown by Ne Win.

FURTHER READING

The Burma bookshelf is short compared to that of other nations of South and Southeast Asia. The fact that books by or about Aung San Suu Kyi form such a large proportion of the total reflects not only her fame and popularity abroad, but also the reclusive nature of the state under military rule and the extreme difficulty of working there as a journalist or academic researcher.

The first biography of Suu to appear was *Aung San Suu Kyi: Toraware no Kujaku*, by Yoshikazu Mikami (1991), which is particularly strong on the Japanese connections of Aung San and his daughter.

Several other biographies have been published subsequently. *The Lady: Burma's Aung San Suu Ky*i by Barbara Victor (1998) and *Aung San Suu Kyi: Towards a New Freedom* by Ang Chin Geok (1998) are slim volumes, and both now very dated. *Le Jasmin ou la Lune* (2007) by the Bangkok-based Belgian journalist Thierry Falise is a fast-paced and fascinatingly detailed account of Suu's career, in French. *Perfect Hostage: A Life of Aung San Suu Kyi* by Justin Wintle (2007) devotes much space to the premodern history of Burma and is often skeptical about Suu's career, blaming her "intransigence" as the reason why she has spent so many years in detention. But the book's main weakness is that, through no fault of his own, the author never actually met the book's subject.

Of Suu's own written work, the most important essays are collected in *Freedom from Fear* (1995), which contains her short biography of her father, her seminal long essay *Intellectual Life in Burma and India under Colonialism*, and other political landmarks such as her first speech at Shwedagon in August 1988. It also contains the tributes of friends, including Ann Pasternak Slater's moving and intimate memoir, *Suu Burmese. Letters from Burma* (1997) is a collection of the pieces Suu wrote regularly for the *Mainichi Daily News* in Tokyo after her release from house arrest in 1995.

One of the most revealing works about Suu's life and beliefs is *The Voice of Hope* (2008), a series of interviews conducted over a period of months by Alan Clements, a former Buddhist monk, in which Suu speaks more candidly about herself than ever before or since.

Mental Culture in Burmese Crisis Politics by Gustaaf Houtman (1999) is a fascinating scholarly account of the role Suu plays in Burmese politics, informed by the author's excellent knowledge of Burma and Burmese. Though out of print, it can be downloaded from Google Books.

For more on other aspects of Burma, the following can be recommended:

INSURGENCY AND DEMOCRACY STRUGGLE

Outrage by Bertil Lintner (1990): a blow-by-blow history by the Swedish journalist, a veteran Burma-watcher, of the great Burmese uprising and its bloody suppression, enriched by numerous interviews and depositions by Burmese in the front line.

Land of Jade: a Journey through Insurgent Burma by Bertil Lintner (1990): the story of Lintner's unique journey with his young and heavily pregnant wife—she gave birth en route—through the war-torn badlands of the Burmese frontier. A gem that deserves to be much better known.

Burma: Insurgency & the Politics of Ethnicity by Martin Smith (1991), a detailed history of the insurgencies that have bedeviled Burma since independence and their causes.

Little Daughter by Zoya Phan (2009): the moving autobiography of a Karen girl born and raised in the thick of Burma's ethnic wars.

Than Shwe: Unmasking Burma's Tyrant by Benedict Rogers (2010): the only detailed biography of the man who bent Burma to his will from 1993 to 2010.

HISTORY

The most readable general introduction to Burmese history is *The River of Lost Footsteps: A Personal History of Burma* by Thant Myint-U (2006), which contrives to bring the region's endless dynastic wars and reversals of fortune to life.

Forgotten Land/A Rediscovery of Burma by Harriet O'Brien (1991) blends personal reminiscence—the author spent years in the country as a diplomatic "brat"—with a pithy yet vivid account of Burmese history.

Defeat into Victory by Field Marshal Viscount Slim (1956) describes how the Second World War unfolded in Burma and includes a memorable account of the British commander's meeting with Aung San.

Two concise and authoritative works on contemporary Burma are: *A History of Modern Burma* by Michael W. Charney (2009), and *Burma/Myanmar: What Everyone Needs to Know* by David I. Steinberg (2010)

RELIGION

In This Very Life: The Liberation Teachings of the Buddha by Sayadaw U Pandita (1989) is the book that Michael Aris gave Suu at the start of her first spell of detention: a bracingly straightforward manual of how to attain wisdom and peace through meditation, hugely influential in Burma and beyond, by a living master.

Burma's Mass Lay Meditation Movement: Buddhism and the Cultural Construction of Power by Ingrid Jordt (2007) is the only scholarly account of this important movement.

Religion and Politics in Burma by Donald Eugene Smith (1965): a scholarly description of the political role played in Burma by Buddhism, before during and after annexation by Britain.

SOCIETY

The Burman: His Life and Notions by Shway Yoe (first published 1882, reissued in 1989): a beautifully written and frequently hilarious exploration of Burmese life from birth to death and beyond, a cornucopia for anyone intrigued by the country. Shway Yoe was the pen name of J.G. (later Sir George) Scott, a colonial administrator who spent many years in the Shan States.

Karaoke Fascism: Burma and the Politics of Fear by Monique Skidmore (2004) and *Burma at the Turn of the 20th Century* edited by Monique Skidmore (2005): two brave efforts by intrepid anthropologists and social scientists to get to grips with Burma, despite great discouragement by the authorities.

MISCELLANEOUS

Burmese Days by George Orwell (1944) and *Finding George Orwell in Burma* by Emma Larkin (2006): Burma, where Orwell served as a colonial policeman, played an important role in the formation of his political ideas, confirming his hatred of colonialism. His first novel is a deeply unflattering portrait of Burma under the British—and Burma under the generals bears a striking resemblance to the world of *1984*. Larkin, an American journalist and Burmese speaker, traveled through Burma in Orwell's footsteps, teasing out the parallels.

From the Land of Green Ghosts by Pascal Khoo Thwe (2002), the vivid memoir of the up-country boy from the Padaung tribe, famous for their "giraffe-necked" women, who fled into exile in 1989 and went on to study English at Cambridge.

The Trouser People: A Story of Burma in the Shadow of the Empire by Andrew Marshall (2002): a witty travelogue entwined with a re-telling of the life story of Sir George Scott (see *The Burman*, above)

The Native Tourist: A Holiday Pilgrimage in Burma by Ma Thanegi (2005): what Suu's former friend did next: a whimsical but informative journey through the country.

CURRENT AFFAIRS

Three news websites run by Burmese expatriates offer the best and most detailed coverage of events inside a country that remains remarkably opaque: The Irrawaddy, based in Chiangmai, Thailand (www.irrawaddy.org); Democratic Voice of Burma, based in Norway (www.dvb.no); and Mizzima News Agency, based in New Delhi (www.mizzima.com).

ACKNOWLEDGMENTS

Many people have helped me in many different ways during the research and writing of this book, but some of my debts of gratitude antedate it by decades. It was Alexander Chancellor, my first editor at the *Independent*, who in 1991 agreed to send me to Burma with the photographer Greg Girard to research an article on the fate of Burma's democracy movement for the *Independent Magazine*. Eleven years on, Leonard Doyle, foreign editor of the same paper, sent me to Rangoon to interview Aung San Suu Kyi and then made a fundamental contribution to the project by introducing me to Mark Farmaner and Anna Roberts at the Burma Campaign UK. Mark and Anna have helped me in innumerable ways since then, not least by reading the first draft and drawing my attention to many errors and omissions, and their colleagues, in particular Zoya Phan, have also been very kind. However, neither I nor anyone else involved in the book's publication is connected to the Burma Campaign UK in any way, and all opinions and conclusions expressed in the book are mine alone.

Suu's English in-laws are understandably shy of publicity, but I cannot avoid mentioning the kindness and warmth they showed me even when they had no idea whether or not I could be trusted. Since then we have become good friends, and they have contributed greatly to the value of the book, not only through endless conversations but by introducing me to other people and by reading the first draft and pointing out mistakes. Once they had read the book and decided it was worthwhile, they also did me the great honor of allowing me to quote from or at least look over certain material of a private nature, and to use a number of family photographs.

Harriet O'Brien, Lady Gore-Booth, Patricia Herbert, Martin Morland, Robert and Pam Gordon, Tom and Danielle White and Anna Allott are others closely associated with Burma and Suu who have been generous with their knowledge and contacts.

I met Dr. Maung Zarni much later in the process of research than I would have wanted, but he made up for lost time by providing me with much information that I could have obtained nowhere else, and by the endless stimulation of his ideas.

My old school friend Steve Weinman, his wife Khin Myint and Khin's sister Tin Tin have made an important contribution to this project. Khin and Tin Tin have been constantly available to correct my errant notions and answer strange questions, and Khin in particular is to be thanked for an introduction which changed the book's prospects.

Bertil Lintner was wonderfully generous with his time and memories when we met in Chiangmai, as was Nyo Ohn Myint in the same city. Gustaaf Houtman and Ingrid Jordt are two Burma experts who in their different ways helped me immensely. Maureen Aung-Thwin of the Open Society Foundations opened her address book for me, to the book's great advantage. My elder son, Mario, lent me his genial company and his photographic brilliance on more than one exacting field trip. Claire Lewis was a fairy godmother whose wishes have yet to be realized but we live in hope. I offer a deep *gassho* to Dario Doshin Girolami for helping me once again to put my feet upon the Way.

Others to whom I would like to offer my thanks include:

Shankar Acharya, Gillon Aitken, Andrew Kidd and their colleagues at Aitken Alexander Associates, Jon Bernstein, Ian Birrell, Archie Bland, Richard Blurton, Vicky Bowman, Ruth Bradley-Jones, Katherine Butler, Mark Canning, Baroness Caroline Cox, Peter Carey, Federico Ceratto, Emmanuele Cappelutti and all my other Dharma friends in Rome, Sir Robin Christopher, Alan Clements, Steve Crawshaw, Jason Cowley, Rana Dasgupta, Cecilia Draghi, George Duffield, Sophie Elmhirst, George Duffield, Anne Gyrithe Bonne, Andrew Heyn, Christo Hird, Andrew Huxley, Laurence Earle, Keith Fielder, Jamie Fergusson, Jared Genscher, Imogen Haddon, Catherine Haughney, Suzanne Hoelgaard, Htein Lin, David Jenkins, Liz Jobey, Joshua, Malavika Karlekar, Simon Kelner, Judith Kendra, Sue Lascelles and all their colleagues at Rider, Paul Mander, Charlotte Middlehurst, Sarah Miller, David Modell, Junko Nakayama, Monica Narula, Terry McCarthy, Ohn Mar Oo, Anders Østergaard, Noriko and Sadayoshi Ohtsu, David Randall, Ann Pasternak Slater, Sam Popham, Ben Rogers, Juliet Rogers, Ros Russell, Debby Stothard and Nita Yin Yin May.

In addition, numerous Burmese people and some foreigners within Burma have helped me in the course of this project, offering me their time, knowledge and friendship at considerable peril to themselves, a peril I will not add to by naming them here.

Finally, my wife Daniela and our son Gabriel have lived with this book since its conception and have participated in its creation in more ways than they, or I, can be fully aware of. Thank you.

Despite all the help I have received, I take full responsibility for any mistakes that remain.

I will donate a portion of the earnings from this book to Prospect Burma, the charity supported by Aung San Suu Kyi which has been helping Burmese people study abroad since the crushing of the democracy movement in 1988, and the Assistance Association for Political Prisoners—Burma.

PERMISSIONS

The author would like to thank the following for permission to use copyright material: Anne Gyrithe Bonne, Bonne Film productions for quotes from *Aung San Suu Kyi—Lady of No Fear* (Kamoli Films, Denmark 2010); Eland Publishing Ltd for material from *Golden Earth* by Norman Lewis (© 1951, reissue 2003); Faber and Faber Limited (2007) and Farrar, Straus and Giroux, LLC (2006) for material from *The River of Lost Footsteps* by Thant Myint-U (© 2006 by Thant Myint-U); Guardian News & Media Ltd for extract from "Review of *Voice of Hope*" by Mary Warnock (*Observer*, May 25, 1997; © Guardian News & Media Ltd 1997); HarperCollins Publishers Ltd for material from *Land of Green Ghosts* by Pascal Khoo Thwe (© Pascal Khoo Thwe, 2002); Gustaaf Houtman for material from his *Mental Culture in Burmese Crisis Politics* (ILCAA, 1999); Independent Print Limited for extracts from *Independent* newspaper articles: "Belief in Burma's Future" by Aung San Suu Kyi (September 12, 1988), "The Road to Manerplaw" (May 25, 1991) and "Welcome to Burma" (February 21, 2011) by Peter Popham and the following by Terry McCarthy: "Burmese Army Coup" (September 19, 1988), "Burma Opposition Will Not Give in to Army Rule" (September 20, 1988); "Fragile Peace Settles on Rangoon" (September 21, 1988); "Ne Win Still Fights for Control" (September 28, 1988), "Rangoon Peaceful for Funeral of Widow (January 3, 1989), "Opposition Vote Leaves Burma's Rulers Stunned" (with Yuli Ismartono, June 15, 1990), "EC to End Boycott of Burmese Junta" (June 15, 1990); Irrawaddy Publishing Group for material from "Memories of 8.8.88" by Dominic Faulder and interview with Gene Sharp, March 2011; Bertil Lintner for material from his *Outrage* (Kiscadale,1989); Lonely Planet for material from *Burma*, edition 4, by Tony Wheeler and Joe Cummings (© 1998, YR Lonely Planet); New York Times for "A Daughter of Burma, But Can She Be a Symbol?" by Steven Erlanger (November 1,1989); Oxford University Press, India for material from *Remembered Childhood—Essays in Honor of Andre Beteille*, ed. Marlavika Karlekar and Rudrangshu Mukherjee (Oxford University Press, New Delhi, 2009); Pan Macmillan for material from *Defeat into Victory* by William Slim (2009); Penguin Group (USA) Inc. for material from *Freedom from Fear and Other Writings*, Revised Edition by Aung San Suu Kyi, Foreword by Vaclav Havel, translated by Michael Aris, © 1991, 1995 by Aung San Suu Kyi. Used by permission of Viking Penguin, a division of Penguin Group (USA) Inc.; Penguin Books for material from *Letters from Burma* by Aung San Suu Kyi (reissue 2010); Penguin Books and Michael Joseph for material from *Forgotten Land*; Rider Books, Random House and Editions Stock for material from *The Voice of Hope* by Alan Clements and Aung San Suu Kyi (2008); University of Pennsylvania Press for material from *Karaoke Fascism* by Monique Skidmore (2004); Washington Post for extracts from "Myanmar Crushes Monks' Movement" by William Branigin (October 28, 1990) and "Myanmar Moves on Opposition, 2 Leading Activists Under House Arrest" by Keith B. Richburg (July 22, 1989); Wisdom Publications, 199 Elm Street, Somerville, MA 02144 USA, www.wisdompubs.org, for material from *In This Very Life* by Sayadaw U. Pandita (reissue © Sayadaw U Pandita, Saddhamma Foundation, 1991); Zed Books for material from *Burma: Insurgency and the Politics of Ethnicity* by Martin Smith (1998). While every effort has been made to trace all copyright holders, if any have been inadvertently overlooked, the author and publisher will be pleased to make the necessary arrangement at the first opportunity.

INDEX

ABOUT THE AUTHOR

A foreign correspondent and feature writer for the *Independent* for more than twenty years, **PETER POPHAM** has reported from locations around the world, including Burma and elsewhere throughout South Asia. He is also the author of *Tokyo: The City at the End of the World* and lives in London.